INSIGHT GUIDES

Pakistan

Edited by Tony Halliday
Directed and Designed by Hans Höfer
Photographed by Heinz Grosse, Ara Güler and others
Editorial Director: Geoffrey Eu

APA
PUBLICATIONS

PAKISTAN

First Edition
© 1990 APA PUBLICATIONS (HK) LTD
Printed in Singapore by Höfer Press Pte. Ltd

ABOUT THIS BOOK

While throughout history Pakistan was always the destination for many peoples, today it receives fewer visitors than one might expect. Even in the 1960s, when the first big waves of travel to the subcontinent began, most people spent little time exploring the Land of the Indus. This may partly be because, until very recently, there has been so little written about the country and travellers were just unaware of what it has to offer. Situated between Central and Southern Asia, Pakistan's vast deserts and plains, its rugged hills and mountains, have conspired with the legacies of the regions's rich past to provide a fascinating land in which to travel.

The task of putting together *Insight Guide: Pakistan* fell to project editor **Tony Halliday**, a British photo-journalist based in Munich who has travelled extensively in Asia. Halliday's own contribution to the book, describing the mountains of the Karakoram and Hindu Kush, reflects his penchant for getting right off the beaten track. He spent four months trekking in the region in 1987, a trip inspired by a 1986 trekking venture through the other end of the Himalayas, namely the remote and largely unknown ranges of Chinese Sichuan.

But the mountains of the north form only a small part of Pakistan. To provide an insight into a country about which so little is generally known, and which is often so misunderstood, a team of seasoned Pakistan experts was assembled. The members are therefore not only widely-travelled in Pakistan, but have also spent many years studying the different aspects of the country.

Beryl Dhanjal's fascination for Pakistan derives from her family connections to the city of Lahore (from Bhagbanpura near the Shalimar Gardens) and also from her having studied South Asian History, Anthropology and Panjabi at the School of Oriental and African Studies in London (SOAS). Besides dealing with the "here and now", Beryl's article on the Panjab delves into the history and folklore of the province to come up with many delightful legends and stories. Beryl also co-authored the article on Sind, as well as writing and assisting with other pieces in the book. She compiled the "Travel Tips" section at the end.

Christine Cottam claims that she was two years old when she first set off for Pakistan, only to be intercepted by her grandfather at the bottom of the garden. Since then, she has spent much time in Pakistan, both in travelling and as a visiting professor of Anthropology at Quaid-i-Azam University in Islamabad. Her work has given her glimpses of Pakistan that tourists seldom see, particularly amongst the Pathans of the Frontier whom she regards as a cheerful and affectionate people. Her articles include "The North West Frontier Province", as well as the section on Karachi and the feature "The Women of Pakistan".

Alan Palmer, a British archaeologist, has visited many of the important sites in Pakistan. Alan wrote the first two chapters, about early civilisation in the Indus Valley, as well as the tour around many of the country's "lost cities". He sums up his fascination for the country like this: "On the one hand is the brutal, stark, yet splendid isolation of the northern mountainous areas, yet on the other is a remarkably sophisticated and complex cultural heritage which invests in this country the right to claim to have been the cradle of civilisation."

The province of Sind, home to the earliest

Halliday   *Dhanjal*   *Cottam*   *Palmer*

civilisations in Pakistan, is rich in history and culture. This article was co-authored by **Mohammad Mian**, a well-known journalist from Karachi. As well as visiting many of the shrines of Sind's Sufi saints (Sufi music and poetry are a passion that Mohammed shares with many of his countrymen), his work has also taken him out into the depths of the province to spend time among the simple folk living on the Indus Plain. Mohammad was also responsible for the pieces "Democracy Rediscovered" and "The Tide of Islam".

Christopher Shackle is Professor of Modern South Asian Languages at SOAS. He wrote about the Pakistanis, their religion, their beliefs, their languages and everything that forges a land of such varied ethnic dimensions into a unified whole. His history of travel in Pakistan also made him the obvious choice to contribute on that side as well. Having spent some time out in Pakistan's western fringes, his offer to write about the province of Baluchistan, with its vast deserts and fascinating history, was gratefully accepted by the editor.

Cris Thomas also has close associations with SOAS, where he obtained an M.A. in South Asian studies. An avid spectator of political events and developments in South Asia; his contributions include the article on the recent history of Pakistan and an account of the British involvement in the area.

Shahrukh Husain was born in Karachi and lived there for the first 17 years of her life. Her work as a freelance journalist has involved her in writing on many aspects of South Asian culture, ranging from mythical folklore to Islamic Art to the very basis of all civilisation – food. Shahrukh has also worked as an adviser and translator for the BBC on Pakistani topics. She provided articles on food and handicrafts, as well as a fascinating thesis on those painted wagons which are an integral part of Pakistan's street culture.

Anthony Lambert hails from England and has travelled widely. Claiming that he has always been fascinated by the precarious presence of man in wild places, he is particularly interested in the remoter and more rugged parts of Pakistan, especially along the Frontier. His account of Pakistan's railways past and present is geared to the buff and uninitiated alike and provides a valuable guide to those out in the field. Anthony has published and edited numerous travel books, as well as travel articles in the *New York Times*, *World* and *Geographical* magazines.

Further contributions came from anthropologist **Renée Holler** who wrote the feature on shamans, and **Chris Lyles** who wrote the piece "A Passion for Cricket".

No *Insight Guide* would be complete without photography. The nature of a country is best reflected in its people, and it was with this in mind that Munich professional **Heinz Grosse** was assigned to capture many of the faces and scenes which appear in this book. Additional material was supplied by other seasoned travellers to Pakistan, notably Ara Güler, Christine Osborne, Simon Hughes and Lyle Lawson. Other valuable contributions came from Wolfgang Fritz, Jimmy Holmes, Javaid Khan, Ernst Steiner, Hans Höfer, Tony Halliday, Beryl Dhanjal, Alain Evrard, Anthony Lambert, Alan Palmer, Bill Wassman, Piero Fantini, Hermann Maier, Gilles Blanchez and Erik Bergendahl. **Chris Bonington** provided the pictures of K2. Thanks are also due to **Mr. S.H.S Jafri** in Islamabad for procuring archive material at the Directorate of Films and Publications.

– APA Publications

Mian   *Shackle*   *Thomas*   *Lambert*

CONTENTS

PLACES AND FEATURES

TRAVEL TIPS

Up in the mighty Karakoram mountains in the north, the River is still young as it cuts its way through some of the most forbidding country on earth. By the time it reaches the plains of Panjab it has matured, slowing right down to old age as it washes the banks of timeless Sind before dying in the Arabian Sea. The journey ends but the flow is eternal. Since the beginning of time, the River has witnessed so much.

Its blood soaked sands have been the playground and burial place of some of the greatest imperialist adventurers – Iranian, Greek, Scythian, Turkish and the British. Alexander, Mahmud Ghaznavi, Timur and countless warlords have furiously fought for imperial supremacy over the rugged land of the Indus valley.

Pakistan, the meeting place of many worlds, has not only provided the theatre for the ravages of invading armies. It has also been the abode of peace and prosperity for humanity on a very large scale. Ancient cities, some abandoned millennia ago and some still thriving in the modern age, are testimony to the fact that the Land of the Indus has provided for many of the world's greatest civilisations.

Since the Harappans, who built the world's oldest advanced civic culture some 5,000 years ago, many have come and gone or come and stayed in and around the Indus Valley. From those early times, through the Vedic and Buddhist eras and on to the world of Islam, the Pakistanis of today are the common inheritors of some of the greatest cultural traditions of humanity.

They are traditions which sail slowly along the river and plough the fields at the water's edge and roll with the simple bullock cart along the endless track of time. They are traditions which have been written down in great epic poems or simply passed down by word of mouth from generation to generation, which are now poured out in song and dance and music and verse. They sing of the call of the mountains and of love in the desert. They beat the drums and even blow the bagpipes at the door of the holy man's shrine.

Emanating from the historical continuity of intensely human values, the cultural strength of the Pakistanis has grown not in spite of but because of the fact that so many people have chosen the Indus as a home, and even invaded it to fulfil their dreams.

Preceding pages: summertime in a northern valley; reaching for the sky; praying in solitude; monuments of the past; monuments in the present; where the river is young.

The dawn of ages: The most enduring testimony to the existence of prehistoric man anywhere in the world are the tools which he left behind. From the first crude hand axes and cleavers made in the Paleolithic age about 500,000 years ago, through to the finest microliths of the Mesolithic age, archaeologists almost wholly depend upon a study of technological developments of stone tools for an understanding of cultural evolution.

Pakistan is no exception, and it seems that from a very early date the first Pakistanis had begun to evolve a particularly high level of organisation in their hunter and gatherer societies. Here, man relied upon chert from the Rohri Hills of Upper Sind and quartzite from the Potohar Plateau and Soan Valley of the Northern Panjab for the raw materials from which he learned to fashion an increasingly wide range of tools. The enormous quantity of discarded chippings or flakes, the waste left over from stone tool manufacture, spread over these quarries, suggests that they were used to produce tools not just for local needs but to serve a very large area. By 50000 B.C. in Pakistan there was already a well-established system of communication and social structure; the tools were mass produced with organised labour.

Man settles down: About 10,000 years ago, as the climate grew warmer, the nomads were encouraged to settle down and grow crops. In Pakistan this was the first of a number of steps which led to the first urban settlements which ultimately blossomed into what is known as the Indus Valley Civilisation.

Exactly where and when the first permanent settlements were established remains questionable. The oldest settlements were believed to have been in the Quetta, Loralai and Zhob valleys in Baluchistan, where a mixture of pastoral and agrarian farming was practised. However, these societies appear to have been semi-nomadic and more recent research suggests that the first permanent settlements are to be found nearer the flood plains of the Greater Indus River System.

Older than Mesopotamia: From Mehrgarh, situated on the transitional zone between the upland valleys of Baluchistan to the west and the Indus flood plains to the east, comes the earliest definite evidence yet of permanent settled agriculture. By 7000 B.C. Mehrgarh was already a sizeable village of 6 hectares – some 1,000 years before the growth of urbanism in Mesopotamia – and by 6000 B.C. it had grown to a small town of 12 hectares

with a probable population of 3,000. The inhabitants lived in houses made of red mud brick, the same material they used to build the granaries in which they stored their grain.

As well as barley and wheat, dates were also grown and soon there was to be cotton too. They relied increasingly upon domesticated cattle, including the water buffalo, rather than sheep, goat and deer which at that time were still wild. Society became increasingly sophisticated and while there is no evidence of palaces or temples, the earliest known ritual burial grounds have been found here. The skeletons, curled up on their sides, were buried with grave goods including tur-

Left, the famous Fasting Buddha from Taxila. Above, the "High Priest" from Mohenjo-daro.

quoise beads believed to have been imported from Turkmenia. Only a handful of sites comparable to Mehrgarh have been discovered, all west of the Indus. It seems that for a while at least, most people in Pakistan chose to continue living as hunter-gatherers or nomadic farmers.

To the Indus: But then suddenly, from about 3500 B.C., communities moved east and permanent settlements began to spring up virtually throughout the Indus River System. The nomads of the day must have seen the advantages of settling on a river plain. Exactly how this all crystallised into an advanced civilisation remains a mystery. Civilisation in the Indus Valley evolved very

slowly and a study of the earliest settlements near the Indus and its tributaries can give clues to the developments. Here, archaeologists have identified different cultural groups largely on the basis of the different types of pottery they used. One such group is typified by the the pottery found at Amri in Sind Province and another by that found at Kot Diji, also in Sind. The fact that these sites were destroyed and only after being rebuilt began to follow the culture of the more mature Indus Valley Civilisation may indicate that the latter was forcibly imposed. Certainly Kot Diji appears to have been deliberately destroyed by fire.

Elsewhere, however, there is evidence of more gradual and peaceful development. At several earlier sites terracotta mother goddesses have been found and evidence of a horned deity also appears on pottery sherds suggesting a continuity of religious belief. On a more material level, sheep and goats were domesticated before the arrival of the Indus Valley Civilisation, copper was already in use and older stamp seals have been found. Furthermore, town walls were already a common feature and the grid layout of the streets at Rahman Dheri, dating back to about 3500 B.C., provides some of the earliest known evidence of advanced urban planning.

Spheres of influence: The Indus Valley Civilisation has become known as the Harappan Civilisation after the site where it was first discovered. Though its heartland lay along the Indus Valley, its influence covered a much broader area; between Afghanistan and what is now Northern India in the north and from the Iranian border as far as to the east of Bombay in the South; an area larger than any encompassed by Ancient Egypt or Mesopotamia, larger than modern day Pakistan. The civilisation lasted, at its height, from about 2500 B.C. to 1500 B.C., but the question of how and why an advanced independant culture grew up in this part of the world is still open to speculation. Where did the inspiration come from?

When the first discoveries were made at Harappa (A.D. 1920) and Mohenjo-daro (A.D. 1922), archaeologists knew almost nothing of the earlier civilisations of Pakistan. They therefore looked at what they did know and through an examination of different artifacts they tried to show that the idea of settlement on the Indus originated from those who had settled on the Tigris, the Euphrates and the Nile. But there is now little to suggest any direct influence although ancient trade links undoubtedly existed. The material remains which the Harappans have left us are remarkable for their uniformity throughout the length and breadth of the civilisation. And much of what was left behind is totally unique; particularly in the fields of architecture and urban planning, Harappan Civilisation sets itself apart from developments further west.

Worlds apart: While the the Egyptians were using slaves to build the Pyramids and in

Mesopotamia the craftsmen were busy constructing magnificent temples, the Harappans were building much plainer more uniform buildings, not from huge stone blocks, but from normal red bricks of the standard 28 by 14 by seven centimetres. The solid brick houses built along roads, avenues and lanes provided a quality urban enviroment for the masses; original blueprints for the modern day urban planner. So which civilisation was more advanced? Certainly the normal everyday working Egyptian would never have lived in anything more substantial than a wattle and daub hut.

The pottery, mostly plain, but often with a red slip and black painted decoration was

uniform script also appears on pottery, suggesting a widespread literacy.

The craftsmen were particularly skilled at making faience from steatite and beads from cornelian and although relatively few pieces have been discovered, especially in comparison to Egypt and Mesopotamia, it has been argued that their overall skill was unique in the ancient world.

The birth of a religion?: But while the uniformity of material goods and town planning indicates a tightly and centrally organised society, this isn't to say that the Harappans enjoyed equality. Far from it. The huge variations in the sizes of dwellings suggest a pronounced hierarchy governed by an elite.

actually quite poor but gives an impression of efficient mass production. However, the Harappan craftsmen often displayed great skill, exemplified by the large numbers of stamp seals, usually made from steatite, a soft stone.

The faces of the seals were usually carved with animal designs, though humans were also occasionally represented. On most of the seals there were written inscriptions which have not yet been deciphered. The

Some have even suggested that this elitism formed the origins of the Hindu caste system. If so, who were the rulers? Is it possible that they are represented by the few stone sculptures so far discovered which had narrow eyes, were bearded and wore their hair at the back in a bun or a plait? Some say that they have a religious air about them and that the Harappans therefore were ruled by a priestly class.

There are certainly some clues about the religion which they may have presided over and these are remarkably reminiscent of certain aspects of Hinduism. The Great Bath at Mohenjo-daro and the recurrence of ad-

Left, a forerunner of the Indian headdress? **Above**, early morning over Mohenjo-daro.

vanced washing facilities in many households suggests that bathing was already a ritual function. Of all the animals carved on the steatite seals, the most beautifully executed was the humped bull or Zebu. The high quality of the work is perhaps an indication that this animal had even then taken on a special association. A prototype of Siva, to become linked with the humped bull in Hinduism, also seems to appear on the seals in a number of guises, and the modern Hindu Goddesses may have their antecedants in the female terracotta figurines excavated on a number of sites. They are heavily adorned with jewellery and sometimes also with elaborate headdresses.

lation of trade which now increased both internally and abroad.

Various centres began to specialise in particular crafts, confident that the well-developed trade routes could provide access to a wide market. Nodules of flint and finished flint blades from the Rohri Hills have been found on sites as far away as Harappa and and Lothal. Balakot and Chanu-daro developed as centres for shell and bangle making, while Lothal specialised in the cornelian beads. Industrial sites specialising in brick and pottery production as well as copper smelting have been located in the Cholistan Desert. Perhaps the most remarkable project of all, however, was the establish-

The capital of the Harappan Civilisation is thought to have been Mohenjo-daro, the greatest known Harappan city which, at its height, had a population of about 80,000. Harappa was probably a twin capital, although the discovery of similarly sized towns at Lurewala in the central Indus Valley and Ganweriawala in the Cholistan Desert suggests rather that a series of provincial capitals were established, including other sizeable settlements such as Kalibangan and Lothal, both in India.

Tradesmen: Throughout the civilisation there was a constant standardisation of weights and measures, implying a firm regu-

ment of the Harappan colony of Shortugai in Afghanistan, near the Badakstan lapis lazuli mines. It seems that the settlement was there solely for the purpose of exploiting the stone.

Meanwhile the volume of raw imported materials increased. There came gold from South India, silver from Afghanistan or Iran, copper from Arabia and jade from Central Asia. There was undoubtedly trade with Mesopotamia too, much of which was probably carried by ship. Although the sunken oblong structure adjacent to the settlement of Lothal may not after all have been be a dock, but a system for providing fresh water for the local people, a number of other sites near the coast west of Karachi must have been ports. Images of ships regularly appear on Harappan seals and there are likely references to sea trade in Mesopotamian texts. No doubt pack oxen were used to cover arduous land routes. Internally the Indus River network must have been vital and carts were also important for local transport as reflected in the copper or bronze models and terracotta toys which have been excavated at a number of sites.

Agriculture: Nevertheless it was the development of an efficient agricultural production which was the basis and backbone of the Harappan Civilisation. At its height, sheep, goats, various strains of cattle, oxen, foul and

even elephants were domesticated as well as buffalo and camels. Then, as indeed is still the case today, as the river and its tributaries receded during the summer months it left behind rich alluvial soil which could yield a full crop the following spring without the need even for ploughing or manuring.

Two types of wheat, barley, dates, field peas, cotton, sessamum and mustard were all grown and rice husks have been found at Lothal and Rangpur. The likelihood is that

Left, a shallow grave at Harappa. **Above**, bronze model of a dancing girl.

wheat and barley were harvested in the spring and cotton and sessamum in the autumn. Yet for all these advances an analysis of the skeletons from the cemetary at Harappa indicates a life expectancy for adults of around 30 years.

Decline and fall: But what could finally have brought this great civilisation to an end? Opinion was greatly influenced by the discovery of skeletons in the upper archaeological levels at Mohenjo-daro. Apparently massacred, they were assumed to have been the victims of invading Aryan hordes. This theory was given extra credence by references in the Rig Veda to *Hariyupuya* the scene of a defeat of non-Aryans by the invaders, which has been linked to the modern name Harappa. However, not only is Mohenjo-daro the only Harappan site for which there is physical evidence of a wild end, but modern dating techniques suggest that the city fell into decline well before the Aryans ever arrived.

Another theory may be that the very success of the Harappan Civilisation led to its downfall in as far as a population boom led to an over exploitation of natural resources and to soil exhaustion. However, as the entire population even after a boom may only have ever been about 400,000, this seems improbable.

Flooded out: Much more likely is the problem created by recurring and ever-worsening floods. The annual seasonal flooding of the Indus was of course a fact of life, but evidence from a number of sites suggests a far worse problem than this. Geologists have suggested that movements in the earth's crust had caused southern Pakistan to become slightly raised, effectively damming the Indus and preventing it from running down to the sea. The Indus would have broken its banks and flooded the surrounding plain, submerging many of the fields. The coastal settlements would have found themselves on dry land, so becoming defunct as trading ports.

The civilisation fragmented into a number of different cultural groups which emerged across the region, bringing to an end this remarkable period of uniformity. In Baluchistan Harappan sites were totally abandoned and the people probably returned to pastoral nomadism, a way of life many Baluchis follow to this day. In Panjab and Sind, as indeed in Kutch and Sarashtra in India, some sites continued to be occupied but there was a marked general decline in standards. At Chanhu-daro, for example, new settlers who followed the Jhukar Culture dismantled Harappan buildings for bricks to build much inferior houses. They were supplanted by followers of the Jhangar culture. The origins of these people remain quite uncertain.

History books: It is with the arrival of the Aryans that the new chapter in the story of Pakistan really begins. Though there is only very scant archaeological evidence of their presence, they are chiefly known to us because of their written texts. They therefore bring the uncertainties of prehistory to an end and usher us onto the very threshold of history itself.

The earliest and most important text for understanding the origins of this people is the Rig Veda, a book of hymns probably written down c. 1500-1300 B.C. The Rig Veda shows that the Aryan tongue was related to the great family of Indo-European languages, and was an early form of classical Sanskrit. Linguistic clues suggest that the Ayrans probably originated on the steppes of Eurasia and seem to have arrived in Pakistan in two principle waves, the first around 2000 B.C. and the second, the larger wave, around 1400 B.C., after they had been displaced from Iran. Exceptionally skilled warriors, they were able to establish themselves quickly in the Panjab.

Searching for cows: There are numerous references in the Rig Veda to the destruction of cities and fundamental to their military strength was the horse and chariot. But initially they did not occupy the cities which they found, but chose to live in small villages. Although they cultivated barley and probably wheat, they were predominantly pastoralists. The very word for war in the Rig Veda is *gavisthi*, meaning "search for cows". They were led by a hereditary king who was at least partly accountable to an assembly made up from the five tribes who fought not only against non-Aryans but also among themselves. They even persuaded non-Aryans to side with them against their own race.

From the beginning of its time in the subcontinent, Aryan society was divided into three *varnas* or "colours" – the *Brahmana* (priests), *Rajanya* (warriors), and *Vaishya* (common people). Soon a fourth – the *Sudras* emerged, who were not entitled to be invested with the sacred thread, and who were gradually denied their privileges. Here were the definite beginnings of the caste system.

Some have even argued that the use of the word *varna* may suggest that divisions were along racial lines, although this is very contentious. Indeed at this stage, divisions were probably merely social, based upon occupations. With time, however, more and more sub-castes were formed which further fragmented and ultimately stifled Indian society. They were increasingly rigid, too, and became linked not to occupation, but to birth.

The Aryans gradually expanded eastwards, reaching the Indus Valley through a mixture of conquest and amalgamation. Once they acquired iron they embarked on a massive programme of land clearance which paved the way for a change from pastoralism to settled agriculture. Archaeology indicates that towns, if only crudely built with mud and wattle and daub, were suddenly springing up: Urban life was returning and with it came increased prosperity.

Aryan culture: Despite their war-like image, the Aryans had always been lovers of music, dance and poetry. In addition to the Rig Veda, three further books of hymns were composed, as well as the great epic poems of the Ramayana and the Mahabharata. The words were almost certainly not written down until centuries after, but were committed to memory and passed down orally from generation to generation. This is all the more remarkable as the Mahabharata is the largest single poem ever created.

From these works, much is learned of the religion of the Aryans. Originally nature worshippers, they believed their gods to be represented by the forces of nature. Fire was especially important to them. Sacrifice played an important ceremonial role, but significantly it was forbidden to sacrifice cows, which were held in special esteem.

Gradually a theory of rebirth was developed as well as the doctrine of *Karma*, whereby one's status in life was pre-determined by one's conduct in the previous incarnation. Through a long process of transition and change, many aspects of Hinduism were to emerge from these early beliefs.

Right, an enduring mode of transport.

Up until the 6th century B.C. Pakistan remained without a powerful, unifying political force. In late Aryan times (or late Vedic times) a number of small principalities emerged, including Gandhara, which lay either side of the Indus, incorporating the Peshawar, Lower Swat and Kabul valleys.

The Persians: These principalities battled with each other for supremacy, but none were strong enough to unify the area into a single kingdom.

The whole region was therefore vulnerable to the attentions of the expanding Persian Empire, the Archaemenian rulers of Iran. Indeed, shortly before 530 B.C., Cyrus the Great crossed the Hindu Kush to receive tribute and within a decade Gandhara had been formally annexed as the 12th satrapy of the Archaemenid Empire, so bringing the independence of the region to a close.

With a base established in the north, the Persians were able to advance down the Indus valley into Sind. Most of Pakistan was under their control by 518 B.C.

Naturally, Gandhara's trade with Iran and the whole of Central Asia began to thrive, largely on the strength of its famous woollen goods, and the area soon became one of the richest satrapies of the whole Empire. The towns blossomed. Pushkalavati (modern Charsadda) developed into a regional capital along with Taxila which was to grow into one of the finest seats of learning in the ancient world, as a centre both for Vedic and Iranian studies. The Kharasthi script, written from right to left, which would later appear on Ashokan inscriptions in the 3rd century B.C. and which would continue to be used in Pakistan up until the 3rd century A.D., was introduced into the area at this time by Persian scribes.

The origins of Buddhism: Meanwhile, important developments were taking place in India, essentially a reaction to the economic and social changes of the times. The growth of towns and agricultural expansion in late Vedic times, particulary in the Ganges Valley, had by the 6th century B.C. produced an accumulation of wealth concentrated in the hands of the powerful few. At the same time, the caste system was steadily becoming more restrictive. Many thinkers increasingly came to question Brahmanical orthodoxy and the authority of the Vedic literature. Among these thinkers were Vardhamana Mahavir, who was to formulate Jainism, and Gautama Buddha, who was the founder of Buddhism.

Their ideas won quick support, especially from the lowly and oppressed castes. Jainism remained restricted to India, but Buddhism was soon to reach Pakistan with profound implications.

Alexander's quick visit: When Alexander the Great brought Persia to her knees in around 330 B.C., there was no power in Central Asia left to resist his relentless march east. No doubt driven on by his natural geographical curiosity, not to mention the tales of fabulous wealth on the Indian subcontinent, Alexander crossed the Hindu Kush in 327 B.C. Once in Pakistan, he found that with the collapse of Persian authority this land had once more fragmented into the control of local rulers and he was able to advance almost at will. He was given a friendly reception at Taxila and the local king offered him a tribute of fresh troops and treasure. Only when Alexander reached the Jhelum River did he encounter any serious resistance, but even then he proved victorious. However, upon reaching the Beas, his troops refused to go any further.

Quite possibly, after 10 years of continuous campaigning, they were exhausted and longing for home. They were also probably intimidated by the prospect of encountering the dreaded Nandas, who are referred to in Greek texts. The Nandas were the formidable army of the great Mauryan Empire which was growing at this time in India. Alexander therefore abandoned hope of reaching the Ganges and sailed down the Indus to the sea from where he and his army returned home. Some went on foot across the Makran Desert and others by ship via the Persian Gulf.

By 325 B.C., Alexander was off Pakistani soil and when he died even the governors he had left behind to rule his conquests made a quick dash back west. Despite this "defeat", the manuscripts of Greek historians have survived to provide us with fascinating glimpses into the development of society. We can read of the practice of *sati* (widow sacrifice upon the death of a husband) and of the poor selling their daughters in the market place. We read too of the splendid quality of the local oxen, so splendid in fact that Alexander had 200,000 of them sent back to Macedonia.

For all the references in the Greek texts to the Indian subcontinent, there is no single reciprocal reference in the Indian texts, and yet his brief rule did have significant consequences. For the first time ancient Europe and India came face to face and consequently new trade routes were opened up.

late Vedic period, from its base in the Lower Ganges Basin. From the 6th century B.C. it had struggled with neighbouring states for supremacy and with the accession of Chandragupta Maurya about 325-321 B.C. the first Indian Empire was born. From its capital at Pataliputna, near Patna, the Empire at its height was to dominate the whole of the Indian subcontinent apart from the land south of Karnataka and parts of Afghanistan to the west.

In Pakistan areas were brought under control which were to elude even the British Empire, and a decisive step forward in achieving this was the successful campaign by Chandragupta in the Indus Valley in 305

A number of new settlements were established in Pakistan, such as Boukephala on the Jhelum and Alexandria in Sind, and although none of these have survived as modern towns, many of the Greek inhabitants remained behind after the generals had left. Important too was the power vacuum which Alexander left for the expanding Mauryan Empire to step into.

The Mauryan Empire: The Mauryan Empire grew out of the kingdom of Magadha, another of the states which had emerged in the

B.C. against Seleucus, one of Alexander's generals who had founded the Seleucid dynasty in Iran. This victory brought the land to the west of the Indus under Mauryan control.

Chandragupta ended his reign to become a Jain and, according to Jaina sources, travelled to south India with a group of Jaina monks, where he carried abstinence to the extreme and deliberately starved to death.

At this time the area of Kalinga, modern Orissa, remained a troublesome thorn in the flesh of the Empire. When Chandragupta's grandson Ashoka, the greatest of the Mauryan rulers, succeeded to the throne, he

Above, a Greek coin minted in Gandhara, with the head Alexander the Great.

waged a bloody and ultimately victorious campaign in this area in 260 B.C. A legend relates that in order to inherit the throne he had been prepared to murder 99 rival brothers, yet he found the experience of Kalinga so disturbing that he adopted the ideas of Buddhism and indeed during his reign Buddhism was to flourish in Gandhara.

As part of his administrative control of the Empire Ashoka issued a series of edicts which he had engraved either on natural rock surfaces or on specially erected sandstone pillars and placed usually along the sides of public roads. For a long time they were believed to carry Buddhist messages, but Ashoka was always careful to differentiate

between his personal leanings and his official responsibilities.

The inscriptions in fact relate to the idea and practice of *dharma* which broadly means working towards the general well-being. Words such as consideration, obedience, generosity and honour are used but the inscriptions also refer to such practical topics as the establishment of medical services, digging wells, building rest houses for travellers and planting banyan trees along the roadside to provide shade.

For 100 years the Indian subcontinent was forged into a unified whole. The system was principally maintained by a land tax and by

trade duties. Internal and external trade blossomed, agriculture was developed and new roads were built to facilitate the movement of goods. One royal highway is said to have linked Taxila with Tamralipti, the main port at the Ganges Delta.

At its height the Empire was also able to support a huge army. According to Pliny this consisted of 9,000 elephants, 30,000 cavalry and 600,000 infantry. The Mauryan Empire was therefore not only the first Indian Empire but also the greatest. Despite many attempts by later rulers to emulate the Mauryans, none were ever able to do so.

Yet within 50 years of Ashoka's death in 232 B.C. the Empire had shrunk back to the Ganges. Some have explained the decline in terms of a revolt of the Brahmins, yet Ashoka never directly attacked Brahminism, although he did attack what he saw as useless ceremonies and sacrifices. Much more likely is that the economic burden of the administration and army simply proved too great to bear.

Bactrians, Scythians and Parthians: Each time that a major political power based in India collapsed, Pakistan moved back into the orbit of Central Asia, and so it was upon the disintegration of the Mauryan Empire. However, following the death of Alexander, power in Central Asia also fragmented, resulting in the formation of a number of kingdoms ruled by ex-Greek generals and their descendants. One such kingdom was Bactria situated in a prosperous region between the Hindu Kush and the Oxus and enriched by its strategic position on the line of a major trade route between Gandhara and the Mediterranean.

In 185 B.C. the Bactrian king Demetrius marched over the Hindu Kush, into the Panjab and down the Indus, so bringing much of Pakistan quickly under his control. Under Menander, the most successful of their kings, who ruled 155-130 B.C. and who was to become a Buddhist, the Swat Valley, the Hazara district and the Panjab as far east as the banks of the Ravi were brought to heel. Menander even made a determined, if unsuccessful attempt to conquer the Ganges Valley. Indeed all Bactrian ambition was soon to be undermined when their home base was itself attacked by a number of nomadic tribes from Central Asia, among them the Scythians.

Nowhere is the constant movement and interaction of peoples across Central Asia and through the Indian subcontinent better illustrated than in this episode.

When Emperor Shi Huang Ti built the Great Wall of China a number of Central Asian nomadic tribes were denied the possibility of raids into China. One of these tribes, the Yeuh-chi therefore turned their attentions to the shores of the Aral Sea from where they dislodged the Scythians. The uprooted Scythians were forced eastwards through Bactria and Parthia, over the Bolan Pass and into the Indus Valley where they arrived around 75 B.C. before some of their number moved on as far east as Delhi. However, was they who finally ushered in a period of stability.

The Kushans and Gandhara Art: The rule of the Kushans was one of the most decisive periods in the history of the whole Indian subcontinent. At their height in the 2nd century A.D. they ruled from the Oxus to the Ganges and yet their influence spread way beyond even these frontiers, for their winter capital was at Purusapura near Peshawar and from this position they had control of the Great Silk Road which linked Rome with Xian in China. With this position, therefore, came wealth.

The real significance of the Kushans, however, was not the size of their empire,

although they had few problems dislodging the Bactrians from Gandhara, they were in essence still a nomadic Central Asian tribe and fell victim to the next wave of migrants to pass through. These were the Parthians from east of the Caspian Sea who arrived and prospered in Northern Pakistan even before the 1st century B.C. was over. Yet they too were in their turn soon swept aside by the Kushans, a branch of the Yeuh-chi, who arrived in Pakistan in the 1st century A.D. It

Left, a Boddhisattva with a distinctly Grecian look. Above, a Gandharan relief depicting the Buddha's Great Departure.

nor the wealth that they accumulated. Rather their significance was the way in which they chose to spend that wealth: they transformed Gandhara into a religious holyland. Although the Kushan rulers themselves appear to have been Zoroastrians, they displayed a remarkable degree of tolerance towards Buddhism and other religions. Buddhist monasteries and stupas were built throughout Gandhara attracting pilgrims from as far afield as China. They were lavishly adorned with statues of Buddha and Bodhisattvas (future Buddhas) and narrative scenes from the life of Siddharta, the historical Buddha, and of his *Jatakas*, or previous births.

From their position on the Silk Road the sculptors were able to draw on a range of artistic influences and it was the particular fusion of Graeco-Roman and Indian styles which produced the distinctive and much acclaimed Gandhara art form. A revolutionary feature of the Gandhara School was the successful representation of the Buddha in human form. Previous attempts in the "Ancient Indian" sculptural schools had been unsatisfactory, or else they had represented Buddha in the form of a symbol, such as a lotus, a tree, a wheel or a stupa.

Significantly it was at this time that a new form of Buddhism developed called *Mahayana* Buddhism in which the image of the

the mid-3rd century A.D. only Gandhara and Kashmir remained to them and by the end of the century even these territories had been swallowed up by the Sassanian king of Persia, reducing the Kushans to mere vassals. As for their lands in India, they were steadily being acquired by the Guptas.

The Gupta Empire: Although it is unlikely that the Guptas ever had absolute control of the Indus Valley and probably never exacted anything more than tribute from the Panjab, it is difficult to ignore this dynasty in a history of Pakistan because the Gupta period has often been referred to as the Classical Age of India. During their rule much of what has come to be recognised as India was

Buddha himself came to be worshipped. Kanishka, the greatest of the Kushan kings, appeared to have given his full support to the new ideas. The message of Buddhism was sent out to the world. Missionaries were sent westwards into Central Asia and also eastwards to China and Tibet via the Karakoram. Still today Buddhist engravings can be seen carved into rock faces along the Karakoram Highway, the physical evidence of the movement of ideas.

Territorially, however, the Kushan kings never fulfilled their ambitions of controlling Central Asia. Indeed after the death of Kanishka their territory gradually fell apart. By

established or consolidated, particularly in the fine arts, literature, philosophy and science and of course all this has great bearing on the evolution of Pakistan.

Patronised by the court, there was a strong revival of Hinduism during which the king himself came to be looked upon as Vishnu. The Brahmins were also keen to foster this image and in return their own authority was strengthened by gifts of land. The caste system continued to be refined and there was a steady increase in the number of sub-castes partly due to the incorporation of the waves of invading foreigners into Hinduism. The numbers of untouchables also multiplied.

Accompanying these developments, progress was made in religious (and secular) literature. The Ramayana and the Mahabharata, the two great Vedic epic poems, were finally committed to writing in the 4th century A.D.

For all this, the origins of the Gupta dynasty are obscure, but from a position of mere local importance, the marriage of Chandra Gupta I into royalty at the beginning of the 4th century A.D. undoubtedly marked a great advance in their pursuit of supremacy. A capital was established at Pataliputra and Chandra Gupta I began to call himself "great king of kings" and yet even after considerable expansion under his son, Samudra Gupta, effective control probably remained limited to the Ganges Valley.

The Empire reached its height under Chandra Gupta II (375-415 A.D.). Following a victorious military campaign against the Scythians in Western India (388-409 A.D.), Sind was brought within its sphere of influence as well as northern India. However, even with these acquisitions the Empire could not rival the Mauryan Empire before it, the main reason being that central administrative control was never as completely established.

The Huns and the dark ages: The Gupta Empire appears to have been steadily weakened by worsening economic problems. Additionally, by the 5th century A.D. there was a fresh threat coming from the northwest in the form of the Huns. Reputedly fierce barbarians from Central Asia, one branch of the tribe had headed west for Europe and ravaged the Roman Empire, while a second had headed east to terrify the Persians from a position on the banks of the Oxus. This second branch then turned its eyes towards Pakistan.

King Skandra Gupta was able to hold back the Huns during his reign, but they eventually broke through the Hindu Kush at around 466-467 A.D. and were reinforced by a second wave of invaders about 20 years later. They quickly established a kingdom which extended into Sind and as far east as Central India. They are considered to have been excellent horsemen and first class archers.

Their ferocity no doubt also contributed to their success: the Huna chief Mihirakula is renowned as an oppressive tyrant who is said to have sought entertainment by having live elephants rolled over a precipice.

Though their rule was short-lived, its consequences were far-reaching. Most immediately Gandhara was sacked and Gandharan art, already well past its heyday, was never to recover.

Buddhism retreated from the plains of northern Pakistan and sought refuge in the Swat Valley where it was to survive until the 16th century A.D. Further afield, the fragmentation of the Gupta Empire introduced a period of political confusion plunging most

of the northern Indian subcontinent into a Dark Age.

Yet, ironically, even this episode made a positive long-term contribution to the development of society both in Pakistan and India. A number of other tribes followed the Huns over the Hindu Kush into Pakistan, some of whom settled and added to the cultural diversity whilst others moved on into India. Among those who moved on were the Huns themselves who, many scholars believe, converted to Hinduism and were to become the forefathers of the great Rajput families of Rajasthan. Certainly to this day some of the Rajputs maintain the title of "Huna".

In A.D. 711, a youthful Arab general Muhammad Bin Qasim rode eastwards along the desolate Makran Coast with six thousand Syrian Arab cavaliers to become the conqueror of Sind. It was an event of great historic significance about which the Italian scholar F. Gabrieli comments: "Present day Pakistan, holding the values of Islam and Arabism in such high esteem, should look upon the young Arab conqueror, Muhammad Bin Qasim, almost as a distant *Kistes* (founding father), a hero of Indian Islam".

Muhammad Bin Qasim's conquests were part of the proselytization and expansion of the Damascus based Ommayid Empire. He was the military commander of Caliph Walid bin Abdul Malik whose domains extended from Central Asia to Spain. In A. D. 712, Muhammad Bin Qasim conquered Sind's major sea port Daibul. Its ruins are situated 40 miles east of Karachi at the mouth of a dried up channel of the Indus Delta. The city had a great Buddhist stupa, a dewal, the root of its Arab name Daibul.

At that time Sind was ruled by Brahmin King Dahir son of Chach, relates the 13th century Persian chronicle *Chachnama*, translated from a lost near-contemporary account in Arabic referred to by later Arab historians.

Dahir's kingdom extended from the Indus Delta on the Arabian Sea to Rur, contemporary Rohri, on the eastern banks of the Indus opposite the modern city of Sukkur. The kingdom had brought about a reassertion of Brahminism over Buddhism, but because the majority of the people were then followers of the Buddhist faith, it had an extremely fragile base. The Arabs came across so many Buddhist idols in Sind that they adopted the word *budd* (Buddha) for the idol in the temple, a word still used in Pakistan.

After taking control of Daibul, Muhammad Bin Qasim continued his advance northwards and conquered Niran near Hyderabad. There the Arabs were reinforced

Preceding pages, foliate decoration first appeared with the Turkish invasions of the subcontinent. **Left**, Friday prayers in Lahore. **Above**, solitary in thought.

by a contingent of four thousand native Jat soldiers. They crossed the Indus by a bridge of boats and challenged Dahir's army near Rawar. The battle of destiny ensued. Dahir's forces were scattered and he died fighting.

The Arabs continued pressing northwards along the Indus. They captured Dahir's capital city Brahmanabad (Brahmin City), where they built their own city Mansura. Next they occupied Rur and continued their advance until they conquered Multan, the most ancient living city of South Asia. Multan, with

its renowned ancient golden temple dedicated to the sun god Aditya, contained so much gold that the conquerors evidently felt that they need go no further. For three centuries it remained the northernmost outpost of the Sind province of the Arab Empire.

The amazing Arab Islamic expansion was not only the result of cavalry forays. They had combined military operations with political means as well. Their offer to proselytize the natives to their own faith and become part of the new Islamic community had a far reaching impact. It was an offer which was open to everybody, and one which was perhaps most readily accepted by the lower orders of Hindus who now had a marvellous opportunity for collective manumission from caste slavery. As a result many Sind tribes accepted Islam, among them the Somra Rajputs. An additional attraction was that religious levies were abolished for those who converted.

A Charter of rights: But the new ruling power in Sind did not impose Islam on anybody. The *Chachnama* has reproduced extracts from the historic Brahmanabad Charter which for the eighth century represents a particularly high level of humanistic social order and values.

Those who did not choose to convert to Islam were treated magnanimously. The after themselves. He showered his new appointees with gifts and gave them seats of honour in the court. On a local level he appointed elders to collect revenue from villages and towns, allowing them complete administrative authority.

The members of the highest caste, Sind's ruling class Brahmins, who obviously saw less reason than anybody to convert, were also incorporated into the Brahmanabad Charter. They were restored to their top posts and much of the administration of the country was left in their hands.

Links with Baghdad: Ommayids were succeeded by the Abbasids who became the new rulers of Sind. From A.D. 750 the Abbasid

charter allowed complete religious freedom to those living in the countryside around Brahmanabad, putting them on par with the status of Jews, Magians and fire worshippers in Syria and Iraq. They were allowed to continue making idols of their gods; Brahmins and Buddhists alike could continue celebrating religious festivals according to the customs of their forefathers. They were encouraged to do business freely with Muslims.

Muhammad Bin Qasim incorporated the traditional administrative and revenue structures into the new order, appointing officials to positions according to their rank and experience, leaving the internal affairs to look Caliphs with their capital in Baghdad sent their governors to rule. Ibn Haukal, who had travelled extensively through the Arab domains around the middle of the 8th century, particularly mentioned the affluence of the people and cheapness of food in Sind. Being a prosperous land, Sind paid substantial revenue to Baghdad. In A.D. 820, Caliph Al-Mamoon had received one million dirams as revenue from Sind.

Culturally, deep interactions had started between the Middle East and the South Asian subcontinent. The Arabic language had made deep inroads into Sind which has the longest tradition of Arabic scholarship in the whole region. Modern Sindi vocabulary abounds in Arabic words. There is mention of Sindi scholars and poets in the annals of Abbasid Arabic literature. There was also a synthesis of Islamic and Sindi living patterns. Local dress was adopted by the common folk from among the new settlers, though the merchants continued to wear flowing Arab cloaks.

Academically there was not only one way cultural traffic. During the rule of Abbasid Caliph Al-Mansur, scholars from the Indus valley were welcomed at the court of Baghdad. Their works on medicine, mathematics, astronomy and philosophy were translated into the Arabic language.

The coming of the Turks: In the north Islam was also making inroads from Afghanistan into the north western regions of Pakistan. Islamic missionaries were actively spreading their faith among the tribes. Peshawar Museum has a stone tablet inscribed with both Arabic and Sanskrit characters from the Tochi valley of Waziristan, which establishes the presence of Islam in the area as early as A.D. 857. With the gradual decline of the Abbasid Arab Empire the Turks now

Left, Kufic Script records the building of a mosque in Banbhore c. A.D. 727-728. **Above**, artisans at work.

entered the imperial arena. First they established themselves in Afghanistan in the late 9th century. In A.D. 962, Alaptagin became the ruler of Ghazni. He was succeeded by Subaktagin who defeated and arrested Lamaghan from Raja Jaipal. After capturing Peshawar, he started developing his new domain by building roads for military as well as trade objectives.

Mahmud of Ghazni: Subaktagin's son Mahmud succeeded his father upon his death in A.D. 977. Mahmud set about the extension of the Turkish Empire into South Asia. He carried his military campaigns into the *Aryavarta* (the abode of Aryans). He was acknowledged as a vassal by the Abbasid Caliph Quadir Billah who presented him a robe of honour and gave him the title "Right Hand of the Empire and the Ruler of the Community". Mahmud's empire extended from Iraq to the Ganges and from Khwarzim to Kathiawar on the Arabian Sea.

The successors of Mahmud of Ghazni consolidated the Empire in the Indus valley and it was extended right up into the Panjab. Lahore replaced Multan as the administrative and cultural centre.

Multan was visited by one of the greatest rationalists of the world of Islam, Abu Raihan Al-Beruni (A.D. 973-1053), the philosopher, mathematician, astronomer and meritorious cultural historian. He has left a brilliant and authoritative work on Indian culture, the *Tahqiq ma lil Hind* (Research on India). Al-Beruni was also a scholar of Sanskrit and was fascinated by the charitable Indians. "It is obligatory with them every day to give alms as much as possible. They do not let money become a year or even a month old, for this would be a draft on an unknown future, which a man does not know whether he reaches or not."

The most benevolent legacy of the age was undoubtedly the movement for mystic brotherhood spread by the Sufi saints including Ali Makdum al Hujwiri, the dispenser of the treasure of spiritual guidance (Data Ganj Bakshs).

Hujwiri preached Islam to all, irrespective of caste. His work *Kashf el Mahjoob* (Exposure of the Esoteric) was written for the layman. He was critical of the age: "The Almighty has caused us to be born in an age when people consider their baser passions to be their religion. They crave for authority and rank. For them their pride and vanity are the marks of honour and knowledge. They interpret their hypocritical and exhibitionist acts of worship as fear of God. They have vengeance in their hearts and pretend to be compassionate and honourable. Exhibitionism and baseness are presented as chastity and purity. Hypocrisy for them is piety."

The Ghaznavid dynasty was ousted by the Ghurids (1148-1206). Muhammad Ghuri was appointed governor of Ghazni by his brother Emperor Sultan Ghayasuddin. He extended the borders of the Empire up to River Jumna; conquered Ajmer and Delhi. His Turkish successors advanced their domains southwards to Bengal. At the turn

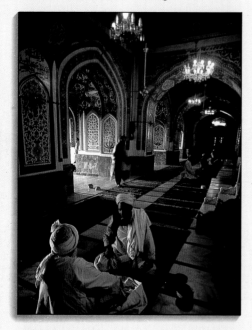

of the 13th century the Delhi Sultanate was established.

The Delhi Sultanate's administration was based on the structures of the Abbasid Empire. The Sultan was source of all power. He ruled his realm with the help of a large army and a vast civil administration. Judiciary was headed by a *Qaziul Qazat*, the chief justice, with magistrates and jurisconsults to dispense justice to all. Police, intelligence and communications were developed. Local people were incorporated in the army and civil administration. Most of the revenue collectors were the traditional village heads. During the Sultanate there was a fruitful fusion of Islamic and Indian culture and spiritual values. The political unity of the subcontinent resulted in economic regeneration and trade on large scale. It resulted in the development of exquisite crafts and high quality of consumer goods. Poetry and music became the passions of the masses. Literary romances and history writing flourished, giving birth to the secular modern literature in prose in various languages.

But with all the pomp and splendour of the Delhi-based Indian Turkish Empire, the spread of Islam was not the result of the military successes of the Sultans, but of the peaceful preaching of the mystics. While in the 14th century, Shia Muslims established important centres in the Deccan in southern India, the imperial centre did not generally attract converts to Islam. It became the religion of the majority only on the western and eastern peripheries, where the mystics were most active and where the Islamic country of Pakistan was to emerge.

The greatest challenge the Sultanate faced appeared as the scourge of Mongols who invaded the northern subcontinent in the 13th and 14th centuries. Firstly there were the Mongol hordes of Ghengiz Khan who reached the Indus in 1221, to be followed in 1398 by the Central Asian conqueror Timur. Both caused havoc in the region. There was death and destruction, chaos and confusion. But then Timur grew weary of the subcontinent and returned to Samarkhand. Under a series of different dynasties the Sultanate survived, until at the beginning of the 16th century when it fell to the displaced descendant of the the house of Timur, the great adventurer Babur.

The Delhi Sultanate lasted for three hundred years. Its administrative, civic and cultural structures continue to this day. The Indian historian Panikar observes: "Islam introduced in India a conception of human equality, a pride in one's religion, a legal system which in many ways was an advance on the codes of the time. The new spirit which the Hindu monarchs of Rajputana and Vijaynagar dynasty displayed as champions of *dharma* and as upholders of religion, was the direct result of their contact with Islam."

Above, formal Islam. Right, the sufis pursued a path of mystical realisation.

44

THE SUFIS

Much of the Koran consists of the regulations which are subsequently elaborated to form the law that governs all aspects of Muslim life. But the holy scripture is much more than a legal text, and many of its most beautiful verses, like "Wherever you turn, there is the face of God", have always been an inspiration to Muslims seeking to draw close to God through directly realised spiritual experience.

These seekers came to be called Sufis from the clothes of wool (suf) which they wore as a badge of their having renounced the world to pursue the path of mystical realisation. The early Sufi masters, who often came into conflict with the strict exponents of the law, developed an elaborate mystical theology which mapped the stages of the spiritual quest towards its ultimate goal of the union of the soul with God. Drawing on a great many sources for its inspiration, Sufism was never a unified movement, rather the product of various schools, each with its different special teachings and techniques passed on directly from a Shaikh to his disciples, some of whom he would appoint Shaikhs in their turn to teach others. Because of the strong disapproval of celibacy in Islam, most Shaikhs were married and thus hereditary links were also important.

Through these chains of succession, the Sufis were organised into different orders, each typically spread through a different territory, through which tombs of the order's saints would become centres of pilgrimage, and where loosely associated laymen would acknowledge the Shaikh and contribute to the expense of his establishment.

This flexible pattern was rapidly extended to India from the 11th century onwards. Although it was the soldiers of the Sultans who conquered the vast territories of northern India, including the heartlands of Pakistan, it was the great Shaikhs (also called Pirs) of the Sufi orders who were responsible for the conversion of so much of the local population to Islam, and it is the shrines constructed around their tombs to which people still turn today. Even though many of those local converts were first attracted as much by the awesome reputation of the Pirs as wonder-workers as by any deep understanding of their spiritual message, the Sufi ideals of tolerance and of gradually bringing people to a greater spiritual awareness were thus what lay behind the most successful missionary movement in the history of the subcontinent.

Within the inner circle of close disciples devoting themselves to the fulltime observance of the Sufi path, the Shaikh's authority was absolute. Every detail of his behaviour would be carefully noted and recorded by his followers. Only he could teach the personalised discipline of the order called zikr or remembrance. This may consist simply of the repetition of a short formula like "There is no god but God" to a prescribed pattern of breathing and chest-beating. A few orders have specialised in fiercer and more spectacular physical mortification, whose advanced practice might allow devotees to pass skewers through their cheeks without lasting pain. In the environment of India, with its elaborate yogic traditions, many individual Muslim faqirs have always rejected the carefully balanced spiritual discipline of the regular Sufi orders in favour of more outlandish practices like wearing heavy chains, or of the quick path to enlightenment through drugs.

Within the mainstream, however, the most popular discipline has been the practice of listening to the singing of mystical poetry in the strongly rhythmic style called qavvali. Particularly encouraged in the Chishti order, this poetry and its music has always had an immense popular appeal, extending far beyond Sufi circles as such. Most of the classic poetry in the local languages of Pakistan is of Sufi inspiration. The Sufi poets often related the agony of the separation from the Beloved and the joy at finding Him using tales of romance as metaphors for their spiritual quests. The divine was always the man and the seeker the woman whose identity is merged in that of her lover. Such romances are still recalled again and again. So even today, when the regular institutional practice of Sufism has greatly declined in Pakistan, the Sufi legacy continues to be a vital part of the country's cultural heritage.

The turn of the 16th century was a busy time. Not only in Central and South Asia, but the world over. Europe in particular was beginning to expand its influence in all directions. In 1492 Columbus sailed to America and with Vasco da Gama, the Portugese had opened up the subcontinent and the far east to sea trade. The world was getting smaller, and everyone, it seems, was in search of new wealth and territory and empires.

Born in 1483, Zahiruddin Muhammad Babur originally came from the principality of Farghana which formed part of an area now known as Uzbekistan in the Soviet Union. He was a professional ruler of the house of Timur whose empire was under threat from the advancing Uzbeks from the north.

Having lost Farghana, and captured and lost Samarkand, his first expedition outside Central Asia resulted in the capture of Kabul in 1504. He had become a ruler without a kingdom and denied the places he loved, turned his gaze south in search of a fitting domain. He was a writer, poet and adventurer and his fantasies resulted in the creation of an empire which represented one of the most glorious epochs in the history of the subcontinent. At the height of their power, in the 16th and 17th centuries, the Moghuls were to rule over 150 million people. The Empire was to become one of the most powerful the world had ever seen.

Sweeping down with his army, Babur seized Kandahar in 1522 and Lahore in 1524. In 1526 in a battle at Panipat, 50 miles north of Delhi, Babur defeated the Afghan leader Sultan Ibrahim Lodi, ruler of the last dynasty of the Delhi Sultanate. It was the first time northern India had seen guns, the matchlocks and mortars which Babur used to annihilate the forces of the Lodi chief. Even with 100,000 men and 1,000 elephants, he didn't stand a chance. Another momentous occasion in South Asia's history; Moghul rule was established and Babur secured a territory stretching from the Oxus in the west

to Bengal in the east, with a southern limit marked by the Rajasthan Desert.

Beyond his military achievements, Babur is particularly remembered for the wonderful gardens he laid wherever he went and for his memoirs the *Baburnama*, a classic autobiography. On arrival in the subcontinent, he seems to have been very disparaging about a lot of what he saw:

"Hindustan is a country of few charms. Its people have no good looks; of social intercourse, paying and receiving visits there is

none; of genius and capacity none; of manners none; in handicraft and work there is no form or symmetry, method or quality; there are no good horses, no good dogs, no grapes, muskmelons or first rate fruits, no ice or cold water, no good bread or cooked food in the bazaars, no hot baths, no colleges, no candles, torches or candlesticks..."

He did, however, see some advantages of his newly conquered territory:

"Pleasant things of Hindustan are that it is a large country and has masses of gold and silver... Another good thing is that it has unnumbered and endless workmen of every kind. There is a fixed caste for every sort of

Left, Babur was a very keen gardener. **Above**, elephants were much favoured by the Moghuls.

work and for every thing, which has done that work or that thing from father to son till now..."

Babur didn't live long enough to really reap the rewards of his military exploits. Who knows, maybe he was homesick. In any event it is said that he gave up his life for his son Humayun who had fallen critically ill in 1530. He offered his own life to Allah in exchange. The wish was granted; Babur died and Humayun recovered.

But Humayun lacked his father's talent and energy. At continual odds with the Afghans, their rebel chief Sher Shah Suri finally forced him to leave India and seek asylum in Persia. Before Humayun was fi-

nally ousted from Indian soil, his wife Hamida Banu Begum had born him a son while they were taking refuge down in Sind in 1542. He was born in the desert town of Umarkot and his name was Akbar. He was to rule the Moghul Empire for nearly 50 years.

During Sher Shah's five year reign, a great deal was achieved in terms of administration and building. As well as making a valuable contribution to the building of the Grand Trunk Road, he also constructed a number of strategic forts to protect the Empire, including the giant Rohtas Fort near Jhelum. His reign is said to represent the longest five years in India's history.

Humayun only took back his father's territory in India on the death of Sher Shah in 1556 and then continued to reign for only seven months. He died after falling down the steps of his library in Delhi! It is said that he took excessive amounts of opium.

The story of Hemu: Even as a young boy Akbar's powers of leadership were put to the test when fighting against the forces of his father's enemy, Sher Shah. Fighting on the side of Sher Shah was a man called Hemu who was a Hindu of very humble birth indeed. He had risen to a high position in the service of a nephew of Sher Shah and was universally liked by Hindus and Muslims and was equally open handed with all. He ran his fief well and maintained a large army which achieved many victories.

He especially appreciated elephants which he saw as an important part of the force. Perhaps because he was an ugly little man and was unable or unwilling to ride a horse, he always led his troops into battle on an elephant. He was too weak to wield a sword, but was always in the thick of the battle, leading his men and calling them on. His disabilities mattered little as people were afraid of his name and reputation and his unbroken line of victories.

When he fought against Akbar, at Panipat, an arrow hit Hemu in the eye and his elephant bolted. Seeing the commander go the troops, as always, withdrew; and so it was that Hemu was captured. Bairam Khan told Akbar, who was then a young boy, to decapitate this enemy. Some accounts say that Akbar did so. Others say that seeing the lad look reluctant, Bairam Khan did it for him.

Securing the Empire: Akbar became Emperor when he was only 13 years old. Throughout his rule he aimed to be the Lord paramount of India. He saw the importance of a strong, highly disciplined army claiming "A monarch should ever be intent on conquest otherwise his neighbours rise in arms against him. The army should be exercised in warfare, lest from want of training they become self-indulgent."

He swept over India and secured an Empire that stretched from the Arabian Sea eastwards to Bengal and from Kashmir in the North to the Deccan Plateau in the South.

The Moghuls had inherited the well-established administration of the Delhi Sultanate and Akbar ensured that the Empire ran smoothly by encouraging the loyalty of his officials. He gave them ranks called *mansabs*. The *mansabdars* were required to recruit and maintain a specified number of cavalry according to rank, extracting sufficient revenue for the purpose from the *jagir*, a piece of land which was given to them in return. The system bred competition among those keen on titles and honour. They remained loyal and ensured that Akbar had his army. The *mansabdar* was also required to send a certain amount of revenue to the Emperor as a kind of tax. Akbar was clever; he continually rotated the *mansabdars* around the *jagirs* lest local alliances grow to threaten the absolute power of the Emperor.

The story of Rupmati: And he didn't stop with his wives either! He very often used to disguise himself and venture into the slums to see how the people really lived. One time he heard a beautiful song, about a lady called Rupmati who was in the harem of Baz Bahadar, the ruler of Malwa. There were many rulers who tended to combine high culture and Barbarism, and Baz Bahadar was no exception!

Akbar brooded on the words of the song and became jealous. He wanted to have Rupmati. In the end he found an excuse and sent an army against Malwa. Baz Bahadar prepared for battle and sent the women of the palace to a safe place, leaving orders that

In Akbar's time, the number of Hindus given official posts increased dramatically. They gained a very large share in the administration of the Empire. The *jizya*, taxes which had previously been levied on Hindus, were abolished.

Akbar's openness towards the Hindus did not stop with administration. He also married a great many Hindu wives, partly to help cement alliances and also to keep his vast empire intact.

Left, Akbar orders the slaughter to cease. **Above**, entering the Lahore Fort.

they were all to be sent to heaven in the event of defeat.

Akbar won the day and Baz Bahadar fled. The swords were drawn and the ladies all slain; all except for Rupmati who was badly injured. When the Moghul commanders came and tried to save her, she took a phial of poison she had hidden inside her clothes and perished. Akbar was sticken with grief.

Since then popular songs have celebrated Baz Bahadar, the faithful Rupmati, and Akbar too.

Influences: Akbar's biographer was his courtier and confidante Abul Fazl who produced the *Akbarnama*, a massive biography.

Apparently Akbar ate one meal a day, comprising 40 dishes!

As his reign went on, Akbar became increasingly keen on discussing religious matters and listened to the debates of various faiths; the Hindus, Parsees and Christians all had an impact on his thinking. In the latter half of his reign, he established the *Din-i-Ilahi*, a new order encouraging a cult of loyalty around himself, elevating himself in some people's eyes to a position of a divine ruler. His experiments with religion were not continued by his successors.

Having the Hindu classics Mahabharata and Ramayana translated into Persian was a measure of his religious tolerance.

In the arts there was a great deal of influence from Persia. Humayun had brought back Persian artists after his period of exile. Akbar continued to foster the Persian tradition and encouraged local artists to fuse it with their own ideas. An Indo-Persian school developed using primarily secular themes such as portraits, court scenes, natural life, historical subjects and legends. Beautiful paintings, the classic Moghul Miniatures, were used to illustrate the *namas* (biographies) of Moghul rulers.

His contribution to architecture is of no less importance and is characterised by a blending of Hindu and Muslim styles. His greatest achievement was Fatehpur Sikri near Agra in India, which became his capital from 1570 to 1585. He then moved to Lahore, which was more strategically located, and built the Lahore Fort. Akbar finally died in 1605.

Jahangir 1605-1627: Developments during the reign of Akbar's son Jahangir were to a large extent directed by his intelligent and very beautiful wife, Nur Jahan. Artists and politicians began to flood in from Persia as never before. Jahangir became a keen collector of art as well as jewels and other priceless gifts which his nobles gave him.

In amongst leading a number of military campaigns southwards to the Maratha kingdom of the Deccan Plateau, intented to extend the Empire still further, Jahangir followed his favourite hobby – collecting and dissecting all manner of species of animals.

Much has been written on his bouts of heavy drinking and brutality. When angry, and especially if his throne was threatened, he was capable of great cruelty, having men flayed alive, impaled, or torn to pieces by elephants.

Once, while hunting, his men inadvertently frightened away the prey. Jahangir was incensed and in his memoirs he relates without shame his radical reaction, "In a great rage I ordered them to kill the groom on the spot and to hamstring the bearers and mount them on asses and parade them through the camp so that no one should again have the the boldness to do such a thing."

The height of Moghul magnificence: On Jahangir's death there followed a very bloody fight for his throne from which his eldest son Shah Jahan emerged victorious.

Shah Jahan's name has gone down in history as the architect of the Taj Mahal, built in memory of his beloved wife Mumtaz Mahal who bore the Emperor no fewer than 14 children, eight sons and six daughters, in a period of 17 years.

Important as it is, the Taj Mahal is only one of the many landmarks of Shah Jahan's reign from 1627-1658, a reign which marks the climax of the Moghul dynasty. For thirty years his throne was never seriously threatened and the realm never invaded by a foreign foe. And with the exception of some moves south into the Deccan where he placed his son Aurangzeb as viceroy, the Empire was not greatly extended.

Shah Jahan was primarily interested in collecting jewels and he took enormous pleasure in a display of courtly magnificence. The opulence of his court was a legend not only in India, but also in Europe. After his formal enthronement, he glorified himself by constructing a peacock throne more splendid and costly than the throne of any other monarch.

It took seven years to build and was in the form of a bedstead on golden legs with an enammelled canopy supported by twelve emerald pillars each of which bore two peacocks encrusted with gems. Between the birds on each pillar was a tree covered with diamonds, rubies, emeralds, and pearls.

In the realm of architecture and art the highest quality of the Moghul period belongs to the reign of Shah Jahan. Preferring marble to the red sandstone favoured by Akbar and Jahangir his buildings are characterised by elegance and the lavish use of costly decoration (Taj Mahal, and the Pearl Mosque in Agra).

The city of Lahore now flourished, with Jahangir's tomb and the marvellous Shalimar gardens, laid out by Shah Jahan, which are among the most magnificient garden landscapes in the world. There was at the time a saying about Lahore, "The Persian cities of Isfahan and Shiraz together are not equal half of Lahore!"

The end of his reign was far from noble, being imprisoned by his son Aurangzeb who, some have claimed, deposed his father partly to put a halt to his architectural extravagances. He died in 1666, a prisoner in the Agra fort.

Aurangzeb 1657-1707: The two most prominent sons of Shah Jahan were Aurangzeb and his older brother Dara Shikoh. They were worlds apart in how they envisaged the Moghul world, typifying two completely opposing arguments. While Dara Shikoh thought that the only way of maintaining the Empire was by joining the oceans of Islam and Hinduism, much in the same vein as Akbar; Aurangzeb justifiably felt that all the wealth, extravagance and idolatry encouraged by previous rulers had led to a degeneration of moral conduct.

He was convinced that the only path ahead lay in a reassertion of strict Islamic principles combined with orthodox mysticism. The argument heralded the beginnings of a split in the unity of northern India. His reign is marked by his constant adherence to his principles, from which he never strayed.

Before their father died, Aurangzeb defeated Dara Shikoh in battle and had him executed when he became Emperor.

Aurangzeb displayed great bravery even as a young boy, stopping a charging elephant which threatened the royal family. He spent the early part of his reign in fighting off the continuous attacks from Persians and Central Asian Turks. He became feared and re-

spected for his vigour and skill, and was regarded by his subjects as a good man and a good, though strict, ruler.

He was a highly educated man and he knew the Koran by heart, following the Islamic law in every detail of his personal conduct. As his reign went on, he spent more and more time in prayer and in living a simple life; he spent a lot of his spare time embroidering hats.

Though he was never frivolous, his wives were, and some of them even drank and tempted him to do the same! Once, they say, he tried to ban fashionable clothes and wine. One of his wives invited the wives of all the learned men to a party. They came in all the latest fashion and accepted the wine. She then showed him all these drunken wives and said, "If the wives of the scholars who decide the law are such, how can you forbid the ordinary women in the family?"

However, he soon lost the support of many Hindus due to a series of unpopular measures. He destroyed their temples: "The richly jewelled idols taken from pagan temples were transferred to Agra and placed beneath the steps leading to the Nawab Begam Sahib's Mosque in order that they might ever be passed under foot by the true believers." He reintroduced the *jizya*. But then he married his son to a Rajput Princess and contin-

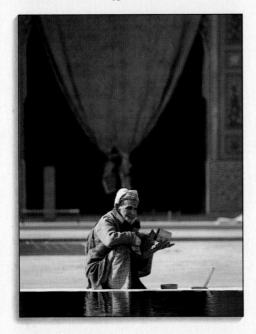

ued to employ Hindu officials. Indeed, no Moghul Emperor employed more Hindu officials than Aurangzeb.

He was anti-Shia, banishing them, prohibiting their long moustaches and appointing an officer to measure and clip off their long whiskers!

Militarily, he was determined to combat the advancing Marathas in the Deccan, making the southern town of Aurangabad his capital from which he conducted operations. The Marathas were led by that legendary figure Shivaji who is still cherished to this day by low caste Indians in Bombay. For the last 26 years of his life, Aurangzeb was em-

broiled in this bitter conflict which proved to be immensely costly. The financial pressure began to show and it strained the whole administration. His absence in the south also prevented him from maintaining a firm grip on the north, and slowly the Empire began to crumble.

An important contributory factor was that the *mansabdari* system created under Akbar had broken down: Land was no longer rotated and this allowed local rulers to take advantage and cement their own alliances. There was less meritocracy in Aurangzeb's reign, and he didn't engineer loyalty towards himself as Akbar had done. He finally died in 1707. His funeral was a characteristically simple affair; it was paid for by the sale of his embroidered hats.

Aurangzeb bequeathed few major artistic splendors to the Empire. His most notable achievement in this field was the magnificent Badshahi Mosque which he had built in Lahore.

Decline and fall: Aurangzeb was the last great Moghul and the disasters of his successors show how much the Empire depended on the strength and character of the Emperors. No Emperor after Aurangzeb had the charisma of the great Moghuls or was militarily able to assert himself. Constant warfare sapped the economy and the Empire drifted into chaos and anarchy.

Successors spent their reigns either fighting off the Afghans, Persians, Sikhs, Rajputs and Marathas, or living lives of decadence, propped up as a symbol by anyone who felt it advantageous to do so, including the British. Territory was lost: the greatest ignominy, perhaps, was the sacking of Delhi in 1739 by the Persians who rode off with Shah Jahan's peacock throne. The Panjab and Kashmir came under the control of the Afghan Ahmad Shah Durrani and remained under Afghan control until, in the early 19th century, the Sikhs pushed the Afghans back to the Khyber Pass.

All the while, however, from small beginnings in Bengal, another power had gradually been gnawing away at everybody else's stake in the subcontinent: The British.

Above, washing pans in the ablution tank of Wazir Khan's Mosque. **Right**, would Aurangzeb have approved?

Early days: The small group of British merchants who came knocking on the door of Jahangir's Moghul court at the beginning of the 17th century were not the first Europeans to start trading in the subcontinent. They had been beaten to it by the Portugese as far back as 1498 when Vasco Da Gama discovered a sea route to India. The Dutch had followed, and continued to set up trading colonies in the East Indies, blocking any chance of the British gaining a foothold in that part of the world. But India was big

enough, and anyone stood a chance of deriving great wealth from the fabulous riches that it possessed.

From their first enclaves in Bengal, the merchants of the East India Company could not have imagined that British presence in India would come to mean anything more than peaceful trading. But then the French arrived in the middle of the 17th century, signalling the beginning of militarisation: the situation in Europe was such that the two sides inevitably ended up fighting on Indian soil. Within 100 years the French were a spent force and the British possessed the most efficient military machine in the sub-

continent, as clearly demonstrated by Robert Clive at the Battle of Plassey in 1757.

As Moghul power declined, British influence increased. The British advanced by making alliances with Indian rulers who very often preferred them to neighbours with whom they may well have been warring for years. Any resistance was easy to crush; there were no problems in defeating the undisciplined ranks of Indian cavalry.

In 1775 the Company was found to be corrupt and a regulating act gave the goverment control over Company officials. In 1784 the India Act left the Company solely in charge of commerce. India was given a Governor General with almost exclusive control, and British policy often reflected the beliefs of this man. Motivated by good old-fashioned Imperialism, the British began to annex states, offering troop protection against aggressive neighbours in return for loyalty and sizeable subsidies. By 1818, Bengal, Bihar, Orissa, and a tract of land north of the Ganges running up to Delhi were firmly in British hands.

A power in the Panjab: Two hundred years after their arrival in the subcontinent the British were well placed to begin playing their strategic games. They now began to determine the future of Pakistan. Eyes turned northwest, to the frontiers of Afghanistan. It was feared that the Russian bear was advancing out of Central Asia and Afghanistan was viewed as an important buffer state.

But any attempt to secure the frontier had to take into account the Panjab and its powerful Sikh ruler Ranjit Singh. The role of the Sikhs in the power struggle in northern India at the time of the British advance had such deep implications for the region's development that no history of Pakistan would be complete without describing how the Sikhs had become such a dominant force.

The Panjab had been the home of the Sikhs since the late 15th century, and their religion was based on the teaching of Guru Nanak. He was followed by a succession of nine other living Gurus. The first five gurus were all noted poets, whose work was collected to form the basis of the Sikh holy book, the *Adi Granth*. There is a tradition that it was Akbar who granted the daughter of the third Guru an area of land in Amritsar on which the Sikhs built their temple in 1577.

Gradually the Sikhs came into increasing conflict with local Governors and they also became increasingly militarised. The Gurus bore arms and were accompanied by armed retainers, mercenaries and the trappings of state. The ninth Guru Teg Bahadar was executed by Aurangzeb.

His son Govind Rai founded an order called the *Khalsa* which was to become the basis of modern orthodoxy. Govind "borrowed" the Rajput title of Singh in an attempt to increase the status of the Sikhs. He was murdered in 1708 by a Pathan horse trader.

Thereafter one of his friends, a curious holy man called Banda Bahadar (Banda = slave, Bahadar = brave) led what was effectively a peasant revolt in the Panjab, marking the beginnings of the chaos and confusion, violence and bloodshed which were to continue all the way through the 18th century. While confusion from within was largely a result of uprisings inspired by the Sikhs, the local governors also had to contend with invasions from the outside.

Apart from Nadir Shah's Persians in 1739, there were a series of nine invasions by the Afghan Durrani between 1747 and 1769, causing havoc in the province. It became more or less impossible to govern at all. The best that the local governors could do was to try and make friends and alliances wherever they could. Sometimes they would attempt to pacify the Sikhs and sometimes they would persecute them. Sometimes they managed to do both, simultaneously.

Throughout the century Sikh warlords emerged, and while they spent most of their time fighting each other, they also fought governors or Afghans where the need arose. At the end of the century these warlords were either dead or very old men. By a combination of clever marriage alliances and tricking or defeating the aged Sikhs, one young man emerged to unite Sikh power in the Panjab. His name was Ranjit Singh.

He was not a handsome man as smallpox had left his face pitted and taken away the sight of one eye. When his Muslim wife

Left, Robert Clive helped turn the East India Company into a military machine. **Above**, not a pretty sight – Ranjit Singh.

Mohran asked "Where were you when God gave out the good looks?", he answered "Whilst you were occupied with your good looks, I was seeking power!"

By 1799 he had taken Lahore where he was pronounced Emperor. Ludhiana followed in 1806, Multan and Kashmir fell in 1818 and 1819, Ladakh in 1833 and Peshawar in 1834. With such a strong presence in the north-west of India, the British could sit back and let Ranjit Singh do all their work for them; the buffer state was there, ready made.

Under Ranjit Singh the Panjab was spared the permanent state of rebellion common to other states. His army, the mightiest in India, was 75,000 strong, contained a hard core of

Pathans and had Italian and French generals who could no longer find work back home. It also contained a fair amount of quality French military hardware smuggled out of Europe after the downfall of Napoleon. Little wonder that he was respected by all, including the British.

The British didn't move in until after his death in 1839, when the Sikh Empire began to collapse. Despite the ensuing anarchy the British were met by fierce resistance from the Sikhs, which resulted in two brief but extremely bloody civil wars known as the Sikh wars. Following the second one in 1849, Governor Dalhousie commented on how vital the Panjab was to British interests; "It is far too near the Afghanistan border for any further risks." From this point on, the Sikhs remained loyal to the British and their support helped the Panjab to become the most prosperous state in British India.

The sowing of the seed: The consequences of the first Sikh war (1846) had major repercussions for another state, Kashmir. Before being taken by Ranjit Singh, it had been ruled alternately by Moghuls and Afghans. Kashmir was then 90 percent Muslim, but after the siege of Multan in 1819 Ranjit Singh wanted to reward one of his leaders, Gulab Singh, a Hindu. He was duly granted the estate of Jammu.

The Indus revisited: Sind was another logical target for the British, who had begun showing interest in the early 19th century when a diplomatic mission under Lord Minto visited the ruling Talpur Mirs in 1809. They signed a treaty by which the Mirs promised not to allow in the French. The British saw the importance of the Indus River, believing it could be an important commercial highway.

A further treaty followed in 1832, whereby the Indus was thrown open to commerce on condition that no armed vessels or military stores passed along it. The British basically ignored this and took Karachi, Sukkur and Bukkur in 1839.

In 1841 Gulab Singh allowed British troops to march through his territory on their way to do battle in Afghanistan. During the Sikh wars he had refused to help the Sikhs , and was once again rewarded, this time by the British. The prize was worth his treachery: in 1846, he received Kashmir by the treaty of Amritsar by which "Maharaja Gulab Singh acknowledges the supremacy of the British government, and will in token of such supremacy present annually to the British one horse, 12 goats and three pairs of Kashmiri Shawls". The granting of the control of Kashmir to a Hindu began a struggle which has not finished to this day.

Sir Charles Napier took over responsibility for the Sind. Described as an "eccentric swashbuckler with no scruples", Napier said of Sind, "We have no right to sieze Sind, yet we shall do so and a very advantageous, useful, humane piece of rascality it will be."

After annexing the province he issued the simple message "Peccavi!", meaning "I have sinned". His four years as governor saw vigourous and oppressive rule, but by 1843 he had secured it for the British.

Discontent: British activities on the subcontinent had not been limited to waging war. There had been a gradual process of westernisation which had effected the whole of Indian society. Western scientific knowledge was beginning to open India to the world of industry and mechanisation. Western education established private colleges and universities.

For India's Muslims, the repression of Persian and the encouragement of Urdu and regional languages, coupled with the introduction of English as the language media at universities, began to undermine the Arab-Persian tradition which had been fostered so much during the height of the Moghul Empire. Many Muslim academics and religious thinkers began to feel that their cultural basis was being destroyed. Some began to distrust the British.

buying and selling; land suddenly had a price and could be bought and sold to the highest bidder. The feudal society was out and the cash economy was in, and the Moghul pyramid of rights, based on rank, came tumbling down. There emerged a pro-British *nouveau riche* elite, which gradually came to replace the rulers of old. Many of the trappings of Moghul glory became superfluous; artisans, courtiers and many soldiers lost their jobs.

In addition there were grievances caused by changes in the right to succession; if a ruler died without an heir, the state would go to the British.

While the British ran India with a lot of collaboration and cajoling, it is clear the

Apart from this, there were a whole number of reasons for various pockets of discontent which began to ferment. While the British had convinced themselves that only their presence could help what they saw as a chaotic, backward India, they actually succeeded in turning the whole fabric of Moghul society upside down. Whenever the British annexed states they made revenue settlements with, or sometimes without, local rulers. The British introduced the notion of

Left, Sikhs fought with the British during the Mutiny. **Above**, a British legacy – the Khojak Tunnel in the deserts of Baluchistan.

annexation of states had caused much resentment among those who gained nothing from it. A major plaintive was the army; after Sind was annexed, soldiers lost the allowance they had previously received for being "abroad". Many soldiers were from Oudh. When this state was annexed in 1856, the British put a stop to all the special treatment and favours which had previously been common practice.

The Indian Mutiny erupted in isolated areas in 1857. There were bloody uprisings in Meerut, Delhi, Kanpur and Lucknow. British reprisals were exceptionally brutal. The soldiers petitioned the last Moghul Bahadar

Shah Zafar, who was officially up to this time the sovereign ruler of the Moghul Empire, to be their figurehead. "Grant me six feet of earth in the lane where my beloved dwells", he pleaded. The British exiled him to Burma where he died in 1862.

The British Raj: Control now passed from the East India Company to the Crown and the Company was disbanded. Westminster was now to have a Secretary of State for India and a 15-member India Council. The Crown's representative in India was now the Viceroy, who had almost absolute authority. Under him was an Executive Council made up of British members and a Legislative Council of British and Indian representatives.

India became the jewel in the Imperial crown. The country prospered under increased agricultural production, rapidly expanding trade, and industrial development. The railway network provided a major contribution, increasing from a mere 200 miles in 1858 to 35,000 miles by 1914. The coalfields of Bihar and Orissa increased production from 500,000 tons in 1968 to 20 million tons in 1920. Jute and textile production boomed in Bengal. Tea exports also rose dramatically.

The Game goes on: Territorially, the only problem remained the North West Frontier. At the far northwest of the Panjab, this was a tribal highland area belonging to the Pathans. Since the Panjab annexation, there had been a bitter and bloody struggle between The Pathans and the British. Beyond settled areas the British initially tolerated a degree of tribal independance, but used hostage taking, blockades, subsidies and punitive expeditions to ensure the area's security.

Given impetus by the second Afghan war (1878-1879), and the steady Russian advance in Central Asia, advocates of more direct control brought about a shift to the Forward Policy, where an extensive network of military outposts and agents was established in tribal territory. The tribal areas of the Afridis, Mashuds, Waziris were now officially ruled by the British.

With the North West Frontier under control, the British then feared that the Russians might somehow come in through the back door, over the passes of the Hindu Kush.

The ensuing hysteria produced Rudyard Kipling's Kim, espionage, intrigue and great excitement; The Great Game was diverted to the Northern Areas of Pakistan. The Gilgit Agency was established as a means of fanning British influence throughout the far northwest, as far as Chitral and Hunza. Hunza actually fell to the forces of Algneron Durand in 1891.

In 1893 the British drew a frontier between British India and Afghanistan. The resulting Durand Line (named after Algneron Durand's brother) cut straight through Pathan tribal territory. Following Pathan revolts in 1897 which needed 35,000 troops to put down, viceroy Lord Curzon created the North West Frontier Province, as he saw it as impractical to rule the whole area as part of the Panjab.

To the west, Baluchistan with its borders to Persia and Afghanistan, was of great strategic importance. The routes through the Bolan Pass to Quetta and beyond were vital. Again the British faced a tribal problem, solved by the same kinds of measures used to subdue the Pathans. By the 1890s Baluchistan was largely pacified and stabilised.

Split factions: On the political front after the mutiny, most factions of Indian society expressed absolute loyalty to the Raj. And despite the fact that the British tried to blame the Muslims for the mutiny, support from the Muslim westernised elite did not diminish. There were speeches thanking God for the enlightened and benevolent rule of Queen Victoria. On the other side of the coin, more learned Muslims saw that they had difficult times ahead, wondering how they should assimilate to developments under the British while still holding on to their traditions. With the disappearance of Bahadar Shah, they suddenly had no figurehead.

Things were a lot easier for the Hindus. Hinduism had become trendy in the West; people began to study it. While abroad Hinduism became accepted as the spiritual force of India, many felt that the Muslims, who had ruled most of India for some seven centuries, were not now recognised as an independent, self-reliant group.

Among the more liberal, already westernised Muslims, Sir Sayyid Ahmad Khan (1818-1898) emerged as the main advocate of reforming Muslim society towards progress, representing a feeling that a rejection of the British would only result in the Muslims of India disappearing into oblivion.

He wanted advantages for Muslims and was keen for a reform of Muslim education. He stressed that science was not anti-Islamic. In 1875 the British gave him a grant to found the Muhammadan Anglo-Oriental college which later became Aligarh University. From here, a stream of educated Muslims went into government service.

First moves: In 1885 the Indian National Congress was formed. The party began to fight for a devolution of power into Indian hands. Although some leading Muslims were members, it was viewed with suspicion by most, including Sir Sayyid, as being a Hindu body which would only ever represent Hindu interests. In 1905, Lord Curzon divided Bengal into two, a predominantly Hindu West and a Muslim East. The Hindu-dominated Congress opposed this move and intense agitation ensued.

In a classic example of Divide and Rule, the British now sought Muslim support. This greatly strengthened the Muslims and in 1906 in Dacca, East Bengal, the All India Muslim League was formed to promote feelings of loyalty to the British and advance Muslim political interests. They petitioned Viceroy Curzon that in any political move

Muslim interests be taken into account. The 1909 India Councils Act rewarded Muslim loyalty. The act gave Muslims separate electorates where they could elect their own representatives to the Legislative Council. Some historians claim that this move foreshadowed the birth of Pakistan.

A slap in the face: Then in 1911, amidst ever-increasing cries of protest from the Hindus, Britain revoked the partition of Bengal, whipping up Muslim resentment. Muslims began to feel isolated, and their fears were boosted by European attacks on Muslim countries. A surge of emotion followed the Italian attack on Libya in 1911, the French in Morocco and the division of Persia

by Britain and Russia. The last straw for Indian Muslims came when Britain fought Turkey in the First World War. The Turkish Sultan was seen as the spiritual head of the Muslim world. They saw Britain leading a Christian crusade against Islam. More and more Muslims decided to transfer to the Congress party. In 1916 the Muslim League and the Congress signed the Lucknow Pact: Congress accepted separate Muslim electorates in return for League support in its cause to drive out the British.

The Quaid-i-Azam: One of the engineers of this liason was Muhammad Ali Jinnah (1875-1948). Born and educated in Karachi,

Left, Sir Sayyid Ahmad Khan. **Above**, thinking about the future – Dr. Iqbal.

Jinnah went on to read law in London. Returning to India in 1896, he opened a legal practice in Bombay from where he turned to politics. He was initially a Congress member and endeavoured to bring about the political union of Muslims and Hindus, earning him the title "The best ambassador of Hindu-Muslim unity".

By the 1920s Gandhi was dominating the Indian political scene. His movement for Home Rule using non-cooperation, strikes, boycotts and non-violence had galvanised India into revolting against the British. Gandhi brought Muslims into his campaign, realising their importance.

Jinnah, however, was opposed to Gand-

hi's unconstitutional methods and his essentially Hindu approach. He left Congress in 1920, but the turning point came in 1928 when Congress leaders ignored Muslim demands for one third of the seats in any future parliament and for separate electorates. This Hindu arrogance crushed Jinnah and with tears in his eyes he remarked to a friend, "This is the parting of the ways."

He left politics and in 1930 left India for England where he lived for five years. In London, Jinnah was greatly influenced by a study on the life of Kemal Attaturk, the Turkish leader. He came to believe that he too could achieve his unfulfilled ambition,

that of leading his people. What he needed was a cause and this was provided for him in the name of Pakistan.

In 1930, Dr Allama Muhammad Iqbal, a renowned poet-politician from the Panjab, proposed a separate Muslim homeland in north-west India. At the same time, the Muslim visionary Chaudhuri Rahmat Ali and a small group at Cambridge University had coined the name Pakistan from P (Panjab), A (Afghans), K (Kashmir), S (Sind) and "Stan", the Persian suffix meaning land. The name also means "the land of the pure" in Urdu.

Jinnah returned to India in 1935 in the new robe of a Muslim politician, having abandoned the role of the ambassador of Hindu-Muslim unity. But he still hoped that Congress would respect and take into account Muslim interests.

Pakistan becomes a reality: Jinnah's hopes were dashed in 1937 when, following British moves to devolve power in the 1935 Government of India Act, Congress made the fatal mistake of not including Muslim Leaguers in the formation of provincial governments. Once again Congress had ignored the Muslims. And now the Hindus had their franchise, but the Muslims did not. Jinnah never trusted Congress again, especially Nehru, who saw the Muslim League as a communal body and would only accept Congress Muslims. From this point on, Jinnah worked furiously to amass Muslim support for the League to show the world that the League and the League only was the true representative of India's Muslims. The party was totally reorganised, opening branches in the remotest villages. His rallying cry was "Islam in Danger".

In March 1940 Jinnah submitted the Lahore Resolution, better known as the Pakistan Resolution. In it was the essence of Pakistan: "The Muslims and the Hindus belong to two different religious philosophies: they neither intermarry nor interdine ... to yoke the two together, one as a numerical minority and the other as a majority must lead to growing discontent ... Mussalmen are not a minority as is commonly known and understood. Muslims are a nation and according to any definition of a nation they must have their homelands, their territory, their state." The new British Labour Government of 1945 determined to solve the "Indian

Problem". The idea of a seperate Muslim state was gaining favour, despite opposition from Gandhi, Nehru and Congress. It led to terrible violence as Muslims and Hindus turned on each other in an atmosphere of unease about the future.

In Calcutta in 1946, some 5,000 were killed in three days. The British, already prepared to grant independence, had to act quickly to prevent further bloodshed. The new Viceroy Lord Louis Mountbatten saw that "giving Jinnah his Pakistan" was the only solution. The problem was in Bengal and Panjab where the population was mixed. Mountbatten refused Jinnah's wish for both provinces to remain undivided and to be-

acceeded to Pakistan, though they were originally designated as part of Hindu ruled Kashmir. When the deadline passed, Kashmir still hadn't decided.

The British had the impossible task of drawing up the new boundaries dividing Bengal and the Panjab. The announcement of the new borders resulted in the greatest migration in human history as some seven to eight million Muslims left India and the same number of Hindus made the journey in the opposite direction.

The migration took place amid terrible bloodshed, suffering, loss and bitterness. Panjab saw the worst of this: 55 percent of the state was Muslim, 30 percent Hindu and

come part of Pakistan. Jinnah thus had to accept a "moth eaten Pakistan" saying, "I don't care how little you give me as long as you give it to me completely."

Independence: Mountbatten announced that Pakistan would receive independence on 14th August 1947. Firstly Indians had to vote: were they to stay in India or join Pakistan? Baluchistan, NWFP and Sind voted to join Pakistan directly. Various kingdoms in the north, including Gilgit and Hunza, also

Left, Jinnah as a young man. **Above**, Jinnah surrounded by a crowd of Muslim students in Kanpur in 1941.

most of the rest Sikh. The new boundary cut between the two biggest cities, Lahore and Amritsar. Trainloads of Muslims fleeing west were held up and slaughtered by Hindus and Sikhs. The same fate awaited Hindus and Sikhs going east. Prior to independence, Lahore, a city of 1.2 million had 500,000 Hindus and 100,000 Sikhs. Very few remained behind after the migration. Conservative estimates put the number of deaths at 250,000: it could well be over half a million.

In Karachi on 14th August 1947, the flag of Pakistan flew for the first time. Governor General of the new Islamic state was Muhammad Ali Jinnah.

Two wings: The Islamic state of Pakistan was geographically unique: No other country in the world was divided into two by 1,600 kilometres of foreign territory. East Pakistan was smaller, comprising one seventh of the total area but its 45 million people represented 55 percent of the population. The only thing that the two wings really had in common was religion: Linguistically, culturally and economically, there were great differences between East and West Pakistan.

The East was the home of the Bengali people, fiercely proud of their culture. The West was made up of a tapestry of peoples and cultures of the four provinces Sind, Panjab, North West Frontier Province and Baluchistan, as well as the semi-autonomous kingdoms of the North. In order to unite the minorities, it was proposed to make Urdu the official state language. The Bengalis objected and within weeks of Pakistan's birth there were demonstrations over the issue.

Inheritance: Kashmir provided the showground for Pakistan's early history and it has remained a bone of contention between India and Pakistan ever since. At Independence, Kashmir with its 80 percent Muslim majority still hadn't chosen whether to join India or Pakistan. Its geographical and religious affinities lay with Pakistan, and to Jinnah and his countrymen it seemed inconceivable that Kashmir could join India.

However, the British had recognised Gulab Singh Dogra as Maharaja in 1846 and his descendants had ruled ever since. Hari Singh could not decide: join Pakistan and he would, as a Hindu, have to abdicate; join India and he would alienate his people. His hesitancy was viewed as an attempt to gain independence for the province. Pakistan leaders felt that unless they made a move for Kashmir they would lose it. Pathan tribesmen led a holy war to save their Muslim brothers and invaded the state on 22nd October 1947.

Preceding pages, the Cabinet Mission in 1946. **Left**, a final salute from Viceroy Mountbatten as Pakistan receives independence. **Above**, a salute back.

Seeing the invaders only 20 miles from Srinagar, Hari Singh panicked and signed an accord by which Kashmir joined India. Prime Minister Nehru, himself a Kashmiri Hindu, sent in 100,000 troops to crush what he claimed was an invasion of Indian territory. Following a ceasefire, a line of control was determined by the United Nations: From the Neelum Valley, a buffer zone in the south known as Azad (free) Kashmir belonging to Pakistan, the dotted line sliced northeastwards to divide the territories of Baltistan

and Ladakh. The headwaters of the Indus and other rivers, the lifelines of Pakistan's agricultural economy, now lay in India. A treaty for water rights for irrigation was only drawn up in 1959.

Survival: Unlike India, Pakistan had inherited no organised, well-tried machinery of government. In all areas the country basically had to start from scratch. The first concern was to ensure the economic survival of the country, something which was achieved through the inspiration of Jinnah, foreign aid, and the resourcefulness of the Pakistani people as a whole. It was no easy task: while Pakistan had always been a main producer of raw materials, the major centres of manufacturing were now in India. There was the additional burden of absorbing the millions of *Mohajirs*, refugees from India. But they soon became integrated into the new society, many of them arriving in Karachi which had been abandoned by the Hindus at the time of partition.

In search of a constitution: On 11th September 1948, Pakistan was plunged into mourning as Jinnah died of tuberculosis. His death had dire consequences as his position had to a large extent held together the opposing factions in Pakistani politics, now seeking to form a constitution.

Affairs of state now became governed by an argument over the role of Islam: Should Pakistan have an Islamic constitution? Some saw Islam as a code of personal behaviour but not necessarily as the base of a political system, while others regarded it as the very essence of the state. The *Mullahs* and Muslim activists led campaigns to try to assert the primacy of Islam against the secular orientated politicians and western educated elite.

Jinnah was succeeded as Governor General by Khwaja Nazimuddin, a distinguished Bengali, with Liaquat Ali Khan as Prime Minister. A close friend of Jinnah, Liaquat Ali was a moderate who believed in a democratic secular state. Before he could proceed far with constitution making he was assassinated in October 1951 by a gunman whose identity and motive have not been officially established.

Nazimuddin stepped in as Prime Minister, with Ghulam Muhammad as Governor General. The leadership now faced militant Muslims demanding an "Islamic purification of national life". Following riots between rival Muslim groups in the Panjab the military had to restore order.

Drifting apart: 1952 saw demonstrations in East Pakistan, once again over the language issue. Bengali nationalism was beginning to grow, with politicians claiming they were neither given enough say in national policy nor enough command over local affairs.

To combat the growing strength of feeling in the east, the four West Pakistan provinces were combined to form a single unit. Elections for a national Assembly were held in 1954, where the new United Front Party in the east routed the Muslim League, demonstrating the gulf between the two wings.

The military takes over: A constitution was finally drawn up in 1956, making Pakistan an Islamic Republic, still within the British Commonwealth. Ghulam Muhammad resigned beause of poor health and General Iskander Mirza became the first President.

The military had been viewing with deep mistrust numerous experiments in constitutional development and the rise of the East Pakistan autonomy movement. Many generals, some of whom had held high office in British India, felt that they could run the country better than the politicians. Tired of 11 years of factionalism, regionalism and sectarianism they decided to act. In 1958 the

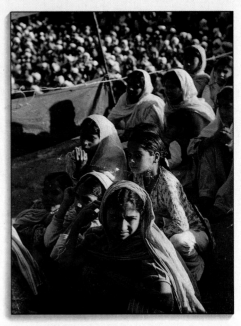

constitution was abolished and martial law was declared. President Mirza was forced to resign and was replaced by General Muhammad Ayub Khan. There were purges on politicians, and army officers replaced civil servants. Ayub Khan's policy was "blending democracy with discipline" and he eventually introduced a new constitution based on village self-government, in which people voted for 80,000 "Basic Democrats" who in turn voted for the president and the assemblies. To the middle and upper classes he brought prosperity. But while business and industry boomed, agriculture developed, and the rich got richer, very little was done to alleviate the plight of the poor. There was very little spending on basic education and other social services. Despite Ayub Khan's increased efforts to give East Pakistanis a liberal share in the administrative and other essential services, the complaints of the Bengalis continued.

Plebicite: Meanwhile, the old problem of Kashmir once more came to the surface. In April 1948, both Pakistan and India had signed a United Nations resolution that the Kashmiri people should decide their own destiny, voting whether to become part of India or to join Pakistan. The willingness of the Pakistanis to comply had never been matched by the same kind of enthusiasm on

He became increasingly isolated and, following an attempt on his life, he handed over power to the Commander-in-Chief General Agha Muhammad Yahya Khan in March 1969. It was Yahya Khan's aim to restore parliamentary democracy, and he set elections for the following year.

The two main contenders in the election were Zulfikar Ali Bhutto with his Pakistan People's Party (PPP), which, towards the end of the 1960s, had gained huge popular support in the West, and Sheikh Mujibur Rahman's Awami League, which had emerged as the strongest party in Bengal.

While the PPP won the majority of seats in the West, Rahman's Awami League had a

the part of the Indians, who in 1964 admitted that they had no intention of permitting a free vote for the Kashmiris. War broke out in August 1965, lasting for a mere 17 days. While the war itself came to an inconclusive end, the overwhelming Muslim majority in Kashmir remained subjects of India.

Restoration of democracy: In Pakistan the war had received a lot of support, but this did not prevent opposition to Ayub Khan. Many people had become disenchanted with policies of centralisation and limited democracy.

Left, Kashmiri women hoping for justice in 1948.
Above, Pakistan defends its territory, 1965.

clean sweep in the East with 167 off 169 seats. Thanks to the East's population majority, the League claimed it was also in a position to dominate the new National Assembly. The two leaders were on collision course, Bhutto refusing to be a member of a Bengali dominated assembly based in Dacca. Yahya Khan desperately tried to hold the country together by delaying the new assembly and seeking a compromise solution. But the dispute led to strikes and then all-out revolt in the East, Rahman declaring East Bengal a separate state in March 1971. Yahya Khan declared him a traitor and inevitable military action followed.

Bangladesh: The ensuing conflict was the culmination of years of growing tension between the two wings. The Government of Pakistan was just as determined to keep the country intact as the Awami League was to break away. The armed uprising in the East resulted in appalling loss of life. Atrocities were committed by both sides as millions of innocent Bengali refugees fled across the border. But it was all over when India declared war on Pakistan on 12th December 1971. Within twelve days, Pakistan had lost half its navy, a quarter of its airforce, nearly a third of its army, and 5,000 square miles of territory. By directly intervening in the conflict, India had supported the creation of the

new independent country of Bangladesh.

Father of the poor: Pakistan was demoralised by defeat, and Yahya Khan resigned, handing over to Zulfikar Ali Bhutto. A rich Sindhi landlord with a western education, Bhutto had been a major figure on the political scene for years. Full of charisma, he was loved by the masses who readily responded to his cry of *"Roti, Kapra, aur Makan"* – bread, clothes and housing.

His PPP had steadily been winning popularity in the villages and poor industrial areas, particularly in Sind. He fought for the masses in a way that no other politician had yet done, being the first to tell the poor that

they mattered. His power base was the trade unions, and left-wing students and activists.

In 1972 he pulled Pakistan out of the British Commonwealth after Britain's recognition of Bangladesh. In 1973, he founded a new constitution based on adult suffrage and gradually Pakistan began to rebuild. There were now closer ties between Pakistan and other Islamic states. Under Bhutto, Pakistanis began to work in The Gulf. He also strengthened ties with China and the Soviet Union, a continuation of the "non-aligned" policy which had begun under Ayub Khan.

At home, he nationalised the major industries and the banks, and he initiated reform of the education and health systems. He also began reforms in the civil service. A believer in a strong, centralised state, Bhutto refused any regional autonomy. Kingdoms in the north, including Hunza, now came under the direct control of Central Government.

There were problems in Baluchistan which had always been a sensitive area, since certain tribal leaders had never wanted to surrender their independence. They now felt that they didn't receive their share of public money and when in 1973 Bhutto cut the power of Baluchi tribal leaders, they revolted. It led to some 55,000 tribesmen fighting 70,000 government troops, resulting in 10,000 deaths. Massive aerial bombardment won the war for Bhutto in 1974, although minor skirmishes continued.

Bhutto's nationalisation of big business incensed business circles. He also angered religious leaders with his essentially secular approach to running the country. And by his personal domination of the party, he alienated the left wing, wanting all power to rest with him. He became The State, and as rival and opposition groups became too strong for him, he had them purged by his paramilitary group, the Federal Security Service.

The fall of Bhutto: In 1977, Bhutto unexpectedly called elections and nine opposition parties joined to form the Pakistan National Alliance. Bhutto's PPP still had by far the most widespread appeal, and he easily won the election with 155 out of 200 seats. A little too easily, thought the opposition, and accusing Bhutto of rigging the results, the PNA led street demonstrations which brought 300 deaths in six months.

Bhutto declared martial law in Karachi, Lahore and Hyderabad, but the country was sliding towards anarchy. On 5th July 1977 General Muhammad Zia ul-Haq placed Bhutto under house arrest and announced that he was taking over as chief administrator of martial law. Once again the military ruled Pakistan.

Zia ul-Haq: "I want to make it absolutely clear that I neither have any political intentions nor does the military want to be taken away from its profession of soldiering. My sole aim is to organise free and fair elections which will be held in October this year." There were no elections and General Zia remained in power until he died in a plane crash in 1988.

General Zia came from a middle class

You take away the ideology of an ideological state and nothing is left." He did not hold elections as promised, claiming that the economic situation was not yet ready for them. More likely is that he knew that in any election the only winner would be Bhutto. Opposition leaders and Zia himself said that Bhutto first had to be tried for murder before he could stand again as a politician. In Zia's words, "Accountability first, elections later." Bhutto was suspected of ordering the murder of a political opponent and on 3rd September 1977 was arrested in Karachi on a charge of conspiracy to murder Muhammad Ahmed Khan Kasuri in Lahore. Despite very flimsy evidence, the Lahore High Court

family who moved from Jullundur in the Indian Panjab following partition in 1947. He had wanted to be a lawyer, but then decided to join the military. A firm believer in law and order, he accused Bhutto of bringing Pakistan to the brink of civil war, ruining the economy and disrupting normal life.

Zia claimed to be a strict devout Muslim, believing that Pakistan could only be saved by adopting strict Islamic principles. "This country was created in the name of Islam.

Left, Zulfikar Ali Bhutto. **Above**, progress in Pakistan; the Tarbela Dam is the largest earth-filled dam in the world.

sentenced Bhutto to death. He filed an appeal in the supreme court challenging the verdict, but it was rejected by four votes to three. Despite appeals for clemency from all over the world, Zia confirmed the death sentence.

Bhutto was hanged in Rawalpindi Central Jail on 4th April 1979. His body was flown to his hometown of Larkana in Sind. When news of his execution came out, his body was already buried in his ancestral graveyard.

Repression: Following Bhutto's execution Zia had 3,000 PPP leaders and workers jailed, many remaining there until his death. Zia then silenced other opponents. In October 1979 he banned all political parties, ordering that party offices be closed and their funds seized. Government was in the hands of Zia and his Provincial Governors.

Zia also appointed the Islamic Ideology Council which spearheaded the Islamisation programme. It sought to Islamise the country by bringing existing laws into conformity with Islamic injunctions. The Shura changed, ammended or nullified about 500 laws on the grounds of their being repugnant to Quranic institutions. Zia did not see this as Islamic Fundamentalism and was quick to refute such allegations saying, "In a true Islamic state laid down on the basis of Quranic instruction, there is no room for fundamentalism." People were now punished according to the Islamic Penal Code.

"Hero": The western world was shocked by Bhutto's execution and by the switch from secularism to Islamification. Zia was gradually becoming isolated when the Soviet Union invaded Afghanistan in December 1979. Suddenly with his pledge to help the Afghans, Zia changed in the eyes of the West; he became bastion of the free world against communism.

Criticism of Zia stopped, allowing him to go ahead with the brutal repression which had begun in early 1979. Zia allowed no opposition. When, in 1981, opposition leaders tried to form the Movement for the Restoration of Democracy, around 15,000 people were arrested. The jails were flooded. Amnesty International listed 15 centres where political prisoners and journalists were flogged and tortured. Deaths were reported of Trade Union leaders following "encounters with the Security Forces".

The Soviet invasion of Afghanistan was a financial godsend for Zia. American and western aid came in billion dollar programmes. It helped an impressive growth rate with significant wage rises. From 1979 the sustained economic growth averaged seven percent. But defence took the lion's share and spending on development was practically nil. A 1984 World Development Report stated that only five countries in the world spent less on education than Pakistan.

But Pakistan's role in helping the Afghan Mujahidin proved vital and was considered at the time to be a major achievement of the Zia regime. Pakistan became the haven for some three million Afghan refugees. The Washington Post wrote in August 1988,

"Without Zia's bold stance, the Kremlin's decision to evacuate Soviet troops would have been unthinkable." His support of Afghanistan also gave him huge standing among other Islamic countries and Zia had the unique honour of addressing the United Nations General Association on behalf of the entire Muslim world.

Zia inherited the traditional discord with India, but sought a tension free relationship. He visited India on several occasions, the most famous being his visit to Jaipur where he met Rajiv Gandhi at a Pakistan versus India cricket match. It led to the term "Cricket Diplomacy". But India continued to accuse Pakistan of helping Sikh terrorists in their fight for a separate Sikh homeland.

Up until 1983, the provinces remained unusually calm under Zia. In that year, the Movement for the Restoration of Democracy launched a mass campaign against martial law and for a return to free elections. The movement only took off in Sind where, due to Bhutto sympathies, there was an intense anti-Zia feeling.

There was a great resentment in Sind to the power and wealth of non-Sindhis in the province, and Sindhis felt they were discriminated against: they provided only a very small percentage of the armed forces and the civil service. On 14th August bombs were thrown in Karachi and within days Sind was aflame. Police were lynched and soldiers attacked. The military responded and unofficial reports claim 1,000 deaths. A total of 21,000 people were imprisoned.

The Sind riots seem to have made Zia think and he announced that elections would be held in 1985. Firstly he held a referendum which asked the country what it thought of the Islamification programme: only 10 percent of the nation voted. The subsequent elections were a farce: parties were not allowed to contest and they were boycotted by the Movement for the Restoration of Democracy. A 53 percent turn out voted for a national assembly; before the new assembly even met, Zia ammended the constitution enabling him to dismiss parliament at will.

Zia indeed sacked parliament in 1988. He died soon afterwards when his plane exploded shortly after take-off.

Right, a poster depicts the demise of General Zia ul-Haq.

70

جنرل اختر عبدالرحمٰن خان شہید

جنرل فیض حسین خان شہید

DEMOCRACY REDISCOVERED

January 1946 was the watershed in the history of the Indus valley. Under popular political pressure, the British colonial rulers had conceded to the people the right of franchise and the first ever general elections were held. Exercising their right to use the ballot, the people had voted for the creation of an independent democratic state. For a society where 90 percent of people had been engaged in the drudgery of agriculture and living under oppressive feudal regimes, this momentous decision was the highest mark of folk wisdom.

Ideals: Muhammad Ali Jinnah whom people lovingly titled **Quaid-i-Azam**, the greatest leader, was a liberal democrat in a society where for thousands of years tribal potentates, priests and mandarins had wielded absolute control over the body and soul of the people. The caste system had subjected the tillers of the soil and the craftsmen to the bondage of a handful of privileged. On top of that the British colonial overlords maintained their empire with the help of a tightly controlled military bureaucracy drawn from the ruling classes.

Jinnah, as if possessed by the spirit of the age, had challenged the caste and colonial prerogatives by direct appeal to the common people to unite and struggle for an independent and democratic state. He had laboured relentlessly for a decade to create a democratically structured political party from the grass roots. By mobilising popular support he was successful in wresting independence from the British on the negotiating table.

The most vital social developments that led to independence were the presence of a democratic political party and people's right to vote. These had led to the election of a sovereign assembly and Jinnah defined its supremacy on 11th August, 1947 when it met for the first time: "...we shall make this Constituent Assembly an example to the world. The Constituent Assembly has got two main functions to perform. The first is the very onerous and responsible task of

framing our future Constitution of Pakistan and second of functioning as a full complete Sovereign body as the Federal Legislature of Pakistan. We have to do the best we can." He was categorial about the absolute authority of the elected parliament: "The first and the foremost thing that I would like to emphasise is this: remember that you are now a Sovereign Legislative body and you have got all the powers." He was emphatic about the democratic rights of the citizens of the independent state: "If you change your past and work together in a spirit that everyone of you, no matter to what community he belongs, no matter what relations he had with you in the past, no matter what is his colour, caste or creed, is first, second and last a citizen of this State with equal rights, privileges and obligations, there will be no end to the progress you will make."

As if he had a premonition of the danger to democracy, Jinnah admonished a group of military officers shortly before he died in 1948: "I want you to remember if you have time enough you should study the Government of India Act, as adapted for use in Pakistan, which is our present Constitution,

Preceding pages: smiles all round, anyone for polo? Devotees celebrate their saint. Left, welcome to Pakistan. Above, all in a day's work.

that the executive authority flows from the Head of Government of Pakistan, who is the Governor General, and, therefore, any command or orders that may come to you cannot come without the sanction of the Executive Head."

Jinnah's counsel was not to be heeded by the traditional ruling classes. For 43 years since independence real democracy has hardly surfaced. For most of that time the military have ruled, in two spells of 11 and 15 years.

That did not daunt the people from the course of their struggle for democracy, for at the end of the 11 years of the second spell of military rule, when general elections were

If the present experiment in elected government succeeds, followed by elections after five years, the system might have a chance. But Benazir Bhutto does not yet have a free hand in carrying out the reforms that the country so desperately needs. The 1973 Constitution has not yet resurfaced in its original representative form. At present, Bhutto's government is subject to the arbitrary control of the unelected President and the restrictive structures left by the military regime. The military bureaucracy wields an enormous amount of power, of which Benazir is justifiably cautious.

Trying to survive: All that she can do is preserve her party's grass roots support and

held in November 1988, their voice was finally heard once more.

Prime Minister Benazir Bhutto, and the Pakistan People's Party was voted into power. Her election mandate – democracy, federalism and social democracy – has won her party enough seats and as leader of the majority party she is the first woman prime minister not only in Pakistan, but also in the entire Islamic world. Out of the four provinces of the federation, her party has ministries in the provinces of Sind and North Western Frontier, while the opposition parties have coalition governments in the Panjab and Baluchistan.

make a bid in the next election to have necessary majority to restore the Constitution and put her blueprint for running the state according to her light. In that endeavour she needs lots of luck and support from her friends from the West, especially in putting Pakistan on its feet economically.

Bordering with the USSR, China and India, and professed strategic vital interest parameters of the US and its rich industrialised partners, Pakistan is precariously poised amidst the summitry of the big powers in one of the most volatile parts of the world.

Whatever its orientation, any government in Pakistan whether democratically elected or despotic has to respond to the overtures of all the big four powers. It is a daunting challenge that Pakistan must take. Its real strength lies within the political behaviour of its own people. If they are organised socially and advanced economically, the independence of the country can be maintained with their active participation.

Within months of her assuming power, Benazir Bhutto had gone to win friends and influence people at the top. She hopes to elicit "grants" and not the loans to build the tattered infrastructure and industry. By "grants" she means free lunch from the US and its rich industrialised allies for voluntary services rendered for the avowed cause of freedom and democracy.

Afghanistan's role: Historically, developments in Afghanistan have always made deep inroads into the Indus valley. Similarly the Indus valley has made its contribution to the material and spiritual life of Afghanistan. The war which still ravages in that country has obviously had a great effect on Pakistan as well.

In December 1979 Russian troops were positioned in Afghanistan. Refugees started to arrive. By December 1988, at least 3,637,000 Afghan refugees were said to be inside Pakistan. A total of 3,270,000 were registered in 340 "tent villages", journalese for the refugee camps. More than 80 percent of these lived in NWFP and Baluchistan. At least 363,000 more were unregistered.

The fighting for Jalalabad in spring 1989 brought further refugees. By June that year, 67,000 new displaced persons had been registered. In one week alone, mid-February 1989, 17,000 arrived in Peshawar. Relief agencies suspect that many "collaborators" were murdered by mujahidin before they could even register. At least one new camp was added to accommodate those in danger.

In the camps, survival needs are met, lost kindred contacted and skills imparted, at all levels from pre-literacy to post graduate. But households have to accept "protection" from one or another of the political parties in exile. Many have decided to chance it outside. Some have been extremely successful. In a decade, entire fleets of rickshaws, taxis and minibus services came under Afghan con-

trol. Company logos like "Afghan Caravan" or "Flying Coach" services show their owners are aware of playing to a global gallery. Others, even with marketable skills, have not done so well, finding work only as night watchmen, bodyguards, or casual labourers. Their plight is desperate.

The educated elite (Afghanistan figures in the world's lowest literacy rates) either emigrated or work in the relief agencies. At the end of 1988 there were 79 of these operating in Peshawar alone. No less than 56 were receiving funds from the United Nations High Commission for Refugees. What their role will be after resettlement is completed is unclear. Many refugee leaders fear

that, even when the fighting is done they will not be independent. As one expressed it "Afghanistan might be liberated from Soviet invasion but it will be invaded by aid agencies." Chances of a speedy end to Afghanistan's troubles seem remote and in the meantime, compassion fatigue has set in. The first refugees were made welcome in Pakistan, as brothers and sisters in Islam. People are now feeling that it's time they went home and worried that they won't, blaming them for everything from drug rackets, juvenile delinquency and AIDS, to deforestation, overgrazing and soil erosion.

A rough ride: Proof of the fact that democracy is at last beginning to function in Pakistan was shown in the relatively orderly way in which the vote of no-confidence in the Bhutto government was carried out in October 1989. The fact that Benazir managed to hang on by the skin of her teeth was not, however, so much due to any policies which she has introduced but rather to the fragmented nature of the opposition.

But with the sudden release of energies which have been subdued for so long, any democratic government would have a hard time in Pakistan. There is so much to complain about! One of the greatest challenges the country now faces is to solve the problems created by increasing urbanisation.

in agriculture. Large scale manufacturing employs only 18 percent of the labour force. While some of the remainder are engaged in small and highly productive workshops, many are still employed in a very inflated and inefficient service sector.

On economic terms: Economically the country is in a tight corner because of uneconomic and unproductive strains on its meagre resources. During the last decade it has accumulated US $15 billion of debts from the West. Very little of this huge sum has been invested in productive development. The bulk of investment goes to unproductive expenditure; defence 60 percent, debt repayment 20 percent, and administra-

While since 1947 agricultural and industrial developments have undoubtedly improved the lot of a great number of Pakistanis, there are also vast numbers who have hardly benefitted or whose plight has even drastically deteriorated, especially amongst the huge numbers of people who have been forced to migrate to the cities in search of work. Pakistan has a birthrate of 3.1 percent, one of the highest in the world. The present population of over 100 million is likely to double by the second decade of the next century.

At present 30 percent of the population is urbanised, while 70 percent is still rural. Fifty percent of the labour force is engaged

tion 10 percent. Out of the remaining 10 percent to be spent on people's welfare, quite a big chunk goes to lining the pockets of the bureaucracy. It is therefore no wonder that basic facilities are very often quite inadequate. Little money has been invested in education, health, transport, recreation, communications, roads, and sanitation. These are a few of the basic services which, in common with other South Asian countries, have lagged sadly behind the level which modern cultural norms demand.

Agriculture and industry: The principal produce of the country is agricultural: Wheat, rice, sugarcane, pulses, oilseeds. There is great promise for the growth of agricultural produce because of the perfect climatic conditions – with enough water and plenty of sunshine. The irrigation of vast tracts of desert, particularly in Panjab and Sind, ensures, for the time being at least, that the demands of a growing population are met.

Pakistan produces some of the finest cattle in Asia outside Japan. It is one of the major exporters of cotton and rice in the world. Both the crops demand a high level of physical labour to which the country folk have become accustomed for thousands of years. Fisheries are also becoming a noticeable source of exports.

Exports of manufactured items are lim-

mill as well as some small cotton ginning factories. The 1950s saw the boom period for the cotton textiles and cotton yarn industries. Side by side foundries and mechanical and electrical workshops grew up from the artisan base.

The country has a steel mill with an annual manufacturing capacity of one million tons of steel. It was constructed with the help of the USSR. The Chinese have built a heavy engineering complex. Ship building, automobile assembling and spare parts manufacturing, telecommunications, railway wagons, machine tools, fertilisers, cement, glass, surgical goods, sugar processing plants, industrial machines, food processing, and

ited. These include leather goods and a limited quantity of cotton garments. Because of its cheap labour Pakistan has become a major exporter of hand-knotted carpets. Indeed Pakistan's artisans, many of whose trades have their roots way back in history, provide a substantial contribution to the country's economy.

Since independence industrial development has taken off from the meagre base of two cement factories, a textiles and a sugar

garments are just some of a huge variety of industries where remarkable progress has taken place.

But inadequate development of mining, power generation, metallurgy, chemicals, mechanical engineering and electronics seriously hampers the industrial take off. Benazir Bhutto has pledged the expansion of the industrial base, with the help of western aid and the private sector.

"Petrodollars": Pakistan's major export is manpower. Pakistan's labour force working abroad numbers 1.5 million persons. The miracle of large scale modern civic development in Saudi Arabia and other oil rich

Left, street life. **Above**, modern Islamic architecture, the Ismaili Centre in Karachi.

Persian gulf states is in part testimony to the toil and skill of Pakistan's artisans. At present measures are being taken to export more labour and technicians to work for the reconstruction of war ravaged Iran and Iraq. Many families rely on income from abroad.

The gypsies of the West are said to be migrants from the Indus Valley. Present day Pakistan seems to be undergoing another large scale migratory spell. There is hardly a western industrial state without a community of Pakistani labour and enterprise. Historically, apart from the nomadic tribesmen of the western deserts, the Pakistanis were a village bound community. It is amazing how they have become worldwide wanderers.

Their return home plays an important role in refuelling the economy with their hard earned foreign exchange; indeed this now constitutes the single largest amount of the country's export earnings.

Many Pakistanis have also chosen to settle permanently abroad, notably in Britain and the USA. The Northern English town of Bradford, for example, has a high proportion of Pakistanis in its population. They are shop owners, successful businessmen, doctors, dentists, lawyers, bus conductors, computer programmers, restaurateurs, labourers and professors.

The brain drain: Many who have moved abroad more recently also have a great deal of expertise. They work in the best universities and hospitals. Among them are deft neuro and cardiac surgeons. One of these expatriate top scientists is the Nobel Laureate in Theoretical Physics Dr. Abdus Salam. The brain drain continues, and while developed countries like the USA are flooded with such scientists, a developing country like Pakistan must muddle through with the skills of those who have either chosen to stay behind or haven't been able to leave.

Life goes on: But Pakistan is by no means a morbid place to live. Far from it. The people are the inheritors of a rich tradition of conventional wisdom of nearly 10 millennia. There was the case of a US sociologist doing research on a village in the Panjab. When the people were asked what it was that they cherished most in life, invariably the prompt answer was their honour.

In religious matters the Pakistanis are generally tolerant. For them love is the most important quality of life. Most of them follow the mystic's way of seeking communion with the sublime through ecstatic love. Priesthood is not strong as it is in the adjoining countries where magian spells still haunt the temporal and spiritual life. Each time the priests contested an election in Pakistan they were rejected by the people.

Aesthetically each village has its repertoire of flute, string, harmonium and drums. The bards and minstrels sing old romances and refrains. Every village has its shrine of the local saint, where the annual festival is held. There is a vibrant literary movement. Poetry is a passion and even the remotest village has its share of poets. In Pakistan, public poetic recitation is an institution.

Some of the world's finest craftsmen still continue to produce exquisite pieces of handicraft.

There are traditional and makeshift modern sports that engage the youth. The remotest villages and back alleys of the cities produce world renowned sportsmen, among whom are the top squash and cricket players of the world. Field hockey is the sport where Pakistan is a favourite, so often tipped to bag the Olympic gold medal.

Above, bagpipes are a relatively new addition to the many musical instruments used in Pakistan. **Right**, cricket in the mountains.

A PASSION
FOR CRICKET

In the back of the jeep which winds its way up towards the precipitous Lowari Pass in the Frontier, sit five Chitrali men with shawls wrapped tightly around them. At 3,000 metres in the late afternoon the air is getting decidedly chilly. The radio they bought the day before in a Peshawar bazaar is perched between them on the mound of rock salt they are taking to their home village of Drosh on the Chitral Valley side of the pass. The commentary has just switched from English to Urdu, enough of which they understand to be able to recognise the gist of what is going on. They crouch and listen. The unanimous roar of a crowd of thousands reaches a crescendo as Imran Khan, one of Pakistan's most famous cricketing sons, races towards the wicket on a hat-trick delivery. It is the 1987 World Cup final being played 800 kilometres away in Lahore, and the Chitralis are transfixed.

The batsman at the other end is the legendary West Indian Viv Richards and there is not a single boy in the entire ground (and probably in the whole of Pakistan) who would not yearn to be in Imran's boots. Everyone of them is dreaming that one day they too might also be a national hero playing on an international stage.

Many Pakistanis are fanatical about cricket. It is partly due to hero worship of players such as Imran Khan that ever more youngsters in Pakistan want to play the game in order that they may emulate their idols. Imran Khan, whose parents both came from Pathan landowning families, lived in Zaman Park in Lahore, a comfortable, wooded, residential district. But not all Pakistani cricketers have such a priveleged background; many players who represent their country learned the game the hard way – in the streets, by the side of the road, in fact on any flat piece of ground that might enable a game of cricket to be played. Should one wander through Iqbal Park in Lahore any day, it would be possible to witness ten or more games being played simultaneously by a multitude of impoverished (but enthusiastic) children, among whom may well be a potential cricket star of the future. The same kind of scenes can be witnessed all over the country, with the youth of Pakistan making the best of the meagre facilities available.

Cricket is now booming in Pakistan. The game received its biggest boost when cricketing relations with India were re-established in 1978 after an 18-year rift. As a result of the political tension between the two countries sporting encounters between them have always engendered passionate emotions. When Pakistan beat India at Lahore, there was jubilation throughout the country and the government even proclaimed the following day a national holiday. In 1986/7 when Pakistan recorded their first ever series victory over India on Indian soil, a crowd in excess of a quarter million lined the streets to welcome their heroes home.

Indeed the depth of interest and emotion felt for cricket in Pakistan is probably more profound than in any other cricketing nation. When Javed Miandad resigned the captaincy at the end of 1987, some people demonstrated outside Imran Khan's house, clamouring for him to come back as captain for the tour of the West Indies (he had previously retired from the game) and some even threatened to go on hunger strike if he did not. In the end it required the personal intervention of the late President Zia to persuade Imran to once again take up the reins of captaincy. Zia said that, whilst he appreciated Imran's decision to leave the game at his peak, the country needed him and sometimes "one had to rise above the self".

It is largely through the influence of television and radio that cricket has attracted such a popular following in Pakistan. While among the less well off televisions are still very much a communal commodity, prosperity has increased enough to allow most people at least a radio, enabling the game to be spread into the remotest corners of the country. The game is still going on as the Chitralis end their journey in Drosh. They alight from the jeep to catch the final moments of the day's play inside, while outside children go on playing their version late into the evening on a piece of flat ground down by the river, overshadowed by Tirich Mir and other peaks of the Hindu Kush looming to the north.

Assuming that they have coped successfully with the culture shock induced in most Westerners by the sheer numbers of people to be seen on the busier streets of any Asian city, the first impression of the Pakistanis likely to be gained by visitors to a city like Karachi or Lahore is of the amazing variety of its inhabitants.

Men in turbans with long flowing beards, dressed in all kinds of colourful regional attire, nudge against clean-shaven men attempting to get to the office, some dressed in

one side of the street, a man with a great drooping moustache and fading pin-striped jacket over his salwar kameez lights his water pipe behind his rows of spices, as the ladies return home with reems of new silk they have just bought from the same shop they always go to.

There are aristoctratic looking people milling around whose ivory complexion indicates that they originate from Turkish or Iranian lands, while the poorer man selling his wares at the street corner may have much

suits and ties, others in the more common *salwar kameez* (the long shirt and baggy trousers which many Pakistanis wear). There will occasionally be women too, with their faces veiled, striding confidently through the bazaars.

There are people from the country, people there to stay, people passing through. There may be youths in T-shirts jumping off fast-moving buses, stumbling across desert tribesmen selling their hand-knotted carpets in the market, where groups of other men with henna beards squat, chatting in a whole variety of languages and accents which nobody else in the vicinity understands. Nearby on

darker, South-Indian looks. There are people whose Caucasian features make them look slightly European, and others who look as if they may even be descended from Ghengiz Khan. From the tall and strapping to the slight and delicate, there is commonly such variety of people on the streets of a Pakistani city that the visitor may well ask himself the question, "Who are the Pakistanis?"

Although this question has been endlessly posed in the debate about national identity going on since the creation of the country in 1947, the Pakistanis, whether rich or poor or middle-of-the-road, are quite happy with the answer "We are all Muslims, and that is what makes us Pakistanis, despite our differences." And that is the answer that most visitors will be immediately content with as well, as the sound of the call to prayer, hailing from loudspeakers clinging precariously to the top of some ancient minaret, gradually loses itself over the hustle and bustle of the city.

Inheritance: Joined together through Islam the Pakistanis, wherever they may originally come from, are as varied a mix of people as one is likely to find anywhere. Some of the differences between them are due to regional origins, to cultural formations and preferences or to specific religious beliefs and values. Others stem from social and economic background, whether in the rural areas which constitute so much of the country or in the cities and towns where ever-increasing numbers of Pakistanis now live.

Although Pakistan lies at the foot of main invasion routes from Central Asia, the lands of Indus which have such a long history of human settlement also border on India. So while past tribal immigrations have left their stamp here and there, the genetic inheritance of most Pakistanis in fact stems from the vast South Asian pool which embraces one-fifth of mankind. The differences between the typically well-built and fair-skinned Panjabis and the slighter and darker inhabitants of Sind are therefore less apparent to an outsider than their shared homogeneity. Only in the mountainous border regions do the Central Asian physical types predominate, as amongst the sharp-featured and fair-skinned Pathans and the peoples of the Northern Areas. The legacy of population movements throughout the ages causes such "non-Indian" features to occur in the majority population as well, but only sporadically.

But as in most parts of the world, the ethnic breakdown of the Pakistanis owes more to cultural than to physical factors. Much more significant, therefore, are the major regional differences. These are only crudely reflected in the administrative division of Pakistan into the four provinces of Panjab, Sind, Baluchistan and the North-West Frontier Province (NWFP), plus the outlying tribal areas and territories, since the boundaries of these units are in many cases simply the product of

arbitrary administrative decisions made in the colonial period, and run across ethnic and linguistic lines. The language issue is in fact increasingly central to the debates within Pakistan about the country's multiple ethnic identities, which can only be followed with some awareness of the relationships between the languages involved besides the characteristics of the regions in which they are spoken.

Languages: In common with most languages of Europe nearly all the languages spoken in Pakistan belong the same great Indo-European language-family. These were originally brought to the subcontinent some 3,000 years ago by the Aryan invaders,

whose language is preserved in the ancient Sanskrit of the Vedas. Spoken across the vast plains which extend from Pakistan through northern India to Bangladesh, the modern Indo-Aryan languages, produced as a result of a long process of simplification and mixture with now lost local languages, are descended from Sanskrit in the same sort of way as French and Spanish are derived from Latin.

This Indo-Aryan family includes Urdu, now the national language of Pakistan, which began life as mixture of the Hindi of Delhi with the Persian spoken by the invading Muslim armies and then developed as the

Left, a man from Hunza. **Above**, the turban is common headgear in Pakistan.

lingua franca of the Moghul Empire. Panjabi is very closely related to Urdu, and is indeed sometimes unjustly dismissed as being Urdu's country cousin, while Sindhi is a more distant relative with many special features of its own. Now recognised as a language distinct from both of these, Siraiki is spoken in south-west Panjab and in the neighbouring areas of all three other provinces. The less widely spoken languages of the Northern Areas, like the Shina spoken in Gilgit, are still more different members of the same Indo-Aryan with a long history of separate evolution.

Within the larger Indo-European family, the languages to the west of Indo-Aryan in the far north, the only other non-Indo-European language native to Pakistan is the Burushaski spoken up in Hunza, a strange survivor which seems to be related to no other language on earth, in spite of crackpot attempts to prove otherwise.

There is thus a rich variety of languages, but as is so often the case in Pakistan this variety is balanced by a number of common elements. In this instance, the most obvious is the use of some form of the Arabic script, of such special significance for Muslims everywhere as the script of the Koran, to write all the major languages, even if special letters and writing styles are used for spelling Sindhi and Pushtu. The shared Islamic heri-

belong to the quite closely related Iranian group, whose most important member is Persian (Farsi). In the north-west, the tribal movements of the Pathans have carved out a still expanding area for Pushtu, famous for its harsh clusters of consonants whose sound is often likened to that of someone talking with a mouthful of stones. Pushtu is less similar to Persian or the Indo-Aryan languages than the other Iranian language of Pakistan. This is Baluchi, spoken in Baluchistan alongside Brahui, a non-Indo-European language belonging to the Dravidian family otherwise largely confined to south India. Apart from the Tibetan Balti-speakers

tage is also deeply imbedded in the vocabulary of all the languages, which draws extensively on Arabic and Persian. In conjunction with the basic grammatical similarities between most of the languages, this common vocabulary (which has of course long come also to include a great many borrowings from English) greatly eases communication and the task faced by most city dwellers of learning more than one language.

Ethnic and social groups: Intercommunication is certainly called for in the cities, for it is there that conflicts between ethnic groups may erupt, particularly in the great metropolis of Karachi. Although it is the capital of

Sind, Sindhis have long been a minority in this continually expanding city. They are far outnumbered by the Pathans and Panjabis, the dominant groups in Pakistan as a whole, who have settled there besides the less numerous Baluch.

Karachi is also the stronghold of Pakistan's fifth major ethnic group. These are the *Mohajirs*, literally "Refugees" the name given to the Muslims who left their homes in India at the time of Partition to settle in the Islamic homeland of Pakistan. Wherever they came from in India, they were almost all united by being native speakers of Urdu, unlike most other Pakistanis, who have to learn the national language in

sions to be expected from the rapid progress of urbanisation in Pakistan, which forces people from different backgrounds into close contact with one another. Pakistan is still, however, a predominantly rural country, with the majority of the population tied to the land. In the outlying mountainous regions, subsistence is at best marginal, and the males of these predominantly tribal societies are often forced to seek seasonal work as labourers in more prosperous regions.

In Panjab and Sind, where intensive agriculture is made possible by canal irrigation, the village remains the centre of social and economic life. Remnants of the traditional caste-system, though without the social dis-

school. Also unlike most other Pakistanis, with their traditional attachment to the land, many of the *Mohajirs* came from urban backgrounds, and on their arrival in Pakistan naturally took over many of the city jobs previously managed by the Hindu minority which was displaced to India. With the increase of education in Sind, this has provoked the feeling among Sindhis that such jobs should go to the "sons of the soil".

This is but one manifestation of the ten-

Left, friendly policemen in Lahore. **Above**, the traditional *salwar kameez* mingles with western shirts and slacks.

crimination still widespread in Hindu India, are to be seen in the specialisation of the artisans, like blacksmiths or washermen, who work for the farmers.

The status of the farmers themselves varies from region to region. In the central parts of Panjab they mostly own the land themselves, but in the Siraiki-speaking areas of south-west Panjab and in Sind they are more likely to be the tenants of great landowning families, whose estates have largely survived attempts at land-reform. Popularly referred to as "feudals", these great families, which may control hundreds of thousands of acres, form an aristocracy which continues to provide Pakistan with many of its leaders, the Bhutto family itself being an outstanding example. The landed power of the countryside is in turn linked to the economic power of the cities, whose own expansion has however allowed fresh fortunes to be made by newcomers to the old world of the "22 families" believed to have controlled virtually all Pakistan's wealth during the Ayub Khan period in the 1960s. The wealthy still thrive in Pakistan, and the English-medium education given to their children in the prestigious schools modelled on the British pattern gives them a rather different outlook to that of most Pakistanis, while ensuring their future social status.

country itself was founded. These effects are felt even by the tiny religious minorities which constitute about three percent of this Muslim country's population.

Besides a few Parsis, the Zoroastrian community which migrated centuries ago from Iran to India, a small number of Hindus from the professional groups which dominated urban life before 1947 still live in Pakistan, mostly in Sind. But most registered Hindus are either tribespeople living in the deserts bordering India, or else those who have rejected conversion to Islam or Christianity in favour of their own *Balmiki* cult. The largest religious minority is that of the Christians, mostly descended from the mass con-

The other main focus of power lies with the army, which has ruled Pakistan for so much of its history. Although its presence is felt throughout the country, most of its ranks are still drawn from the old recruiting grounds of British India, the naturally poor districts of north-west Panjab and the adjacent Pathan areas of the NWFP. Pathans also make up an important part of the officer corps, which is however dominated by the strongly nationalist background of the Panjab squirearchy.

Religions: The one great force whose effects are felt throughout Pakistan is the Islamic religion in name of whose ideals the

versions of former untouchables carried out during the British period by the missionaries of many different churches, from Roman Catholics to Seventh Day Adventists. In addition there are some Anglo-Pakistanis of mixed race and Goanese Catholics.

Islam itself is much less monolithic than is all too often supposed by non-Muslims. The truth of this is amply demonstrated by the variety of Pakistani Islam, which stems not only from recent developments but from the earliest period of Islamic history. Soon after the death of the Prophet Muhammad, a major split arose between the followers of his son-in-law Ali, the Shias who believe Ali and his descendants to be the Imams divinely ordained to absolute leadership of all Muslims, and the majority party, the Sunnis who believe Ali to be only one of the Caliphs appointed to head the Muslim community which is to be guided by the sunna or example of the Prophet.

First introduced into Sind by the early Arab invasions, later massively reinforced by the full-scale Muslim conquests of medieval times, the prevalent local version of Islam has always been the Sunni one, more precisely the version of Sunni Islam which follows the *Hanafi* school of Islamic law. In the majority of mosques in Pakistan, whose number was so greatly expanded by the

tively as *Ulema*, individually as *Maulvis*, or more disparagingly by those out of sympathy with their traditionalism as *Mullahs*. Numerous clerical groupings have emerged from the reform movements of the 19th and 20th centuries founded on the ideals of restoring Islam to its original pristine state or restating these in modern terms. Many have political ambitions, the best known being the *Jamaat-e-Islami* which was particularly influential in the Zia period. The *Jamaat* has long been at the forefront of agitation against the *Ahmadiyya*, a group founded in 19th century by a Panjabi cleric whose claims to succeed the Prophet Muhammad, the focus of such very special veneration throughout

orthodox policies of the Zia regime, the daily prayers are therefore performed in accordance with the *Hanafi* ritual, which will also be observed by the majority of believers at the great community prayers held on the major festivals at large mosques or specially constructed *Idgahs*.

As in other Sunni Muslim countries, religious leadership is provided by the clerics trained in Islamic law who are known collec-

Left, reception on the lawn. **Above,** in a world dominated by Islam there are minorities – the Kailash of the Hindu Kush.

Pakistan, have caused his followers to be officially classed as non-Muslims.

Besides the Sunnis, there are also substantial Shia minorities. Most follow "Twelver" Shiism, the official religion of Iran, which claims that the line of living Imams came to an end with the twelfth. Although many of their beliefs are shared with the Sunnis, Shias have a particular reverence for *Sayyids*, the title given to all those who claim linear descent from the Prophet. The Twelver Shias are spread through many parts of Pakistan. They have their own clerical leaders, tend to worship in their own mosques, and have as the high point of their religious year the spectacular mourning ceremonies of *Muharram*.

More distinctive in their observances are the Ismailis who believe that the Aga Khan is the living *Imam*, and who practise their worship in the special buildings called *Jamaatkhanas*, which are prominent features of many cities in Sind. At the other end of the country, the efforts of early Ismaili missionaries also converted the inhabitants of Hunza to their version of Islam.

Shrines: Since the numbers of immigrants from other parts of the Muslim world were never that large, even before the flow virtually dried up with the collapse of the Moghul Empire, most Sunnis in Pakistan too are the

descendants of local converts. In this great missionary enterprise of medieval times, a much lesser part was played by the orthodox clerics than by the *Pirs*, saints who followed the mystical teachings of Sufism.

The shrines constructed around the tombs of the great *Pirs* have for centuries lain at the heart of the religious life of the country, as magnets for devotion attracting both those in spiritual need of the aid of the saint, and many petitioners making vows in the hope of gaining his support for more practical or even material ends. While a mosque is always attached to a major shrine for those who wish to offer formal prayers, it is to the

tomb, typically covered with flowers lying on a sheet, that petitioners come to make their requests, to stroke the surround or grille to establish contact, to raise the hands in a silent prayer, typically the *Fatiha* which stands at the beginning of the Koran, and to leave a cash offering.

The holy reputation of the *Pirs* has ensured the hereditary devotion of families or even tribes of followers, and as a consequence a continuing status of immense importance for the leaders of the great *Pir* families. These are often themselves long-standing members of the "feudal" elite, enjoying very substantial incomes even after the formal nationalisation of the vast endowments of the shrines. The patronage of wealthy devotees has ensured that the older shrines are often complexes of unique architectural beauty and interest, while even those which came more recently into existence around the tombs of saints buried within living memory leave the passerby in no doubt as to the importance of what lies behind the eye-catching extravagance of their garish exteriors.

Some idea of the continuing importance of the shrines in bringing Pakistanis of all types and backgrounds together may best be gained from visiting them on Thursday evenings, when crowds gather to listen to the rhythmic singing of mystical songs, called *qavvali*. Even more unforgettable is the sight of the annual festivals held to mark the anniversary of the saint's death, or rather his "marriage" with God. These festivals – *urs* – may attract thousands of pilgrims of both sexes, often brought from distant provinces by special trains and buses. The accompanying *mela* (fairs) are an additional attraction on these occasions, bringing in all sorts of other people, including many whom one suspects seldom if ever choose to step inside a mosque for the performance of the prescribed prayers. Open to everyone, whatever their needs or wants, the great shrines provide the opportunity for the visitor, bewildered by the seemingly chaotic hustle and bustle outside in the street, to step inside, if only mentally, to try to establish contact with that other reality which may connect everybody at one time or another.

Above, a man reading the Koran. **Right**, the other side of Islam – inside a shrine.

THE WOMEN OF PAKISTAN

The election of Benazir Bhutto to her country's premier post in 1988 shows that gender in itself is not a problem for women aspiring to high office in Pakistan. The first ever female Prime Minister of an Islamic state, at the time of writing Ms Bhutto is also one of only five female premiers in the entire international community.

Political prominence of women is nothing new in Pakistan. Muslim women played a leading role in the struggle for independence and have been elected or appointed as the people's representatives in local regional and national governments ever since. They have reached the highest offices in state administration.

Pakistan was amongst the first countries to appoint women ambassadors, and today the country's professional women enjoy an exceptionally high profile. Many, like Maleeha Lodhi, editor of *The Muslim* (a newspaper published in Islamabad), are well-known figures. The aspirations of any women wishing to work in Pakistan are backed by the nation's constitution which encourages the participation of women in all spheres of national life and prohibits discrimination on the basis of gender. (The relevant articles antedate United Nation's declarations on women's rights by 40 years!)

Unlike certain neighbouring countries, Pakistani women are not limited to certain 'feminine' occupations like teaching in a girl's school or nursing in a women's hospital. There are woman doctors, lawyers and bankers. Women work as executives in advertising, personnel management and public relations. They are employed at senior management level by international corporations and the development organisations. Women also run their own highly successful enterprises. Emancipated women, with a good education and training, can go a long way in Pakistan. No other major international airline employs as many female pilots as PIA. Islamabad's universities alone have more female professors than the universities of the United Kingdom put together.

This is not to say that women with professional ambitions have always had a smooth ride. During the years of military rule the activities of women's groups were monitored. Associations of professional women, such as the Women's Action Forum, claim to have been harassed by the police. Some women have complained of sexual harassment at work. Many assert that women's cause has not been advanced by past or present governments. This, of course, the latter deny.

Most Pakistani women, however, lead very traditional lives. Their background dictates that they will have little chance, let alone desire, of entering into professional fields of work. Official statistics show that only 14 percent of women have had any schooling at all. Latest figures show that in 15 out of Pakistan's 75 districts, less than one percent of women can read and write.

With only 960 women to every 1,000 men, Pakistan's sex ratio is one of the world's lowest. Female life expectancy is 52 years, 20 years less than in Scandinavia. In the less developed areas, where families have to battle for their livelihood, the birth of a girl is often considered a misfortune. Girls are more at risk than boys from all childhood ailments due to inadequate nutrition. The typical woman can expect to be married at the age of 14, to carry nine pregnancies to full term and maybe lose as many again. Attempts by national and international development agencies to increase educational and healthcare provision for women are often hampered by traditional attitudes towards women's role in society. They are attitudes which can often be just as strong in the cities as in the rural areas.

Amongst "feminists" in Pakistan and elsewhere, there has been a tendency to equate Islam with the denial of rights to women. For their part, the *ulema* (religious leaders) assert that concern for a woman's rights is a central feature of Islam. Unlike non-Islamic doctrines (like orthodox Judaism, Hinduism and Christianity) Islam actually insists upon a woman's right to education and a livelihood, to own and inherit property separately from her husband, as well as to personal maintenance from him. These rights are enshrined in the *shar'ia*, Islamic law, they say.

The situation in practice is a little more complex. Whilst the Pakistani legal system incorporates many tenets of the shar'ia, the customs and traditions of the local community tend to take precedence over it. Learned sources report that Mohmand Pathan women cannot own or inherit land or houses, for example. Their consent is not asked in marriage negotiations, they retain no rights in the marriage settlement and cannot ask for divorce, under any circumstances. Even a woman's rights over her personal belongings, like clothes and jewellery, are subject to her father, husband or other male guardian's wishes.

Some or all of these practices are found in Pakistan's other rural areas. They may be relics of folk religions pre-dating Islam, borrowings from other south Asian religions, or simply misunderstandings of what the orthodox teaching really is. Whatever, they are not sustained by Islamic law.

Islam emphasises women's rights to run their own affairs, but it is hard for most women to act independently. Their decisions are generally enacted by a male spokesman, after consulting with male kinsmen. This is due to a set of customs, known as *purdah*, which are deeply rooted in the traditional way of life.

A survey shows that 82 percent of urban women and 47 percent of rural women say they keep purdah. Purdah means curtain or veil, but keeping purdah involves sexual segregation. Unless they are close relatives, men and women should keep their distance from each other. When meeting strangers of the opposite sex, modesty is preserved by avoiding eye contact, speaking formally and keeping the interaction short.

Traditionally minded families consequently divide social life into two domains, the private (household) and the public (non-household). In public, a woman should be chaperoned by a man, another woman or at least a child and should veil herself. In private, veiling is not required, though in very religious families women keep their hair covered when men are present. The household is women's realm, *harem* (forbidden) to male outsiders. As a result, specific areas are set aside for the men to receive male visitors. In the Tribal Areas, each village has a *hujra* (guest house). In the towns, every house has *baithak* (sitting room). In some places, for example amongst traditional landowning families of Sind, it is the women who keep to their own quarters, the *zenana*.

In the modern urban centres, high socio-economic status is often linked with freedom from such traditional constraints on mobility. In cosmopolitan Karachi, Islamabad and Lahore, women from the elite groups go about unveiled and may even wear Western style dress at home. This is seldom the case in the provincial cities and towns which tend to be a lot more conservative.

In Baluchistan and NWFP, to see any woman out and about on urban streets is uncommon. Those who do appear in public are often concealed by the all-enveloping *burqa* (like a nun's outfit) or *chaddar* (a sheet wound around the head and body, barely revealing the eyes).

Segregation is less pronounced in the rural areas, as women must move among males to work in the fields. Women do 75 percent of Pakistan's agricultural work. With work ranging from sowing, reaping and threshing to fetching water, the more conservative forms of veiling would be quite impractical. The women of rural Panjab and Sind usually wear a *chunni* or *dupatta* (a scarf draped around the head and shoulders) to signify modesty when men are present. Women of nomadic tribes do not wear veils. They scorn purdah as *bazaari* (towns-people's) practice.

Purdah is primarily the preserve of the provincial middle classes and for them it is a particular source of prestige. It shows they are wealthy enough for their women not to have to work. It also states their claim to a distinctive status based on religious piety.

For a woman who keeps purdah, whatever her background, her status exists in the approval of her immediate social circle. She is awarded points for chastity before marriage and fecundity afterwards. Her reputation is built on her good nature and common sense. She is serene in the knowledge that, whatever happens, her menfolk will look after her. She is often envied by less fortunate women who have to go out and work in order to supplement the family income.

One unexpected result of economic development is that many rural women who have never kept purdah are now secluded in their homes. Recent studies have shown that this is often the women's choice. It beats hard work under the hot sun in the fields all day, no question about it.

It is difficult to decide which of the almost endless catalogue of dishes from the subcontinent can be identified as specifically "Pakistani". Indeed Pakistan shares its culinary heritage with India, so menus overlap. If there is a difference (apart from those resulting from religious constraints) it is that the food in Pakistan is generally less hot than traditional Indian fare. This is partly because Indo-Muslim cooking, heavily influenced by Arab, Turkish and Persian food, makes lavish use of yoghurt which has a slightly neutralising effect on the strident sharpness of chillies.

Indo-Muslim cooking, developed in the Muslim courts of India and widely known as "Moghul" cuisine, is part of the stock national repertoire. It relies for its flavours on a blend of the more exotic herbs and spices such as saffron, cardamom, sesame and poppy seeds (the last two often roasted). The subtly bud-bursting quality of the resulting tastes and fragrances would be forfeited by the over-liberal use of chillies, consequently this food is perhaps the best choice for palates unaccustomed to very hot food.

Most menus will offer a selection of meat and poultry served in a variety of spicy sauces. The word *Mughlai* (à la Moghul), often a misnomer, is frequently appended to the name of the dish to emphasise its aristocratic origins and indicate the school of cooking described above. Other words pertaining to cooking methods appear as part of the name given to dishes – *bhuna gosht* (meat sautee – in which the meat is fried with a variety of spices and comes in a paste rather than a sauce), *machli ka salan* (fish curry) or *bheja masala* (devilled brains). The ubiquitous *korma*, (meat in spicy yoghurt gravy) may be suffixed with the word *mughlai* or *zafrani* (with saffron) or indeed the name of a chef, establishment or region. *Khara masala gosht* (whole spice meat), *dopiaza* (two onion) chicken or mutton which requires onions to be added at two different

stages of the cooking process and *roghan gosht* (garnished meat) are just a few more popular dishes. These are variously garnished with fried onions, raisins, cashewnuts, pistachios and slivers of almonds. Sliced tomatoes and boiled eggs, shredded lettuce, and raw or lightly cooked onions are also used to make presentation more attractive and colourful. As the restaurant becomes cheaper, the luxury elements in dishes are replaced with larger quantities of cheap ingredients such as tomatoes, onions,

garlic, ginger, turmeric and chillies, making the food correspondingly hotter.

Another legacy from the Moghul era is the celebrated *haleem* claimed to be much loved by the Emperor Akbar. It contains succulent pieces of meat, cooked in seven grains including rice, wheat and various lentils ground to a sensuous, velvety texture. Its variant *khichra*, ground meat cooked with similar ingredients is a much "stodgier" concoction, equally if not more popular. Both are available from shops and stalls in disposable earthenware pots as are many other foods bought from street vendors and cheap stalls. *Dalcha* is a more mundane

Preceding pages: going shopping; bridal wear; waiting to be cooked. **Left**, street vendor. **Above**, at a wedding party.

version consisting of meat and *channe ki dal* (yellow split-pea lentils) in a brown gravy, and may appear on some menu cards.

Another perennial favourite is *nihari* which consists of large chunks of beef from the head and shoulder, with brain, tongue and marrow added to a highly seasoned gravy. Traditionally *nihari* was eaten at breakfast by workers to sustain them throughout the day. Ironically it is now a much sought-after delicacy and available only from select restaurants on specific days. It is served with slivers of ginger, fried and raw onions, fresh chillies, chopped coriander and lime juice and eaten with *naan*.

Pakistan's most famous contribution to the international gourmet scene is probably *tandoori* chicken, a chicken quarter steeped in marinade and barbecued in a *tandoor* (underground clay oven) from which it derives its name. *Tikka kebabs* made from cubes of chicken, mutton, fish or king prawns and sometimes beef, are a constant favourite and come in an enormous variety. Most *tikkas* and *kebabs* are barbecued on skewers or baked in the *tandoor* oven unless the cooking method is specified as in *karhai kebab* (fried with onions and spices, in the wok-like *karhai*). *Seekh-kebabs* are succulent sausage-shaped tubes of mince cooked in a *tandoor* or barbecued, after being moulded directly onto the skewer (*seekh*). Also commonly found and convenient to carry is the *shami kebab*, a meat rissole sometimes filled with a mixture of finely chopped onions, mint and coriander seasoned with lemon juice.

Nargisi koftas (meatballs) are coated in a spicy meat-paste and deep fried. Sometimes these are served in an onion sauce. *Ghulvan kebab* (dissolved kebabs) and *dam kebab* (steamed kebabs) are rarer and highly prized for the melt-in-the-mouth quality of their minced meat which is softened literally to a paste with the aid of natural tenderizers such as raw papaya or *kachri* (a species of melon).

Traditionally *kebabs* are eaten with *naan*, bread baked in a *tandoor*, or its variant *kulcha* sprinkled with sesame seeds. The *paratha* is also a popular alternative. Depending on the chef's recipe they can range from circles of airy, layered, puff pastry to a thicker, fried version of the ordinary *chapati*. *Parathas* also come stuffed with mince meat or vegetables. The versatile *puri*, a small, puffed circle of bread is enjoyed with meat, vegetables and lentils as well as desserts. Some places boast of special breads such as *shirmal* cooked with milk and eggs, which like *naan*, is one of the few yeast-baked breads. *Roghni* bread is soft and slightly sweet and is also another favourite *kebab* accompaniment.

Biryani, rice cooked in rich meat-sauce (or chicken, fish or prawns) possibly tops the national popularity polls and is reserved for special occasions due to its festive character. Like various sweetmeats and other celebration foods it is often decorated with finely beaten edible silver paper and partly dyed an attractive orange with saffron.

Pulao is a lighter version of biryani and may contain meat, chicken or fish cooked in simple bouillon.

Cloves, cardamoms, peppercorns and cinnamon are used to increase the aroma of rice dishes. Rose-water and *kevra* sprinkled over rice and other foods add further fragrance. The humdrum *khichri,* a mixture of rice and *channe ki dal,* is also favoured with aromatics. A mushy version is eaten with a sauce of mint and natural yoghurt to cure diarrhhoea.

Traditionally most rice dishes are served with *raita*, yoghurt sauce seasoned with salt, pepper, ground fresh coriander and a sprinkling of chillis. Grated cucumber and mint flavoured *raita* is probably the most famous one worldwide. Elaborate recipes of *raita* may include fried vegetables, such as *okra*, aubergine or pumpkin and an infusion of fried mustard or cummin seed with turmeric.

Yoghurt is also a crucial ingredient of the pungent, strongly flavoured cuisine eaten at brunch or tea. The spicy *chaat* (literally "lick") dishes fall into this category and it is astonishing to see what can be achieved with boiled potatoes and chick-peas or gram flour. They are doused in yoghurt, chillies, and *chaat-masala* (a combination of roasted hot spices), sprinkled with fruit, chopped green chillies and onions, topped with hot red-chilly sauce, sweet and sour tamarind or green chutney made from mint or coriander in a base of lime juice and ground green chillies.

"Chutney" is the word for hot tangy dips made from ground ingredients and served in place of relishes and ketchup. Easy to eat finger foods perfect for filling gaps, include *pakora*, deep fried balls made from a batter of pale yellow gram flour, flavoured with spices and *bhajia*, batter-fried vegetables. These come with piquant chilli chutneys, spiced yoghurt or tamarind sauce. *Samosas* are also good finger foods, and come mainly in filo of puff pastry with meat or vegetable fillings. *Kachori*, a crisp, round pastry filled with lentil paste is a delicious alternative. The authenticity of these tastes is an experience available only from the stalls of street-vendors and can rarely be replicated at home. Other cheap, convenient snacks from barrows include roasted peanuts (*mumphali*) and gram pulses (*channa*) available in slim paper cones. *Kabuli channa* is seasoned with salt, powdered red-chillies and lime juice.

mango, water-melon and a berry called *falsa*, among others.

A range of curried and extremely spicy breakfast dishes include *Khagina*, eggs scrambled in oil spiced with onions, chillies, garlic, ginger and tomatoes. Like most recipes these vary slightly from place to place. Devilled kidneys (*gurda*), liver (*kaleji*), brain (*bheja*) and sweetbreads (*kapoora*) are delicious flavours for those who enjoy offal. They are eaten with *paratha* or ordinary *chapati*. *Alu-puri* (spicy potatoes with *puri*) are also popular at breakfast which is often rounded off with *suji ka halva* (semolina pudding) also eaten with *puri*. *Jalebi*, crispy whirls of saffron flavoured syrup are also on

Lassi, a yoghurt drink (savoury, sweetened or fruit-flavoured) is recommended with all these dishes since it is cool and soothes the effect of the chillies. The bubbles from aerated drinks bursting on over-stimulated taste-buds exacerbate the discomfort. Ice helps by numbing the tongue. *Nimbu pani* (freshly squeezed lime juice) and a variety of other fresh fruit juices are seasonally available from shops and barrows. These include sugar-cane, pomegranate,

sale in the morning. *Jalebi* and other sweet-meats are mostly sold in cups made from dried leaves bound together with twigs. Karachi is particularly well known for *habshi halva* a dark brown, sticky sweetmeat available only in Sind, and *halva* of *akhrot* (walnut), a similar looking, lighter brown confection. *Sohan halva*, a pistachio and almond studded disc of stickjaw-style toffee is also widely available. The rare and subtly delicious *andey ka halva* is a taste not to be missed if the chance presents itself. Other desserts include *shahi tukra* (imperial pieces), a national version of bread pudding, coated in cream and slivers of pistachios and

Above, some of the basic ingredients used in Pakistani cooking.

almonds and *gajar ka halva,* a delicious dessert made from carrots and popular with wrestlers and body builders for the vitality and strength they claim to get from it.

Pakistanis prefer meat to vegetables so the order of priority on social occasions is meat, poultry and seafood. Lentils and vegetables are regarded merely as accompaniments although some of these are delicacies in their own right.

Chicken is the most expensive meat in Pakistan, mutton is next and beef, which is not very popular, is considerably cheaper except in five star restaurants where it may be imported from Argentina or Australia and priced correspondingly!

Regional specialities: Local preferences are obviously directly related to the local agriculture and geographic location. Unfortunately, few restaurants in the largest cities, Karachi, Rawalpindi and Lahore, offer regional specialities.

Rice and fish are the staple food of the Sindhis living along the banks of the River Indus, which gave India its name. Their favourite fish is the magnificent *palla* and white salmon from the river. The coastal regions of Sind, particularly Karachi, are known for their high quality seafood. Trawlers bring in enormous catches of fish, lobster and king prawns to Karachi Fish Harbour each evening which are comparable to the

Most meat is killed according to the *halal* process of slaughtering and draining the animal's blood. Butchers carefully remove all the fat from it to preserve its freshness longer in a hot climate. In spite of the marked national fondness for meat, certain days are designated meatless.

The main meal for an average Pakistani family probably consists of meat, poultry or fish cooked in gravy with a dish or two of vegetables or lentils, plain boiled rice and *chapatis* or its puffed variant *phulka,* the commonest of all Pakistani breads. Poorer households may forego meat in favour of more filling food such as potatoes.

best in the world. Pomfret, a popular sea fish, is fried or baked in a coating of garlic, ginger, turmeric and red-chilli paste and served with lemon wedges. King-sized prawns, creamy, full-flavoured and as large as chicken drumsticks are also widely available at ludicrously low prices.

The Sindhis have a predilection for tangy flavours. Sindhi recipes often quote the ingredient *amchur* (powdered raw mango) which provides a lemony piquance to their vegetables. A huge variety of mangoes grow locally so Sind boasts a delectable range of mango-based pickles, condiments and preserves unique to the region. Perhaps the most exciting taste of the area is *sajji* – roast lamb or sometimes beef, prepared in a yoghurt marinade and generally cooked over a bed of rice into which run all the juices. *Sajji* is also widely available in Baluchistan.

The Panjabis dislike the sourness of tamarind, lime and raw mangoes, preferring the sustenance provided by energy giving meals of potatoes, meat and the great regional favourite *dal* (lentils). When one of the many varieties of *dal* is infused with garlic, red-chillies, curry-leaves, cummin seed or onions fried in *ghee* (clarified butter) it is known as *tarka* (or *baghar*) and regarded as a great delicacy. Bread is perhaps the most vital part of the Panjabi meal and in rural

(meal). Panjabis often cook meat with added vegetables; favourite combinations are with tomatoes (*tamatar-gosht*), potatoes (*alu-gosht*), cauliflower (*gobi-gosht*) or spinach (*palak* or *sag-gosht*). Meat may be left out altogether and vegetables mixed together to produce, for example, the renowned *alu-gobi*. The celebrated *sarson ka sag* (mustard leaves) is traditionally cooked in an earthenware pot and served with unleavened cornmeal bread. *Channa Bhatura* (chick-peas with potatoes), eaten with a course variant of the *puri,* is another regional speciality.

In and around Lahore the River Ravi yields the prized fish *bekti* which is deep-fried in batter or spices. A number of local

areas, is sometimes accompanied with little more than raw onions and a green chilli or two washed down with a pot of fresh milk or *chach*, a buttermilk variant of *lassi*. This may be followed with a lump of the fudge-like *gur* (a product of boiled sugar cane) which is used as a sweetener instead of refined sugar.

Bread is made of several different grains in the Panjab, including millet and maize. This probably accounts for Panjabis referring to meals as *roti* (bread) rather than *khana*

Left, the baker's oven. **Above**, vendor surrounded by nuts.

specialities are available outside the walled city of Lahore. Crisp-fried or stewed mutton known by the blanket term *karhai gosht* (pan meat) is a great favourite. For the more adventurous palate there is *kalla pacha* – a local variant of *siri-paya*, highly flavoured, soupy and made from the head and hooves of cattle. This has a high gelatine content and gives a sticky texture to the gravy which some may find off-putting.

Naan-kebab is the staple food of Pathans who also have a penchant for *biryani* which they satisfy when they can. The celebrated *chappli kebabs* of Peshawar are named for their shape which resembles *chappals* (slippers). As the terrain gets higher and rockier the choice becomes restricted to coarse bread eaten with locally grown beans and home-made cheese called *paneer*. Chicken is very often the only meat option.

Fruit from Quetta and the valleys of Hunza and Swat is legendary for its succulence. Pakistan boasts a huge range of melons and citrus fruits. Plums, apricots, peaches, walnuts, mulberries and grapes grow in the temperate regions as do apples and pears. Pomegranates, papayas, guavas, sugar cane, bananas and mangoes grow in the plains. The *Sindri* is among the most superior species of mangoes along with the smaller *alphonso* and the green-skinned *langra*.

Most cultures attach some rituals to eating and this is also true of Pakistan, essentially a food-oriented culture. Traditional menus are set for festivals such as the two Eids, when *sevayyan* and *sheer khorma* (vermicelli puddings) are cooked while *biryani* and *korma* provide the standard wedding menu.

Pakistanis eat sweets and confectionaries to celebrate happy occasions much as a bottle of champagne is popped in the west. Hence the demand of "*mithai khilao*" (distribute sweets) directed to people with reason to celebrate. A wide variety of milk based sweets is available from "sweet marts". The commonest of these are *barfi* (a

fudge-like sweet which comes in coconut, pistachio and almond squares), *pera* (a similar, round sweet, harder and more crumbly in texture, *Karachi halva* (gelatinous squares of flamboyant pink, yellow or green, studded generously with nuts, round, syrupy *gulab-jamun, rasgullah* and *cham-cham*. *Laddoos* (moist, yellow balls) of several kinds are also popular.

Most of these require a seasoned palate and a definite sweet tooth but are frequently on offer when visitors come. Refusal to eat may be interpreted as refusal of friendship and is taken as a slight. However, a token morsel of food or a sip of water is considered sufficient indication of goodwill. Most Pakistanis are very hospitable and tend to press food on guests, prefacing their offers with the remark "you haven't eaten a thing". Though somewhat daunting to the uninitiated, this springs from a desire to ensure that guests do not leave the table hungry due to a sense of formality.

Tea is also freely on offer in homes and also in many shops where the client may be expected to spend a little time on selection. *Chai* stalls are strategically located in all the bazaars, providing a chance for the traveller to recuperate. Tea tends to be very sweet and is often cooked with milk, sugar and allspice (nutmeg, cinnamon, cloves, cardamoms). If milk is served separately it is always hot. *Sulaimani chai* (Tea Solomon) is black and meals are sometimes followed with *sabz chai* (green tea) or jasmine tea, light, fragrant and claimed to be good for the digestion. Tibetan tea churned with butter is available in Baltistan.

The ubiquitous *paan* (betel leaf) is worth a try. It is available from stalls on every street corner. A variety of fragrances and tastes are wrapped with chopped betel nut into the leaf and this is generally eaten after meals. Those addicted to it eat it at all times of day except directly before meals and spit out the red-stained liquid, much like tobacco chewers.

All in all then, exciting taste sensations await the more adventurous visitor to the country, while fast-food chains, food-stores and middle-to-expensive restaurants cater to more international tastes.

Above, "Dessert, anyone?" **Right**, pensive mood in a sea of greens.

Local handicrafts are perhaps the most striking expression of the individuality of Pakistan's regional identities. The colour, shape or style of a craft item instantly evokes its region: the bright patchwork quilts of Sind, the *kaghazi* (paper-thin) pottery of Bahawalpur, the ceramic tiles of Hala and Chiniot.

Handicrafts are part of the daily domestic routine in the lives of most of Pakistan's rural dwellers who account for roughly 70 percent of the country's population. Although some

items such as bed-covers and floor coverings inevitably perform a dual function much of this output is functional. Baluch women, for example, keep their pots, pans and spoons in specially woven wool or cotton-net bags which can be easily suspended from a cart or an animal when travelling. Hammocks provide a convenient resting-place for babies when hung from poles but can be put away when necessary, and so the list continues.

The revitalisation or decline of a craft at a particular time provides clues to social change. The decrease in woven camel-coverings in Sind and Baluchistan over two centuries, for example, indicated the deci-

sion of several nomadic tribes to settle. Corresponding increases in the production of floor coverings have confirmed this. As the trend to settle escalated, the motifs of cloth woven for animal coverings were nostalgically transferred to rugs produced and used by settled tribes, yet another pointer to their altered needs. The beams upon which pivot the trestle-style looms found in Sind, Panjab and Bahawalpur, are supported by forked branches fixed to the ground. This likewise bears witness to settling tribes re-

placing their collapsible, tripod-style weaving looms. Similarly the disappearance of the basketry flute-bags of Umarkot in the Thar Desert denotes the emigration of its substantial yogi snake-charmer population following drought and famine.

Influences: Changes and developments in the crafts similarly have a valuable story to tell about the social structure, its altering pattern and the history of the country and its people. The Arab conquests beginning in the 8th century are recorded in the universally encountered geometric patterns from the Islamic world. The Perso-Turkic invasions left their imprint in the form of floral and foliate motifs widely used in every conceivable area of decorative art. From gold jewellery to wool carpets, craft products bear the hallmarks of Islamic art and architecture blended with the more free-flowing asymmetric compositions and mellow forms of indigenous South Asian art. The tree of Life encountered in Islamic art across the world is frequently replicated in Pakistan. Much of this art is inspired by the magnificent architectural monuments seen in the Muslim world from the Iberian Peninsular through the Arab heartlands and Ottoman Turkey to Persia and South Asia, displaying splendid examples of ceramic tiles, elaborately filigreed metalwork and inlays of precious

metal, gems and ivory. These continue to feature in the range of handicrafts and jewellery found in Pakistan's craft markets.

The impact of British colonialism in turn left its mark, corrupting the taste of the urban population who have tended for years to favour European design for home and wear to the detriment of indigenous crafts which, paradoxically, made a permanent impact on

Preceding pages, the woodworker's craft; a mosque in Skardu. Far left, camel skin work on vases and lampshades in Multan. Left, blue-glazed ceramics from Hyderabad. Above, fine metalwork on display.

the paisleys, dancing figures and geometric emblems of occidental fabric design. The change in taste reflected the desire of the urban rich and the newly rising to affirm their education and consequent "westernisation" which had become synonymous with notions of modernity and success. Another aspect of modernisation was a clearly stated admiration for scientific achievement and its contribution to the economic improvement of the industrialised nations. The contempt felt by urban and wealthy Pakistanis for regional handicrafts clearly lay in the fact that they were produced and used by rural communities and the working classes. Together these factors prompted a move away from the patronage of handicrafts and indigenous products to factory-made goods. Many city-dwellers still favour various grades of imported china, glass and crystalware while hundreds of village smithies in the countryside continue to hammer out a great variety of brass and copper tumblers, trays, bowls and pots, part of the everyday kitchen paraphernalia of rural dwellers.

Tribes too were once well supplied by their own craftsmen such as the Luri Baluch who combined the two vital roles of armourer and minstrel (easily reconcilable since the latter meant chronicling the war experiences of their tribes in the form of songs). As armoury became redundant the Luri turned their hand to the making of pots and pans. Classical craft both functional and decorative therefore became increasingly confined to its area of production, attracting little respect or regard from the wealthy, although there were notable exceptions such as carpet-weaving.

Home-grown items, however superbly crafted, were consigned to tourist-orientated emporia selling mostly "curiosities" with functional value. This resulted in hybrid products new to the culture but drawing on traditional techniques such as leather embroidery. A proliferation of belts, hand-bags and wallets replaced the embroidered and embossed sheathes, gun-holsters, animal decoration and saddlery no longer much in demand. Hand-painted camel-skin lamps and vases echoing the stained glass colours and patterns of Iraqui and Syrian Mamluk mosques bear testimony to the lost skill of archery and the consequent redundancy of the quiver-maker. Velvet satchels appliqued with the gold or silver arabesques and mirror-work flowers of the Pathan's ceremonial waistcoats, nestle in urban emporia among large quantities of round Sindhi caps with tiny sequins, sunbursts and eight-point stars of cerese, green and yellow.

All this provides evidence of the changing world of ethnic craftspeople as the ever-increasing demand for handicrafts transforms the wherewithal of their daily lives into curios and souvenirs for tourist and commercial consumption.

While the movement within a craft area chronicles events, however, it may itself slip out of existence without note. The year 1974 therefore heralded a vital, if long overdue

porated into stranded necklaces of pearls, emeralds and rubies in the form of pendants and clasps. In addition to such items, essentially part of the common South Asian heritage, are the more solid, rustic examples. Mostly made of solid silver, these consist of chokers, coarsely moulded collars and long necklaces and chains, often representing the total wealth of the wearer. These may occasionally be mixed with base metal and studded with semi-precious stones with a marked preference for blue and red. Frequently women, particularly tribals and those living in mountainous areas, pierce their ears along the outer ridge in order to wear several hoops and studs in conjunction with drop ear-rings.

move to restore status to the handicrafts of Pakistan with the inauguration of the Institute of Folk Heritage in Islamabad. The various projects of the institute included research into the development of various national crafts. This no doubt promoted greater familiarity with the crafts and their quintessential qualities at last bringing about a desirable fusion of the traditional with the contemporary.

Jewellery: The richest and most elaborate items of jewellery seen in Pakistan are those inherited from the Moghul period. These include gold chokers, bracelets and ear-rings enamelled and inlaid pieces are often incor-

Bangles and rings are particularly popular in Panjab where gold is highly rated as are pearls and rubies. The *damani* (jewelled headband), *tika* (jewel worn in hair-parting suspending a pendant on the forehead) and *jhumar* (clustre of chains or jewelled strands fanning out from the parting over the side of the head towards the face) continue to be popular bridal and dowry items. Jewellery still acts as a bank for rural families who feel more secure when they consolidate their savings in the form of gold or silver.

Metalwork: Other items of gold and silver are available for the wealthy in the shape of platters, trays, serving vessels, chalices and *pan-dans* (containers for betel-leaf serving paraphernalia). In fact metalware is available in many grades of workmanship. The country boasts a flourishing production of metal *objets d'art,* many modelled on famous medieval pieces, in the full range of chased, repousse and inlaid metal from furniture to vases, jugs and wall-hangings. Gujrat and Sialkot (Panjab) are notable for their *koftgari,* (the laying of base and precious metal wires on metal objects – damascening) and Multan, Karachi and Hyderabad for their coloured glazes and enamel inlay work. The most popular metalware design is probably the intertwined flowering vine composed of rosettes and arabesques seen on

(parcel gilt) pieces from Rawalpindi and Karachi. Filigree work, another metal speciality, can also be achieved with wood on doors, window-frames, grills and folding screens. The techniques of engraving and damascening with metal and other substances can also be applied to wood-carving.

Woodwork: The wood-worker's skill has long been celebrated as fit for kings, mentioned alike by travellers, diarists and poets. Hasham Shah, an early 19th century Panjabi poet describes in his famed epic poem of the tragic love-affair of Sassi and Punnun, a chest in which a king places his infant daughter before floating her downriver in consequence of a prediction that she would one

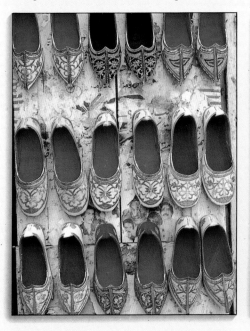

a large number of objects in the Panjab. The crescent moon, the eight-point star and other Islamic symbols appear in fascinating contrast to the stock motifs of lion and elephant heads and fish recently augmented by the reintroduction of human forms from authentic Gandhara art. *Bidri,* silver inlaid on a metal amalgam, produces a dramatic silver-on-black effect which has commanded admiration since its apogee in the 17th century. Other silverwork includes the *ganga-jamni*

day bring disgrace upon his name.

Now from the Master who for Sassi
Built a chest with skill
Would Plato or Aristotle
All artistry have learned
The beauties of the East took each
Adornment's craft from him.
See, Hasham, with what craftmanship
Each piece he makes is turned

A block of sandal was procured,
On which the master wrought
Entwining arabesques of gold,
Bejewelled and begemmed.

Left, Sindi hats. **Above left**, these slippers look very Turkish; **right**; geometric designs are of Arabic origin.

Muslim wood-workers emigrated at Partition from Kashmir and made their homes in Swat, Peshawar, Karachi, Lahore and Pindi. They are particularly remarkable for their inlay work with metal, buffalo-horn and ivory. The wood-workers of Dera Ismail Khan and Chiniot are highly respected for their brass inlaid products, the latter particularly for their bold freehand designs, specifically those incorporating scrolls.

Pottery: Potters like metal-workers frequently draw their inspiration from antique objects, having inherited from within the family techniques handed down by the ancient master-potters of Persia and the Arab heartlands. The blue on white ceramic glazes eros, leopards, bulls, bears and dogs found in 2500 B.C. in Mohenjo-daro still flourish as do terracotta game boards, inlaid with shell and cast with marble and ivory dice. Astoundingly, the foot-driven pottery wheel of Mohenjo-daro is used to this day although artefacts are fired in the open rather than in the kilns of old. Most Bahawalpur pottery is natural terracotta but the full range of glazed and enamelled ceramics is widely available. Sind is noted for its black and maroon, pre-firing glaze. Sindhi artisans are celebrated also for their lacquerware decorated in patterns of blue, mustard and brick-red providing a welcome and lively contrast to their desert environment. In Panjab, the two-col-

were perfected in Iraq and Syria more than 1,000 years ago and those authentic techniques are still applied to the making of the magnificent turquoise tilework of famous Persian mosques and the impressive Multan *idgah*. River mud formed into tiles is painstakingly hand-crafted through each stage of glazing and baking by a handful of family tile-makers surviving around Hyderabad, noteably in Hala. The *kaghazi* pottery of Bahawalpur similarly adheres to age-old techniques. The famous lattice designs enjoy continued popularity while calligraphy, and miniature paintings are a recent addition on vases, plates and wall-pieces. The rhinoc- our lac turnery of Jhang and Sargodha is further embellished with mirrors.

Basketry: Another widely practised craft is basketry. Mats, blinds, fans, slippers and caps are woven from the leaves of the date-palm, wild rushes, reeds and wheat-stalks. This continues to be the work of women who traditionally wove bread-baskets for keeping warm the bread they cooked in large quantities. Other useful domestic paraphernalia included winnowing-fans and lattice-work baskets for storing and carrying. Interestingly however, they were barred from weaving the hats and baskets used by the snake-charming communities of yogis and

Hindu tribespeople, loth to allow women to participate in the making of their ritual equipment owing to notions of pollution linked to menstruation. Decorated basketry bearing intricate geometric patterns woven from pre-dyed grass, reeds and leaves is commercially the most in demand. Basketry shopping bags are seen in use in most of the markets in Pakistan. Basketry screens are often used to curtain off domestic and work areas.

Several agencies have opened up in rural areas all over the country and encourage the mass production of basketry goods providing spare-time jobs for women, men and children. But on the whole, it remains the

products found in Pakistan is a strong feature of its cultural profile.

Another of the most widely travelled concepts of the "ethnic" Pakistani craftwork is the patchwork quilt. Adopted by contemporary Sufism as a symbol of fusion and synthesis the *rilli* originated among the fishertribes of Manchhar Lake (Sind), now largely migrated to Kheenjar Lake. Women of all ages can be seen sitting in the sun, sewing together small squares of old cloth to create multi-coloured chequered *rillis* to be handed down as family heirlooms. The *rilli* is found all over Sind today, some areas favouring more structured patterns and colour combinations than others. Lower Sind for example

preserve of women done at night after their chores are over or during a break in the day's routine when they may chat as they work.

Women and handicrafts: The contribution of women to hand-crafted produce in Pakistan is far greater than is generally recognised. Women of various regions and tribes produce exquisite embroidery and are capable of applying their skills to materials as diverse as floor coverings, leather sandals and handloom cotton garments. In fact the intricate and infinitely varied range of embroidered

Left, women help themselves – a small industries centre in Quetta. Above, Baluchi rugs.

sticks to basic black and white patchwork set out in a clear pattern. Some *rillis* may come decorated with shells, gold thread and beads.

Carpets: Tribal rugs of camel and sheep hair mixed with cotton come flat-woven, embroidered or piled. Baluchistan is perhaps the major source of folk carpets and rugs of various types. Like most other rural crafts these are produced primarily for their own use. As a result some types of floor-covering such as the Baluchi *jhool* based on the animal covers of old, have become so rare that they are regarded as irreplaceable even at the source of their origin. Such pieces, characterised by their central square and a quarter square in each corner, are valued highly as heirlooms and patched with leather in order to be carefully preserved as long as possible. One cause for the lost art is the apparent intolerance of certain women carpet weavers who received such acclaim that they were unwilling to risk their reputation by delegating to apprentices. However the *farashi* rug, generally made from a combination of sheep and camel hair with bleached cotton, remains a popular item. Women carry the pattern intended for the rug under production in their minds discussing between them details of colour and pattern before starting. It is not unusual for a change of mind to occur halfway through the job and occasionally

whose help is invaluable in vital peripheral areas such as spinning, winding thread and working the looms. Children, with their tiny fingers are extremely adept at tying the fine knots required to create patterns and as a result are also popular in the artisan-controlled area of carpet-making. Here the master-weaver remains in control of the work, designing the piece and calling out instructions to the workers who knot and weave the pattern, sight unseen, to completion. Traditionally the master-weaver would call out an instruction to create a barely perceptible flaw in the design. This was meant to avert the evil eye attracted by a too-perfect piece. The *chappay-walas* of Lahore

this can be seen in the finished item adding to the human charm of the whole article.

Common design features include interlocked tapestry weave, striped and banded ground decorated with squares, stars enclosed incrosses, cartouches, octagons, borders and dunes. Rows of stylised camels are understandably popular among the Baluch tribes. It is rare (although not unheard of) for tribal males to weave carpets. A unique regional speciality is the chamois leather rug from Sind, embroidered in multi-coloured silk, gold or silver.

Like most domestic crafts, carpet-making is a family occupation, drawing in children

and the folk-artisans of Karachi remain acknowledged masters of their art. Quetta, Multan and Peshawar also boast thriving handloom carpet-making communities.

Contemporary artisans favour the jewel-like beauty of the floral carpets conceived in Persia and developed in India during the Moghul period. Medallion carpets, bearing a vase-like central motif echoed in quarter-circles in each corner, also continue in popularity as do hunting or animal rugs. A recent addition to classic carpet design is the Kalashnikov symbol, once again reflecting events in the lives of the makers, this time in the shape of Afghan border problems.

Organisation: An increasing demand for local handicrafts prompted national welfare and development agencies to patronise traditional artisans and buy what they could of the handicrafts available. They found that demand infinitely exceeded supply. As a result agencies such as APWA (All Pakistan Women's Association), the PIDC (Pakistan Internal Development Corporation), and the PTDC (Pakistan Tourism Development Corporation) began commissioning items found to be most in demand.

They found that more people were required to meet the demand and recruited women to be trained by the existing practitioners in villages and craft teachers in urban duced by women substantially swelling the number of skilled female artisans who began to move into handloom work, block-printing and related work. Along with male artisans they were organised into numerous groups nationwide which catered primarily to the handicraft export industry. But this group of cottage industries workers, although never short of work, do not command nearly the sort of income that may be expected from so thriving a field.

Craft co-operatives too provide opportunities for artisans from the various craft communities but inspite of the booming demand, Pakistani handicrafts remain low-priced compared with those of other coun-

centres. APWA's training programme spilled over into their Patient's Welfare Project, under whose aegis the wives and grown up daughters of men hospitalised over a long period were taught a skill, often embroidery or sewing. Table-linen, mats and other items produced during training were sold to finance the project and the women subsequently helped meet the demand for such items. The Raana Liaquat Ali Industrial Home, begun under the auspices of APWA, fostered the growth of goods pro-

Left, piece by piece. **Above**, sewing a *rilli* on Manchar Lake.

tries. This has increased the demand further with the advent into Pakistan of western charities and trade organisations who buy cottage industry produce to sell as novelty and gift items such as brassware, wooden boxes and linen direct and by mail order to the consumers in their own countries.

But in spite of occasional attention in the arena of international trade, Pakistani handicrafts remain largely unknown in the rest of the world. Thus, the visitor may harvest a rich and unique yield of products at remarkably low prices, for beyond the organised small industries are the rural artisans and the tribespeople at the periphery of the country.

A guide book to most countries of the world would not normally warrant a special section featuring vehicles. But in Pakistan the common truck and bus have been transformed into works of art.

The traveller is transported to a land of make-believe through colourfully painted heavy goods vehicles bearing scenes of snow-capped mountains beneath purple-streaked skies; emerald valleys with trees of flaming orange; gleaming yellow trains winding through mountain passes against

brated painted trucks of Afghanistan clearly provide the model for the larger Pakistani vehicle and looking further back to the original mode of mercantile transport it would be even more tempting to explore the similarities between the function of the medieval camel and the contemporary heavy goods vehicle.

Conditions along trade routes remain remarkably similar today with very few facilities provided in the form of police or army for the protection of the traveller from thugs

brilliant red sunsets. Trucks and lorries and buses display vividly coloured slogans and symbols. Birds, animals and fish nestle along with floral and foliate motifs amid curlicued frames of stylised hearts or ribbons. In addition the vehicles are swathed in tinkling chains, artificial flowers and good luck charms reminiscent of the camel decor of the medieval Middle East. Hundreds of similarly decorated motor rickshaws wind in and out of the traffic like gaudy cabs escaped from a circus whirligig.

A variety of themes adorns all sides of the vehicle and it is fascinating to ponder on the origins of this unusual art form. The cele-

or political unrest and only rarely a fuelling station or resthouse to break the journey. In the old days good luck charms, bells and chains were hung on camels to ward off evil. Prayers and symbols invoking God's name too, provided potent protection against natural disasters and misfortune. Today trucks and lorries replace camel caravans but the bells, chains and amulets remain.

Indeed, the notion of Divine Protection cannot be dismissed even today and is provided through depictions of holy locales which appeal to the religious sentiments of the driver, who travels lonely and dangerous routes burdened with the goods of others, as well as the businessman who is attracted by his confirmation of piety.

Allah is the word perhaps most commonly seen on vehicles, flanked by stylised peacocks, fish or flowers or framed with an arabesque. The *burraq* (half woman half winged-horse) is another popular image reminding Muslims of the Prophet Muhammad's ascension to Paradise – his one miraculous experience, celebrated widely by Muslims as *Shab-e-Me'raj* (The Night of Ascension). Mecca, the land of the holy pilgrimage, Medina, the city of the Prophet's birth, holy shrines and mosques, particularly those reminiscent of Moghul architecture, are also commonplace.

sion justifying the expense of lavish decoration from the business angle. Trucks and lorries, mostly goods transporters, service the same business circuits and trade routes. Their flamboyantly painted company logos are intended to expand business by attracting the maximum possible attention.

The decoration of vehicles is obviously an important method of advertising. The brighter and more highly decorated the vehicle the more convincingly it indicates the driver's pride and success in his profession. Cheery painted messages of "Be happy!" and "Keep smiling!" and saucy lines from film lyrics and poetry create goodwill in much the same way as commercial sponsor-

The pictures exude an aura of dreamy exoticism, achieved by clouds of powder-blue and candy-floss pink and yellow, surrounding pure white constructions which overlook lakes or nestle in lotuses. Undoubtedly these reaffirm the faith and allay the fear of the driver by night, while offering his sand-sore, heat-stricken eyes relief and coolness by day.

Alongside these morale-building endeavours is the crucial commercial dimen-

ship does through television.

Buses can also be very eye-catching. Those which belong to private fleets undergo a complete transformation to their bodywork. Indeed by the time the specialists are through with the job, the bus which pulls in at a stop on its way from Islamabad to Rawalpindi bears little resemblance to the vehicle which originally came off the production line. The interiors often look more like a shrine than a bus.

The more shining and outlandish the better as the eager conductor alights shouting "Raja Bazaar, Raja Bazaaré". Soon, the bus noses out into the traffic with a full load,

Preceding pages, heading up country. **Left**, a truck driver from the north. **Above**, ideals and fantasy.

leaving another, older jalopy to take its place and vie for less choosy passengers.

Driving is a popular occupation, particularly for tribesmen of independant character, such as the Pathans, who value the opportunity to work without supervision. Some migrants from the countyside too, find it more amenable to work in the open, seeing their work as the contemporary offshoot of bullock or tonga driving. Even those lacking education can swiftly acquire skill and expertise at the job, allowing them more flexibility and pride than the average domestic servant or factory worker.

The truck driver is employed by a boss who owns the transport company controlling understand the escapist depictions of rural life seen particularly on heavy goods vehicles. Cascading waterfalls against lush greenery, bird-inhabited trees, bushes in the height of flower, all vie for space with scenes of the farmer peacefully involved in husbandry assisted by able-bodied bullocks, while other healthy farm animals graze contentedly in the background. The hides of the animals glisten, the streams look clean, the crops plentiful, the living places strong and the people happy. In fact life in the home left behind is idyllic, reflecting the homesickness of the driver now committed to earning his living in the city.

As the choice of these elaborate rural set-

the vehicles. He earns a salary with bonuses for safe and efficient work. The rickshaw driver rents his vehicle from the owner of a motor-rickshaw fleet. The meagre amount of money left over after service, maintenance and fuelling of his vehicle goads the driver on to work several shifts per day, sometimes up to 16 consecutive hours. It is the dream of many a rickshaw driver to own his vehicle. Ownership is the symbol of his success and brings him close to the dream which drove him from his motherland to the travails of city life.

It is through such deeply human experiences and expectations that we can begin to tings reflects the migrant's nostalgia for the simplicity of his rural lifestyle, so the sanitised cityscapes help him cling to his premigration vision of city life. Romantic cities commanded by Moghul-style buildings overlook clean and neatly laid out streets. The occasional orderly bus sails along empty, litter-free roads, unhampered by clusters of frantic office workers desperate to reach work on time.

Airports with aeroplanes flying overhead in clear blue skies, railway stations sporting elegant clock-towers, spotless, deserted platforms with deserted trains gliding smoothly in, all perpetuate the urban dream that propelled him here to seek his fortune. Massive passenger ships docked in superbly maintained harbours revive his ambition.

The disappointments of both, the life he left behind and the one he has chosen, are effectively banished with the help of idealised pictures he carries around on his vehicle. Alongside this personal fantasy are pictures from national mythology. Famous heroes and mythical beasts locked in combat contrast sharply with adjacently placed pictures flaunting the modernity of telephones, overhead cables and rockets. Political leaders sometimes find space amid rows of tulips, strings of beads and bouquets of roses and very rarely, an artist is inspired to paint a political picture.

Created in blatantly hoarding-style brushstrokes, popular film stars and seductive women with kohl-decorated eyes and highly glossed tresses display their allure.

The influence of western commercial art of the 1950s is quite evident in the paintings on vehicles. Like most street art they contain imperfections which must ultimately contribute to their quintessential character. The figures and animals are disproportionate and primitively drawn. The content is heavily stylised and lacks originality. The choice of colours is basic often showing the influence of Indian religious posters produced for mass consumption.

The women and men who create these works of popular art regularly supplement their income by designing and painting hoardings including those for the cinema industry. The artists also get seasonal work from printers specialising in calendars, diaries and notebooks. In addition pictures are commissioned for domestic use or placed in galleries as examples of pop-art. Although untrained, many artists achieve sufficient fame to warrant signing their pictures.

When working on a vehicle, they function in a highly organised and efficient manner, working from samples and templates to suit every imaginable part of the vehicle, although some artists do specialise in painting specific parts only. No space is left blank: bumpers, mud-guards, windscreen surrounds, mirror frames and handles and all

parts of the seat are decorated. Tiara shapes adorn the bonnets at the front of the trucks and buses and Suzukis alike while plaques, circles, squares and corner triangles are used to enhance the overall effect.

The painter is clearly not short of work and his income far exceeds that of the average driver who commissions him. To supplement the painting, artists and specialist garages stock ready made items like plastic daisy chains, and a variety of motifs etched or drawn on different shaped plastic mats of various colours including gold and silver.

These brash examples of consumer culture contribute dramatically to the *kitsch* and gaiety of vehicles. Like mobile art galleries,

they are flaunted in villages, deserts and cities, carrying impressions of urban life to the rural population and vice-versa, compounding the mystique of unknown places and affording the driver a sense of security, albeit temporary.

Admittedly, the clean orderliness of pop-art cityscapes flagrantly contradicts daily reality, the vehicles themselves contributing in no small measure to traffic congestion in towns. But there is no doubt that while sitting helpless and trapped on a hot and dusty city road, the mind is pleasantly beguiled by this flamboyant, almost outrageous display of national street culture.

Left, a bus ride across the desert. **Above**, getting about town on a scooter rickshaw.

It doesn't really matter where one happens to be in Pakistan, whether scrambling up the final metres of a 5,000 metre pass in the Karakoram or getting lost in the hustle and bustle of some ancient bazaar, the general appeal of the country remains the same; it is a land of adventure and huge contrasts.

Perhaps nowhere in Pakistan is there more contrast than in the province of Sind. There is the modern bustling city of Karachi representing the aspirations of a country looking towards the future, while out in the country life very often seems to go on just as it always has done, whether in the rich fertile plains of the Indus, or the barren and arid tracts of the Thar Desert. For all those interested in Sufism, Sind is the place to go, to see dervishes and devotees as they sing, dance and celebrate at the shrines of their saints.

Five tributaries of the Indus flow through the Panjab, mostly a vast irrigated plain where new prosperity can't conceal the fact that it was once the backdrop to glorious imperial fantasies which have left their unmistakable mark on the region. There are the splendours of the Moghul city of Lahore and earlier works of art and architecture in Multan. There are cities that have died and cities that still flourish, all amidst ancient legacies of legend and romance.

West of the Indus Basin, Baluchistan could be said to be the most forbidding part of Pakistan. With its vast inhospitable deserts it has always been on the borders of mainstream developments further east. But its history and the culture of its tribal peoples provide a wealth of things to discover for the most adventurous of those tempted to get right off the beaten track and head out to the Frontier.

The adventurous have always been lured by the North West Frontier Province: as the land of the Khyber Pass, the fiercely independent Pathans and that wonderful Central Asian city of Peshawar, all set in a history stretching from Buddhism to the British, NWFP has few rivals for its utter fascination. And it isn't all as barren as one might at first think; the Swat Valley is as green as they come; surrounded by snow-capped mountains, many regard it as a kind of mini-Switzerland.

But such a description would not do justice to the most spellbinding backdrop of all to Pakistan; the mountains of the Karakoram and Hindu Kush which rise in the north of the country, dropping, briefly, to the valleys of Baltistan and Gilgit, Hunza and Chitral. There is nowhere else on earth with such a concentration of high mountains, where trekkers and mountaineers follow along in the footsteps of past great adventurers and in the shadows of the Great Game.

Preceding pages: K2, viewed from The Ogre, soars high above all other peaks; the vast landscape; kite-flying – a nation-wide festival celebrated in spring; celluloid heroes and heroines. **Left**, ready for the road.

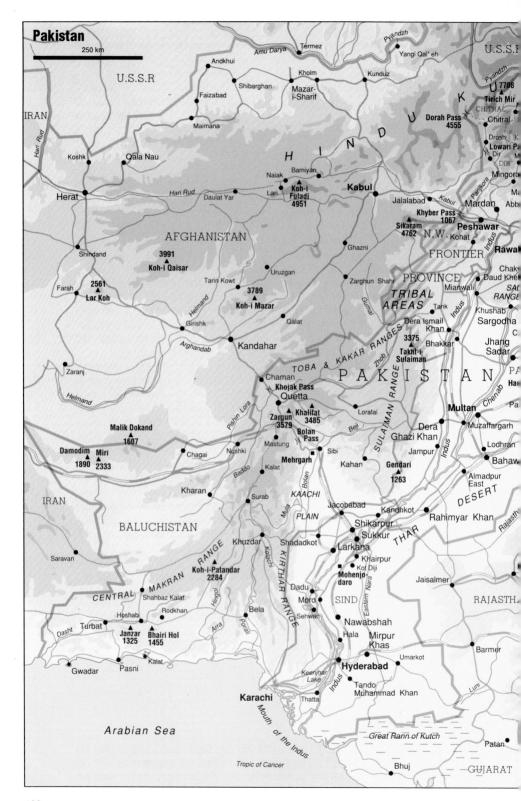

Pakistan

250 km

U.S.S.R

IRAN

Pyandzh

Amu Darya
Termez
Yangi Qal'eh
U.S.S.R

Andkhui
Kholm
Kunduz
Pyandzh
U

Faizabad
Shibarghan
Mazar-i-Sharif
7708
Tirich Mir

Maimana
CHITRAL
Chitral

Dorah Pass
4555

Qala Nau
Drosh K
Lowari Pa
Dir
M

Koshk
DIR

Mingora
Ma

Naiak
Bamiyan
H I N D U K

Hari Rud
Daulat Yar
Lari
Koh-i Fuladi
4951
Kabul

Herat
Jalalabad
Mardan
Abb

Khyber Pass
1067

Shindand
3991
Koh-i Qaisar
Sikaram
4762
N.W.
Peshawar
Kohat

2561
Lar Koh
Tarin Kowt
Uruzgan
Ghazni
FRONTIER
Rawal

Farah
Zarghun Shahr
PROVINCE
Chak
Daud Khe

3789
Koh-i Mazar
Qālat
TRIBAL
AREAS
Mianwali
SAL
RANGE

AFGHANISTAN

Girishk
Tank
Khushab
Sargodha

Zaranj
Arghandab
Dera Ismail Khan
Bhakkar
Jhang Sadar
C

3375
Takht-i-Sulaiman

Kandahar
PA
Ha

Helmand
TOBA
& KAKAR RANGES
Zhob
P A K I S T A N

Chaman
Khojak Pass
Quetta
Loralai
Multan
Pa

Malik Dokand
1607
Zargun
3579
Khalifat
3485
Beji
Muzaffargarh
Lodhran

Damodim
1890
Miri
2333
Chagai
Nushki
Bolan Pass
Mastung
Sibi
Dera Ghazi Khan
Jampur
Bahaw

Kalat
Mehrgarh
Kahan
Gendari
1263
Almadpur East

Kharan
Surab
KAACHI
Jacobabad
Kandhkot
Rahimyar Khan
DESERT
Rajasth

PLAIN
Shikarpur
Sukkur

IRAN
Khuzdar
Shadadkot
Larkana
THAR

BALUCHISTAN
Kot Diji
Khairpur

Saravan
RANGE
Koh-i-Patandar
2284
Kolachi
Mohenjo-daro
Jaisalmer
RAJASTH

CENTRAL
MAKRAN
Shahbaz Kalat
Rodkhan
Dadu
Moro
SIND

Hoshab
Bela
Sehwan

Turbat
Janzar
1325
Bhairi Hol
1455
Nawabshah
Barmer

Dasht
Hala
Mirpur Khas

Gwadar
Pasni
Kalat
Umarkot

Hyderabad

Keenjhar Lake
Tando Muhammad Khan
Luni

Karachi
Thatta

Arabian Sea

Mouth of the Indus

Great Rann of Kutch
Patan

Tropic of Cancer

Bhuj
GUJARAT

132

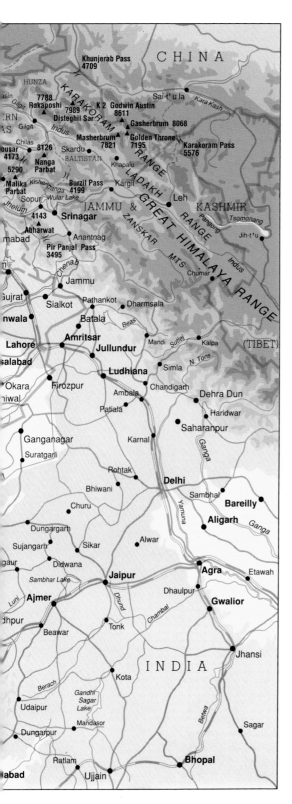

ISLAMIC REPUBLIC OF PAKISTAN: FACTS AND FIGURES

Provinces:
Sind, Panjab, North West Frontier Province, Baluchistan, mountainous areas of Kashmir belonging to Pakistan (The Northern Areas, including Gilgit, Hunza and Baltistan)

Capital city:
Islamabad

Provincial capitals:
Karachi (Sind), Lahore (Panjab), Peshawar (NWFP) and Quetta (Baluchistan)

Total area:
891,940 sq km

Mountains and deserts:
Approximately 450,000 sq km

Highest point:
Mt. K2, which is 8,611 metres high

Hottest place:
Sibi, Baluchistan
(over 50°C in summer)

Major rivers:
Indus, Jhelum, Sutlej, Chenab and Ravi

Main languages:
Urdu (national language of Pakistan), Sindhi, Panjabi, Siraiki (South Panjab and Sind), Pushtu (NWFP) and Baluchi (Baluchistan)

Religions:
Muslim – 97.2 percent (80 percent Sunni , 20 percent Shia), Hindu – 1.0 percent, Christian – 1.5 percent; 4,000 Buddhists and 10,000 Parsis

Population:
c. 108 million

Population growth:
3.1 percent

SIND

Bounded by the endless sands of the Thar Desert to the east, the barren Kirthar Mountains to the west and the Arabian Sea to the south, the province of Sind is aptly named after the great river, the Indus, whose fertile plain has provided for countless peoples ever since the Harappans devised the world's first large scale agrarian civilisation nearly 5,000 years ago.

The Indo-Aryans believed the river flowed from *Sinh-ka-bab*, the mouth of a lion. Because of its huge size, they named it Sindhu, in Sanskrit meaning an ocean. The Greeks called it Sinthus, the Romans Sindus, the Chinese Sintow, the Persians Abisind. The Arabs called it Sind, assigning the name Hind to the lands beyond in the east. Pliny gave the river the name Indus from which India gets its name.

At the time of the Harappan Civilisation, the Indus in flood must have carried a much larger volume of water because of far greater rainfall. The Sind plain was covered with a thick growth of forests and grasses, swarming with tropical wild life. On the ancient seals of Mohenjo-daro elephants and tigers are depicted. In those days the forces of nature were feared in a land where the blazing sun burned over a rugged terrain, which the River drowned in floods when in spate up to 50 kilometres in width. But the floods were a great help for they not only fertilised the land but also scattered seeds. And Man gradually brought the land under control, planting it with wheat, barley, oilseeds, cotton, vegetables and fruits. Similarly it was wrested from the wild beasts – the tigers, elephants and snakes – to be populated with all kinds of domestic animals.

The Rigvedic incantations conjure up the image of the Indus: "Selfmoving river of golden hue, roaring down the snow-clad mountains, rushing through fine forests, passing along fair fields and expanding into vast waters into which the sun sank."

Masson, the British traveller who traversed Sind on foot between 1827 and 1831, arrived from the north-west to find: "an orderly and well regulated country in comparison to the turbulant lands left behind." One morning, as he arrived in a hamlet, the people insisted on his sharing their breakfast. He recounts: "some sixteen or seventeen brass basins of porridge of crushed wheat or rice boiled with milk, seasoned by sugar or salt along with bowls of buttermilk. I laughed, as did the villagers and to avoid offending, sipped a little of each and commending their hospitality departed."

Entering Sind, the Indus passes through the low limestone range north-west of Sukkur and flows by the town of Rohri for around 70 kilometres to the south. North of Sukkur lies the Gaddu Barrage and at Sukkur the Indus was dammed in 1932 by a splendid stone masonry structure. Further south at Kotri is the third barrage. Between these three reservoirs, the flood water is stored to feed the network of irrigation channels. Finally, the Lion River has been tamed, its devastating floods harnessed for well-organised agriculture.

Today, during the cold season, Sind's plain, irrigated by perenial canals, is swamped by fresh dark green wheat, golden stalks of harvested millet and the snowwhite pods of cotton swinging in the breeze, waiting to be harvested. There are large orchards of the choiciest quality mangoes, guavas, citrus and other fruits. The water courses, humming with the flow of precious life, sap towards the fields afar. The tapestry like regularity extends to the length of 500 kilometres downstream and varies in breadth from 50 to 130 kilometres. It is the handiwork of Sind's industrious peasants whose hamlets and threshing floors adorn the idyllic man-made landscape. The most fertile land lies on the banks of the river, submerged by the annual floods which still deposit new layers of silt to revitalise it. The floods regularly replenish a number of tanks, lakes and marshes providing shelter to wild ducks, geese and various species of water fowl.

There are still patches of thick tamarisk forest, which, being the natural flora of the region, give a good idea of how Sind must once have looked.

Above the level of the irrigated and cultivated area, nature's niggardliness still makes its presence felt with its own creations: nowadays instead of the thick jungle there are sandhills, with wild growths of thorny bushes and weeds covering broken ground. Expanses of loose grey and almost white powdery sand is the source of great abrasive torture when adrift in a hot gale. But even here the twiggy, almost leafless broomlike plants and the *ak* plants with their broad leaves and white-lilac flowers thrive in their harsh environment. *Aks* thrive anywhere.

There are salt flats nearly devoid of vegetation, so forlorn and vast to display the curvature of earth, as barren and devoid of life as the surface of the moon. But even here the life creating ingenuity of Sind's peasants prevails against nature's failings. They first leach this soil with the canal water and

Preceding pages, a harvest of cabbage. Left, a morning stroll.

136

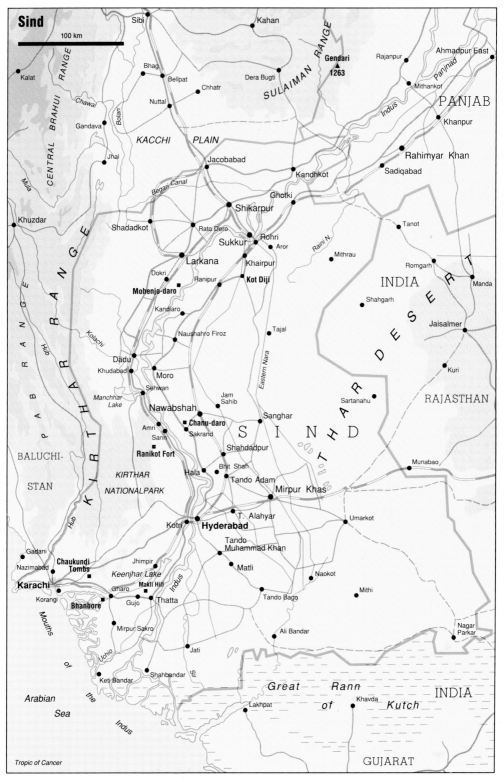

Sind

100 km

Kalat

Sibi

Kahan

CENTRAL BRAHUI RANGE

Chawal

Bhag

Bellpat

Chhatr

Dera Bugti

SULAIMAN RANGE

Gendari
1263

Rajanpur

Ahmadpur East

Panjnad

Mithankot

Indus

PANJAB

Khanpur

Gandava

Bolan

Nuttal

KACCHI   PLAIN

Jhal

Jacobabad

Kandhkot

Sadiqabad

Rahimyar Khan

Khuzdar

Begari Canal

Ghotki

Shikarpur

Shadadkot

Rato Dero

Tanot

Sukkur

Rohri

Aror

Raini N.

Mithrau

Romgarh

Manda

Larkana

Khairpur

INDIA

Dokri

Ranipur

Kot Diji

Mohenjo-daro

Shahgarh

Jaisalmer

Kandiaro

THAR   DESERT

Naushahro Firoz

Tajal

Kolachi

Eastern Nara

Kuri

Dadu

Khudabad

Moro

RAJASTHAN

Sehwan

Jam
Sahib

Sartanahu

Manchhar
Lake

Nawabshah

KIRTHAR RANGE

Amri

Chanu-daro

Sakrand

Sanghar

S I N H D

PABB RANGE

Sann

Ranikot Fort

Shahdadpur

Munabao

BALUCHI-
STAN

KIRTHAR

NATIONALPARK

Bhit Shah

Hala

Tando Adam

Mirpur Khas

Hub

Kotri

T. Alahyar

Umarkot

Gadani

Hyderabad

Nazimabad

Chaukundi
Tombs

Jhimpir

Keenjhar Lake

Tando
Muhammad Khan

Matli

Naokot

Karachi

Gharo

Makli Hill

Indus

Mithi

Korangi

Bhanbore

Gujo

Thatta

Tando Bago

Mouths

Mirpur Sakro

Nagar
Parkar

Uchio

Jati

Ali Bandar

of

Arabian

Keti Bandar

Shahbandar

Sir

Great   Rann

INDIA

the

Sea

Indus

of   Kutch

Khavda

Lakhpat

Tropic of Cancer

GUJARAT

137

then grow quality rice on it. There are alluvial deposits which are parched after the flood. They are bone dry and bone coloured. These are the havens of ugly, untidy thorny bushes which survive on the minimum of moisture.

Beyond Hyderabad, the Indus flows south to its swampy delta east of Karachi. It is covered with tamarisk, scrub and salt water rushes and marshland overgrown with mandrake stretches towards India. Indus flood water is so heavily loaded with silt that it discolours the Arabian Sea up to 16 kilometres from the coast. Its channel continues through the last deep canyon it has carved in the sea bed.

History: Alexander came this way after 10 months of voyaging down the rivers. Although he decided to take the overland route back to Babylon, along the Makran Coast, he sent some of his men by ship, passing Manora and anchoring in Karachi Harbour on the way. The fleet commander Nearchus described the harbour as "large, circular, deep and sheltered from the waves, and the entrance into it was narrow."

Others came Alexander's way and settled on the Indus, like the two Scythian tribes, the Jats and the Meds who invaded from the north. The Jats still retain their name, identity and tribes, in spite of their being of greatly mixed blood. The Meds have disappeared excepting the Mohana fishing folk of Sind who still call themselves Meds.

A line of dynasties: The Indus Valley of Sind has played host to many dynasties. Buddhism and Brahminism once flourished. Islam arrived when Sind was brought under the rule of Ommayid Caliphate in A.D. 711 by Muhammad Bin Qasim and it remained on the borders of the Caliphate under the Abbasids. The effect of Arab rule is considered to have been beneficial in spreading education and improving agriculture and commerce. Arab domination of the area was thrown off by the Somra Dynasty (1058-1249) who were indigenous, Sindi Muslims. There are many tales about the Somra rulers, and there are known to have been 21 of them during a 300-year period. In the 14th century, they were replaced by the Samma Rulers in Lower Sind (1351-1517). The Sammas were fiercely independant and rebelled against Delhi Sultanate. They reached the height of their power during the reign of Nizamuddin, the Jam Nindo (1461-1509) who is still recalled as a hero, and his rule as a golden age. The Capital of all the early dynasties was the city of Thatta.

Persian replaced Arabic as the official language and as it did so, the floodgates opened to Sufi mysticism and poetry of a very high order was produced. It was during the Samma rule that Humayun came to Sind. The Sammas were replaced by the Arghuns (1519-54) and Turkhans (1554-1625), both dynasties from the North.

In 1555 a Portuguese fleet of 28 ships arrived at Thatta, sacked the city and carried off much wealth. In 1592 the Turkhan ruler was defeated and Sind was annexed by the Emperor Akbar. The Moghuls added their distinctive stamp to the area and many beautiful mosques and monuments remain.

Boats on the Indus.

In 1739, the Moghul Empire effectively collapsed when Nadir Shah plundered Delhi. Thereafter, it only waited for the death of Nadir Shah in 1747 for new Sindi dynasties to rise – the Kalhoras with their capital at Khudabad and later Hyderabad, and finally the Talpur Mirs. Talpur Mirs from Baluchistan had been employed by Kalhoras in their army. Wonderfully decorated mosques and mausoleums, forts and many other structures in Sind owe their existence to these local dynasties.

At the end of the 18th century, Sind had a strong neighbour in the Panjab, when that area came under the control of Ranjit Singh. He had ambitions to expand his empire but respected the Mirs and moved in other directions. When the Afghan war broke out in 1838, the British were concerned about Sind and in spite of opposition, took it under their protection in 1839 (the year Ranjit Singh died). The Mirs of Sind resented the high handed British action in totally disregarding their wishes and resorted to arms. But after initial success, they were beaten on the battlefield at Miani and Sind was annexed by Sir Charles Napier in February 1843. Napier commented: "The brave Baluchis, first discharging their matchlocks and pistols, dashed over the bank with desperate resolution; but down went these bold and skillful swordsmen under the superior power of the musket and bayonet." It was a battle between medieval tribal feudalism and the burgeoning British industrialised power.

The British set about organising the area with their customary gusto – barrages and irrigation canals were commenced, in order to control the treacherous flooding river and to irrigate the desert, to provide more farmland. And of course, the roads, and railways...and all that went with it. Under the British, Sind was attached to Bombay Presidency until 1937 when it was made an autonomous province. In 1947, many of the educated elite and middle class of Sind, being Hindus and Sikhs, left the area. A large number of Muslim immigrants arrived from India.

Such vessels have been used for thousands of years.

PAST MEETS PRESENT

Perhaps nowhere else in the subcontinent does there exist a population of such ethnic diversity as in Sind. Sindhi people are the followers of the world's oldest religions: Hinduism, Jainism, Buddhism and Zoroastrianism, as well as its newer ones: Christianity, Islam, Sikhism are all to be found here. Most of Pakistan's non-Muslim minorities, some four million people, are "Sindhi".

The heartland of the province is the Indus Valley and along the banks of the river live aboriginal fisherfolk whose way of life has

simplest furniture: cots of wood and rope (*charpoi*), cotton mats (*durri*), colourful patchwork bedspreads and quilts, earthenware pots and hubble bubble smoking pipes.

Both men and women are dressed in long tunics and baggy trousers. Handcrafted textiles are exquisite confections of brightly coloured needlework. The women are skilful in embroidery and decorate their tunics with colourful patterns studded with pieces of mirror. Mirrorwork is also used to embellish the embroidered skull caps worn by the men.

hardly changed for thousands of years. Their houses are simple and spartan, nothing more than bundles of river reeds lashed together. Both the men and women wear loosely tied turbans to keep off the heat from the sun. People claiming Arab, Afghan and Turkish descent reside in the ancient mansions of riverside towns and cities. The common name "Shah" applied to many settlements commemorates the Arab invaders who brought Islam to the subcontinent.

The flood plains are inhabited by a number of agricultural castes and tribes: Samma, Jat, Sumro, Mohana, Rajput, Baluch and many more. Villagers live in adobe huts with the

It is the woman's job to fetch the water, milk the goat, cow and buffalo. The woman helps in harvesting, cotton picking, chasing away birds from the fields, gathers sticks and makes dung cakes for fuel.

Against this idyllic picture, huge demographic changes are occurring in Sind, promoted by rapid industrialisation which attract people to the cities as well as the equally rapid developments in modern farming. Modern irrigation works convey Indus water to the cotton and sugar plantations of central Sind. Here, 20th-century peasants live the life of medieval serfs. Agrarian relations are feudal: sharecroppers must surrender up to

80 percent of the crop to Baluchi, Jat and Rajput landlords. Many Pakistanis assert that, since the British administrators and the Hindu moneylenders left, the stranglehold of the landlords has tightened. Mechanised agriculture drives away those who have worked the land for centuries. Smallholders have to sell their plots and leave. Peasants are used as private armies by warring landlords; unlisted casualties of the Green Revolution.

The peoples living on the peripheries of the province have been less affected by these developments. Western Sind, the region of the Kirthar Mountains, is inhabited by tough, nomadic peoples. Here jagged ranges zigzag through stony plains and sand dunes. In

herds of sheep and goats. The women grow grains and gather roots and berries along the dried up courses of former rivers. They plait palm leaf sandals, mats and baskets, sold by their menfolk in the towns, knot beautiful rugs and saddle bags and stitch brilliant embroidery, embellished with cowrie shells. Life is harsh, yet the nomads are renowned for poignant poetry and lovesongs: slain heroes, parted lovers, shattered dreams...

On the other side of the Indus, in the sandy Thar desert, live a variety of peoples: the Vaghri, Bhil, Meo, Mina, Koli and many others. There are also tribes of Hindu Rajputs. They live mostly in conical huts made from desert brushwood, herding sheep

summer temperatures exceed 50°C in the shade. Tribes like the Marri, Bugti, Brahui and Hur resemble their neighbours, the Pathans, but are led by hereditary chieftains, the maliks. These reside in fortified houses by the few permanent springs. Plots of date palms, soft fruits, succulent vegetables and green fodder for cattle advertise their wealth. Horses are kept – just for the prestige.

Meanwhile, the common people follow a wandering life. Shelter for them is a goat hair tent or lean-to of leaves. The men watch

Left, heading for the city. **Above**, returning from the well.

and goats, and sometimes scrawny, undersized cattle. Donkeys are used as beasts of burden and camels for ploughing. There is cultivation wherever and whenever water is available – the economy depends on rain.

The women weave blankets, the men make tiles and pottery. Sometimes the Rajput women, who claim direct descent from the royal line of Ujjain now in Indian Rajasthan, can be seen striding through Karachi's Old City, unmistakable in their voluminous skirts, backless bodices and tight leggings. They disdain veiling their faces: "The sight of her nose struck my heart like a sword..." a famous Rajasthani poem commences.

KARACHI

There was nothing much at Karachi until the Mirs of Talpur seized it from the Khan of Kalat in 1795 and constructed a mud fort at Manora. Under its protection, a small town grew up, whose population had reached 13,000 by 1818. Not much happened thereafter until 1st February 1839, when a British ship – the Wellesley – anchored off Manora. Two days later the little fort surrendered without a shot being fired on either side. The fickle finger of fate had suddenly shoved the sleepy backwater towards becoming a megalopolis, a world city.

Wrested from the swamps: The settlement was remote and swampy, isolated by hundreds of miles of bleak desert in every direction but the sea. Nonetheless, within four years, the capital of Sind was transferred there and building began in earnest. By 1847 the Napier Barracks (now government offices) were completed. A census next year showed that the population had already reached 50,000. The filth and squalor proliferated, everything became plastered with smelly black mud from the mangrove swamps, so a Municipal Committee was formed to levy funds and provide public utilities. In 1848 the municipality's income was Rs.6,000; in 1849 it was Rs.18,000 and in 1850, Rs.27,000 – an increase reflecting the mind-boggling population explosion.

The committee laid out a whole network of roads, named after itself, in what is now Central Karachi. Preedy Street was named after the Revenue Commissioner; McLeod Road after the Collector of Customs and so on. Even in those days Karachi had a traffic problem. There were so many carts and carriages that the roads had to be paved with gravel chippings (an unheard of refinement, way ahead of London.) The streets were watered daily by municipal bullock carts, to damp down the dust. As revenues increased, public works were undertaken on a grand scale. **Frere Hall** (a museum and library) was fin-

ished in 1865, Mereweather Clock Tower in 1867, Boulton Market in 1883, Empress Market in 1889... The town turned into a city.

As people poured in, the drinking water problem, always difficult, became acute. There is no natural source of water in Karachi; all water consumed there must be fetched from somewhere else. Last century, water drawn from the Indus was brought by camel train to the cantonment. The wealthier merchants sent mule carts to the sweetwater springs in nearby Clifton. Less fortunate people bought drinking water from municipal watercarriers until household pipes could be laid. Though provision proceeded apace, demand has always been ahead of supply. Karachi's poor, in places like Korangi, are still waiting for safe drinking water.

At the turn of the century a public tram service commenced from Saddar (the cantonment) to the new harbour at Kiamari. The horses wore straw hats to avoid sunstroke and water for them was provided by the philanthropic "Drink-

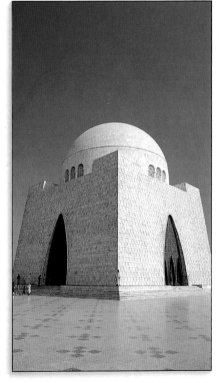

Left, Islamic influences in modern architecture – the Pearl Continental Hotel in Karachi. **Right**, the Mausoleum of M.A. Jinnah.

ing Trough Society of Karachi." The troughs can still be seen here and there in the city. Modernising the harbour commenced in 1860, proceeding by fits and starts. By 1882 the Mereweather Pier was completed and pilgrims for Mecca no longer had to embark at Manora. By 1900, Karachi was one of the the biggest and best outfitted ports in the world. Nonetheless, it continued to be troubled by the ague and the plague until the sanitation system was completed, just after the first World War.

The war itself brought immense prosperity to Karachi's merchants. Clifton's promenade, pier and park were gifted to the city by Sir Jehangir H. Kothari OBE in 1919. The complex cost Rs.300,000 to build, an absolute fortune in those days. Other public parks, including the **Zoological Gardens** on Garden Road were laid out at this time. Even more new roads and buildings were constructed in the interwar period. As the population approached the quarter million mark, those who could moved out to the suburbs, building houses in a style best described as "South Asian Hollywood." Commuting arrived with a vengeance and one of the world's first rapid transit systems was inaugurated.

Melting pot: The building of Karachi attracted Goan cooks, Anglo-Indian bartenders, Sikh bricklayers, and Chinese washermen. Parsi, Hindu and Jain merchants came from Gujarat and Rajasthan. Until Partition, their camel caravans regularly crossed the Thar. The Parsis built a Tower of Death out at Korangi. A few of the merchants' big mansions still remain downtown. The Lebanese community became sizeable. People of African descent can also be seen in and around Karachi. Tradition has it, they escaped from a shipwrecked Arab slaver at the mouth of the Hub River (hence their nickname "hubshi").

At Partition, Hindus, Armenians and Jews left the city en masse. Muslim refugees from India, calling themselves *mohajir*, migrated in by train, boat, air, truck, even on foot. It is not known how many millions arrived. Karachi, new capital of a new country, was so pushed

Karachi was built by merchants.

for space that its government servants had to sleep in the public parks and gardens in tents! The Mohajir further diversify the ethnic mix of the city. Many English stayed on, their ranks now depleted by age. Vintage couples can be spotted at their usual watering holes, the **Metropole Hotel** and the statelier clubs in the early evening.

Subsequent decades have seen the influx unabated. The Karachi Development Authority instituted the upgrading of amenities on a massive scale: new housing colonies, public buildings, roads, schools, colleges, markets, bazaars, business centres, to keep pace with development needs. Cycle rickshaws have now been replaced by thousands of scooter-rickshaws.

After Pakistan's civil war in 1971, thousands of Biharis (Urdu-speaking Muslims from Bangladesh) arrived by boat. In the 1980s Afghan refugees joined migrant workers from the Frontier who have laboured as dockworkers and porters for decades. Meanwhile, "economic refugees" from Pakistan's less developed areas, like Gilgit, Chitral and Hunza head for Karachi in search of jobs. The original Sindhi speaking population is now a minority in the city.

Gas supply lines from Sui in Baluchistan were laid, the Hub Dam Scheme extended the Greater Karachi Water Project and the Circular Railway was completed. In the 1960s, two huge industrial areas were built, at Sind Industrial Estate and Landhi and in the 1970s three more: the Export Processing Zone, Pakistan Steel Mills Complex and Muhammad Bin Qasim Container Port. In the following decade, work on KANUPP, Karachi's nuclear power station, was inaugurated. Industrial growth has been spectacular.

Rich and poor: Original home of Pakistan's film and music industries, Karachi in the 1980s made more films and exported them to more countries than Hollywood. It houses the very latest in modern technology. The city works and sleeps in a haze of brick dust as buildings barely 30 years old are relentlessly torn down and replaced with something more up to date. The population of seven, maybe eight, million now extends over several hundred square kilometres along the coast and into the desert, residing in modern apartment blocks, prestigious cooperative housing societies called "Colonies", seaside mansions and sprawling shanty towns on the outskirts, areas of such appalling poverty that it is difficult to see how residents will ever be extricated from their plight. Working 16 hours a day, poor youths toil like slaves, earning a pittance to produce elegant costume for the city's elite.

Piles of rubble surround new homes, hotels and condominiums. Limousines and rickshaws alike must pick their way through scaffolding jungles as artisans with age old skills produce ever more new buildings. Sometimes these are exquisite, and Karachi's modern architecture is the showcase of Asia. Foremost amongst modern buildings is the **Masjid-i-Tuba** at Defence Housing Society – a vast and beautiful white marble flying saucer, the widest diameter dome in the country. If you stand just

Frere Hall.

inside the entrance and whisper against the wall, the echoes ricochet around the dome and set the chandeliers tinkling. The Housing Societies themselves contain a good deal of interesting domestic architecture, especially around the Golf Course. The Influence of Buckminster Fuller, Frank Lloyd Wright and friends is pronounced.

The Mausoleum of the Quaid-i-Azam on M.A. Jinnah Road is another impressive white marble construction. Last resting place of the founding father of Pakistan, 12 tonnes of bronze were used in its arches as reinforcement against earthquakes. Following custom, the bodies of the Quaid and near relations lie in a subterrananean chamber. The rail around the replica "grave" above is made of solid silver and the chandelier a gift from the Muslim Association of the People's Republic of China. Outside, 15 pools line the walkway back to the road. Downtown, in Karachi's central business district, the new **State Bank Building**, the **Habib Bank Plaza** and the international class hotels (especially the Taj Mahal Hotel and the revamped Metropole Hotel) are striking examples of modern architecture and interior design. When **Holy Trinity Cathedral** was built in the last century, there was public outcry over its "dangerous" high spire. Nowadays, buildings of 20 storeys or more are commonplace. **The Avari Towers Hotel** is the latest addition to Karachi's skyline, owned by a wealthy Parsi businessman.

The traffic is mad, the pavements thronging, yet Karachi is extremely likeable. It has a vibrant cultural life: lots of theatres, museums (including the National Museum of Pakistan) libraries, art galleries and interest groups. Every kind of club is found here, including the extremely exclusive **Boat Club**, **Sind Club** (for politicians and civil servants) and **Gymkhana Club** (for business people). The majority of Pakistan's voluntary agencies are also based in Karachi. Its **Leper Hospital** headed by Dr. Ruth Pfau, is world renowned for its rehabilitation work and welcomes vistors, by appointment

The old city is a maze of bazaars.

please. Dr. Pfau works out in the shanty towns, doing all she can to curtail the disease amongst Karachi's ever-increasing poor population.

A stroll around town: Despite the hustle and bustle, central Karachi is probably the nicest Pakistani city in which to walk around, enjoy the street life and sample the cuisine. The restaurants offer a wide range of ethnic menus centred on locally caught fish and shellfish. The Goan Restaurants, selling Portuguese-cum-South Indian food (try the blisteringly spicy vindaloo) and Chinese, even Lebanese restaurants are probably the best in Pakistan. They are located in **Saddar Bazaar**, the central shopping centre, roughly approximate to the rectangle formed by Abdullah Haroon Road and Zaibunissa Street (familiarly known as Victoria Road and Elphinstone Street).

The southern end of the complex is called **Zainab Market**. Here, amongst more mundane businesses like typewriter servicers are interesting little knick knack shops selling copper and brass goods, embroidered shawls, lacquered and inlaid woodwork and marble boxes. Famous Sindhi specialities, like painted camel skin lampshades from upcountry, handglazed blue tiles and pottery (shipping can be arranged), handloom striped cotton cloth (*sussi*), applique bedspreads (*rilli*), hand-blocked maroon and indigo cloth lengths (*ajrak*) and mirror-worked embroidery are all sold hereabouts. A few shops have antique jewellery, traditionally sold by weight.

The northern end is known as **Bohri Bazaar**. This sells cloth fents, ready made outfits for men and women, cheap accessories, genuine leather briefcases, sandals and shoes. In the streets between Zainab Market and Bohri Bazaar and leading off the main thoroughfares, are a series of mini markets, where shops and stalls selling old and new carpets, maps or books mingle with others selling secondhand spectacles and broken radios. One man's old junk is another man's antique, after all.

St Patrick's Cathedral, Convent

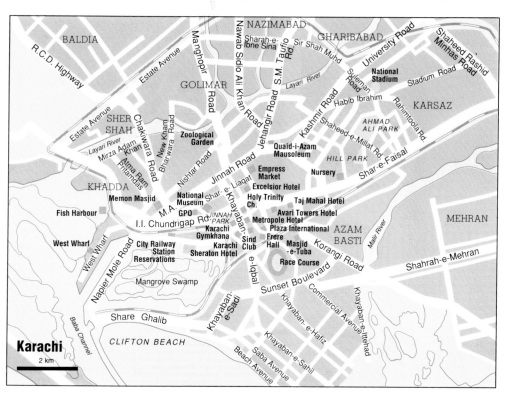

Karachi

2 km

and Bishop's Palace, spiritual home of South Asia's largest Roman Catholic congregation, is a few minutes walk to the east. Its school has educated Pakistan's ruling classes of all denominations since the last century. **Holy Trinity Cathedral** and **St. Andrew's Church** mark the ends of **Saddar**, the former British shopping enclave.

Just to the north is **Empress Market**, a covered bazaar whose clock tower and arcades exactly resemble the market halls of the North of England. On this site in 1857, 15 "mutineers" or patriots of the war of independence, were executed by cannon fire (hence the alternative name Shahid – Martyrs' Market). Inside and around its walls are grocery, fruit and vegetable stalls, brightly coloured, eyecatchingly displayed. The best Chinese restaurants are nearby.

The **Old City Markets** are down M.A. Jinnah Road towards the harbour. Their street cuisine is renowned. **Lea Market**, **Boulton Market** and **Napier Road** are the places to saunter through traditional oriental bazaars, get a way-side shoeshine or haircut and try authentic regional snacks like *nihar* (panfried brains) *pursindah seekhi* (skewered lamb fillet) *sajji* (roast leg of lamb) and *machli pakora* (deep fried fish in batter.) The **Sarafa Bazaar** is right in the middle of these markets. This sells copper, brass, silver and goldware – a good place to look for antique dishes and utensils, some salvaged from shipwrecks and restored. Often they carry the name of well-known ships or shipping lines.

Down by the harbour: The **Fish Market** is on **West Wharf**, at the far end of M.A. Jinnah Road, going west. This is another Victorian market hall. The local catch is auctioned every morning and evening. Karachi's fish and shellfish (especially lobsters, crabs and prawns) are then flown daily to grace the tables in Islamabad or shipped out fresh, dried, tinned or frozen all over the world.

Outside, throngs of little sailing boats called *bheddi* and *hora* (slightly bigger) bob up and down in the creek, three or four deep at the quayside. The boats

**Left,
St. Andrew's
Church.
Right,
new heights
attained.**

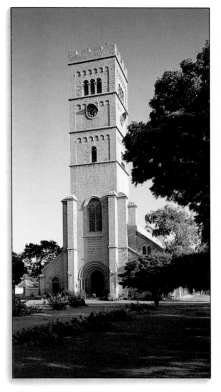

have traditional lateen sails as well as diesel engines and are gaudily painted, with their rigging tricked out in bunting and tinsel. Designs feature swordfish, sharks and huge eyes (to ward off the evil eye), helicopters, fighter planes and guerillas with missile launchers, presumably an influence of the Afghan War. They can be hired by the day for deep sea fishing, scuba diving, etc.

The cranes of the new **Container Port** can be seen behind the Fish Wharf. The old harbour is across the creek at **Kiamari**, reached via the Napier Mole, the extension of Napier Road along the East Pier. Boats can be hired to sail along the coast, mooch around the harbour, or go crab fishing. This is another experience not to be missed. The skipper provides the lines and bait to catch the crabs and cooking pots, potatoes, onions, tomatoes and spices with which to cook them. Dinner is served when the passengers have caught it.

The boats drift gently down **Ghizri Creek** for an hour or so towards the sea, passing the **Hindu Ghats** (bathing steps) on the way. The women's bathing place is secluded from public gaze by wooden screens. On longer trips, the boats anchor off the **Oyster Rocks**, between Clifton and Manora Lighthouse. On the largest rock, a small island really, is a little Hindu Temple.

Clifton is a "posh" seaside suburb. It was developed as a health resort by British officers and administrators with private incomes and wealthy businessmen in the last century. It was thought that the brisk sea breezes dispersed the marshy vapours of Karachi proper's extensive mangrove swamps (known as fever trees.) The Pakistani ruling classes continue to patronise Clifton. The Jinnah family once kept house here, at the Mohatta Palace; the Bhuttos still do. Some of the villas are palatial. Designed to impress, they would not be out of place in Palm Springs or Miami.

In addition to very desirable residences there is an aquarium, zoo, and a not-even-once-used casino. **Jabees Playland** is an air-conditioned amusement hall for children and young

At the water's edge.

people. **Funland** is an amusement park with dodgem cars, mini-train rides etc. again for the young at heart. There is also a bowling alley. On Thursday afternoons and Fridays, all Karachi brings its children for camel and horse rides along the beach, picnics in the gardens and bracing walks on the promenade.

Behind the beach, steps up a low hill lead to the green painted **Ziarat of Qazi Abdullah Shah** who died in the 16th century. Round about it are stalls selling garlands of rose and jasmine petals, strings of *patasi* (sweets made of candied sesame seeds) and shawls to lay over the saint's grave. Devotees scoop up water from the sweet spring at the foot of the hill. *Qavvalis* are held late into the night on Thursdays. Travellers should be appropriately dressed and ready to make a small donation.

At **Manghopir** there is a shrine to the Muslim saint of that name, guarded by crocodiles. These are a snub-nosed variety, quite different from the long-nosed *gharials* of the Indus. Legend has it that the *pir* brought the crocodiles

from Arabia in the 13th century, in the form of lice in his hair! Maddened by the itching, he stamped his feet and two pools were formed, into which the crocodiles jumped. The pools are fed by hot sulphur springs which are alleged to cure skin complaints, rheumatism and frigidity. Bath houses are provided.

Manora Lighthouse marks **Manora Head** (also known as Manora Point and Manora Island.) This is the end of the **Sandspit** protecting the harbour from the open sea. The cannons of the ancient fort on the point formerly commanded the channel and it is here that the Talpur Mirs surrendered. Between July and November, when the monsoon winds blow onshore from the Ocean, giant turtles lay their eggs along the seaward side of the spit. The turtles are a protected species and are easily frightened away forever. Karachi's representative of the World Wildlife Fund (contact through All Pakistan Women's Association on Garden Road) is glad to advise on appropriate procedures for viewing these amazing reptiles, which otherwise never leave the sea.

Along the coast: Between Sandspit and Paradise Point, a distance of about 50 kilometres, is a series of beaches, some crowded, others deserted. **Sandspit Beach** is a very popular seaside resort, extremely busy at weekends. On full moon nights in the hot weather it is a great place for *purdah* parties. Groups of ladies in head-to-toe black *burqas* (a bit like European nuns' outfits) accompanied by excited children, thermos flasks and picnic baskets drive out from the city to cool their toes or more in the briny. The shore is crowded with kiosks, tea huts and hawkers selling cigarettes, or camel and horse rides, fortune tellers, snake charmers, performing monkeys, dancing bears...

Along the coast, in the direction of Paradise Point, is **Hawkes Bay**. This is named after a British Officer who built a beach house out here so that his ailing wife could convalesce from an attack of the dreaded vapours. Hawkes Bay is now lined from end to end with beach huts. Some are sadly dilapidated, giving the Sandspit end of the bay the feeling of

Sharks are a common catch.

a ghost town. Further down though they are smartly kept up, very 1930s in their pistachio-tinted cement walls, and sun-lounges. They have "all mod cons" and can sometimes be rented.

The bigger consulates and multinational companies based in Karachi maintain rather splendid beach houses at the far end of the bay, where the golden sands are cleaner, the swimming better (it can be dangerous at Sandspit in July and August) and the journey a little too far for comfort by public transport. It takes about a couple of hours by infrequent and unreliable buses to the stop at Dada's Chai Shop. The exclusive French Beach section of Hawkes Bay can only be reached by car and travellers arriving on foot are turned away by the watchmen.

Eventually, the houses thin out and cease altogether. From here on travellers should take their own food and drink to the beach. There are no hawkers. After **Baleji Beach**, the road winds inland to avoid the Nuclear Power Station, passing through arid scrubland dotted with occasional hamlets. Beyond, the road returns to the coast and rough tracks lead down to quiet little rocky bays. Though charming, all these beaches are remote therefore travellers should not swim or sunbathe alone. The undertow is tricky. At **Paradise Point** the road follows the clifftops out towards Cape Monze and ultimately Gadani Beach, about three hours drive from central Karachi on the other side of the **Hub River**.

Plans are afoot to turn **Gadani Beach** into a "package tour" holiday resort, with smart hotels, swimming pools, fancy shopping plazas and so on. At the moment it is better known for its 150 or so shipbreaking yards (see Baluchistan). Gadani's fishermen catch the largest and most succulent prawns in the world. In winter, they net stingray (pichar), which are sold in Karachi by local middlemen. The flesh is sold for eating. *Hakim* (traditional healers) use the poison from the ray's tail to make homeopathic preparations which are exported all over the Middle East.

Big smiles.

LOWER SIND

Leaving Karachi towards Hydera-bad, there are two routes. The Super-Highway and the older, National High-way. The 164-kilometre Super High-way is fast but not very interesting. The main site of interest reached from the road is the Kirthar National Park. The Super-Highway also crosses the Kotri Barrage, the lowest of the trio of bar-rages which control the Indus.

Relics of a prosperous past: Following the National Highway, about 27 kilom-etres from Karachi are the **Chaukundi Tombs**, an area that seems to have been a graveyard since antiquity. There are hundreds of tombs, with a variety of intricate motifs carved on brown stone. Foliate and jewel designs embellish the tombs of women while horses and swords decorate those of men.

Sixty-four kilometres from Karachi, near Gharo on the Highway, lies **Bhan-bore**, noted for archaeological investi-gations and the discovery of ancient settlements of various periods; Parthian, Hindu-Buddhist and Islamic. Some finds are similar to items discov-ered at Taxila. It is also claimed as the site of ancient Daibul, where the Arab invaders under Muhammad Bin Qasim landed in 711 for their incursion into Sind. It is now some distance from the coast, due to silt deposited by the Indus.

At **Gujo**, about 87 kilometres from Karachi is a site where pottery from the chalcolothic age has been found. The carved symbols on rocks bear a striking resemblance to the famous seals of Mohenjo-daro. A turning from Gujo leads to **Haleji Lake**, a reservoir which is a winter haven for migratory birds. A track beside the lake leads to a rest house and facilities for bird watching. There are crocodiles in the lake.

The Highway reaches the ancient town of **Thatta**. Like many a town in Pakistan Thatta has seen changes in its fortunes. Today, it is a small town and new buildings are going up. The old town is delapidated and dusty with a lot

Chaukundi Tombs.

of ruins among the hills, purplish dunes and cactus plants. It was for many years the capital of Sind, said to have a large population, a busy port, and as many as 400 institutions of learning. Yet even the River Indus deserted it and moved its channels several miles away!

Although Thatta is very ancient, the main period of greatness was during the 16th and 17th centuries. It was a great cultural centre, but the glory passed away in 1742 when it was sacked by Nadir Shah and his Persians. The Kalhoras moved the capital to Khudabad and later to Hyderabad.

The historical importance is recalled by the splendours of the **Jamia Masjid** built by Shah Jahan, finished under Aurangzeb. Legend has it that the splendid Masjid recalls Shah Jahan's gratitude to the locals for their hospitality shown to him when he had taken refuge in the town, getting away from his irate father. The masjid is very large with more than 90 domed compartments. These apparently aid the acoustics for it is said that the prayers said before the Mihrab can be heard all over the building. It covers about 6,000 square metres and is covered with exquisite calligraphy carved in golden stone and patterns in glazed brick and tilework, local materials, and it is quite a contrast to other buildings of the time.

Another well known mosque is the **Dabgir Masjid** built in the 16th century by Amir Khusro Khan, the Governor of Thatta. The mihrab is carved with such delicacy of touch that it looks like sandalwood rather than stone.

West of the city lies an enormous graveyard, the **Makli Hills**, claimed to be the world's largest cemetery. It measures about 15 square kilometres and is usually described as a "necropolis" which is a good word for an area said to contain about a million graves. The interesting monuments fall into three main periods. The earliest are tombs of the Sammas, rulers known as the Jams who ruled from mid-14th until the early 16th century. The second period are Turkhan and Arghun rulers and the last are Moghuls. The **tomb of Jam**

Islamic art at its finest – Shah Jahan's Mosque.

Nizamuddin dates from 1508. Some of the decoration is very much in the Hindu style and there are arches planned to support a dome which was apparently never built. The arches are an early example of efforts by Hindu craftsmen to create a true arch. The building is partly despoiled but what remains is still very fine. There are excellent specimens of local craftsmanship in carved stone.

Near the road is the **tomb of Mirza Isa Turkhan** built 1573. He was the first of a dynasty of Turkhan rulers of Sind. This particular tomb appears on the back of the 10 rupee notes. It is richly decorated with surface tracery.

There are a number of other Turkhan tombs, some carved with roses and sun flowers. Tombs of later rulers are ornamented with tilework, and also with glazed bricks in blue and bluey-green shades. In fact the area is full of exquisite tombs of rulers and holy men and is testimony to the huge wealth that the dynasties possessed.

South of this area is a twelve pillared verandah in front of a Lake; the setting for a romantic tale – rags to riches for a ruler. Jam Tamachi fell in love with a fishermaid called Nuri.

Keenjhar, one of the largest man-made lakes in Pakistan, is 125 kilometres from Karachi. There were originally two natural lakes and these have been combined (for irrigation purposes) and an embankment built. A beach road along the lake leads to a picnic resort and it is possible to swim and fish. A boat service is available for visitors who wish to see the island shrines on the lake. The area is noted for an abundance of game birds. In recent years a new recreational complex has been under development. Air-conditioned cabanas have been erected and a range of sporting activities provided. There are also some older facilities, so there is plenty of accommodation. As Keenjhar Lake is only 24 kilometres from Thatta and 83 kilometres from Hyderabad, it is a good centre from which to explore.

Fishermen: The river between the coast and Hyderabad is rich in fish. Indus fishermen still use the same kind of boats as their ancestors thousands of years ago. The most picturesque scene on the river is *palla* (Indus salmon) fishing during August and September. The simple gear used consists of a sturdy eight foot pole with two "V" shaped prongs at the top, to which a small net is fixed. The open end of the net can be closed by pulling the string which is tied to the top of the pole. This fishing gear is wielded by a single, loin-cloth clad fisherman with a turban upon his head. He is equipped with a harpoon, a bag for the catch and a gourd float tied to his belly. With this gear, he plunges into the river, floating on the gourd. He swims to the current in mid-stream, where he dips the net pole into the water where the palla fish swim upstream toward the spawning grounds. Once a fish is caught in the net, the fisherman closes the open end, harpoons the fish, and throws it into the bag.

Hyderabad: Moving up the highway from Karachi towards Lahore, **Hyderabad** is 190 kilometres from Karachi. The town is one of the largest in Paki-

The British left their mark in Hyderabad.

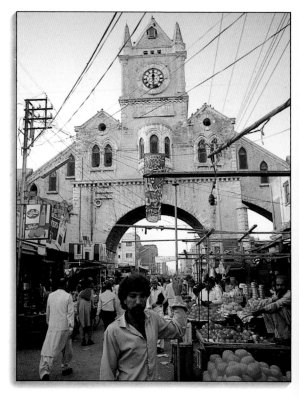

stan. Its ancient name was Neeron Kot, Neeron's Fort. It was a Buddhist town at the time of the Arab conquest. But its main importance is more recent. In 1757, the Indus changed its course and flooded the then capital, Khudabad. The Kalhora ruler Ghulam Muhammad then moved to this location and named the place Hyderabad. In 1783 the Kalhoras gave way to the Talpurs and the Talpur Mirs rebuilt the town.

The British annexed Sind from the Talpur Mirs and added their town. They needed their administration and offices. The town also has a huge bazaar, the longest in Pakistan, congeries of alleys where almost anything may be purchased. The British ornamented it with a rather dashing clocktower.

The houses are interesting for having characteristic *badgirs* or windcatchers attached to the rooftops to catch the breeze. The breeze is directed into the room below and cools the home.

The old fort rising above the town dates from the Kalhora and Talpur period but it was destroyed by an explo-

sion in 1906 when the British were using it as an arsenal (as usual). Only one decorated room survives, which is a great pity as descriptions of the fort and court when it was in its heyday sound splendid. Sir Charles Napier used it to hold grand durbars (court) too.

There is another "Fort", the **Shaikh Makai Fort**. Shaikh Makai was a dervish (holy man) who came from Mecca and settled here in about 1260. His mausoleum was built much later, in 1671, and is housed inside a mud fort.

The town also contains mausoleums of past rulers, decorated with tile work and paintings. The Kahhora tombs date from the late 1700s. The Talpur monuments date between 1823-1878. There is a private Talpur Collection which may be viewed, as well as a museum.

At Miani, near Hyderabad, the British defeated the army of the Mirs and annexed Sind. Nowadays, the one time battlefield is a picnic place. There is a memorial to the fallen of Napier's force.

Fishing is possible in the lakes around Hyderabad.

The dynasties of Sind built enormous tombs on the Makli Hills.

TALES OF THAR DESERT

Beyond the irrigation channels to the east of the Indus plain lies the **Thar Parkar Desert**, its sand heaped up and hollowed out with the regularity of sea waves in parallel ridges by the south west wind from the sea coast. In between the dunes there are valleys having an alignment from south west to north east following the wind direction. After the summer monsoon rains it is covered with lush green vegetation which provides fodder for cattle and goats. Crops of coarse grains are raised in depressions where rain water accumulates. Within this desolate wasteland small lakes are formed following the monsoon rains. If the rains come, for every year the spectre of famine looms. "Expect one bad year in two and famine every three years" they say, but after rain the Thar Desert truly blooms. It is a region which also comes alive with local romance and legend.

One very popular local song of the Thar is the romance of the local native girl Marvi who declined to be the wife of Omar, a Somra Rajput Prince. Sind's most revered saint and poet Shah Abdul Latif recalls the tune in one of his many poems. Confined in the palace, Marvi pined for her simple desert life and her commoner lover:

People must be overjoyed,
It's rainy season in the Thar.
Some shear, others card,
Heaps of wool everywhere.
Happily on their looms,
Blankets they weave.
Beautiful plants in desert bloom,
I have no share in the season's joys,
My girl friends in oases roam,
Must be missing Marvi, their
friend....

How sad to think,
People gossip about my elopement.
Let someone ask my beloved,
If he ever thinks of me.
I wish he would come back to me,
Dressed in his desert homespun rags.

Born in the desert: From Hyderabad it is possible to travel out into the Thar Desert to visit the birthplace of the Emperor Akbar at Umarkot. The road passes through **Mirpur Khas**, 67 kilometres from Hyderabad, a town founded by the Talpur Mir Ali Murad Talpur. The town rose in importance due to the British, being conveniently situated close to the railway and the Jamroa Canal. A heap of ruins known as Kahu-jo-daro and a Buddhist stupa attest a previous civilisation locally.

Umarkot was the local centre until Mirpur Khas took over in 1906. It is said that Umarkot was founded by a ruler called Umar. The most conspicuous building in the town is the Rajput Fort. It houses a museum concerned with the life of Akbar, but there is not a great deal to see there. Indeed, the visitor's book is full of travellers' laments expressing the anticlimax of the place. There is no entry for Humayun.

Outside the town Akbar's birthplace is commemorated by a pleasant monu-

Left,
a Rajput girl
hides her
secrets.
Below, the
monument to
Akbar's birth,
Umarkot.

ment made of stone. Akbar was born here in 1542. His parents, fleeing from their enemies, had to march all the way from Jodhpur, where they had been tricked by the ruler, who pretended to be friendly but in fact, planned to sell Humayun out to Sher Shah Suri. Akbar's mother, Hamida Begum was only 15 years old and was seven months pregnant when they fled with a few faithful retainers. Bleak and grim it must have been. The couple were given all possible assistance and shown kindness by Rana Virsal Prasad the ruler of Umarkot. But Humayun was much given to pleasure in those days and lost the Empire and was forced to flee to Persia, despite the assistance he was given at Umarkot.

There is a romance associated with the town and another, later Umar. Umar and Omar are popular Rajput names.

The lovers were the Princess of a neighbouring state called Momal and a courtier called Rano. The Princess, seeking to choose a husband, arranged a complex series of tests around her pal-ace. There was a moat, which was actually shallow but appeared deep due to a system of mirrors underwater and also the fact that the water came from the sea through special channels so that it always looked turbulent. Then there were some realistic looking stone lions, which appeared real and ferocious. Finally there were seven beds, six of which had weak cotton threads and only one was properly strung with cord. Hopeful suitors had to pass all these obstacles. Many men failed. Umar, King of Umarkot came upon the scene with his court. Umar gave up, though his vizier Rano was more stouthearted. Rano tested the depth of the moat with his lance, found it shallow and crossed. Once across the moat, the lions seemed awfully still. He prodded one and found that it was stone. In the end, he solved the mystery of the beds by similarly prodding them with his lance.

The couple were married and were very happy, but the King of Umarkot was jealous and insisted that Rano stay with him. Rano used to slip away every **A faith-healer in Umarkot.**

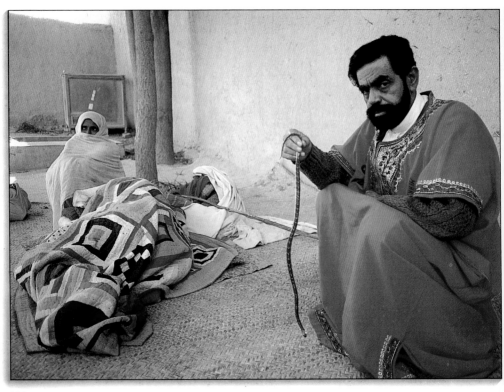

night and ride to the neighbouring state to join Momal. One night however, there were special guests and Rano was unable to get away. Momal, alone, imagined all manner of things, finally convincing herself that the only reason for his absence could be his infidelity. Eventually, he did come but as he approached her bedside he was horrified, seeing another figure lying beside her.

The next day, realising that he had been there, she ran in search of him but found that he had taken up the life of a hermit and refused to speak to her. She died of a broken heart a day or two later, unable to explain to him that the figure lying beside her was her younger sister, dressed as a man to punish him for the unfaithfulness he had never committed.

Of Hindus and Jains: The region contains a wealth of ancient Hindu and Jain sites, especially around **Nagar Parkar**. There are some Jain temples near Virwah in the Nagar Pajar district, and a block of carved marble from the site is on display in Karachi museum. There is another Jain site at Gori, where there is a marble temple. At Bhodesar, seven kilometres from Nagar Parkar are more Jain temples said to date from 14th-15th centuries. A tank nearby was said to have been excavated in the 14th century. It proved not to be watertight and the builder apparently remedied this defect by sacrificing his son as an offering to the Goddess of the town.

Sardhara is situated in the Karunjhar Hills near Nagar Parkar. On *Sivatri* (Siva's night), an annual fair used to be held at the local temple to Siva (Mahadev). The nearby pool and fort are both held to be very ancient. About two kilometres away is the stone statue of a cow carved out of the rock. Water flows from the stone udders into a nearby tank! Another place of Hindu pilgrimage was nearby Ancheleser, which was also associated with Siva, and held to be one of his lungs. There were tanks filled by springs and a flight of more than a hundred steps led to another spring in the hills. In general, this area is one where a good many Hindus have continued to live.

The Rajput Fort has many a tale to tell.

UP AND DOWN THE INDUS

From Hyderabad the traveller can return to Kotri via the Super Highway and follow the western bank of the Indus, or continue due north up the eastern bank. **Bhit Shah** is 55 kilometres away, and about 3 kilometres east of the National Highway.

The town's main attraction is the shrine of the revered Shah Abdul Latif. He was born in 1690 and here he lies buried, the uncrowned king of Sind. His shrine is situated on a *bhit* (mound) and hence the name of the place Bhit Shah, the Mound of the King. The Saint had forsaken a life of material comfort for he was born to a background of wealth. As is usual with holy men of the region, Shah Abdul Latif was generally on the side of the devout poor and his songs have made very deep impressions on the lives of common people. For those who thirst for temporal power and tyranny he expressed his abhorrence:

Clean in dress, dirty of soul,
Donkeys' worthy slaves they are.

His own attitude to living was:

Try to be dead from now on,
Everyone's dead in the end.

The tomb of Shah Latif was raised by the first of the Kalhoras and subsequently beautified by the Talpur Mirs. It is lavishly decorated with blue glazed tiles. Pilgrims throng to the annual festival of Bhit Shah to pay homage to the saint. His words have universal appeal:

Arise! You have no voice,
God hearkens to the meek.
Sing and play music for your Lord,
Ask him to grant your wishes.
Don't let the strings rust,
Play the lute, beat the drum.

What does the Lord care for name and
pedigree,
He favours those skilful in
their trade.

**Left,
dusk on
the Indus.
Right,
Hala's
famous blue
tiles used
in the
construction
of the local
mosque.**

The **Bhit Shah Cultural Centre**, consists of 8 hectares of ornamental trees, gardens, and the Kirar Lake. There is an auditorium, library, museum, and rest house.

On the main Highway where the road to Bhit Shah branches off, is the **Shah Abdul Latif Highway Memorial Centre**. This includes an arts and crafts centre, restaurant, filling station etc. The complex is devoted to the life, teaching, poetry and music of the Saint.

Continuing northwards, there are two settlements at **Hala**, One ancient, one modern, dating from 1800 and founded by one of the Mirs. Hala is famed for the mausoleum of Mir Makhdum Nuh, another well known Sindi saint who died in 1592, though the present tomb dates from 1790. Hala is also notable for arts and crafts, pottery, tiles, laquer work. There is a pretty tiled mosque.

On the road from Nawabshah to Sakrand, three ancient mounds have been discovered at **Chanhu-daro**. Excavations have led to the discovery of remains of a drainage system not

unlike that of Mohenjo-daro. Painted pottery, bead making equipment, seals, copper and bronze models and toys have also been found.

On the national highway, about 35 kilometres south of Rohri, lies **Kot Diji**, another important archaeological site. One of the sites is on a hill, which is also the location of an impressive 18th century Talpur Fort. The hill area seems to have been the preserve of the higher class citizens. The hoi polloi inhabited the nearby plain. The civilisation here was earlier than that of Mohenjo-daro and appears to have ended in an enormous fire.

Upper Sind: The town of **Rohri** stands opposite Sukkur across the river. It is a much smaller place and less busy. Rohri has a goodly collection of historic buildings. The **Jamia Masjid** was constructed in 1564 by Fateh Khan, a courtier of the Emperor Akbar. The **Idgah Masjid** dates from 1593 and the **Mau Mubarak** building was erected in 1545 for the reception of a hair from the beard of the Holy Prophet.

The many forests in the area were originally planted by the Talpurs and the British; the wood was useful for fuelling railway engines. The remains of the ancient city of **Aror** are situated eight kilometres east of Rohri, on the eastern edge of a low range of hills of ancient churt rocks which provided flint tools in the Stone Age. The road connecting them passes over an ancient bridge, claimed as one of the oldest in the country. Nearby is a dried up riverbed where two stones mark the ancient course of the Indus. The river moved in A.D. 960 as a result of an earthquake. During his expedition Alexander had a prolonged stay in Aror. He ordered the place to be garrisoned and reinforced its citadel before sailing down the river to the Delta. Hsüan Tsang, the renowned Chinese Buddhist pilgrim visited Aror in the 7th century. Muhammad Bin Qasim defeated its Hindu ruler in 712.

The town of **Sukkur** is on the opposite side of the river and it is best known because of the Sukkur Barrage. There is a massive international aid programme

The 18th-century fort at Kot Diji was built by the Talpur Mirs.

in progress to repair the headworks and extend the canals. Above Sukkur the width of the channel is only 200 metres whilst on the plain, when in spate, the river is sometimes twenty kilometres wide. Seven major irrigation canals lead off from the barrage in the massive irrigation scheme. One canal (the Rohri Canal) is larger than the Suez or Panama Canal and much longer. It irrigates more than 2.5 million hectares, most of which was desert before the scheme.

Bukkur is one of several islands in the river. A limestone rock surmounted by a fort with gates facing Sukkur and Rohri, Bukkur seems to have been viewed as a strategic spot to hold on to by early dynasties. There was certainly competition to rule it between the local dynasties and the Delhi Sultans, and it did change hands. It was strengthened by various people, prized by the Moghuls, Afghans, Kalhoras and Talpurs. In 1838 the British demanded it, and were obliged. They used it as an arsenal and as a prison for Baluchi robbers. Nearby are two other islands, one

Washing day in Sukkur.

is sacred to Khwaja Khizr and has a mosque. Khwaja Khizr is called Zinda Pir "the living saint" and venerated by Hindus and Muslims alike. He became something of a water god in mythology. The other little island, Sadbela was a Hindu shrine with a Udasi monastery. (Udasis were an order founded by one of the sons of Guru Nanak.)

Nearby are two very important bridges. The **Lansdowne Bridge**, a suspension bridge between Sukkur and Rohri, is 250 metres long, and the **Ayub Bridge** is among the world's largest railway arch bridges. It was opened by President Ayub Khan in 1961.

Sukkur grew because of the activities of the British. However, there are local antiquities, including mausoleums from the Kalhora period and also a leaning tower – the **Masum Tower**. It is said to have 84 steps; to be 84 feet high with a circumference of 84 feet.

From Sukkur, the road to Sibi and Baluchistan leads through **Jacobabad**, a town whose name recalls General John Jacob (1812-1858), of the Scinde

Irregular Horse. He was one of those eccentric and far larger than life Victorians. It was his headquarters and still bears his mark; the roads he laid out, the house where he lived and the tomb where they laid him (mourners came from miles around and the sound of women tearing their hair and men wailing was "indescribable"). The town is also the location of a five-metre high pyramid – the grave of Jacob's horse "Messenger".

Down the West Bank: South of Sukkur, **Larkana** is one of the more important modern towns of Sind, probably best known as the location of "Al Murtaza" the home of the Bhutto family and background to their dramatic lives.

The area is well irrigated from the Sukkur Barrage and Larkana is a pleasant garden city. Rich too! In fact Sindis say that rich men should visit Larkana. The avenue of trees lining the road to the family tomb demonstrates what could be achieved elsewhere in the province, were the resources made available. Most people however, would go to the area in order to visit **Mohenjo-daro** where the most impressive remains of the Indus Valley Civilisation can be seen (see page 168). **Dadu** is mainly important as an administrative centre. In the area though are several mounds containing the remains of cities contemporary with, and earlier than, Mohenjo-daro. There has been much excavation at **Amri** of an eight hectare site preceding the Indus Valley civilisation.

Continuing down the highway, **Khudabad** experienced a brief moment of glory in the 18th century when the Kalhora ruler, Mian Yar Muhammad built his capital there, but soon afterwards the capital moved to Hyderabad. Now, it is a small town, though there is a large mosque dating from Mian Yar Muhammad Kalhora's day, a massive building lavishly decorated with some wonderful glazed tile work. The ruler's tomb is also situated locally, and there are many other old tombs and mosques.

On a conical mound lies the historic town of **Sehwan Sharif**. The town is very old; on its outskirts are the ruins of

Left, sailboats crewed by Mohana fishermen. Right, Bukkur Island.

a huge fort founded by Alexander as he passed through this way. It was also the capital of a Buddhist ruler, a brother of Chandragupta II, who ruled this area in the 4th century.

The town owes its greatest importance to the **Mausoleum of Sheikh Osman of Marwand**, known as Lal Shah Baz Qalandar (Red Royal Eagle) who died in 1274. He arrived here from his native Marwand near Tabriz in Iran in 1260. He belonged to the Qalandar denomination of Iranian Sufis, who clothed themselves in coarse woollen raiment, their waists tightened by bark girdles, their right hands holding an almond wooden crook, signifying renunciation and living as wandering gypsies without home, family or trade. Practising austerity and contemplation, they transported themselves into violent ecstasy. Osman lies buried in a side chamber where devotees lay flowers and light incense sticks to seek favours through prayer.

The building is covered with blue glazed tiles. It has been enlarged and decorated by generations of rulers of various dynasties. So parts are gifts from Turkhan rulers and their successors. Features such as the wooden gates, encased in hammered silver are gifts from Talpurs, as are the silver spires on the domes.

From his Sehwan shrine Osman still holds great sway over the minds of the people. The booming copper drums in the courtyard announce daily the majesty and supremacy of the spiritual realm of the saint in the shrine, in the same way as that of temporal kings from their palaces in the past. The saint has his devotees among both the Muslims and the Hindus. For the Muslims he represents a protest against temporal tyranny and steel frame ritual constraints. Muslim *fakirs* sit around in the yogic posture, arms adorned with metal bangles. The saint has a great following among the people of Sind and other regions of Pakistan.

Osman was a Qalandar, which in Persian language means uncut and unpolished, implying a fearless Sufi not

The Mausoleum of Shah Lal Baz Qalandar in Sehwan Sharif.

bound by rituals. To his devotees, he is Red Qalandar, the Ecstatic. He declares his creed in one of his lyrics sung by his devotees with music during their ritualistic ceremonies:

From whither I behold within my
beloved's (God's) countenance,
And proud I'm dancing before my
beloved.
Blessed be the unbelievers, trampling
piety under their feet,
Look at me here I dance dressed in a
holy man's habit.
Behold! I'm Osman of Marwand, an
accomplice of Mansur,
The world passes by and I reel from
the gallows.

There is a pun, for "Mansur" in Arabic means the "victor" and it was also the name of a Sufi who was hanged for his unorthodoxy.

Each year Osman's followers celebrate the anniversary of his death by holding his marriage (with God) ceremonies on three successive days. Mar-

riage processions come to the shrine, on the first day from the house of the hereditary Muslim keeper of the shrine, on the two successive days from two different Hindu houses who also enjoy the privilege on an hereditary basis. They bring the nuptial presents and a platter of henna paste which are left near the tomb for the night. In the morning the platter bears the mark of two palms sunk in the paste implying acceptance of betrothal.

People come from all over to celebrate the festival. There is constant music, singing and dancing keeping pace with the booming of the big copper drums. One party follows the other and the ritual continues from morning to the evening. The drums thunder, men and women celebrate the occasion by ritual dancing and achieve grace with quick steps, forward and backward, hands flailing above shoulders. The singing girls of whom Qalandar is patron saint gyrate furiously, tossing their heads and swinging their long hair, drenched in sweat, panting in frenzy to reach the state of *la hoot la makan*, no self no space, perfect union and peace with the Divine.

West of Sehwan Sharif is **Manchar Lake**. The lake is in a large natural depression and is fed by flood water from the Indus. When the flood level falls, water runs back again from the lake to the river. It is noted as a bathing place for fairies and mermaids. There are several islands in the lake and an interesting collection of fauna and flora. An extraordinary number of birds are to be found in the area.

There is also a colony of fishermen, owners of large, high-prowed wooden boats. Such traditional craft can be seen along the banks of the Indus too. The fishermen use nets and submerged lines to catch fish in the traditional manner, though there are references to a noisy form of communal fishing whereby a flotilla of boats scare fish into a net. The local folk have a rather peculiar method of catching water fowl. Men wade out with stuffed egrets on their heads to act **A devotee** as a decoy. The fishermen of Manchar **of the Royal** Lake are believed to be the direct de- **Red Eagle.**

scendants of the Indus and pre-Indus culture of Sind.

To the Kirthar Mountains: Continuing down the west bank, about 90 kilometres north of Hyderabad is a small place called Sann. There is a track from Sann leading about 20 kilometres across uninhabited territory, absolute wilderness, to **Ranikot Fort**. The Fort is claimed to be the largest fort in the world. It might well be so, too, as the wall around the circumference measures 24 kilometres, and it looks like the Great Wall of China stretching across the landscape. It stands on a trade route through the Kirthar Mountains. It is ancient, origins unknown, though some of the more modern construction seems to date from the Talpur Mirs. There is barely a track to it, so it is best reached by camel.

Beyond Ranikot, the **Kirthar Mountains** are remote, on the western border of Sind stretching 250 kilometres in a continuous rampart down to the coast where they finish in mangrove swamps. The Kirthar limestone rocks are of pale,

Life on the water at Manchar Lake.

bright grey and almost off white colours and provide quality building stone blocks. Though the hills look like stony wilderness, they actually support quite a variety of vegetation to provide grazing for large herds of cattle, sheep, goats and camels.

The hills are the location of the **Kirthar National Park**. The Park is the habitat of some rarer species including the Sind Ibex, Chinkara, Gazelles, Leopard, wild sheep and a number of other animals. The Government have provided facilities for tourists to visit the park, though animal spotting is not very easy.

Fire-walking, a custom more well-known in South India, is practised in the Kirthar region. A trench ten yards long is filled with embers covered with the sage green leaves and purple flowers of the ak. In some parts of the world, fire-walking is a testimony of faith. Here, it is an ordeal undergone by those who have been accused of theft. The one who walks through the fire with no blisters is considered to be innocent.

MOHENJO-DARO

Clouds of dust emerge above the rooftops as the buffalo return from a day's work in the fields, pulling their carts through the unpaved streets. Evening time, and the sun begins to set over to the west, behind the hill. In a back lane a group of children finish their last game of marbles and then go indoors.

Finishing their shift, a group of workers emerges from a manhole; they have spent the whole day unblocking a drain which has caused a neighbouring back lane to flood. Father arrives home, tired after a day's work in the pottery and mother starts complaining about a cracked drainpipe. Water is seeping through the walls. They will be here with a replacement first thing in the morning. Very efficient. Life in the city 4,500 years ago.

In those days it was a lot greener at Mohenjo-daro. More could grow. The climate was cooler and there was more rain than there is today, here 20 kilometres south of Larkana in the province of Sind. But the hill is still there, and so is a lot of the city. At Mohenjo-daro are the most impressive remains of the Indus Valley Civilisation. The Indus River flows to the east, five kilometres away.

The first excavations on the site were carried out by the Indian Archaeological Survey and began in 1922 under the directorship of Sir John Marshall. It was really an accidental discovery; the only visible evidence of civilisation was the Buddhist Stupa on top of the hill. But gradually, parts of a city were unearthed under successive archaeologists. Under the rubble of millennia. Today, with a bit of imagination, it is just about possible to picture that thriving, teeming, well organised city.

The rulers and the ruled: Mohenjo-daro, "The mound of the dead", is divided into two distinct parts. There is the hill, the mound, over to the west and the larger lower city down to the east, where most of the people lived. The

A guide at Mohenjo-daro.

whole city is about five kilometres in circumference. The mound, the so-called citadel, is man-made, built purposefully higher than the rest of the city, so that the people who lived there, the rulers, could have a clear view out over their domain. Equally, the normal burghers living down the hill could always be reminded that they were subject to a greater power. Like the town halls, tax offices and other hubs of today's bureaucracy, the mound must have been an intimidating sight.

The citadel appears to have been heavily fortified as indicated by the presence of a series of towers running along its south-eastern perimeter. It is unclear as to whom the potential enemy might have been, but clay pellets were found by one of the parapets, presumably missiles for some kind of sling.

While no excavation work has actually been carried out under the relatively modern Buddhist stupa, several major buildings have been unearthed on the flanks of the mound.

The Granary: One of these is a large structure now believed to be the base of a huge granary. Being such an important commodity the city fathers must have felt that it was a good idea to have all the grain centrally located under their watchful eye, doling out the rations to the masses as they saw fit. The structure, originally measuring about 45 metres by 23 metres, was later enlarged even further. A huge building, the base is made up of a total of 27 large brickwork piles, forming a rectangle of nine by three. The spaces in between provided the ventilation for the grain stored above. The grain was transferred into the granary by means of a brick loading platform on its northern side. There is nothing left of the wooden superstructure.

The Great Bath: The most celebrated of the citadel buildings, however, is the Great Bath, which was built later than the granary; its construction destroyed half of the loading platform of the granary. It measures 12 metres by 7 metres and is 2.5 metres deep. Steps lead down into into the bath at either end.

Restoration work at Mohenjo-daro, the "Citadel" in the background.

The Harappans seem to have gone to a great deal of trouble making the bath watertight. The bottom and the sides were made out of fired bricks which were bound together by gypsum mortar. The sides were also sealed by a course of bitumen. The sophistication of the bath was such that the steps, also made of fired brick, were originally fitted with timber treads laid in either bitumen or asphalt. The bath was drained through a brick arch about two metres high and was probably filled from a large well found close by in one of the adjacent rooms.

Rooms actually line the bath on three sides. A staircase was found in one of them, indicating that they were probably two-storied. The excavators also recorded discovering charcoal and ashes which may have been the remains of a wooden second floor. Rather ominously, the northern part of this complex was later filled in with solid materials, perhaps to counter the effects of rising flood waters!

Across the lane to the north of the main complex, there were six small bathrooms measuring only 3 metres by 2 metres. The bathrooms themselves were solidly built, furnished with neatly arranged brick floors and linked up to the central drainage system. There is no doubt that the architects and masons of the age were capable of producing extraordinary quality. None of their entrances overlooked that of another, suggesting a respect for privacy and perhaps even a hint of exclusiveness.

A priestly class: Some have read even more into the evidence than this. Mackay even suggested that a priesthood lived on the second floor above the bathrooms, descending to perform water-based religious rites whilst laymen performed their own more public rituals in the Great bath. Given the prominence of ritual bathing in modern Hinduism, it is very tempting to agree with this interpretation. He even went on to speculate that a building to the north-east of the bath was the residence of a very high official, possibly even the high priest himself, or perhaps a college

The Great Bath.

of priests. The building includes an open court with verandas on three sides and a series of dwellings which resemble barracks.

The Assembly hall: Other areas which have been excavated are in need of re-excavation with the benefit of modern techniques. One such case is the so-called Assembly Hall in the southern part of the citadel. It was originally divided into five aisles by rows of brick plinths which probably supported wooden columns, but later underwent a number of alterations. The floor was made of fine sawn bricks similar to those used in the Great Bath.

A rare stone statue of a seated male was found in a room to the west and close by were a series of large stone rings which may have been architectural pieces or even part of a ritual stone column. Could the Assembly Hall actually have been a temple? From these three buildings alone, enough information has emerged for one to assume that it was here on the citadel that the power of the secular and religious administrations lay. There is even a strong hint that there was no real distinction drawn between them.

Down the hill: The lower city of Mohenjo-daro, where the houses, shops and craft workshops were located, is a fine example of good urban planning. The main streets are about nine metres wide and run at right angles to each other, dividing the town into roughly rectangular blocks measuring about 360 metres by 240 metres. Between these main streets run a series of lanes, also at right-angles, usually about 1.5 to 3 metres wide. There is therefore a sense of strong administrative control which is reinforced by a number of small, single-roomed buildings on street corners. These could well have been the night watchmen or policemen's posts.

Advanced drainage: Though the streets were unpaved and presumably very dusty, a series of brick drains ran through them, which were not only of unique quality among contemporary societies, but even today would be the envy of much of Asia. Clearly these drains were sometimes subject to block-

age, but they appear to have been regularly cleaned to judge by the brick manholes which were located at intervals along their length. Earthenware pipes ran from the houses, sometimes built into the walls themselves, to link up with these main drains. The pipes came in lengths which slotted into each other much in the same way as modern drainpipes.

Water was provided by public wells in the streets. Today some of these wells stand tall like chimneys. With the passage of time the ground level rose as new buildings were built on the rubble of the old. The archaeologists, excavating down through the rubble, have exposed the full length of the well shafts and left them standing as they found them. It is an interesting exercise to examine the declining standard of the brickwork of the wells from the good quality at the bottom, representing the early period, to the poor quality at the top, representing the later period.

Privacy: Besides these public wells, many houses also had their own private

A well.

wells. Indeed privacy is a recurring theme at Mohenjo-daro. House doors opened into the lanes rather than onto the busier main streets. Windows were rare and the fragments of lattices of alabaster and terracotta which have been found suggest that the few windows were fitted with window screens. The houses of the more well-to-do actually looked inwards onto a central courtyard which, combined with the occasional dog-legs in the lane, gives an air of an introverted and secluded society. The tendancy for the houses to have small alcoves by the entrance reinforces a sense of reserve.

Construction and amenities: During the height of the Harappan period, the overall quality of domestic accommodation was very high. Fired bricks were usually used for the construction of the walls in the modern "English bond" style. There is evidence that internal walls were plastered, though the rendering to the external walls is not certain.

Most houses were equipped with a flight of stairs which presumably led to either a second storey or at least a flat roof. These upper storeys were made of wood, as indicated by the presence of holes in the masonry which probably supported timber beams. Bathrooms were common and occasionally houses also had private seated latrines quite similar to those used in the west today. Although some were much larger than others, virtually all buildings in the lower city had the same basic plan.

Not only houses: But some of the remains have walls which are a great deal thicker than the majority of buildings, indicating that they had some special function. It has been suggested that the citadel did not have a monopoly over religious rites and that temples also existed in the lower city. Just inside the gateway to one such building, archaeologists discovered a ring of brickwork just over one metre in diameter. Given the occasional evidence for tree worship at this time, the ring has been interpreted as possibly being a protective enclosure around a sacred tree.

Furthermore, even though sculptures

Found at Mohenjo-daro, a seal depicting the "Zebu".

172

are rare throughout the Harappan Civilisation, one was found, as well as the fragments of a second, in and around the precinct of this building. The figures had much in common. Both were bearded with a headband across the forehead, and in both cases the eyes were designed as if to be inlaid with another material, perhaps shell or faience. The first was that of a man's head, carved from white limestone and standing 17.5 cm high.

The second sculpture was a seated or squatted figure, reminiscent of that found close by the Assembly Hall on the citadel, and made of alabaster. It was found in three parts. First the body was found on top of the wall above the western flight of steps. A fragment of the head was then excavated in a lane about 15 metres to the north, and the remaining part was then discovered in the central courtyard of a nearby house. Re-assembled, this figure measures about 42 cm in height.

While all three pieces were found in archaeological layers belonging to the

final stages of occupation of Mohenjodaro, it has been suggested that the style of the statue actually belonged to the the early period of occupation. It was a treasured object, passed down from generation to generation before being finally broken and scattered.

Industry and commerce: Some of the buildings or rooms lining the street appear to have had industrial or commercial use, as indeed is common in the cities and bazaars of today. One discovery is of a room which had five shallow conical pits lined with wedge-shaped bricks built into its floor. These have been interpreted as being stands for large jars with pointed bases, suggesting that the room may well have been a public restaurant, or even perhaps that the assumed jars were dying vats.

What was initially believed to have been a range of shops has also been discovered. Further observation, however suggests that these were probably workmen's quarters. They were arranged in two parallel rows of eight, and each was divided internally into a front

A terracotta model of a bullock cart. Similar vehicles are still in use in Sind today.

and rear, possibly a bedroom. A central passage ran between the two rows, separating all but the end couple. It may be significant that this end pair were also different in that they were slightly larger than the others and their internal division was more elaborate. If these rooms were workmen's quarters, it is tempting to see the end pair as being occupied by supervisors.

Indeed the complex could be the accommodation for the attendants of the nearby "temple", or even for a priesthood, similar to that which was built around the great bath. It is perhaps significant that most of the front rooms had good bathing facilities, though these need not have had any special associations and may purely be testimony to the remarkable overall standard of civilisation attained by the Harappans.

The discovery: Central to the debate on the decline of the Harrapan civilisation has been the fate of Mohenjo-daro. On at least three occasions the extent of flooding was so severe that the city was swamped making extensive rebuilding

necessary. The levels of floors and courtyards kept having to be raised with packed mud. Furthermore, as is clearly illustrated by the wells, there was a general decline in building techniques, as indeed in the overall quality of planning. Houses must have become more and more overcrowded; increasingly, buildings and even courtyards were divided and then sub-divided again. Space available for occupation was diminished due to the steadily rising levels of the Indus. The twist in the tale, however, is provided by the discovery of five groups of skeletons, and of one individual; men, women and children, 38 in all. They date from the end of the occupation. They met a violent death. Some were found in the streets, some on the floors of houses, others on a staircase. Some had broken skulls, all were contorted and there was little effort to bury them. Who the killers were remains a mystery, as does their motive. From this point on Mohenjo-daro remained quite uninhabited.

The bitter end: It is a sad reflection that this great archaeological site is rapidly disintegrating. This is largely due to the effects of the rising water table. When excavations began in 1922, the water table was 7.5 metres below the ground level. Now in the summer season it comes to within 1.5 metres of the surface. As a result the natural salts in the soil below the ground are being dissolved by the water and turned into salt crystals. These are reacting with the clay bricks, causing them to disintegrate even at the touch of a hand.

Despite efforts by UNESCO to preserve the site, priceless evidence is therefore being lost daily. Not only are the standing remains being affected, but so too are unexcavated buildings still below ground. Perhaps the greatest loss of all, however, is the pre-Harappan settlement which is believed to lie directly under the Harappan site. Previous attempts to reach these lowest levels have invariably failed due to the difficulties encountered with the high water table. With the water table ever rising, the lowest levels will now almost certainly be lost forever.

Left, a drainage system nearly 5,000 years old. **Right,** Mohenjo-daro crumbles.

178

THE PANJAB

The name Panjab is derived from the words *panj*, meaning five, and *aab* meaning waters and the province of Panjab is crossed by five major rivers. When Pakistan came into being in 1947, a part of the eastern Panjab went to India but the major portion of the state was awarded to Pakistan.

The rivers are the Sutlej, Beas, Ravi, Chenab and Jhelum. They are all tributaries of the Indus and have all played their part in converting the Panjab into the richest and most fertile province in Pakistan. The population has now grown to over 50 million, more than half the population of the entire country.

Before the turn of the century, when the British brought their technological skills to bear on the area, Panjab was by no means the fertile breadbasket it is today; on the contrary much more of the land was desert or semi desert. The rivers were dangerous as they were prone to flooding and changing course when swollen with water from the hills. The shifting rivers presented considerable dangers to anyone or anything in their path and just how dramatic the changes in courses of rivers was can be seen quite clearly. In Lahore the Ravi used to run by the Fort. Now its course is a couple of miles away.

Khwaja Khizr, the water God who lived underwater with the crocodiles needed offerings to placate him. If well pleased he might allow a man to reap an easy harvest without much effort from the rich alluvial soils of the river. Alternatively, he might wash everything away. It led to the saying "*Ik sal amir, Ik sal fakir*" meaning "A rich man this year, and a beggar the next." Another traditional saying warns that "Living near a river is as risky as handing a baby to a witch."

In the past, people in the Panjab have been constantly on the move just to stay alive. The area was once dotted with sites which were once flourishing cities and are now no more. Many of the towns are relatively new having been established as British cantonments or markets for canal colonies. Old towns were washed away by the rivers and replaced by new towns on safer ground. Some have just died; Bhera, near Sargodha, for example, used to be a flourishing place. It was an ancient town where Sher Shah built a beautiful mosque. There were shrines which attracted pilgrims. Bhera was a centre of Moghul local government. It was plundered by the Durrani, repopulated by the Sikhs and prospered under the British when it became the most important city for miles around. Then as the canal colonies flourished, other towns grew and Bhera waned. Local Government moved. Having sustained a lot of damage in 1947, it is now a ghost town.

The breadbasket of Pakistan: Today, agriculture is the most important industry in the Panjab. Wheat, rice, sugar, fruit, tobacco, cotton and many other crops flourish. But visitors may be surprised to see how much industrial development there also is. There is a policy of attracting industry to rural areas so quite large enterprises are to be found dotted around the landscape outside the urban areas. The factories of the Panjab produce anything and everything. Apart from food processing and textiles, there are also furnaces and foundries and chemical plants. Everything from agricultural tools to zips is produced in the Panjab.

All these developments are explained by a quick look at a detailed map. It is impossible not to notice how much of the Panjab is criss-crossed by canals. Surrounded by desert, most of the Panjab is now a huge oasis of green where there are hundreds of new settlements with practically no historical reference.

Canal colonies: Quite what a spectacular feat was achieved by irrigation and the creation of these settlements – the canal colonies – can be judged by driving along the edge of an irrigated area. On one side of the road lies the green cultivated area, with trees, homes, and civilisation; and on the other side there is sand and not much else.

The canal colonies must be one of the most astonishing projects ever carried out by the British. Such canals which had been built previously were on a far smaller scale, more for gardens and enjoyment than for public water supplies. The project involved science and canal engineering and radical social engineering too; creating farming land and moving population to inhabit it. The British began construction of the Upper Bari Doab Canal in 1860-61. The waters of the River Ravi were led a hundred miles from the hills to water the fertile and densely populated areas of Lahore and Amritsar.

In 1870, water was similarly diverted from the Jumna to South Panjab.

The first major colonisation experiment was undertaken in 1886-88 when an effort was made to irrigate 76 thousand hectares of wasteland in Multan district using water from the Sutlej. The idea was to settle immigrants from surrounding areas on the land. This early experiment was not a complete success because the flow of water could not always be guaranteed. But meanwhile, the skills of canal engineering had advanced and a plan was made to harness the Chenab to irrigate over a million acres. The lower Chenab Canal opened in 1892, was a great success and a turning point in the economic history of the Panjab. From 1905-17 an incredibly ambitious project was carried out to irrigate the desert South West of Lahore. The Ravi had already been tapped, so a complex system of three canals was built linking the three rivers, Jhelum, Chenab, and Ravi, which opened up huge areas for irrigation.

This was how it began. Since then the system has been further developed, skills and technology have advanced and projects to irrigate more land continue. Nowadays, the map of the Panjab has been totally altered by the changes brought by irrigation.

But the Panjab isn't all green fields and desert. In the north of the province lie the time-warped remains of the ancient Salt Range, the weird forms of the Potohar Plateau and the lush green Murree Hills, which are the foothills of the Himalayas.

Preceding pages: the Alamgiri Gate built by Aurangzeb; the bread basket of Pakistan.

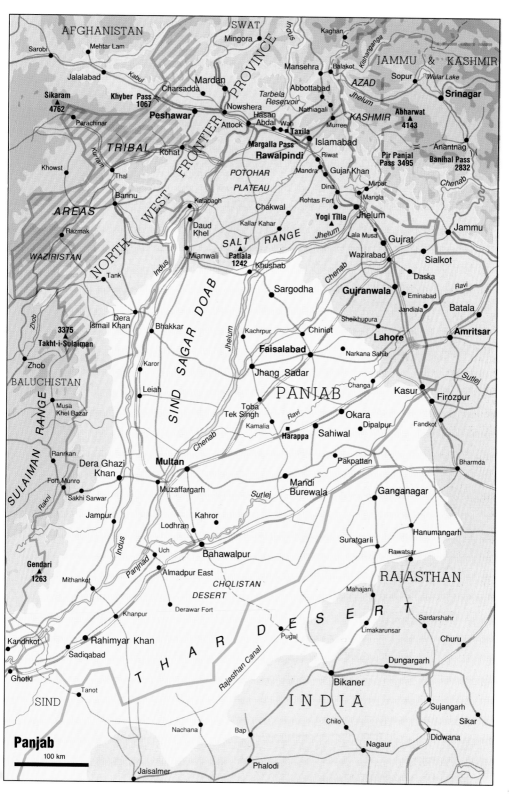

Panjab

100 km

181

ISLAMABAD AND THE MURREE HILLS

Twin Cities: The latest and most ambitious attempt to build a completely new settlement in the Panjab came with the decision to replace Karachi as the capital of Pakistan. The result is the city of **Islamabad**, situated in the north of the province on the Potohar Plateau, beneath the **Margalla Hills**. Work started on the city in 1961 and it is still far from finished; new bits are being added all the time.

The name of the new capital means "the abode of Islam" and reflects the Islamic ideology in Pakistan. Islamabad is new, planned, spacious, leafy and green. The wide roads, detached houses and gardens contrast somewhat with an old Pakistani city. Islamabad's twin city of Rawalpindi, for example, has plenty of crowds, narrow winding bazaars and ancient buildings all huddled together.

Islamabad is so spacious, however, that transport is a necessity. The distances are too great for it to be much fun otherwise. And in Islamabad there are no scooter rickshaws or *tongas* – traditional Asian forms of transport. Options available are Suzuki vans, Transit vans, taxis and hired cars.

Most of the buildings are low, many single storey, and some of the homes really are quite extraordinary. The homes of the super rich are very elegant indeed, and much more fun when they are a flight of fancy.

The city was envisaged by Ayub Khan on an entirely new site which he thought suitable. Lahore might well have been the new capital but for its proximity to the Indian border. As it is, Islamabad is convenient, bordering on two states, Panjab and NWFP, near to the hills with a "healthy" climate. The British found the area healthy as opposed to the climate of fever-ridden Bengal.

Islamabad is best viewed from the Margalla Hills which provide a pleasant backdrop to the north of the city. The **A view towards Islamabad.**

road up into the hills via **Daman-i-koh** to **Pir Sahava** winds, climbs and bends through alarming hairpins and the corners can be scary to the novice driver.

The road, however, is used by rather aged buses and Suzuki vans. The buses are always packed to capacity, and the Suzukis have so many men clinging to them that the front wheels seem in imminent danger of losing contact with the road surface at times. However, the male passengers come in handy; they push the vehicles which are unable to cope with the steep gradient.

The hills are good for walking, riding or trekking along the well-established system of trails which wend their way through dry semi-evergreen shrubs and trees, as well as some more exotic species which have been introduced. There are numerous birds and some animals, mainly monkey and deer.

Islamabad lies spread below. On the left is **Bari Imam** and **Quaid-i-Azam University**. The university can be picked out clearly by the white ceremonial archway at its gate.

Bari Imam is in a village called **Nurpur**. A 17th-century saint, Syed Abdul Latif Shah lived there and his mirror studded shrine still stands. His most famous miracle was bringing 70 dead cows back to life. The village is always bustling with people, dogs and goats and the colourful small shops sell glass bangles and souvenirs.

Rawal Lake lies looking as tranquil as a Chinese painting. It is a pleasant spot for a walk or picnic. Fishing is possible, but a permit is required from a small hut near the dam. **The Islamabad Club** is situated to the west of the lake. Facilities include golf and riding.

Looking across, one can see the hills of **Shakarparian Park**. This is also a recreational area with some formal gardens and play areas. There are viewpoints, a rose and jasmine garden and a model of the plan for Islamabad. In the park is **Lok Virsa**, the National Institute of Folk and Traditional Heritage containing examples of arts and crafts – costumes, jewellery and musical instruments. Lok Virsa also holds festivals

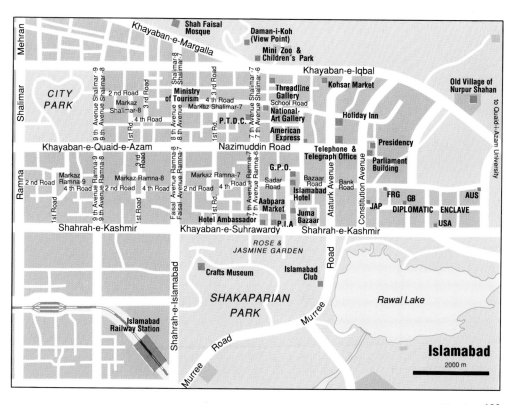

and prepares tapes, films and books which are available for sale from the Lok Virsa shop in Supermarket. Not far from Shakarparian park is **Zero Point** - the point from which distances in Pakistan are to be measured.

At the bottom of the hill, beneath Daman-i-koh, is the popular Islamabad Children's Playland which is a large and superb play area with equipment given by the Japanese to the people of Pakistan.

On the right hand the sweeping roofs and the massive minarets of the **Faisal Masjid** dominate the scene. The minarets remind one irresistably of space rockets. The sweeping roofs, designed to look like a a tent in the desert, are wide enough to accommodate 15,000 people.

Designed by the Turkish architect Vadat Dalokay, it is said to be the largest mosque in the world. The US$ 50 million it cost to build was mostly donated by the Kingdom of Saudi Arabia. The complex also houses an Islamic Research Centre, university, library,

museum and various other facilities. Islamabad has some good shopping areas, especially **Jinnah**, **Aabpara**, and **Kausar** Markets and **Supermarket**, the latter being a shopping mall with an assortment of small, independant retailers offering a wide range of goods. There are groceries and food stores. The bakers sell bread, spicy pasties and some superb cakes and pastries. There are chemists, carpet stores, jewellers, ready-made garment stores and bespoke tailors, bookshops and second-hand bookshops.

Threadlines at Supermarket is a government sponsored handicrafts shop. It sells beautiful things at very reasonable prices.

The markets are always fun. In Islamabad there is a **Juma Bazaar** (Friday Market) and an **Itwar Bazaar** (Sunday market). Juma Bazaar closes down at lunchtime as the people go to attend their prayers at that time.

There are an enormous range of things on sale – fruits and vegetables, fish and chickens; colourful spices, do-

The "space rockets" of the Shah Faisal Mosque.

mestic necessities, pots and pans, fabrics. There are many secondhand stalls selling fabrics, curtains, clothing and shoes. The secondhand sock vendors are a curious sight! Cassettes of popular music are also on sale. Toys and novelties of all descriptions.

At Juma Bazaar it is also possible to see carpet vendors, with their wares spread out, ready to bargain. Many also sell items of jewellery, earrings, bracelets, a taviz with a holy quotation engraved on a semi precious stone. Some of the carpets in the modern era have new designs incorporating helicopters, missiles, planes and *kalashnikovs*. Recently, many vendors also had piles of Russian hats, money, medals and buttons.

City of bazaars: Rawalpindi is the twin, (though much older) town to Islamabad. It is famous mainly for its bazaars and lacks much in the way of historical sites to visit. But for the visitor, a wander through the **Saddar** and **Raja Bazaars** is what visiting a Pakistani city is all about. This, as opposed

to the planned wide open Islamabad, is how a traveller imagines an eastern city to be. Interesting chaos! In the narrow crowded streets with vendors selling jewellery, brass and copper, inlaid furniture, Kashmiri embroidery; it is possible to buy almost anything.

Liaquat Bagh is a park on the site where Liaquat Ali Khan, the first Prime Minister of Pakistan, was assassinated in October 1951. There is an auditorium, and a library and art exhibitions, cultural shows and theatrical performances are staged. Beside the Grand Trunk Road is the **Ayub National Park** which is a popular recreation centre. The park covers 932 hectares, and there is a boating lake, aquarium and gardens as well as a play area for the children and an open air theatre.

Murree and the Panjab Hills: Murree is 2,300 metres above sea level and lies in the foothills of the Himalayas 60 kilometres north east of Islamabad. It is one of many hill stations developed by the British. Just as the Victorians used it as an escape from the heat of the plains, so too is it popular today with Pakistanis. Murree was the summer headquarters from 1850 to 1876 when the summer capital transferred to Simla. There is a good road up into the hills and it takes approximately two hours to drive up from Islamabad.

There are a number of small settlements along the road and beyond the village of **Tret**, the hillsides are covered with pine trees. There is a bridle path from the road to **Nandkot** where there was once a military camp but it was abandoned because of the vast numbers of snakes in the area. It is said that the snakes killed too many soldiers and that there are a lot of graves in the vicinity.

A *ghora* is a horse and **Ghora Gali** which lies at 1,500 metres is the place where they used to change the horses in the days when horse drawn vehicles used to ply up this road. There are a number of official institutions in the hills, police and army depots and educational centres.

Murree Brewery is a curious ruin on the hillside. The name of the brewery was Dyer and Meakin and it was de-

Rawalpindi

1000 m

stroyed in 1947. The Dyers were, in fact, the family of General Dyer who was responsible for the Amritsar Massacre in 1919.

Murree is very popular and crowded in the summer. In winter it is cold and there is snowfall, something which is a novelty and thoroughly enjoyed by Pakistani visitors to the area. A jam, with cars stuck in the snow is an occasion for great enjoyment here.

The centre of activity in Murree is the mainstreet, called **The Mall**. There are shops, restaurants and people parade up and down. There are a number of hotels, and because the hill stations were the rest and recreation centres for the Raj, Murree has quite a lot of churches. There is a very curious story that an ancient grave on a hilltop is that of the Virgin Mary.

There are a number of hill resorts in the area going towards Abbottabad. These are called **The Galis**.

The area is visited for its scenic beauty and countryside. The settlements are not very large, and apart from British period hotels and churches, the buildings are mainly residential. Many of the old homes have corrugated iron on the roof. They look tatty and have very English names. So far, the Murree Hills are far less spoiled than hill stations in India.

The hills present an ever changing prospect, however, as one drives through. There are sometimes very steep precipices on one side of the road and tall pine trees on the other. Pine, maple, oak and chestnut trees grow in the forests and some trees are huge and evidently very ancient. There are meadows here and there, grassy stretches and wild flowers. In any possible place there are terraced fields.

There are resthouses and hotels at most of the settlements, but the most popular places are Nathiagali, Thandiani and Ayubia. The Galis offer endless opportunities for walking and riding.

From **Nathiagali** on a clear day it is possible to glimpse **Nanga Parbat** away to the north.

Ayubia is named after Ayub Khan and a recreation complex is being developed in the area. This includes chairlifts which are a great novelty and an exciting attraction for visitors.

Thandiani is reached from the Abbottabad-Nathiagali road. It was a hill station many years ago, but fell into neglect and disuse and has only been reopened in recent years. From here, the views of the mountains are the most impressive of all.

It is possible to drive from Islamabad through Murree and along the Galis to Abbottabad in the Hazara district of NWFP, and then to return via the impressive **Tarbela Dam** and Taxila on the Grand Trunk Road.

At 1,250 metres, **Abbottabad** lies below the lush pines of the Galis, although it still has a pleasant climate. It was founded in 1853 and named after James Abbot, the first Deputy Commissioner. For those wishing to venture to the Northern Areas either via Balakot and the Kaghan Valley, or via the Karakoram Highway, this is where the journey could be said to begin; it is where the hills start.

Left, retreat in the Galis. **Right**, a steep road in Murree.

186

THE GT ROAD TO ATTOCK

In Rudyard Kipling's famous novel Kim, the Grand Trunk Road is described as being "the backbone of all Hind". The Grand Trunk Road connects Kabul with Calcutta.

"All castes and kinds of men move here. Look! Brahmins and *chamars*, bankers and tinkers, barbers and *bunnias*, pilgrims and potters – all the world going and coming. To me it is a river from which I am withdrawn like a log after a flood. And truly the Grand Trunk Road is a wonderful spectacle. It runs straight, bearing without crowding India's traffic for fifteen hundred miles – such a river of life as nowhere else exists in the world."

To the immediate west of Pindi, the **GT Road** passes through the **Margalla Pass**, used by Babur on his invasion.

The pass is not all that impressive, the road slices through the rocks. A large obelisk on the hill is a memorial to John Nicholson, a general who fought against the Sikhs, gained respect from them, and eventually made a magnificent dash to Delhi in 1857, where he fell. The obelisk recorded that he was "mourned by two races with equal grief". So well regarded was Nicholson that he left a religious group of followers called Nikalsenis.

Just beyond the Margalla Pass is a small preserved section of the GT Road as built by Sher Shah. The holes in some of the rocks along the highway are caves and are used for residential purposes. Just beyond the Margalla pass is **Taxila**. While the main attraction here are the archaeological remains of great cities and stupas, the valley in which it all lies is one of the most beautiful in the Panjab. It can take days to explore the whole area on foot, so one of the most comfortable and relaxing means of transport is the *tonga* (horse and cart). Their drivers await the traveller in the main Taxila bazaar.

The best parts to visit include **Sirkap**, the second, Bactrian Greek city which is

There are many destinations along the GT Road.

← TO GRAND TRUNK ROAD TO →

RIWAT 11 MANDRA 21	SANGJANI 13 TAXILLA 21
GUJARKHAN 30 MISSAKESWAL 35	HASSANABDAL 28 HAITIAN 43
JHELUM 67 CUJRAT 100	CONDAL 48 ATTOCK 56
WAZIRABAD 108 CUJRANWALA 128	CAMPBELLPUR 59 NOWSHERA 78
LAHORE 171 DELHI 483	PESHAWAR CANTT 185

a pretty site for a walk and a picnic. But watch out for nasty prickly acacia twigs on the grass. They catch in the clothes and are horribly scratchy. It is possible to climb the hill beyond the city via some steps. The layout of the excavations can be appreciated from the top.

The **Dharmarajika Stupa** is quite a pleasant stroll across a little stream to the extensive remains. The **Jaulian Buddhist** monastery is quite a steep climb up the hill. There is a large stupa surrounded by the bases of many smaller ones covered with delicate sculptural decoration. To the left of the main stupa is a Buddha with a hole in the middle of his belly. It was for healing; the supplicant put his finger in the hole and prayed for health. Nowadays tourists often make a wish.

Taxila has a number of shops selling local, decorated pots and there are some stonemasons who sit hammering at rocks, carving out pestles and mortars which are for sale. The masons are friendly souls. Taxila Museum contains a wealth of finds from the area (see page 191). Beyond modern Taxila is the small town of **Wah** where a small turning to the left leads into a Moghul garden. The garden is no rival to Shalimar but is nonetheless a very pleasant place. There are many springs in the area. Akbar was apparently so stirred by the beauty of the surroundings that he said "Wah!" (not unlike "wow!" – an exclamation), and the name stuck. Wah has grown enormously in recent times. It has enlarged so much that it now joins Taxila and Hasan Abdal. Wah has a considerable amount of industry and some rather up market housing areas.

Hasan Abdal is half way between Rawalpindi and Attock. It is an interesting spot with a collection of buildings, the most important of which being the *gurdwara* called **Panja Sahib**, the temple of the Guru's palm.

The tale is told that Guru Nanak and his disaster prone disciple, Mardana were passing the area when Mardana became thirsty. The Guru sent him to the summit of a nearby hill to ask Baba Wali Kandhari who lived there, for

Attock Fort.

water. Baba Wali Kandhari declined to help and three times in all Mardana laboured up the hill and back. On the third occasion the Guru struck the ground with his staff and a spring of water burst forth. Meantime, Baba Wali Kandhari discovered that he no longer had water in his well! He was so angry that he hurled a large boulder at the Guru and Mardana, and the Guru stretched out his hand and stopped it.

Until this day the boulder is marked with the Guru's handprint. The boulder and tank area have been enclosed so it is impossible to see how large the boulder is, but one can climb down into the water and examine the palm print. Be careful! Hold the handrail, for it is slippery under foot. The water gushes out with considerable force from under a stone. There are some huge fish swimming in the pool.

The other buildings in the complex are kitchens and hostels where pilgrims used to stay. Nowadays people come on the festival of *Baisakhi* on 13th April, and there are few other visitors. Some

lovely green parrots can be seen perched on the buildings and phone wires.

Baba Wali Kandhari's shrine is on the hilltop and it is possible to visit it. Adjacent to the *gurdwara* is a mosque where Baba Wali Kandhari is said to have fasted for 40 days. There is a Moghul tomb nearby which according to Jahangir was that of a courtier of Akbar's day. There are a couple of pools, one of which has more big fish, a kind of carp. These are believed to be mentioned by Jahangir in his *Tuzuk*. The emperor caught the fish and put gold rings or pearls in their mouths and let them go again.

Continuing through the gardens, there is a walled garden with the tomb of the mysterious Lala Rukh. Some say she was a Moghul princess.

Continuing up the GT Road, **Attock** is 100 kilometres from Pindi. The first interesting building in town is known as **Randhi Ka Muqbara**, the whore's tomb. It stands in the middle of the road. It is said that a Moghul Governor was well pleased with her singing and granted her wish that she should have a tomb by the wayside. (Whores in Asia were known for their cultural pursuits; they sang, danced and recited. Such occupations were not for respectable ladies.)

More spectacular is **Attock Fort** which sprawls across the hillside looking over the River Indus. The Indus here enters a gorge and continues through it for some miles down to Kalabagh. The Fort rises in steps reaching a great height above the river. The outer stone walls are nearly two kilometres in circumference. The Fort was built by Akbar in 1581 when he was having trouble with a rebellious brother who was holed up in Kabul. Attock superceded Rhotas. It was taken by Ranjit Singh and by the British. It was also the birthplace of Sir Anthony Eden.

Unfortunately it is not possible to visit the Fort or to photograph it as it is still in use by the Army, so it is considered a military installation. Nearby, the muddy brown waters of the Kabul River join the blue waters of the Indus. Attock used to be rich due to trade with Russia until the revolution.

Cycling home.

TAXILA

Thirty kilometres north-west of Rawalpindi out along the Grand Trunk Road lies Taxila, one of the most important archaeological sites in the whole of Asia. Its name is said to be derived from that of Taksha, Prince of the Serpent Tribe who, according to Puranic verse, was consecrated here. However, the origins of the site itself actually go back to the mesolithic age since which time there has been quite a remarkable continuity of settlement through to the Islamic era.

Taxila first rose to international fame as a major university town after Gandhara was brought under the control of the Persian Archemenian Empire in the 6th century B.C. Situated strategically on a branch of the Silk Road which linked China to the West, the city flourished both economically and culturally. Spurred on by the advent of Kushan rule, marked by the building of a new city, Taxila reached its greatest heights between the 1st and 5th centuries A.D. Backed by royal patronage, Buddhist monuments were erected throughout the Taxila Valley which was transformed into a religious heartland and a destination for pilgrims from as far afield as Central Asia and China. Undoubtedly badly shaken by the arrival of the Huns into the area in the mid-5th century A.D., the city finally plunged into decline when quarrels among the nobility undermined royal power in the 6th and 7th centuries. Nevertheless, the remains of three wonderful cities can still be visited today along with a multitude of Buddhist monasteries, stupas and temples.

The Bhir Mound: Local tradition asserts that the first city at Taxila is to be found just south of the modern museum on the Bhir Mound. In fact Archaeologists have located an earlier urban site nearby on the opposite side of the Tamra rivulet, which dates back to before 1,000 B.C. However, there is much more for the visitor to see at Bhir Mound.

Taxila landscape.

It is clear, even from a casual glance, that the settlement, which dates from the 6th century B.C., was never pre-planned as the later urban site of Sirkap was to be, but gradually evolved in response to the growing needs of an ever-increasing population. But even in this earliest of cities, there is evidence of considerable sophistication.

The eastern part of the site so far excavated appears to have been chiefly a residential area. It evolved as a series of squares, each one possibly the focus of a trade or profession, around which the domestic quarters were arranged. Stone foundations which remain embedded in the floors suggest that the houses originally had wooden pillars to support their roofs. Houses situated on busy crossroads often had their corners reinforced with stone pillars, presumably to protect them from potentially damaging knocks from passing traffic.

A number of smaller lanes appear to have been walled off, possibly to secure a greater degree of privacy. The citizens were well supplied with municipal rub-

bish pits along with both public and private soak pits for the disposal of sewage. While the wider streets ran from north to south, the lanes tended to run from east to west. One building in particular merits special mention. Made up of a series of rooms it is immediately noticeable because it appears semi-octagonal in plan and it assumes an air of extra importance as it is situated at the junction of two of the wider streets. It is just possible that this building was the administrative centre of early Taxila.

The western part of the site, by contrast, appears to have had ceremonial importance. Crucial to this interpretation is the so-called **Pillared Hall** or **Temple**, a rectangular building with three square pillars running down its middle. A veranda runs along its eastern side and adjacent to this is an open court, cobbled in the south-east corner, containing a platform for a bath and a drain. In the adjoining rooms to the north is a square tank and at least three pedestal bases. Perhaps most significantly of all, however, are the terracotta reliefs of male and female deities holding hands in and around the Pillared Hall which were intended as souvenirs for pilgrims. This evidence, taken together, has led to the remarkable suggestion that here on Bhir Mound may have been the earliest Hindu shrine yet discovered.

Sirkap: The city of **Sirkap**, or "Severed Head", chronologically the second major city of Taxila, is to be found spreading down the Hathial Spur and onto the plains of the Taxila Valley about 1.5 kilometres north-east of the museum. It is bound to the west by the Tamra rivulet and to the north and south by the Gau rivulet which today has been almost completely obliterated by a modern road and water channel.

The present layout of the city was established by the Bactrian Greeks sometime around 180 B.C. and takes the form of a wide and open grid system. A main street running north to south and a series of lanes running east to west and crossing at right angles divide the city into neat blocks.

In all, the archaeologists have recog-

A record of developments over the centuries.

nised seven major building phases at Sirkap, the earliest of which appears to have been pre-Bactrian and contemporary with the occupation of the Bhir Mound. These seven phases can be seen in section in the walls of a deep trench in the north-west corner of of the excavated site. Most of the visible standing remains today, although essentially following the Bactrian Greek plan, belong to the Parthian period and post-date a devastating earthquake which struck the area sometime during the first half of the 1st century A.D. They are built in a style of diaper masonry which replaced the rubble masonry used in the earlier periods.

The city is encompassed by an almighty wall over five kilometres long and up to six metres thick. Although fairly straight along its northern and eastern sides, it is particularly irregular to the west. There may well have been an entrance on all four sides originally, but today the only one evident is the northern wall and it is through here that today's visitors would normally enter

Bartering for Buddhas.

the city. The gateway itself consists of a hall, eight metres by 11 metres, and four guardrooms, two against the outer face of the city wall and two against the inner face. Although an underground drain ran out through the gateway, Sirkap is remarkable, as was the Bhir Mound settlement before it, for not having refuse drains or water wells. It must be assumed that the nearby rivulets were considered enough to carry out both functions.

The main north-south street was slightly but nonetheless deliberately misaligned with the gateway, but once the street is reached a clear view is afforded right down the full length of the city. Much of the main street may have been lined with shops. They were interspersed with stupas and fronted blocks of buildings which chiefly comprised of domestic quarters and areas of light industry.

Having passed blocks of rather poor quality housing both to the left and right built up against the city wall, the visitor encounters the first of the stupas on the

eastern side of the street. Although little more than a square base remains, it is typically located in an open courtyard which has rooms on four sides. The remains of three further votive stupas can be picked out in the courtyard. On the opposite side of the main street are a number of well-planned spacious houses behind which are a series of disorganised structures. They are thought to have been made up of a goldsmith's workshop largely on the evidence of 66 copper dies for the manufacture of ornaments which were discovered inside.

Three blocks further south, back on the eastern side of the main street, is the **Apsidal Temple**, perhaps the most impressive building to be seen at Sirkap. Its rectangular court, measuring 70 metres by 40 metres stands about 1.5 metres above the street level and is surrounded by an enclosure wall of diaper masonry almost two metres thick. It is approached from the main street by a double flight of steps on either side of which are small chambers, probably for temple guards. The temple itself, raised on a platform, consists of a porch, a nave and an apse and is encircled by an ambulatory passage. It therefore bears a striking resemblance to the **Chaitya** congregation halls of South India. The stupa is assumed to have stood in the apse, although regretfully it has been destroyed.

The importance of the Apsidal Temple is reinforced by its interruption of the grid layout of the city, for it extends into the space which by rights should have belonged to the residential block to the north. The houses within that block are consequently poorly aligned and give the impression of having been squashed into the remaining available space. One block still further south on the western side of the main street are the remains of the most unusual shrine. Again approached from the street by a double flight of steps, which can perhaps be taken to be a mark of some importance, its platform was reinforced internally by both cross and diagonal walls. Almost certainly not a The "Sun Temple".

stupa it has been suggested that this building may have been a **Sun Temple**.

Diagonally across the street is the remarkable **Shrine of the Double Headed Eagle**, enclosed within a quadrangle to which access is gained via a single flight of steps. Only the base of the stupa now remains but this is fascinating in itself for the array of artistic influences which it betrays. A series of pillasters are spaced around the base, a number of which are adorned with Corinthian capitals. Between the pillasters on the western face are six niches, three on either side of the central stairway which led up to the top of the stupa base. The two niches closest to the steps are decorated with Greek triangular pediments, while the two central niches display ogee arches as found at Ajanta, and the outside two show early Indian *toranas* or gates. Furthermore, above each of the ogee arches is perched a double-headed eagle, which have provided the shrine with its popular name, an emblem which was probably introduced by the Scythians. Immediately

south of the shrine is the probable accommodation of the monks, a huge house of 30 rooms built around six small courts.

Continuing southwards along the main street, passing another stupa in the next block on the right hand side and a number of blocks of domestic quarters of various standards, the visitor will arrive at a spacious block on the left hand side which contains the so-called **Palace**. Syrian Christian tradition asserts that St. Thomas, or Doubting Thomas, visited Sirkap and the court of the Parthian King Gondophares in about A.D. 40. If there is truth in this tradition and if this building is indeed a palace, then St. Thomas would almost certainly have stayed here. In some respects the building is certainly very impressive and fronts the main street for over 100 metres. However it is noticeably better built towards the south, where the walls are thicker and better planned. It is made up of a series of courts with living rooms built around in a way which basically reflects the pattern of the smaller do-

Shrine of the Double-Headed Eagle.

mestic quarters at Sirkap. The recent excavation of coin moulds from the poorly preserved building just to the south may give an indication to the presence of a mint. If so, the so-called palace may actually have been the administrative headquarters of Sirkap which otherwise has so far evaded the trowel of the archaeologists.

Continuing southwards along the main street, the remains of the **Kunala Monastery** and stupa are to be found at the top of the Hathial spur. A little beyond here, but also within the city walls, at the top of the next hill is the **Ghai Monastery**.

The Dharmarajika: No visit to Taxila would be complete without a visit to **Dharmarajika** for the **Great Stupa** is one of the largest and most impressive throughout Pakistan and is conveniently situated just two kilometres east of Bhir Mound and Sirkap. The original stupa here was reputedly built by the emperor Ashoka in the 3rd century B.C. to house the relics of the Buddha himself. But this is likely to have been destroyed in the earthquake of the 1st century. Its rubble probably underlies the present structure which was built and added to through a number of different periods up until the 4th or 5th centuries A.D. In the 19th century its relic chamber was broken into by robbers, the result of which is the large gash still seen in the stupa's west face.

The Great Stupa consists principally of a circular drum standing about 14 metres high which is reinforced by the construction of 16 walls radiating from its nucleus to its outside wall. In plan this gives the drum the appearance of the *Dharma-cakra* or the wheel of law. Four staircases situated at the four cardinal points provide access to the top of the stupa base. This whole structure is then encircled by a paved ambulatory passage.

Great importance was clearly attached to the Great Stupa, an impression reinforced by the host of smaller votive stupas, chapels and chambers which cluster around it, sometimes even crowding onto the ambulatory passage.

The Dharmarajika Stupa from a distance.

196

Built at various times from the 1st century B.C. to the post Kushan period, these structures display a wide range of designs. Quite probably they were donated by pilgrims and possibly represent various schools of Buddhism. A number of the votive stupas were found to have their relic chambers intact, from which were recovered some remarkable items including a gold casket which contained a ruby bead, coral, silver leaf and a tiny bone relic.

Amongst other important structures in the vicinity is a rectangular tank just north of the Great Stupa, reached from its northern side via a flight of steps. Although clearly intended to supply a source of water, its precise function is not clear and it was even filled in during the Kushan period to allow for the building of additional stupas.

To the west of the Great Stupa is an **Apsidal Temple** dating from the 1st century A.D., the octagonal shape of which was used to house an octagonal stupa. The original **Monastery** on this site was located towards the river, although it then shifted around to the northern side of the Great Stupa, beyond the complex of stupas and chapels. It was built in stages up to the 7th century around a series of quadrangles in which stupas were erected.

In the heyday of Dharmarajika the monks' quarters were spacious and even luxurious, but around the 5th century appear to have been destroyed by an enemy, possibly the Huns. The buildings which replaced them were significantly smaller and to judge by the extra thickness of the new walls, may even have been built with defence in mind. However, they too were later burnt and destroyed, probably in the 7th century. Ominously amongst the rubble, archaeologists discovered six graveless skeletons, some of which had even been decapitated.

Jaulian: About five kilometres east of Sirkap is found the Buddhist monastery of **Jaulian.** The visitor is more than recompensed for the journey out here. There are wonderful views of the Taxila Valley from the top of the spur on which

Jaulian Monastery.

the monastery stands, some 100 metres above the plain.

The complex itself has three principal components: the Lower Stupa Court, the Court of the Main Stupa and the Monastery. The entrance leads into the Lower Stupa Court, and by taking the five steps leading up to the south, the visitor arrives in the **Court of the Main Stupa**. Of the Main Stupa itself, only the circular base of the drum, set in a square plinth, and the flight of steps which provided access to the top of the base from the north, have survived. Very little is known about the stupa's original size and form. However, still around its base are a series of plaster reliefs of large seated Buddhas in the pose of meditation dated to the 5th century A.D. They are separated by pilasters which themselves incorporate smaller images of the Buddha.

On the eastern side of the steps is a further seated Buddha known as the **Healing Buddha**. It is said that sick pilgrims used to insert their fingers into the hole at his navel in the hope of being cured of their ailments. On the pedestal immediately below is a Kharasthi inscription naming the donor monk as Buddhamitra Dharmanandin.

Around the Main Stupa are 21 smaller stupas all set on square plinths, the bases of which are beautifully decorated with stuco reliefs, generally arranged in three tiers. In the lowest tiers frequently appear lions alternating with A*tlantes*, whilst in the upper two tiers are Buddhas and Bodhisattvas. These figures are often within niches framed by Corinthian pilasters in the lower two tiers and *Persepolitan* pilasters in the upper tiers. On a number of the bases can be traced the names of certain bene-factors written in Kharasthi, indicating that this script continued to be used right up to the 5th century.

Lining the walls of the Court of the Main Stupa are 28 chapels which probably had wooden roofs. They originally contained stories from the life of the Buddha or Bodhisattvas in scenic relief, usually in clay.

Passing back to the **Lower Stupa**

Buddhist reliefs at Jaulian.

Court which contains a number of stupas and chapels showing the same characteristics as those just described in the Court of the Main Stupa, further steps lead through the eastern wall towards the **Monastery** itself. Here, a large open courtyard is surrounded by 28 monks'cells which vary in size and only some of which have windows.

Their floors are made of packed stones and mud and their walls were originally plastered and possibly painted. One of the cells along the northern side was converted into a chapel and from another is a stone stair-case which led up to a second storey. In front of some of the cells, sculptures stood in alcoves, some of which are still to be seen, notably immediately to the south of the entrance into the monas-tery. Here a headless Standing Buddha is surrounded by 12 figures amongst whom is a man wearing a pointed cap and typical Central Asian clothes.

It is clear that the stupa courts and monastery chapels were once provided with statues and ornamentation. Indeed taken along with the bathroom in the corner of the Monastery courtyard, and the Assembly Hall, kitchen, refectory, scullery and latrine built immediately behind the eastern cells, it appears that Jaulian catered well for monks and pil-grims alike.

Further sites: In addition to these sites, there is still much more for the visitor to see at Taxila. Just 2.5 kilometres north-east of Sirkap is the third city of Taxila, **Sirsukh**, which is believed to belong to the Kushan period. Though still largely unexcavated it is apparent that, like Sirkap before it, it was built as a forti-fied settlement.

To the north of Sirkap are four temples, all standing on earlier mounds and overlooking the city. They are all in the style of Greek temples. The best to visit is probably the one at **Jandial**, 1.5 kilometres north of Sirkap. Instead of the rows of columns which might have been expected to surround the building there is a continuous wall punctuated only by windows. Otherwise this temple could almost have been lifted straight from the Aegean.

There are also several more Buddhist monasteries which are worth a visit. Just to the south-east of Dharmarajika are arranged four monasteries as if they are on the four corners of a square. They belong to the early Kushan period and may have been built to cope with the needs of a rising population of monks at this time.

In the cases of three of these monas-teries the main stupas are outside the court containing the monks'cells and only in the later fourth case was the stupa built within the court. This com-plex has therefore been important in understanding the evolution of the monastic pattern in Gandhara.

Of all the remaining sites and monu-ments which cannot now be discussed, mention must at least be made of **Kal-wan**, the largest Buddhist settlement at Taxila. Found about two kilometres south-west of Dharmarajika, it is a remarkable complex of monasteries, stupas, chapels and shrines. Kalwan had a long history and continued to grow well beyond the Kushan period.

The Buddha in meditation.

THE GT ROAD TO LAHORE

The Potohar plateau: Taking the GT Road from Rawalpindi in the direction of Lahore, the traveller realises that the the landscape resembles the fantastic scenery of a science fiction film. This strange planet scenery is the **Potohar Plateau**, a fantasy in improbable colours. Stones, rocks, boulders, ravines. In certain places not much grows apart from Acacia bushes. Hungry vultures settle in flocks if an animal gets injured on the roadside. Wherever there is a possible space though, the land is used for cultivation with little fields of wheat or spinach among the huge boulders.

The plateau is indeed very old with signs of early man and many fossil remains.

There are many small towns and ancient settlements along the road. At **Riwat**, which is on the GT Road 15 kilometres south of Pindi, there is an early 16th century fort. It was built by a tribe called the Ghakkars as a defence against the Moghul emperor Sher Shah. With walls 10 metres high, it is tiny compared to Sher Shah's giant Rohtas Fort. Inside the fort are a mosque and a mausoleum. There is a grave in the centre which contains the remains of Sarang Khan who was flayed alive by Sher Shah's generals. His daughter was forcibly married to one of them. Sarang Khan lost 16 sons in the wars but a couple more were still left to carry on the line. There is a curious rocky outcrop beside the fort and it is possible to climb onto the walls and the rocks. Friendly local children will accompany every move.

Past Riwat is the Buddhist site of **Mankiala**. There is a legend that the Buddha offered his body to hungry tigers and the remains mark one of the four great stupas of North West India which commemorated the event. Another legend is that Alexander's horse Bucephalus died there.

The town of **Dina** is more or less par for the kind of settlement found along

Resting at a wayside *dabba* **(truckstop).**

the GT Road. Congested and cluttered – a lot of traffic, buses, cars and trucks, camels and donkeys, pools of stagnant water, litter, bits of vehicles, general pandemonium, hawkers and an abundance of people. Dina serves as an important crossroads. There is a turning on the right side of the road which leads to **Rohtas**. The turning on the left leads to **Mirpur**, Mangla and the dam.

The Mirpur area is not very exciting for the visitor, though it is the home of many of the migrants who live in the Northern English town of Bradford. The **Mangla Dam** is about 15 kilometres east of Dina. One of the largest earthfilled dams in the world, it is situated on the River Jhelum. It is one of the results of the Indus Basin Treaty drawn up between India and Pakistan in 1959 to secure Pakistan's irrigation rights to rivers having their source in Indian territory. The dam is covered with the most enormous pebbles.

The road to Rohtas is rather narrow to begin with and threads between little shops and graveyards where mangy, dozy bitches suckle their pups. The road has far too many speedbreakers (sleeping policemen). Rapidly the road peters out altogether leaving one in the dried up bed of the River Kahan. (At least it is to be hoped that it is dried up!) The river bed is no problem for a vehicle like a landrover. Cars may be driven as far as possible, then park and walk. Sometimes it is possible to get a lift. People are very kind.

Proceed with caution across the river. The **Fort of Rohtas** is enormous, but invisible! Suddenly it can be made out, brooding and sinister and with massive walls. The fort now appears to be in the wilds of nowhere, but at the time it was built it was an important site. It was built by Sher Shah Suri who ruled from 1539 to 1545 and guarded the main north south route at the end of the Salt Range, on the original part of the GT Road which Sher Shah built. The Fort was named after the famous victory he achieved at Rohtas in Bengal. It was built as a defence against Humayun and against the Ghakkar tribe, but was

Rhotas Fort.

quickly rendered superfluous to the defence requirements of the Moghul Empire. Ten years after Sher Shah's short reign, in which so much was achieved, his successors had proved incompetent and Humayun returned. Rohtas never saw action; the commander surrendered. Humayun lived less than seven months, falling down the stairs of a building in Delhi also built by the industrious Sher Shah. Akbar came to the throne and his frontier post was Attock. Jahangir admired the strategic location of Rohtas. The GT Road has since been moved.

The wall of the Fort is about five kilometres in circumference. The gate which was clearly the place for triumphal entries is the Sohail Gate, which is large and richly decorated. By walking along the wall from the gate it is possible to reach a tower where there is a strange block and a hole. It has been said that this was the place of execution and the victim was thrown down the hole.

Some ruins remain of a palace constructed by Raja Man Singh – one pavilion approached by a steep flight of steps with no handrail. There is a great deal about the ruins in Rohtas which is bad news for people with vertigo. There are a couple of wells, one with a flight of steps descending into darkness.

There is a modern village inside the middle of the Fort.

The Salt Range: On the very southern brink of the Potohar Plateau and to the immediate west of Jhelum, a welcome break is made by the gaunt outlines of the Salt Range. There are two lines of hills and they run in a westerly direction towards the towns of **Mianwali** and **Kalabagh**.

The Salt Range is an interesting area for the geologist, recording 600 million years of the earth's evolution. The region is known as the "Museum of Geology". The terracotta hills, the strange rocks in colours of grey, green and brown, and the salt lakes as the road winds along make it a most extraordinary place. The Salt Range is trekking country, and the southern escarpment where the hills fall steeply to the **The ruins at Ketas.**

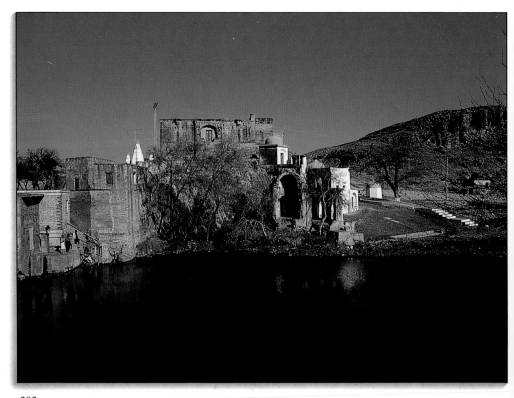

Panjab plain is most dramatic. The Salt Range is mentioned in the Hindu epic, the *Mahabharata*, as the location of the people in exile. These mountains were the high home of the yogis.

The Salt Range gets its name from the locally occuring salt and at **Khewra** is one of the world's biggest salt mines. It is possible that salt was mined before the Moghuls. Certainly it was mined by them and by the British after 1850. It is possible to visit the mine.

The eastern extremity of the Salt Range is reached through Rohtas Fort along a track which winds ever upwards via a series of very sharp hairpin bends. It is not a route for anything except for sturdy vehicles. It is steep, rocky and difficult, but on a clear day there is a spectacular view down onto the plains. The track leads to the top of **Yogi Tilla**, nearly 1,000 metres in height. There is an army firing range and a urial breeding project on the mountain.

At the summit are the remains of a very famous yogi centre. It was the centre of *Kanphat* (split ear) yogis who were associated with Gorakh Nath, a Guru about whom little can be said with certainty except that he lived between the 9th and the 12th centuries. The yogis used to sport large earrings.

There are pools, one with two towers crowned with *chattris*, and considerable areas of building, most of which are not in very good repair. Some have paintings on the walls. The PTDC are constructing a restaurant and doing some restoration and preservation. It is not much visited, has a tranquil atmosphere, and is dramatic indeed in a storm.

Tilla is often mentioned in folklore. Puran Bhagat, Ranjha and most heroes are supposed to have gone to Yogi Tilla and there is also an extraordinary tale about an elephant running up the hill to tell the king to desist from opposing Alexander the Great. The elephant is said to have spoken in human speech. It is not recorded how long it took the animal to run up, nor what the king was doing on the peak. A likely tale. But then if an elephant could make it all the way up Yogi Tilla, who knows what it might not have said?

Kanphat yogis lived in the Salt Range.

There are some other quite lovely spots which can be reached by turning off the GT Road at **Mandra** towards **Chakwal**. Drive with care, the road has a tendency to take a sudden sharp turn across the railway line. The landscape is rather flat and featureless for miles, until the craggy outlines of the Salt Range become clear.

Choa Saidan Shah (the spring of Saidan Shah) is held to be a beauty spot. It is rather a lively little place with a lot of hustle and bustle. Saidan Shah was a local holy man and his shrine is here. The town is noted for perfume distilled from roses. There are orchards and loquats grow. Nearby are a number of ancient Hindu sites. These include Malot, Shiv Ganga and Ketas.

Ketas is an extensive and fascinating site, situated beside a pool which was held to be bottomless. The pool was said to have been formed from a tear which fell from the eye of the Hindu God Siva who was desolate at the death of his beautiful wife Sati. *"Ketas"* is said to have meant "weeping eyes".

Ketas is also traditionally associated with the Kaurava and Pandavas of the *Mahabharata*. It was a Buddhist site associated with Ashoka and there was a palace of Raja Hari Singh of Kashmir. Now, just about all of the buildings are ruins, apart from the odd ones in which people have made their homes.

The ruins are enormously interesting to explore. It is possible to get inside the old temples and climb up on the roof from where there is a good view of the whole site. It is weird inside. Some decorations and carvings remain here and there; plastered and painted surfaces remain to tell how stunning the place must once have been.

Ketas is beside the road, so there is easy access. There are other temples at **Malot** where it is possible to climb onto a spur of the Salt Range where there are the remains of a fort and temple, and five kilometres north east is **Shiv Ganga** where there is a Kashmiri style temple. Some Buddhist period finds from this area are in Lahore Museum.

Kallar Kahar is on the way from **Chakwal** to **Khushab**. The place is described in the *Baburnama*. Babur says that he stopped amongst the "fields of densely growing corn". He described the Kallar Kahar as "a level land shut in among the Jud mountains. In the middle of it is a lake some six miles round, the ingatherings of rains from all sides." Babur found a spring and had a garden made there. The spring of warm water is still there. Of Babur's garden there is no sign, though there are many orchards on that site. There is a stone which is said to be Babur's throne and the shrine of Abdul Qadir Jilani is nearby, with its silvery dome. Among the wealth of birdlife locally, there are many peacocks which thrive due to the local belief that anyone harming them would go blind.

The lake is salty. According to legend, the water was once sweet. One day Baba Farid ud din Ganj-i-Shakar of Pakpattan passed by and asked the local women for a drink. The women said that the water was salty. "If you say so, so be it!" replied the saint and went away. And ever since the water has been salty.

An abandoned Hindu Temple.

204

Endless plains: The town of **Jhelum** is 110 kilometres from Pindi. It is held to be of great antiquity and mentioned in the *Mahabharata*. There was a fort in the Sikh period, in Andarkot. The town flourished under the British as a military encampment and the military are still there. There is an improbably English looking (Anglo Gothic) church which appears like a mirage alongside the river. Can it be real? It is! It has been there since 1857.

Jhelum is a natural border, for a radical change takes place in the landscape. The Potohar plateau comes to an end and the traveller arrives on the plains of the Panjab which stretch away to the south, beyond the Sutlej, down into India. Each to his own – those who appreciate wide open spaces may find the plain to their taste. It lies flatter than the proverbial pancake with a monotonous, ruler-straight, empty horizon.

Where the land is irrigated, there are rich fields. Where there is no water, the land is hostile, covered with spiky acacia bushes. Visually the landscape is not particularly interesting. But this plain was the backdrop to Moghul splendour; the heartland of the Sikhs; and more recently, the setting against which the British chose to act out their favourite fantasies.

In South Asia the village is important as most people live in the countryside. Now the village is changing; while at one time people lived behind thick mud walls used for defence, increasing wealth has resulted in the construction of fine new buildings; new homes. No more mud, only solid brick is good enough for the Panjabis of today.

The houses are two storeys high and the walls are adorned with fancy brickwork and inscriptions which announce who lives inside. Every village has a mosque and in many places there is also a shrine, where people recall some holy man, and perhaps even quote some of his poetry. The locals gather to exchange gossip at a tea stall. There may be a pond, reflecting an abandoned Hindu temple. There are plenty of trees around the village. It was policy from medieval times to plant trees to shade

roads, so they shade a narrow country road, where the cyclists ride onto the dusty shoulder to allow cars to pass. Often three huge banyans might shade a roadside pool.

Elsewhere the countryside is dotted with isolated, stunted trees. In some places there is a passing railway with a train so slow that passing cars inevitably race it and win. And nowadays lest this sounds too much of a rural idyll, there are increasing signs of industry – an unexpected factory is just as likely to pop up as an ancient shrine.

Further down the GT Road, **Gujrat** is 50 kilometres from the town of Jhelum. Indeed, there are tales about the remote past of the city, which is thought to have been founded by a daughter-in-law of Raja Rassalu (see Sialkot on the following page).

Like most towns in the area it has been ruined and rebuilt several times over. In Akbar's day it was called Akbarabad, and was garrisoned by Gujjar tribesmen. It was the scene of the final battle in the Sikh wars when the British under Lord Gough triumphed on 22nd February 1849 and thereafter annexed the Panjab. In the centre of the town there is an old fort and bath house of Akbar's period.

Gujrat is notable for ceramics, which brings to mind the fact that the town was the setting of the famous Panjabi romance, Sohni and Mahival.

Sohni was a potter's daughter who used to swim across the river to meet her lover, Mahival. She used a pot as a buoyancy aid. One night her sister-in-law swapped it for an unbaked pot which dissolved. Mahival, hearing Sohni's cries flung himself into the water but was too slow to be able to save her. Unable to face the prospect of life without her, he let himself go and joined her in death.

Just south of Gujrat, **Wazirabad** rose in importance as a railway junction, though there was an earlier settlement which was called after Shah Jahan's Prime Minister, Wazir Khan. He is mainly remembered as the builder of the Wazir Khan Masjid in Lahore. The town was rebuilt by General Avitabile, one of Ranjit Singh's many European officers. Avitabile was an Italian, a Governor of Wazirabad and later Peshawar (where for his first few days he hanged 50 brigands per day, before breakfast!). Avitabile's Wazirabad residence is still standing and is occupied.

Nearby, there is an impressive railway bridge across the Chenab, which was opened in 1876 by the Prince of Wales (Edward VII). It was then one of the longest bridges in the world.

Rasul Nagar was a favourite resort for Maharaja Ranjit Singh who built a *baradari* (pavilion) and garden beside the river. In Sikh times, it was called Ram Nagar, Ram being a name for God. God's City. Now it is Rasul Nagar, the messenger, the Prophet's city. It has reverted to its earlier name. The famous cannon Kim's Gun, the Zam-zama, which can now be seen in Lahore, was once captured nearby.

Sialkot lies east of Wazirabad, near the Indian border. It has the usual semi-mythical history going back to the *Mahabharata* where it is supposed to be the residence of one of the uncles of the Pandavas.

But the area is mainly associated with the folklore cycle concerning Raja Salvahan and his sons Puran Bhagat and Raja Rassalu. These folk tales were retold by folk singers and poets, by villagers, and in more recent times by R.C. Temple, Flora Annie Steel and other collectors of folk tales. The Temple collection can be purchased from Lok Virsa in Islamabad.

There is a fort reputed to go back to the time of Raja Salvahan, whose eldest son Puran Bhagat was thrown into a well by his wicked stepmother. The well in question is called Puran well and it is on the road which goes to Pasrur. It was said that bathing in the water aided childbirth. The area was ruled by Raja Rassalu but then cursed by Puran Bhagat and deserted for centuries.

The town was occupied by various waves of conquering armies including Timur and Babur and there was an upset in 1857 when the British were forced to seek refuge in the fort. The building was

Sohni swims to Mahival.

partially dismantled in 1866. Allama Iqbal, the great hero and poet of Pakistan, was born in Sialkot and the house where he was born and lived as a child is a great attraction.

Modern Sialkot is a major producer of sports gear and many of the tennis rackets and cricket bats available in western shops come from Sialkot – as does a great amount of other high class, branded sports equipment. In Moghul times, the area was famous for the production of swords and daggers, for which there has been a gradual slump in demand. The craftsmen have cleverly adapted their skills to produce surgical instruments and cutlery. There are also manufacturers of musical instruments in Sialkot.

Continuing on the GT Road **Gujranwala** is 70 kilometres from the provincial capital of Lahore. Gujranwala lies in very fertile farmlands, especially famous for growing blood oranges. In common with other local towns the name bears witness to importance of the tribe of Gujjars.

In medieval times, the principal city in these parts was situated near the small town of **Eminabad**. Friendly villagers claim that the town was called after a lady, Emina, who founded the place. They also point out what they say is Emina's tomb, a tumbledown structure with snakes snoozing in the brickwork.

Nowadays, there is evidence on the ground that there was an enormous inhabited area locally, though it would be accessible only to an archaeologist. Nothing remains standing.

Gujranwala took over from Eminabad and prospered during the Sikh period. It was the home of Maharaja Ranjit Singh's father, Mahan Singh. Ranjit Singh was born here and it was his headquarters before he took Lahore. Their ashes are contained in a mausoleum in the old part of the city.

Gujranwala has expanded in modern times. It is a busy, bustling town on the GT Road, and has an enormous amount of industry manufacturing rubber, soap, and plastics. There are steel works and foundries and engineering works.

A trap for fish in the canals.

LAHORE

Lahore has a friendly, relaxed atmosphere. It is a fine place to watch the world rush by. The improbable mix of painted trucks, cars, bullock carts, buses, handcarts, scooters with whole families aboard – mum riding side saddle at the back, holding a baby, a toddler standing in front of dad, holding on to the steering, and possibly more children too, lodged precariously, hanging on for dear life. Motor bikes carry at least three youths, sharp dressers – skinny knees sticking out in a row.

There are *tongas*, scooter rickshaws with engines pop-popping madly as they weave perilously through the other traffic. There are women in *purdah* and women not in *purdah* carrying enormous bundles on their heads. The bullock carts are often loaded, overloaded, with metal. Heavy industry seems to use primitive transport.

Lahore is undoubtedly ancient. Legend had it that it was founded by Loh, son of Rama, the hero of the Hindu epic, the Ramayana. Some others think that the name means Loh-awar, meaning a "Fort as strong as Iron". It waxed and waned in importance during the Sultanate, as at times Dipalpur and Multan were more important. But Muslim rule began here when Qutub ud din Aibak was crowned in Lahore in 1206 and thus became the first Muslim Sultan of the subcontinent.

But the real flowering of Lahore was during the Moghul period. It was Akbar's capital from 1584 to 1598. Jahangir loved the town and he and his wife Nur Jahan are buried at Shahdara. Shah Jahan was born in Lahore and added buildings and even Aurangzeb, not noted for fine buildings, gave the town the Badshahi Masjid and the Alamgiri gateway to the fort.

During the eighteenth century, as Moghul power dwindled, there were constant invasions. Lahore was a *suba* – a province of the Empire. There were *subadars*, provincial rulers with their own court. These Governors managed

as best they could, though for much of the time it must have been a rather thankless task to even attempt. The 1740s were years of chaos, and between 1745 and 1756 there were nine changes of Governor. Invasions and chaos in local government allowed bands of warring Sikhs to gain control in some areas. Lahore ended up being ruled by a triumvirate of Sikhs of loose character and the population of the city invited Ranjit Singh to invade. He took the city in 1799. Holding the capital gave him some legitimacy; he became Emperor.

The Sikh period was bad news for the protection of ancient buildings. Some survived, misused and knocked about a bit, and a few new ones were added. Nevertheless, descriptions of Lahore during the early 19th century refer to it as a "melancholy picture of fallen splendour". Henry Fane mentions marching ten miles "chiefly through the ruins of the ancient capital". The Sikhs carted off large large amounts of material from Moghul buildings to use in decorating Amritsar. The British added

Left, Lahore street scene. Right, full moon over minaret of the Badshahi Mosque.

a great many buildings, plenty of "Moghul Gothic", as well as some shady bungalows and gardens. Early on, the British tended to build workaday structures in sites like the Fort, though later they did start to make an effort to preserve some ancient buildings.

The Moghul City: Lahore was a city with twelve gates and although most of the wall has now gone, some gates still stand. The largest and easiest building to start with is the Fort. **Lahore Fort** illustrates the full history of Moghul architecture.

The earliest parts associated with Akbar are the sandstone balcony and marble pavilion in the **Diwan-i-Am** (Hall of Public Audience). The balcony is the one on which the emperor appeared every morning to show himself to his subjects, some of whom would attend daily. The sandstone brackets, showing Hindu influence, are typical of Akbar's time. Behind the balcony is Akbar's **Diwan-i-Khas** (Court of Private Audience), which was built in 1566. There are still traces of painted

and gilded stucco work. The marble work is the oldest in Lahore. To the east, the **Masti Gate** with heavy bastions and battlements dates from the same reign. To the north of the **Diwan-i-Am** is Jahangir's quadrangle, begun by Akbar and finished by Jahangir.

Buildings from Jahangir's time include his "House of Dreams" – the **Khwabgarh-i-Jahangir** on the north side. Now it houses a museum with coins and miniatures.

Jahangir's bath house was called the **Ghusalkhana**. "Ghusalkhana" was the name of the Moghul "cabinet", for the chief ministers and courtiers used to attend upon the Emperor and conduct business in the bath house. Only the very highest in the land were admitted!

Shah Jahan was the builder. One of the most superb examples of his period is the **Shish Mahal** (Palace of Mirrors), which was built as a home for the Empress. The mirrors are arranged in beautiful mosaics. The building also contains examples of gilt work and *pietra dura* – inlaid floral patterns in

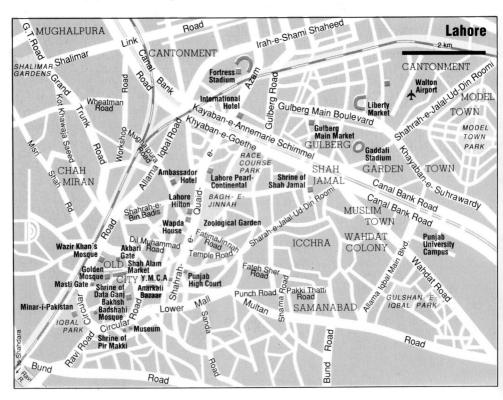

semi precious stone set in a marble background. In addition there are wonderful *jalis* – the marble screens which cover the windows.

The **Naulakha** is another striking building. It is a pavilion with a curvilinear roof in the Shish Mahal Court. It is also wonderfully ornamented with *pietra dura*. Another elegant and graceful building is the **Moti Masjid** built in 1645. It is called *Moti* – the Pearl Mosque – because of the glowing white marble of which it is constructed.

Lahore is unusual in that there are buildings dating from Aurangzeb's reign. The **Alamgiri Gate** built by Aurangzeb in 1673 is massive, with high semi-circular bastions. These are improbably based in lotus petals and crowned with little *chuttris*.

The wall beside the **Shah Burj Gate** of the Fort is covered with lively tile mosaics. Patterns are interspersed with pictures illustrating court life. There are scenes of elephants, camel and bull fights, polo players and blue dragons.

Another building by Aurangzeb

stands opposite; the **Badshahi Masjid**, which has an imposing gateway. This leads into a massive courtyard on the opposite side of which are the three great marble domes, and beneath them the principle hall. At each corner are towering minarets of red sandstone. It is undoubtedly one of the splendours of Lahore.

Most visitors will want to visit the **Shalimar Gardens**, which are situated to the east of the city, five kilometres towards the Indian border. Laid out by Shah Jahan in 1642, the gardens consist of three terraces, lakes, waterfalls, and more than 400 fountains. There are also huge fruit trees and little chipmunks scamper about. The gardens were used as a palace and, as the court was often in residence for weeks at a stretch, there are buildings to accomodate the Emperor and his family.

Wazir Khan's Mosque was built by the Governor of the area during the reign of Shah Jahan, whose title was Nawab Wazir Khan. The Mosque dates from 1634 and is justifiably famous for

In the courtyard of the Badshahi Mosque, Lahore.

BACKSTREET MARKETS

Anarkali Market: The most famous bazaar in Lahore is Anarkali – a maze of lanes and alleys which stretch northwards from the Mall at the Central Museum end. Anarkali has atypical, rather wide alleys, capable of taking a row of parked bikes and motor bikes, and heaps of *gandagi* (rubbish) and still leaving room for other bikes, scooters, rickshaws, cars, bullock carts and pedestrians. Sometimes a man scatters water to lay the dust.

The shops are an odd mixture of east and

Bazaar offers a whole bazaar full of bookshops and stationers.

Anarkali is convenient for visitors to go shopping. No one is likely to get impossibly lost and it does contain a range of shops to supply most requirements. And the shopkeepers are mostly patient and very kind.

Old City bazaars: The bazaars in the old city are the ones people dream about – tiny alleys, some of which will admit a rickshaw, a string of donkeys or carts – and pedestrians have to leap into doorways to give room. Some al-

west. Some are organised with fronts and windows and are recognisable shops. The Bata shoe shop is no different from a shoe shop anywhere else. There may be a chemist which is also recognisable, but interspersed with these are colourful bangle sellers and alleys of stalls offering dupattas in all the colours of the rainbow. A man may be embroidering a dupatta in makash, silver patterns. He will sell it to you right away, and an absolute bargain it is, too.

The bookshop is recognisable as such, but covered in earnest slogans, exhorting self-improvement and erudition in a way no longer fashionable elsewhere. Actually, Urdu

leys are only possible single file.

The Shahi Mohalla, behind the Fort is the Tart's Quarter and contains the places where gentlemen can see dancing girls. In this area are some splendid embroiderers. The alleys give access to tiny booths which have a counter and a bench for potential customers to perch on. If one shows interest, the proprietor sends for tea, immediately. Over tea, he displays his wares, producing suit after suit, piece after piece, lengths of rich cloth, satins and silks, velvets and chiffons – embroidered in various styles and colours. Enough to bring out the sybarite in a puritan!

Fashions are discussed: Perhaps madam

would like silver thread on black velvet? flowers? or geometrical designs? what kind of neckline? And on the sleeves? These purchases take all day, the shopkeeper noting the details in his book. And the cost, for what is no mere dress, but rather, a work of art, is moderate. It is possible to buy ready made too. In fact, orders may take too long to be feasible for passing travellers. Similarly, one can spend an age at the goldsmith.

What more could anyone want? Spices, vegetables, books, gold and silver, brass, jewellery, junk jewellery, antiques, carpets, kitchenware, brooms and buckets, feather dusters, shoes, pots and pans, garlands of money (for weddings or as presents to

material. There are cages of smelly chickens. Sellers of make up, *kajaal* (eyeblack) and *Swiss Miss* lipsticks and nail polishes. Pictures of Imran Khan and other idols. Oranges, juice sellers, chunks of sugar cane piled in fancy shapes, cane juice, parched grain, sheep's head, and meat buzzing with flies whilst a man hacks with a large cleaver. A man produces a basket of scorpions or a snake; their venom is used for making "Sunday oil", an aphrodisiac.

Washing lines dangle, odd spaces are occupied by a cud chewing buffalo or a few goats. There are sellers of tobacco, stalls where parts of the hubble bubble hukkas dangle. There are so many cloth sellers,

whores), garlands of flowers for shrines, blacksmiths and locksmiths, carpenters and furniture vendors, tea shops, snacks and food vendors, milk shops with huge vats of milk, South Asian fast-food, and piled displays of those highly coloured, rather substantial sweets. There are assorted quacks – *hakims* and vaids, and specialists of all kinds, to give one a beautiful complexion or sort out sexual disfunction or minor aches and pains. There are tooth pullers and streetside dentists, false teeth makers with alarming advertising

Far left, relaxing with a pipe. **Left**, shave without the frills. **Above**, garlands for many occasions.

selling cloth for *salwar kameez*, for what you will. The vendor will pull down and throw open so many bales with a careless gesture. It is hard not to make a purchase when the man has displayed half the goods in the shop – pressure salesmanship! There are sellers of suitcases and bags, travel agents. Cats and dogs dine under stallfronts under stollen discarded offal. Kite-flying kids stand on top of the houses and every year on kite flying day they put powdered glass on their kite strings to cut those of their rivals. The streets below are thronging with people, many of whom are kind and friendly and enjoy stopping to chat with a stranger from another land.

the colourful fresco and tile decorations which adorn both interior and exterior of the building.

Anarkali, meaning "pomegranate blossom", is best commemorated by the lively and bustling market which bears her name. And it is appropriate that she should have such a memorial. But there is also a tomb which is associated with her. The story is told that one day Akbar, in the reflection of a mirror, saw her exchange a secret smile with Jahangir. He had poor Anarkali walled up alive. The tomb was later inscribed by Jahangir "Ah! Could I behold the face of my beloved once more, I would give thanks to my God until the day of resurrection."

The building was subsequently used by the British as a Protestant church, St James's Church, Anarkali!

The other spectacular Moghul site is **Shahdara**, just across the River Ravi. There are three mausoleums, those of Jahangir, his wife Nur Jahan and her brother Asif Khan, who was the father of Mumtaz, the lady of the Taj Mahal at Agra. Asif Khan's tomb has retained little of the splendour that there must have been at one time. **Jahangir's Tomb** is magnificent and decorated with *pietra dura*. The 99 names of God are inlaid in black on the marble and there are beautiful *jalis* which admit patterns of light. Jahangir's tomb was built by his son, Shah Jahan.

Jahangir's wife Nur Jahan was a power in the court and apparently much loved. It is said that when Jahangir was a young man, he handed the lady two of the royal pigeons to hold. While pigeon flying may not be a cult in many countries, it is a sport enjoyed by the gentle folk of the subcontinent. When Jahangir returned for his birds, one had flown. He was surprised. "But how did it fly?" he asked. "Like this!" She laughed and let go the second bird. They say that from then on he was enchanted.

Nur Jahan's Tomb was stripped down to the bricks by the Sikhs, but it has been restored this century. In buildings of this sort, the grave is underneath the mausoleum, in the cellar.

If friends in the city have a say in the matter, no visitor will leave Lahore without visiting the shrine of at least one of the major local saints. The three most important from amongst a galaxy are: **Data Ganj Bakshs**, **Madho Lal Husain** and **Mian Mir**.

Ali Makdum Al Hujwiri was an intellectual. He came to Lahore with Masud, son of Mahmud of Ghazni, and died in A.D. 1072. He was called *Data Ganj Bakshs* (the bestower of treasure) because Khwaja Muin ud din Chishti, Saint of Ajmer, meditated for 40 days at the tomb and then enunciated a verse, which translated means "The bestower of treasure in both worlds, reflector of the splendour of God. An accomplished spiritual guide for the learned and a guide for the ignorant."

And many people have gone there in the hope of the treasure of both worlds. It is said, "he who calls at your shrine never goes away disappointed."

Five kilometres east of Lahore is the **Shrine of Mian Mir**, who died in 1635. He is considered to have lived to an old age by holding his breath. It is said that he inhaled only once or twice a night

The tomb of Jahangir from the outside...

and as he got older, the rate rose to four times. The tomb was built by Dara Shikoh, who was devoted to Mian Mir. But Dara Shikoh was murdered by his brother, Aurangzeb, when the job was only half done. Aurangzeb took the material from the tomb and built the Badshahi Masjid.

The story of Madho Lal Husain is unusual. Husain was a Sufi, who having studied hard, thought that he had found the secret of God. It is said that he threw a Koran down a well. When people were angry at this heresy, he called the Koran which returned to his hand, dry. Husain took to singing, dancing and drinking.

He wore red clothes and was called Lal Husain – *Lal* meaning red. When he preached, a Brahmin boy, a Hindu called Madho, came from Shahdara to hear him and an attachment developed between the two.

Madho's kinfolk tried to stop the relationship. Apparently, seeing them sleeping together they wanted to kill them, but due to Husain's powers they couldn't find the door to the room. At one point, Husain went to get Madho and found people lamenting. Madho lay dead. "Why do you lie there?"he cried, and Madho jumped up and left the house with him. Never to return.

Husain is said to have been a drinker and died relatively young. First he was buried at Shahdara, but then the river overflowed and Madho had the corpse reburied at Baghbanpura near the Shalimar Gardens, and was himself buried beside his lover.

Chiragh Mela, the festival of lamps, is held at this shrine on the last day of March each year. Pilgrims light thousands of lamps and spend the night at the shrine. There is also a fair.

The Sikh Period: In front of the Alamgiri Gate is a garden, the **Hazuri Bagh**. The little *baradari* (pavilion) in the middle was constructed by Maharaja Ranjit Singh, who plundered the material from the tomb of Zeb-un-Nisa, the learned and charming poetess daughter of Aurangzeb. She used the pen name "*Mukhfi*" meaning the concealed one. Poets use pleasing pseudo-

...and the splendour of Moghul art inside the building.

nyms in Asia. The *baradari* used to have another storey, but it was struck by lightning.

There were a few additions made to the fort during the Sikh period, such as the massive outside wall. There is also a museum in Rani Jindan's quarters, which houses the Princess Bamba collection. Princess Bamba Sutherland was the last surviving grandchild of Ranjit Singh and her collection included some of his possessions including his umbrella and a collection of horse trappings.

There are some massive paintings of the court of Lahore at the time of Ranjit Singh, by August Theodor Shoefft, as well as pictures of members of the family. The most singular exhibit is a large silver model showing the Maharaja riding in state upon an elephant. The plinth is decorated with hunting scene and a scene outside Lahore Fort with Europeans, Sikhs and soldiers.

Close to the fort is a Sikh complex containing **Dera Sahib Gurdwara**, the **Sikh Temple** with the golden dome. It is on the site where Sikh tradition has it that the Fifth Guru, who had been tortured, slipped into the River Ravi and disappeared. Nearby is the *Samadhi* (cremation site) of Ranjit Singh, marked by a lotus. Surrounding lotuses commemorate the 4 wives and 7 maid servants who were *satis* (burned alive with him), as well as a couple of pigeons who were presumably accidentally incinerated by getting too near the flames.

A great deal of the *Samadhi* was hacked off by Sikh reformers, and the temple was well whitewashed to cover the paintings. There are some other nearby buildings which are *Samadhis* of Ranjit Singh's family, including his grandson Nau Nihal, whose promise was lost when he was killed by falling masonry at Lahore Fort.

The British City: For English-speaking people, Lahore is Kipling's "City of dreadful night". The theme uniting loneliness, fever and the sleeping city originally came from a poem by James Thompson. Sleeplessness, silent multitudes and tropical night combine in a

Sunset over Shalimar.

recurring theme in Kipling's early writing. His father, John Lockwood Kipling was direct and less poetic in his observations: He said that visitors within the walls were assaulted by an assortment of such evil odours "as would rob a Bermondsey tanner of his appetite".

It seems impossible to find places associated with Kipling. The family lived in a bungalow jokingly known as Bikaner Lodge because the Kiplings had no plants or trees about the place, considering them unhealthy. The desert aspect of the garden was reminiscent of Bikaner. The newspaper office where he worked has been redeveloped.

There is **Kim's Gun**, Zamzama – the massive cannon. Kim is perching on the cannon at the beginning of the novel. Nowadays it is in the middle of the road between the University and the Museum and is surrounded by a moat and fountains to dissuade any other children from copying Kim. This gun was cast in 1760 for the Durranis and used at the battle of Panipat in 1761. It was also swung into action at the siege of Multan in 1848, but was damaged after firing only two rounds. It is believed that whoever holds the gun holds the Panjab.

Lahore Central Museum has Kipling associations because his father was the curator. He was the original "keeper of the wonder house" from Kim. The pen case given to the keeper of the wonder house by the Lama can be seen at Kipling's house *Batemans* in England.

The Museum was originally the "Industrial Art Museum of the Panjab". Lahore was important because of the key position of Panjab in the Indian Empire. Recently annexed, efficiently administered, in less than 30 years there had been progress in irrigation, land settlement and afforestation. The British were also keen to foster, develop and support local craftsmanship. Many projects were undertaken.

It seems a shame that there are no remains of the amusement of the day. In Lockwood Kipling's time "rinking" was popular – the Sahibs and Mems had a roller skating rink!

Kim's Gun.

The Museum lost a large part of the collection at partition but the Curators have been making noble efforts to fill lacunae.

There are Gandhara, Hindu, Buddhist, Jain, Indus valley and Islamic collections, wonderful paintings from Moghul times and from the Panjab Hills, and many wonderful examples of handicrafts, rugs and carvings. The collectsions of calligraphy are also very fine.

The Museum's most famous exhibits include a Koran which is a thousand years old, and several sculptures including the emaciated fasting Siddhartha from Taxila, the miracle of Sarasvati, and the green goddess, Athena. There are some fine prehistoric displays showing archaeological finds half a million years old from the area around Islamabad, and the struggle for Pakistan is well documented.

The British left plenty of evidence of their presence. The architecture is "Moghul Gothic"of which there are plenty of examples including Aitchison College, (a renowned public school), The

High Court, Government College, National College of Arts, Tollington Market, Montgomery Hall, Panjab University and the Provincial Assembly. At **Charing Cross** there is an elegant pavilion that used to house a statue of Queen Victoria. She is now on display in the Museum.

Lahore is still growing, and just like any other city, there is incessant redevelopment. Old buildings become replaced by modern concrete architecture. Modern sites of interest include the **Minar-i-Pakistan** which marks the spot where the Pakistan Resolution was passed on 23rd March 1940. It is located in **Iqbal Park**. The tomb of the philosopher and poet is in the **Hazuri Bagh** beside the Badshahi Majid. The **WAPDA** building is an example of a modern office block, with a glass dome and a roof garden. Some of the new blocks are more interesting than others.

The **Fortress Stadium** is an attempt to combine the style of merlons from a fort like Rohtas with a sports stadium. The Stadium is the site of the famous Horse and Cattle Show in March. This includes a display of livestock but also many spectacular feats of horsemanship, tentpegging, dressage, camel dancing, racing, folk dancing, pomp and pageantry. It is accompanied by exhibitions displaying Pakistani craftsmanship and industry and is one of the most colourful of Lahore's events.

Perhaps the best places to see new buildings are the suburbs being developed by returning migrants, which are a happy blend of influences and styles from the world.

Lahore has plenty of fine parks and a zoo. Other leisure areas for the city have been developed in the vicinity. These include **Changa Manga**, a man made forest, originally planted and irrigated by the British to provide wood for railway engines. Nowadays there is a miniature, steam driven railway and an artificial lake with boats on.

Jallo National Park is more recent. It is also a recreational and picnic site, with a zoo, childrens's play area, a lake with motor and rowing boats, and other kinds of amusement.

**Left,
the Minar-i-
Pakistan in
Iqbal Park.
Right,
a veteran of
the times in
Panjab.**

AROUND LAHORE

Sheikhupura is 35 kilometres west of Lahore, and is believed to be of great antiquity. There are piles of ruins around the area. Pakistan could offer a life's work for the world's archaeologists and still have spare capacity. Certainly there was a Moghul presence and Jahangir was fond of the spot. The most interesting building is the **Hiran Minar**, (The Minaret of the Deer). The Minar, erected in 1616, is a monument to Jahangir's pet deer Mansaraj. There is a large tank (as artificial lakes are called in these parts) in front of the tower and a *baradari* (pavilion) in the centre. There are boats on the lake, including a speedboat which zips about wetting passengers with its spray.

The Hiran Minar gardens are a popular picnic spot.

Sheikhupura Fort was constructed by Jahangir, a quadrangle with a watchtower at each corner. The area was subsequently a favoured resort of Dara Shikoh (oldest brother of Aurangzeb) and it is said that the place was called Shikohpur after him which subsequently became Sheikhupura.

In Ranjit Singh's time, the fort was used as a home by one of his wives, Rani Nakayan. Her tomb is also in the area.

Sheikhupura district also produced the two greatest poets of the Panjab – Guru Nanak and Waris Shah. Waris Shah's tomb is at **Jandiala**, 12 kilometres from Sheikhupura.

Waris Shah completed his *Hir* in 1766. It is a living institution. It transcends all barriers. It is a perfect image of the Panjab, captured on paper - the physical and spiritual, ephemeral and eternal, the people, attitudes, folk lore, jokes and tragedies.

Nankana Sahib is on the railway line south west of Sheikhupura and is the birthplace of Guru Nanak, the founder of the Sikh religion, who was born in 1469. There is an enormous complex of buildings. The most important site is the actual site of the birth, which is now

Kite-flying is particularly popular in the Panjab.

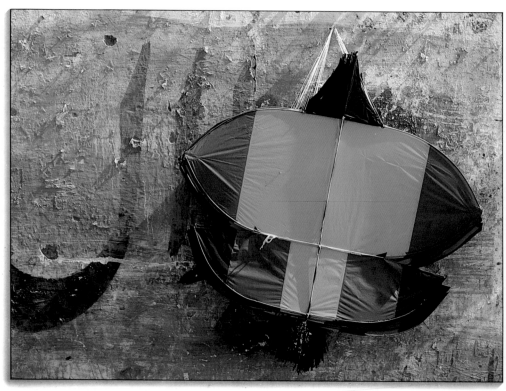

220

surmounted by a gurdwara. There is a well, associated with the Guru's sister, and some sites associated with people who were killed in disputes over the control of Sikh shrines when there was conflict between the traditional guardians of shrines and Sikh reformers in the 1920s. The fighting at Nankana was especially brutal and savage. There are several other Sikh shrines in the town, sites where tradition locates some events in Guru Nanak's childhood.

The next district is **Faisalabad** which was previously called **Lyallpur**, 140 kilometres from Lahore. Founded in 1890, Lyallpur was named after Sir James Lyall, the Lieutenant Governor of the Panjab. The present name commemorates the Saudi King, Faisal.

The original town was laid out on the lines of a Union Jack, like Khartoum in the Sudan. A clock tower occupied the centre with eight main bazaars radiating outwards. The town is called the Manchester of Pakistan; is very busy and has expanded enormously in modern times.

Chiniot is 35 kilometres north of

Faisalabad in the direction of Sargodha. There is a legend about a founding princess who hunted in men's clothing. There are claims that there are references to Chiniot in the Ramayana.

The area was once famous for boat building, but no such industry is seen nowadays. The most enduring craft here is stonemasonry. Masons from Chiniot were employed in the building of the Taj Mahal in Agra and Wazir Khan's Mosque. The main architect of the Golden Temple at Amritsar was also from Chiniot, as were the craftsmen who built the much more recent Minar-i-Pakistan. The town is still famous for arts and crafts, especially woodcarving, doors, brasswork, inlays and furniture. The skills are passed down from father to son.

Panjabi Romances: To the west of Faisalabad, adjacent to the River Chenab, lies the town of **Jhang**, which contains nothing of particular interest except for the tomb of Hir, heroine of the Panjab's most famous romance. The tomb itself is not much to look at, on the

HIR AND RANJHA

Ranjha's family lived at Takht Hazara. There were eight sons and Ranjha was the youngest. He was very handsome and undoubtedly his father's favourite. He was permitted to lead a life of ease, playing the flute, while his older brothers worked the land.

When their father died, things changed. The elder brothers' wives engineered quarrels with Ranjha and many unforgivable words were uttered. The sisters-in-law taunted him to go and find himself a wife such as Hir, a girl famed for her beauty.

Ranjha had been given the worst of the land as his inheritance. Now, he left even that and went wandering in the wilds, where he was sustained by the Five Pirs (holy men). He finally came to the bank of the River Chenab. He looked for a boat to continue his journey and finally, a ferryman, enchanted by Ranjha's flute playing, agreed to take him across the river. Once aboard, Ranjha found that there was a bed on the boat and being exhausted, he asked to lie down. The boatman said that the bed belonged to Hir, and that whilst she allowed him to ferry people across the river, she would not tolerate people using her bed. But he finally gave in – mainly at the insistence of his wives who were very taken with Ranjha! – and Ranjha stretched out on the soft cool bed and he was soon fast asleep.

Hir and her girl friends passed their afternoons playing games down beside the river. This time, when she came and boarded the boat, she was enraged to find a strange man lying in her bed. She roundly berated him and Ranjha, opening his eyes and seeing her replied only "Oh, Beloved".

She was, of course, very beautiful and the poets vie to produce their descriptions of her loveliness. She was soon enchanted by the flute player. Her anger vanished. It was love at first sight.

Hir wanted Ranjha to stay and so she arranged for him to work as a herdsman and care for her father's buffaloes. In the afternoons, Ranjha would take the buffaloes down beside the river where the animals would wallow and graze and each day, Hir would slip away and bring him food and they would talk of love and he would play his flute.

Hir had an uncle named Kaido, a twisted, evil man. He was crippled and people said that it was because he never had been able to find a wife or love. He was a troublemaker and a gossip and he hated young lovers. He was nasty to Hir, whose reaction was to beat him and rip up his clothes. Seeking revenge, he told her parents all about Ranjha. Hir was shut up in the house and Ranjha was sent away though as the buffaloes pined for him and would not eat, the villagers wanted him recalled. Meanwhile Hir's family decided to marry her to Saida, a man she had been betrothed to as a child. The marriage took place though Hir did not consent, and she was carried away in a litter, bemoaning her fate. She refused to have anything to do with her husband. Ranjha, was so distraught that he went to Yogi Tilla and decided to become a yogi.

The Five Pirs said that they would reunite the lovers and Ranjha arrived at Saida's house. Saida's sister, Sehti helped the couple. Hir pretended that she had been bitten by a snake and Sehti announced that she knew of a young Yogi who could cure snakebites, and she brought Ranjha. The three of them laid their plans. Sehti and Hir crept out of the house one night. Sehti ran away with her own lover. Hir and Ranjha also fled, but they were pursued and caught. They were tried and Hir's marriage to Saida was declared to have been invalid, for she had not freely consented to it. It was also agreed that she could marry Ranjha and he was told to go and prepare his wedding procession.

But meanwhile, the wicked uncle Kaido had been telling Hir's father that as the people had seen Hir leave with Saida after the first marriage, and to now permit her marriage to Ranjha would dishonour the family. So, as the preparations for the marriage were completed, Hir was given a cool drink which unbeknown to her, contained poison. She fell dead.

A message was sent to Ranjha and he hurried to Jhang to find out what had happened. He was taken to Hir's tomb and unable to bear the grief, he also fell dead upon her grave.

outside a garish concoction of jazzy pink and green tiles.

Illicit love is the backbone of Panjabi romance – and the lovers are always doomed. These stories are rather like pantomimes – everybody knows what happened, the interest lies in the quality of the telling. The poetry is the thing; the emotion it stirs; the delicacy or robustness of the writing as the poet recounts tragic or dramatic events; the heartstopping moments; the indescribable beauty of the heroines.

The stories have often been used by Sufi poets. The love of men and women is passing and ephemeral. The real, everlasting love is the love of God. Still, the agony, suffering in separation suffered by star crossed lovers is often used to describe the soul suffering in separation from the beloved – God.

South-west of Lahore: Beyond Changa Manga forest, near **Okara**, **Dipalpur** is believed to be very ancient indeed; perhaps there is even an Indus Valley site under the mound. Scythian coins have been found here. It was an important town when the Muslims conquered Sind and Multan in the 8th century. It was the site of a battle in 1285, when the son of the Sultan, Balban was killed and Amir Khusrao the poet and courtier, taken prisoner.

At the time of Timur's invasion, Dipalpur was the capital city, reputed to have 84 towers, 84 wells and 84 mosques. Babur captured it and the Mahrattas and Sikhs did too. Thereafter it lost its importance and has decayed to the state which it is in now, all that remains are the ruins of the ancient buildings.

Sahiwal is half way between Lahore and Multan. While the town is relatively modern with lots of industrial development – it grew up as a canal colony – only 20 kilometres to the West lie the remains of one of the most ancient cities in Pakistan. **Harappa** lies alongside the railroad, where slow trains ply across the flat landscape. Harappa is an important archaeological site of the Indus Valley civilisation. It is somewhat less complete than Mohenjo-daro as it was used as a site for collecting bricks in order to build the nearby railway. The engineers apparently had no curiosity as to why there should have been such huge and convenient supplies of bricks buried locally!

South of Sahiwal, **Pakpattan** was a principal ferry across the Sutlej used by Mahmud of Ghazni, Timur and other invaders. Pakpattan means "Ferry of the Pure". It is mainly famous as the residence of the Saint, Hazrat Baba Farid ud din Ganj-i-Shakkar, or Shakkarganji, meaning "Treasury of Sugar". There are various stories to account for this unusual name. It is said that his mother used to encourage piety by hiding a piece of sugar candy under his prayer mat. After prayer, he was allowed his reward. One day however, she forgot to put the sugar in place and was amazed when she found that the child had not been denied his treat – the sugar was miraculously in place. He was a famous Chisti Saint. He died in 1265 and writings by one of his successors are included in the Sikh holy book, the Adi Granth.

Left, love under the tree. Right, women winnowing paddy.

SOUTH PANJAB

There is a much quoted old saying about the four gifts of **Multan** – heat, dust, beggars and burial grounds. It can get warm, and when the wind blows, it is dusty. As to beggars, there are not many in Pakistan. Those there are, are so seriously disabled that it is hard to imagine what else they could do. As to burial grounds, Multan seems only average.

There are many tales of the undoubted antiquity of Multan. People claim that Multan is as old as Mohenjo-daro; that when Adam was thrown out of the Garden of Eden, Multan was where Satan landed. Some even say that the Rigveda was written there. Captured in 712 in the advance of Islam, Multan remained under Muslim rule until 1818.

Multan was once famous for a sun temple which occupied the centre of the citadel, but it was destroyed in the 10th century, and the replacement was again destroyed by Aurangzeb who proceeded to erect a mosque on the site. This was blown up when the Sikhs used it as a powder magazine.

There was a Moghul fort at Multan with ditches filled with water from the Ravi, which at that time flowed nearby. The fort was destroyed during the second Sikh war.

Miraculously though, there are some wonderful examples of pre-Moghul architecture, in particular the tombs of the Sufis. That of **Sheik Rukn-i-Alam** is a great octagonal tomb, of red brick, ornamented with azure navy and white tiles. Traditionally, it was built for the father of the Sultan Muhammad Tughlaq and given to Rukn-i-Alam. The other nearby tomb is that of Sheik Bahauddin Zakaria (1182-1264) who was the grandfather of Sheik Rukn-i-Alam. He was an educated man who worked hard and brought people to Islam. He also promoted agriculture and trade, dug wells and canals to help the common man. He spoke out against a tyrannous ruler to the Sultan in Delhi.

These Sufis were political. Sheik Rukn-i-Alam used to visit Delhi often, his palanquin roof heaped with documents relating to the cases of needy people whom he wanted to recommend for consideration.

He was aware that he was exposing himself to accusations of worldliness and once when he met another Sufi, he was told afterwards that the other master had bathed and changed his clothes after embracing him! His humility was such that he observed that this had been the correct thing to do, since he himself reeked of the world, whilst the other master was unpolluted by it.

Near these tombs are the remains of a Hindu temple of the *narsingh* (man-lion) *avatar* (incarnation) of the God Vishnu. The temple was destroyed by the explosion of the powder magazine.

The shrine of **Shams-ud-din Tabriz** stands separately, on what was the bank of the Ravi. The story is told that Shams ud din was the master of the celebrated Sufi saint Maulana Jalal ud din Rumi, founder of Sufi derveshes of Quinia. A

Left, the city of Multan. **Right,** creativity and colour in South Panjab.

bizarre legend about his martyrdom is that he was flayed alive and wandered about for four days thereafter with his skin in his hand. His descendants lived at Multan and in 1787 built the tomb there. There are still descendants there, including some singular looking lady *malangs* (devotees) in masculine attire. But they are jolly and good natured.

One welcome thing about Multan and the South Panjab generally is the use people make of colour. If ladies are in purdah and wear a *burqa*, in the north it is black or a drab colour. In Multan, burqas come in jazzy pink or orange, with primitive pleated cloth, and little points on top of the head. They are worn with great elan, sometimes tossed back!

Where *chaddars* (shawls) worn in the north are as huge as sheets and drab, in the South Panjab they are an excuse for wearing a flimsy, colourful accessory. Clothes are very colourful. A man completes his ensemble with a nice piece of cloth wrapped round his head, a cloth with a black or blue background and a vibrant pattern of roses.

A good place for shopping, Multan has a modern shopping mall and also some grand markets around the British clock tower. Here the business of the day goes on; men buying oil to beautify themselves; men gossiping; roadside false teeth manufacturers; a man embroidering a fine *chunni* (the gauzy veil worn by Panjabi women) on a frame. The area is famed for camel skin work, pottery, and cotton fabrics.

Perhaps the name of Multan will mean history to many people, but be warned – Multan is still very much a going concern and there is considerable industrial development, including the largest fertiliser factory in the whole of Pakistan.

Bahawalpur was a princely state founded 1784 by Nawab Bahawal Khan I and named after him. The town of Bahawalpur is a flourishing place and rather pleasant, with wide roads. Richly decorated cycle rickshaws ply for trade and men haul past, carrying entire families, the rider's saddles at an unusual, *vertical* angle.

The Mausoleum of Shams-ud din Tabriz.

The **Cholistan Desert** extends towards India. There are perhaps as many as 400 archaeological sites of the Indus Valley era along the long dry bed of the river, the classical Saraswati of Indian legend which ran through the area.

Derawar Fort is also in the desert, the residence of the Amirs of Bahawalpur. It is necessary to have permission, a guide and a four wheel drive vehicle to visit it. The **Lal Suhanra National Park** is 48 kilometres from Bahawalpur. There are many birds and animals and plans to reintroduce some of the rarer ones.

Recently, some new winter tours have been conducted in the area. These special tours will be of interest to those who wish to see wildlife. There are jeep and camel safaris and expeditions to hunt the wild boar.

There is one ancient city in the area which is well worth a visit: **Uch Sharif** is one of the oldest centres of learning and culture in Pakistan. Uch used to be at the confluence of the rivers with the Indus, but in 1790 the rivers deserted

Uch for Mithankot. The first learned man to settle in Uch in the 10th century, was Shaikh Saifuddin Ghazruni who had the location picked for him by his camel. His uncle had told him to go and settle where the animal would take him. It chose Uch.

Uch boasts some especially beautiful tombs and shrines. The best preserved is the octagonal tomb of **Bibi Jaiwindi**, daughter of another holy man, Hazrat Jahanian. Unfortunately, these wonders are in very poor shape and are falling down and there seems little chance that they will be preserved.

There is one place of pilgrimage in better condition; the shrine of **Hazrat Jalal-ud-din Surkhposh Bukhari** (The Saint of the Red Robes from Bokhara). He came at the call of Hazrat Bahauddin of Multan, whose example he emulated and he also spent much time in Delhi. The shrine has a painted roof which is quite breathtaking. The glorious patterns are picked out in red and blue lacquer. The shrine also has a tranquil and loving atmosphere, aided

The Tomb of Bibi Jaiwindi in Uch Sharif.

by the attendants who are kind, welcoming men of God.

There are said to be some important relics at Uch including a turban which belonged to the Prophet Muhammad.

Mithankot is the home of one of the most famous shrines of the whole area. This is the tomb of **Hazrat Khawaja Ghulam Farid** (1845-1901), holy man and great poet of the Siraiki language, (the language of Multan). He is famous for his *kafis* (lyrics). He was much attached to the Thar Desert. He spent years there, and married a girl from a nomad tribe. In his poetry he frequently refers to the romance of Sassi and Punnun. This is thought to relate to this area and it is a tale used by Khwaja Farid as well as by many other Sufi poets as an allegory for their love of God. The poet describes Sassi suffering the dual torments of the hot dry desert and the agony of separation as she seeks her beloved.The couple were blighted lovers who perished in the wastes.

Across the Indus: About 140 kilometres north of Mithankot lies **Dera Ghazi Khan**. The town is now reached by a bridge over the Indus from the direction of Multan. Formerly there was a ferry and a bridge of boats, but the original town was destroyed by the Indus in 1911 and the present town was built 15 kilometres from the river.

The local shrine is that of Ghazi Khan, the founder of the town. The town provides a gateway to Baluchistan via **Fort Munro**, through the **Sulaiman Mountains**. There are the occasional groups of men squatting by the roadside. Where do they come from? Where do they go? On the road to Fort Munro is the **Shrine of Sakhi Sarwar** who died in the 13th century. Sarwar is a character who appears in many Panjabi folk tales and songs.

He was left some land and his brothers demanded a share on the pretext of wanting to be with him. He allowed them to divide the land. They, of course, took the best and gave him a poor piece. Nevertheless, his crops were far better than theirs. Ten times better! The brothers then begged for grain from him,

A desert comes to life at Sakhi Sarwar.

which he willingly gave and the last of the grain, the little that the brothers did not take, he gave to the needy.

The brothers then took him to Multan to the Governor, Ghanu. Ghanu saw that Sarwar was a saint but decided to test him and sent an empty bowl and jug on a tray. When Sarwar removed the cover, both receptacles were full. Seeing that Sarwar was such a holy man, Ghanu gave him gold coins, a special robe of honour and a stallion. Sarwar fed and clothed all of the poor in the city.

Once the gold was exhausted, meeting more needy people, he gave the horse and robe to be sold to feed them. Hearing that Sarwar had disposed of his gifts, Ghanu was furious and called for Sarwar to explain. Sarwar prayed and the horse and robe were restored to him. Ghanu, now knowing what a holy man Sarwar was, asked him to marry his daughter. The wedding took place and they lived happily ever after. God provided for them and the gifts that God gave to Sarwar were always directed on to care for the poor and needy.

Music maker at the door of the shrine.

The poor and needy (and many others) still go to Sakhi Sarwar. There is a fair held in spring, in March-April time which goes on for a couple of weeks. The painted buses career across the desert, packed full of people and with further passengers on the roof, banging painted *dholaks* (drums) as they go. The buses park in the dried up river bed. The town is thronged with people. The streets, too narrow to admit vehicles, are crowded.

The environs are packed, and so is the shrine. There are dramatic looking men with turbans dancing in a circle, forward and back they step, swinging their arms in the air. There are women going into trances, men blowing the bagpipes, and drumming, drumming and more drumming.

It used to be the popular custom to write petitions on the wall of Sakhi Sarwar's shrine.

Further along the road, **Fort Munro** is the gateway to Baluchistan and was founded as a hill station by Colonel Sir Robert Sandeman.

Most travellers to Pakistan will see little more of Baluchistan than the apparently endless vista of brown and bare-looking rocks which stretches beneath the main western flightpath into Karachi. Such glimpses from the dubious comfort of a Jumbo cabin of a decidedly uncomfortable-looking environment below are no more misleading than most first impressions, for Baluchistan is indeed very large and also very barren.

Baluchistan covers some 343,000 square kilometres within frontiers whose often geometrical straightness indicates that they were first drawn with a ruler by long-dead bureaucrats in distant imperial offices. It is the largest province of Pakistan, accounting for about 42 percent of its total area. But with a population of barely four million at the last count, much less than that of the city of Karachi alone and making up only 4 percent of the national total, it is very sparsely inhabited indeed. Within Baluchistan, only Quetta, the provincial capital in the north-east with over 100,000 inhabitants, can be called a city, and other urban settlements are hardly more than dusty townships.

Only in the production of natural gas, coal and minerals does Baluchistan make a major contribution to Pakistan's economy. Outside Quetta, Baluchistan otherwise still comes bottom of the provincial league in terms of development by almost any criterion which can be established from official statistics, whether in terms of basic infrastructure and housing or of the per capita income, literacy levels and health of its inhabitants. This situation is likely to persist for the foreseeable future in spite of the great efforts to develop the province, begun in recent decades after the long stagnation of the colonial period and its immediate aftermath. There are plans to exploit Baluchistan's touristic potential, but the very size and hostile nature of the province makes the task of any development extremely difficult.

Geography: A glance at the map will serve to show that the provincial frontier marking the boundaries of Baluchistan with the other three provinces of Pakistan is much shorter than the long international frontiers with Afghanistan to the north and Iran to the west. In terms of its physical geography too, most of Baluchistan has more in common with western Asia than with the subcontinent proper. This factor partly underlies its potential appeal as an exotic region for tourism, now that travel in the neighbouring countries has become difficult or impossible.

The north-eastern border of Baluchistan is marked by the lofty Sulaiman Mountains, to the west of which range upon barren range, all continuations of the massive mountain systems of NWFP, swoop down in a great south-westwards arc to reach the highest points in the province just to the east of Quetta with the peaks of Zarghun (3,578 metres) and Khalifat (3,487 metres). The Sulaimans are briefly broken above the flat Kacchi Desert extending

up from Sind towards Sibi, providing access to the legendary Khojak and Bolan passes, the most feasable route from the lower Indus valley through to Afghanistan.

The Kirthar Range runs along the south-eastern edge of the province, continuing in the lower range of mountains marking the northern boundary of the barren Makran Desert which reaches right along the long coastline of the Arabian Sea to the frontier with Iranian Baluchistan. To the north-west, the thousands of square kilometres along the borders with Iran and southern Afghanistan have always been an Empty Quarter permitting only sparse human settlement. The terrain is flatter, and even more arid, and such rivers as run through the deserts terminate in massive swamps like the Hamun-i-Maashkel.

Baluchistan lies outside the monsoon system on which agriculture elsewhere in Pakistan relies either directly or through canal irrigation from the great rivers. The climate is therefore excep-

Preceding pages: at Gwadar on the Makran Coast; the bus pulls in.

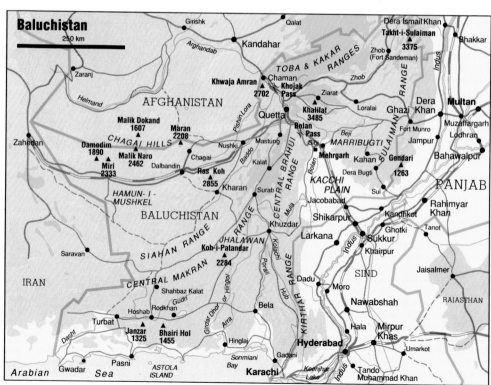

tionally dry, with annual rainfall generally hardly exceeding 15 centimetres, much less along the Makran Coast. When rain does fall, it often comes in dangerously heavy doses, sweeping all before it in the sudden spates which flow through the normally dry river beds or the narrow mountain clefts called *tangis*.

Since the mountains of Baluchistan themselves mark the southern end of the great wall which protects Pakistan from the rigours of the Central Asian climate, the province is exposed to strong winds which are ferociously hot in the summer and bitterly cold in winter. Extremes of temperature are thus added to the general aridity. In Quetta and the surrounding plateau regions it snows in the winter, with temperatures dropping below freezing, while in the summer the mean temperature is only a tolerable 25°C. In lower-lying regions the temperatures are much higher, with an annual mean of 30°C along the coast, while in the Sibi plain the thermometer regularly reaches 50°C in the shade.

Kajaal looks good on the eyes.

Except in the north-east, therefore, the climate combines with the natural features of the geography to form one of the world's most daunting environments for successful human habitation. Many observers have thought that its deserts and stark mountains make Baluchistan less like the earth than the moon, while an official team of U.S. geologists concluded that it was remarkably like the surface of Mars. The more succinct verdict of a common local saying is that Baluchistan is the dump where Allah shot the rubbish of creation.

History: In spite of the intrinsic hostility of its landscape and climate, archaeological discoveries have confirmed that Baluchistan was already inhabited in the Stone Age, and the important neolithic site at Mehrgarh is the earliest (7000-3000 B.C.) on the subcontinent. Until its overthrow by Alexander the Great, Baluchistan was part of the Persian Empire, whose records refer to it as "Maka".

In 325 B.C. Alexander led part of his army back from his Indian campaign to Babylon across the Makran Desert at the cost of terrible suffering and high casualties. Thereafter Baluchistan lay for centuries on the shadowy borderlands of the Zoroastrian rulers of Iran and the local Buddhist and Hindu dynasties of western India. Few remains of any significance date from this period, although the Hindu past was kept alive until 1947 by the annual pilgrimage to Hinglaj on the Makran coast, the last holy place of the Hindus towards the west. This pilgrimage to Hinglaj, believed to be the place where the crown of the dismembered goddess Sati's head fell, was part of the initiation of the *Kanphat* yogis, distinguished by the splitting of their ears to accomodate their huge wooden earrings.

Islam was brought to Baluchistan in 711 when Muhammad bin Qasim led the army which was to conquer Sind across the Makran route, but the area was always too remote for firm control to be exerted by any of the later local dynasties. It accordingly receives only very passing mention in the court histories of the time. The connections of the inland areas were variously with Iran, Afghanistan and India, those of coastal Makran rather across the Arabian Sea with Oman and the Gulf.

The name "Baluchistan" only came into existence later with the arrival from Iran of the tribes called Baluch (usually pronounced "Baloch" in Pakistan). Just how and when they arrived remains a matter of hot debate, since the traditional legends of their Middle Eastern origins, supposed to have been in the Aleppo region of Syria, have been further confused by cranky theories either that like the Pathans they may descend from the Ten Lost Tribes of Israel, or that they originated from Babylon, since "Baluch" is phonetically similar to the names of the god Baal or the Babylonian ruler Belos.

Better evidence is suggested by the Baluchi language, which belongs to the same Iranian group of Indo-European as Persian and Kurdish. This suggests that the Baluch originated from the area of the Caspian Sea, making their way gradually across Iran to reach their present homeland in around A.D. 1000, when they are mentioned with the equally warlike Kuch tribes in Firdausi's great Persian epic, the *Book of Kings*:

Heroic Baluches and Kuches we saw,
Like battling rams all determined on war.

Warlike the history of the Baluch has certainly always been. As the last to arrive of the major ethnic groups of Pakistan they were faced with the need to displace the peoples already settled in Baluchistan. Some they more or less successfully subjugated or assimilated, like the Meds of Makran and other now subordinate groups. From others they faced a greater challenge, notably from the Brahui tribes occupying the hills around Kalat.

The origins of the Brahuis are even more puzzling than those of the Baluch, for their language is not Indo-European at all, but belongs to the same Dravidian

Power of the past: the Khan of Kalat.

family as Tamil and the other languages of south India spoken over a thousand miles away. One theory has it that the Brahuis are the last northern survivors of a Dravidian-speaking population which perhaps created the Indus Valley civilisation, but it seems more likely that they too arrived as the result of a long tribal migration, at some earlier date from peninsular India.

As they moved eastwards, the Baluch were initially successful in overcoming the Brahuis. Under Mir Chakar, who established his capital at Sibi in 1487, a great Baluch kingdom briefly came into existence before being destroyed by civil war between Mir Chakar's Rind tribe and the rival Lasharis, whose battles are still celebrated in heroic ballads. Although the Baluch moved forward into Panjab and Sind, even as far as Delhi, the authority of the Moghuls stopped them establishing permanent kingdoms there, although the names of Dera Ghazi Khan in Panjab and Dera Ismail Khan in NWFP are still reminders of the Baluch chiefs who conquered

these lands in the 16th century. The Baluch who settled in the plains gradually became largely detribalised, forgetting their native language and increasingly assimilated to the local population, with their tribal origins remaining little more than a proud memory.

In Baluchistan itself, which came only briefly under the authority of the Moghuls, the tables were turned on the Baluch by the Brahuis who succeeded in re-establishing their power in Kalat. Throughout the 18th century, the Khans of Kalat were the dominant local power, with the Baluch tribes settled to the west and to the east of them being forced to acknowledge their suzerainty.

The greatest of the Khans was Mir Nasir Khan (1749-1817), whose military success owed much to the regular organisation of his army, with its separate divisions recruited from the Sarawan and Jhalawan areas which constitute the northern and southern parts of the Brahui homeland. The Khanate of Kalat became the nearest thing there has ever been to an independent Baluchistan. This extended beyond the modern boundaries, since Mir Nasir Khan's authority ran as far as the then insignificant town of Karachi. Although dominated by the Brahuis, they themselves became increasingly "Baluchified". Today, for instance, the Brahui language only keeps the first three of its old Dravidian numbers. From "four" upwards Brahuis count in Baluchi, in which most are anyway bilingual.

With the British expansion into western India and their disastrous first Afghan war (1839-41), internal power struggles within Kalat prompted the first British military interference, and the signing of a treaty in 1841. The British annexation of Sind in 1843 from the Talpur Mirs, themselves a dynasty of Baluch descent, and the subsequent annexation of Panjab meant that Kalat and the other regions of Baluchistan were now part of the sensitive western borderlands of British India, where the possibility of Russian interference induced a permanent state of imperial neurosis. Although the eastern Baluch

Tribes-men of yesteryear.

ROBERT SANDEMAN

The present shape of Baluchistan owes its appearance less to geographical features or indeed to any innate unity between its very varied peoples than to the efforts of one remarkably effective colonial official.

Colonel Sir Robert Sandeman (1835-92) was born into a Scottish family otherwise chiefly memorable for one of his ancestors having founded the fervent Presbyterian sect of the Sandemanians. Sandeman followed his father into the Indian army, where as young man he saw action in the 1857 Mutiny. He then transferred to the Panjab administrative service where he found the perfect outlet for his immense energy in working for the settlement of the tribal areas on the western boundary of the province.

His appointment as district officer of Dera Ghazi Khan in 1866 was to lay the beginnings of Sandeman's professional reputation through his successful handling of the Baluch tribes on the district's borders, though only at the price of suffering the personal tragedy of the death of his wife and two young children in a diphtheria epidemic. Sandeman had no time for the previous British policy of leaving the tribes alone until they got out of hand, when a military expedition would be sent in to exact reprisals for a raid. Instead he set out to work with the tribal leaders, thus reinforcing the authority of the Sardars by promising them the support of the colonial power, while at the same time recruiting small forces of tribal horseman to act as guides and for local policing.

This was the beginning of the so-called "Sandemanian" system of frontier management. Its success was largely due to Sandeman's own charisma as the epitome of the Victorian administrator. Known for his courage and utter honesty, and admired and trusted by the chiefs he would ride out unescorted into the hills to deal with any problem man to man. This personal style enabled Sandeman to bring off such coups as ending a longstanding blood-feud by arranging for a marriage between the families of the bitterly hostile chiefs. The impression made by this extraordinary man on the tribesmen who found his Scottish surname so hard to pronounce is recorded in ballads of the time celebrating the deeds of "Sineman Sahib".

On hearing of our ruler's coming,
Our souls were filled with heartfelt joy.
The Frankish army pitched their camps
The rebel strongholds to destroy.
For bringing peace to this my land
May Sineman rewards enjoy!

Sandeman's career really took off when his reputation as a Baluch expert made him the obvious person to deal with the chaotic situation on the sensitive western borders of British India caused by increasingly bitter disputes between the Khanate of Kalat and other Baluch chiefs. As a result of Sandeman's two missions to Kalat a treaty was signed in 1876 which confirmed the Khan and the chiefs of Kharan, Makran and Las Bela as rulers of princely states, while handing over Quetta and the Bolan Pass to British control. Through Sandeman's efforts and his unshaken confidence in the loyalty of the Baluch, the whole area remained peaceful during the hard-fought second Afghan war of 1878-9.

As a result of this war, the Pathan areas lying to the north of Quetta were brought into the British sphere of influence. By succeeding in quickly reaching agreement with the local tribes, he rebutted all those critics who had long said that Sandeman's methods, which had been so successful with the Baluch, would have no chance with the fiercely independent Pathans. His services were acknowledged by a knighthood and the renaming of the headquarters of the new agency as Fort Sandeman.

The rest of Sandeman's life, when not on leave in Ireland and penning memoranda on problems of the Irish fishing industry, was spent in Baluchistan administering the vast and varied areas under his control. He died in 1892 in the southern state of Las Bela, where he had gone to resolve a dispute between the heir and ruling Jam, who erected a dome over Sandeman's grave in Bela.

tribes were partially pacified by the efforts of Sir Robert Sandeman, it was thought easiest to leave the Khan and his subordinate chiefs in control of most of the rest of Baluchistan.

A further treaty was signed in 1876, which forced the Khan to "lease" the strategic Quetta region to the British, but left him in control of the rest of his territories with the aid of a British minister. Granted the rank of a 19-gun salute to mark the size if not the wealth of Kalat, the Khans were for a while content to pursue the eccentric lifestyle characteristic of so many Indian princes of the time. One Khan became legendary as a passionate collector of shoes, and made sure no pair would ever be stolen by locking up all the left shoes in a dungeon below the Fort at Kalat.

With the last ruler of Kalat, Mir Ahmad Yar Khan (1902-79), the Khanate again briefly entered the political arena. Exploiting the opaque clauses of the 1876 treaty, which left some doubt as to just how independent Kalat was supposed to be, he refused to join Pakistan in 1947 in the hope of going it alone. In spite of a spirited call to arms by one member of the royal family, the brief independence of Kalat finally ended in 1948 when the Khan was forced to sign the necessary merger documents, followed by his formal removal from power and the abolition of the state's boundaries in 1955. The present shape of Baluchistan was finally rounded out in 1958 when the Sultan of Oman sold Gwadar, given to one of his ancestors by the Khan of Kalat, back to Pakistan, its only territorial gain since 1947.

Peoples: The remoteness and apparent poverty of Baluchistan long allowed the kaleidoscope of peoples who had come to settle during its turbulent, if often shadowy, history to pursue their various traditional lifestyles with hardly any outside intervention. Principally concerned simply with keeping the tribes quiet in this border region, the British were more than content to reinforce the old order. The colonial regime thus had much less i. pact here than in the more developed parts of Pakistan.

Only its military presence served to curtail the long established tradition of supplementing meagre tribal resources by sallying out to raid the richer lands of the plains.

Since rainfall is generally so sparse, the traditional way of life for most of the Baluch and Brahui tribes in the interior has always been nomadic. The need to escape killing extremes of temperature and to find grazing for their flocks of sheep and goats involves movement over great distances, as in the annual winter migration down from the Kalat highlands to the Kacchi plain in the east. The wealthier tribesmen have horses, mares being preferred, and horse-racing is the chief sport. Donkeys are also kept, more carefully than camels, hence the saying that if you see a donkey, you've found a camp, but if you see a camel, you're lost!

Besides the goats, whose black skins give the nomad camps their distinctive appearance, it is sheep which provide the main resources. Such resources include those likely to come the

Left, "Sineman Sahib". Right, time for reflection.

visitor's way, like woollen rugs with their vivid tribal patterns, or *sajji*, marinated leg of lamb cooked on upright wooden skewers in front of open fires. *Sajji* incidentally is the leading culinary speciality of the Baluch.

The tribesmen's long hair and magnificent waving beards give them a quite distinctive appearance. The typical shape of their heads is due less to genetic inheritance than to the practice of carefully moulding them by bandaging and stroking during babyhood, so as to avoid the dreaded ugliness of an egg-shaped skull. Their white clothes are suited to the climate, being long and loose. The huge floppy turbans (*pag*) may take up to 20 metres of cloth, and the loose trousers (*shalwar*) worn under the long robe (*jama*) up to no less than 40 metres.

The one plant which is able to thrive in the bleak landscape is the dwarf palm called *pish*, whose heart is eaten and whose leaves and fibres are exploited for an amazing variety of uses, providing tents and mats, even shoes. This is one of the tasks given to women in this rigidly segregated society whose ideals are so heavily male-oriented, and where the unquestioned punishment for female adultery is death.

The Baluch code of honour or *mayar* centres on the entrenched ideas of loyalty backed up by the defence of honour through revenge called *ber*. In the words of a proverb, "A Baluch's revenge remains as young as a two-year old deer for two hundred years."

Baluchi ballads keep these values alive with their countless tales of the savage heroes of the golden age of Mir Chakar. One of the best known tells of how after the chieftain Bijar was killed by a Buledi tribesman, his ribs were roasted and thrown to the kites. In revenge, his kinsmen captured the Buledi chief Haibat Khan, cut off his head and used his skull as a drinking cup.

Tempered only by the more charitable ideals of hospitality (*mehmani*) and defending to the death all those who seek refuge (*bahut*), the revenge principle gave rise to permanent feuds, with

The seasonal migration.

one killing only to be wiped out honourably by another.

Although these values are certainly quite similar to the fierce tribal code of the Pathans, the Baluch tribes are differently organised, with great authority and respect being given to the hereditary tribal chiefs or Sardars and the subordinate leaders called *waderas*. One of the ways in which the Khans of Kalat sought to bring some order into their unruly kingdom was by trying to abolish blood revenge by substituting payments of possessions which could be valued in money, like land, sheep or girls, with double compensation for the killing of a Sardar. The British further increased the powers of the Sardars as agents of the imperial power, and the maintenance of strict hierarchy after violent death was reflected in the late 19th century by the blood compensation of a Sardar being reckoned at 20,000-100,000 rupees, as against only 1,500 for an ordinary tribesman.

Loyalty to the Sardars has therefore been the main organising principle of Baluch society. Disputes within the tribes are settled by their judgements, given in accordance with the customary law called *riwaj*, which may still involve trial by fire ordeal. This code has always been much more important to the Baluch than the detailed commandments of Islamic law.

The British tried to extend the principle of the *jirga*, the tribal council of the Pathans, to deal with intertribal disputes. Success was limited by the deep seated hereditary enmities between neighbouring tribes continually involved in disputes over grazing territory. Even today, those tribes which have best maintained their proud identity, like the Bugtis and Marris whose tribal territory lies off limits to outsiders to the east of Sibi, still proudly continue their longstanding fierce rivalry.

Though they give Baluchistan so much of its local colour, the nomadic Baluch and Brahui tribes have never been an absolute majority of the population. Their songs are sung by the professional minstrels called *loris*, while other subordinate groups, typically assigned menial tasks, descend from slaves captured in war. The limited cultivation possible within their territory was sometimes given to special ethnic groups, like the Persian-speaking Dehwars of Kalat.

Outside the Baluch areas, the Pushtu-speaking Pathans incorporated into Baluchistan by the British live up in the Quetta region and beyond, well known for its picturesque orchards of apricot, peach and apple trees. Here better agriculture is made possible by the underground water channels called *karez* which tap the subsoil water through an ingenious system of tunnelling. In the plains of the east, where farming by the more conventional method of canal irrigation is usually practised, the inhabitants of the land are mostly Siraiki-speaking Jat peasants.

Finally, along the 750-kilometre Makran Coast, whose Baluch population lives alongside such longer settled peoples as the Meds, fishing has always been the mainstay of the economy, backed up by the cultivation of dates in

A village in the Bolan Pass.

the valleys and oases of the hinterland. Due to its isolation, sea-links with Arabia have always been important to this region, and the African slaves imported by Arab sailors have left their genetic mark on many of the local inhabitants.

Baluchistan Today: In 1952 an enormous field of natural gas was discovered at Sui in the Bugti country. Pipelines now deliver this to all the major cities in Pakistan, for whom Sui gas is by far its most important indigenous source of energy. Subsequent exploration has revealed very considerable reserves of coal and sulphur around Quetta and minerals of all sorts in remoter regions, like the previously unknown cliffs of onyx out at Dalbadin in the north-west. The economic exploitation of these resources has led to a considerable increase in basic infrastructure to supplement the railways and roads constructed for military purposes by the British. There was a massive growth in the size of Quetta, largely through immigration from elsewhere into the provincial capital.

Since the mines were largely manned by immigrant Pathan labour, rather few benefits were experienced by the Baluch. They were provided with further cause for resentment when traditional grazing grounds in the east were opened by irrigation to cultivation by new settlers from the plains. As a result of the fact that the Baluch were rapidly becoming strangers in their own land, with feelings whipped up by local tribal leaders angered by the abolition of their tribal status, a serious conflict erupted in the 1970s. Massive military force was needed to suppress an uprising by some of the major tribes, notably the Mengals and Marris. No sooner was this unrest dealt with than the Russian invasion of Afghanistan took place. This caused the influx of hundreds of thousands of refugees into Baluchistan, and decisively tilted the ethnic balance of the province in favour of the Pathans, thereby exacerbating the tensions inevitable in a poor and backward society adjusting to rapid modernisation from the outside.

Wheeling and dealing in Chaman.

242

INTO THE DESERT

In an area where the rule of law has always run somewhat uncertainly, and where banditry is far from being a thing of the past, tourists are much more restricted in their movements than in most of the rest of Pakistan. Permits are required to travel anywhere outside Quetta, and most of Baluchistan off the main routes is basically off limits to all foreigners, as much for their own safety as for any other consideration. So only a limited number of possible routes is described here, with the advice to stick to the road and stay on the train.

For those with only a day to spare, the nearest place of interest just within Baluchistan, about 50 kilometres from Karachi, is **Gadani Beach**, once just a fishing village but enterprisingly transformed by the new capitalism and Pathan labour into the improbable site of the world's largest shipbreaking yard. As their turn arrives for destruction,

Fruits of the desert.

ships acquired from all over the world are driven onto the beach in a final burst of power, before being winched up to be cut apart by gangs working round the clock, and to make potentially huge profits for the entrepeneurs in times of high metal prices.

Although it has no lack of "unspoilt" beaches and blazing sun, it is hard to envisage the vast wilderness of the **Makran Coast** as especially attractive to tourists. Yet plans are being made to develop sites including the fishing port of **Gwadar**, now also a naval base and duty-free centre for imports from the Gulf, which is linked to Karachi by air.

Travellers on the main route up from **Jacobabad** in Sind across the flat and salt-encrusted desert of the Kacchi tribal territory to Quetta are advised to avoid the summer, since **Sibi**, whose inhabitants are said to need overcoats in hell, is best known as one of the hottest places on earth. Its jail has searingly bad memories for political detainees. Sibi's only remarkable building is its 16th-century fort, which is given some colour only by the formal tribal gathering held there in February.

Just beyond the town, the important neolithic site of **Mehrgarh** lies at the foot of the **Bolan Pass**, whose dark grim rocks bring home even more vividly than the more famous Khyber the natural obstacles to be faced by any army seeking to cross the mountains of Pakistan's western frontier. The steepness of the Pass is best appreciated on the return rail journey with its alarming sequence of slip lines built to catch runaway trains.

After the coaldumps and mines at the top of the Pass, which are just as unattractive here in Baluchistan as anywhere in the industrialised world, the valley in which the provincial capital of **Quetta** lies at an altitude of 1,675 metres comes as a welcome relief, especially when the fruit trees are in blossom after the winter snows. The pleasantly tree-lined streets of Quetta, rebuilt after the earthquake of 1935, offer little historical interest, although the food and goods on sale in the bazaars give it a certain Central Asian feel. The many

THE QUETTA EARTHQUAKE

The spacious and planned look of downtown Quetta today, whose widely spaced low-rise buildings and broad streets provide such a contrast to the appearance of most other Pakistani cities, is the direct result of the great earthquake which devastated the city in 1935.

The strategic desirability of controlling Quetta at the head of the Bolan Pass had been evident long before the arrival of the British. Under its old name *Shal*, it had been fortified by the Khans of Kalat as their northern capital. Its modern name actually means "fort", being derived from the Pashto word *kwatta* which has the same etymology as the "*Kot*" which forms part of so many Pakistani placenames.

Less desirable is the other implication of its location on the major rift between the Central Asian landmass and the inexorably approaching rocks of the Indian peninsular. The general susceptibility of Baluchistan to frequent earth tremors, which often do little damage simply because very few people live there, was therefore calculated to wreak havoc when a large population came to be concentrated at this nodal point of geological tension.

Not much thought had been given to planning the city which had grown haphazardly to the south of the cantonment housing 12,000 troops, the largest garrison in British India. Alerted to inspection by earlier tremors in the region, such as that which brought freedom to some inmates of the jail in nearby Mach in 1931, experts had been appalled by the slovenly way in which most of Quetta's buildings had been constructed, with bricks inadequately bonded by inferior cement. But virtually nothing had been done to implement their recommendations when a major earthquake struck without warning at 3.03 a.m. on Friday 31st May 1935.

Sufficiently violent to throw the seismograph at Calcutta, 2,250 kilometres away, out of adjustment, the passage of the 45-centimetre high shockwave, which lasted for no more than 30 seconds, was extraordinarily concentrated in its force. Though the seasonal intake of summer visitors made it impossible to estimate what proportion of the city's residents were killed, the casualty figures were colossal, with an estimated death toll of over 20,000 people out of some 60,000. Perhaps another 6,000 died in the neighbouring villages of the Quetta valley and Kalat.

Although the Air Force base to the west of town was engulfed in the general destruction, casualties would have been higher still had it not been for the natural obstacle of the two ditches, the Habib Nullah and Durrani Nullah. These stopped the shockwave from going beyond the city and the official buildings of the Civil Lines to the cantonment, whose troops were thus spared to clear up the ruins in a massive relief operation. If all too few survivors were rescued, the huge task of clearing some five square kilometres of total devastation was accomplished with remarkable speed. Survivors were gathered in a camp set up on the racecourse, and some 20,000 evacuated to prevent the outbreak of epidemics. The city was sealed with military strictness in a wire fence to allow the soldiers to get on with the grim job of digging out the bodies, to be disposed of by burial or cremation in accordance with the presumed religion of the dead.

Once the panic (which led to hurried plans to relocate the city) was over, the task of supervising the rebuilding of Quetta was given to Henry Oddin-Taylor, an engineer who had made his name with the building of the Sukkur Barrage in Sind. Although major re-planning was ruled out by the official decision to respect the rights of all property owners, the new Quetta was made far safer than the old by Oddin-Taylor's insistence on improved building standards involving the vertical bonding of brickwork by the insertion of metal bars, a technique later successfully used for the construction of bomb-proof buildings in Britain in World War II.

If the results were buildings in themselves architecturally unremarkable, the main goal of stability was achieved, as proved by a violent earthquake in 1941 which left them all standing. In spite of the many subsequent tremors which have hit Quetta from time to time, the buildings re-erected on Bruce Road in 1930s still look just as strong on the Jinnah Road it has since become.

Afghan refugees have brought with them fresh crafts like the distinctive Hazara rugs, to add to such traditional items as Baluch mirrorwork.

In the cantonment north of the city, in Staff College Road, there is a small military museum in the bungalow occupied by Field-Marshal Montgomery when he was an instructor at the Quetta Staff College, the academy which trains Pakistan's military elite. The same route out of town leads after 11 kilometres to the favourite picnic spot of **Hanna Lake**, with its island shrine, after 22 kilometres to the flowers and orchards of **Urak Tangi**.

Longer journeys from Quetta are best taken by explorers who find it more interesting to travel than to arrive, since there is little to expect at the end of many hours of looking out of a bus for the occasional tribal group or feature of natural beauty to break the monotony of most of the landscape.

On the road back to Karachi via **Bela**, 122 kilometres south of Quetta, lies **Kalat**, a small town dominated by the **Miri**, the dilapidated stronghold of the Khans which is still a more impressive monument to their greatness than the Quetta Fort they once also controlled.

To the west, one can take the train through 720 kilometres of territory exceptionally barren even for Baluchistan to **Taftan** on the Iranian border.

A livelier glimpse of one of Asia's last true frontiers can be gained by the shorter journey north along the road which winds its twisting way up through the Pathan country and the arid hills lining the **Khojak Pass**, beyond which lies **Chaman**, 130 kilometres from Quetta, but only 24 from the Afghan city of Kandahar across the border. Refugees fleeing the long war in Afghanistan have brought a new bustle to this once dozy town, whose dusty streets are now the scene of energetic wheeling and dealing. Like most such townships along Pakistan's borders, Chaman is a smuggler's paradise.

Although there is a road running north-east to link Quetta with Peshawar, this runs through tribal territory and is closed to foreigners.

The last of the routes radiating out from Quetta is therefore that which runs east to **Dera Ghazi Khan**, 460 kilometres away in Panjab, via the barren flatness of **Loralai** and **Fort Munro**, the "gateway to Baluchistan" up in the Sulaiman hills. Most travellers go no further than the 123 kilometres up to **Ziarat**, a hill-station 2,450 metres above sea level. Though snowbound in winter, its pleasant summer climate and surviving juniper forests make it very attractive to Pakistani holidaymakers able to afford its expensive hotels.

The most popular excursion point is five kilometres away at **Prospect Point**, a 2,700-metre high rock recommended to those able to overcome any fear of heights sufficiently to enjoy the magnificent view of Baluchistan's highest peak, **Mount Khalifat**. Jinnah himself was Ziarat's most famous visitor, and the Residency where he spent his dying summer in 1948, the first year of the country he had brought into existence, is preserved by the nation as a memorial to the revered Quaid-i-Azam.

Left, monument to those who died in the Quetta Earthquake. Right, typical merchandise in Chaman.

THE NORTH WEST FRONTIER PROVINCE

A bullet whines past the hero's head and kicks up a puff of dust: "Cover me!" he snarls, and fires back. The wily Pathan falls. "Got what he deserved!" The Fort is relieved. The Governor personally congratulates Captain Carruthers (played by Errol Flynn or Tyrone Power). Simpering ladies are led to safety, swishing their satin crinolines. The train chugs off into the hills... Everybody knows about the North West Frontier, through scenarios like these. Or do they?

What is it really like? North West Frontier Province lies along the border between Pakistan and Afghanistan. It was a British invention, an administrative convenience brought about by bureaucratic in-fighting in distant Panjab.

The predominant colour of the landscape gave us a new word in English: khaki, derived from the word for "dust". Khaki replaced the bright scarlet of British military uniforms, all too visible against the monotonously drab landscape and allowing soldiers to be picked off easily by snipers.

Much of the North West Frontier is indeed very dusty. Areas are so dry, rocky and barren that the province has been described as a gigantic slagheap. This is a little unfair, for it does possess great beauty. Coming from the direction of Attock by plane, road, or train, on a clear day the Vale of Peshawar ahead looks like a huge grey bowl with a green bottom and three chips out of the rim: the legendary Khyber, Kohat and Malakand Passes.

The climate is extreme, even in this country of extremes. Intensely hot, dry summers and bitterly cold winters, often freezingly foggy, encourage an astonishingly wide variety of vegetation, providing there is sufficient water. Where water is not a problem, the world's most important food staples – wheat, maize, rice and potatoes – can all be grown here.

Sugar beet, a temperate crop and sugar cane, a tropical crop, are cultivated side by side on enormous estates around Charsadda, Swabi and Mardan to supply Charsadda's sugar mills. In the orchards of Nowshera, Pabbi and Jehangira, mangoes and apples flourish in adjacent fields. Some domestic gardens in Peshawar have hedges of banana plants, sheltering patches of carrots and cabbages. Springtime, in February-March is delightful, with fruit and nut trees seemingly in bloom simultaneously: apricots, pears, plums and peaches, almonds, walnuts and pistachios, lychees and loquats, lemons and oranges, even cherries and delicious mulberries.

But it is the people of NWFP who draw travellers back again and again. One of Kipling's most glamourous characters is Mahbub Ali, "who came from that mysterious land beyond the passes of the North." He is the original "wily Pathan".

The Pathans: The majority of people who live in the frontier belong to the Pathan group of tribes. It is the world's largest tribal society. Their very names:

Wazir, Mahsud, Khattak, Bangash, Afridi, Mohmand, Yusufzai, are surrounded by legend and romance. Inhabiting NWFP as well as adjacent areas of Afghanistan they speak a language called Pushtu or Pukhtu. Most Pathans agree that the northern tribes, especially the Yusufzai, speak the correct or "standard" version.

Many origins have been attributed to the Pathans: Aryan, Greek, Persian, Arab, even ancient Jewish. Pathans themselves claim descent from a common ancestor, believed to have lived 20 or 30 generations ago. His name was Qais and he met Muhammad, the Holy Prophet of Islam, in Medina. Pathans say the Holy Prophet gave Qais the name "P'thun" (in Arabic, it means the keel of a ship) because he would transport Islam back home with him.

After his return, Qais married and, as the Holy Prophet promised, had many children and grandchildren. One of them was called Afghana and he had four sons. When they grew up, they left Afghanistan (Afghana's country) to seek their fortunes. One went towards Dir, Swat and Hazara. One went towards Lahore and into Hindustan. One went down to Multan and the other to Quetta. Every Pathan knows this story and believes that one or another of the brothers is his ancestor.

Each tribe takes its name from a founding father. For example, the Yusufzai claim descent from one Yusuf (zai means son) who apparently existed seven or eight generations ago and is a descendant of the brother who went to Dir, Swat and Hazara. The Mohmands claim descent from Mohmand, another descendant of this brother, and so on. The Wazirs of the far south of NWFP add a nice twist, saying they are lost tribes of Israel who escaped from Babylon and so have an earlier, more prestigious origin than the rest.

The stories are mythological rather than authenticated fact, but they do give every Pathan a place on a family tree which covers between 12 and 18 million people. It is this which permits a sense of unity despite so much ethnic diversity. A Yusufzai from Swat other-

Preceding pages: in memory of the fallen, Khyber Pass; Pathan settlements are heavily fortified. Left, the Pathans are still guardians of the Frontier.

250

wise has little in common with his Bangash "cousins" from Kohat or Mahsuds from Wana. They do not even look alike. Yusufazai men traditionally wear their hair short, almost shaved, Bangash men in a shoulder length bob with thick fringe and Mahsud men in almost waist-length "ringlets". When not temporarily allied against an outside threat, they are most likely to be fighting each other. The word "cousin" also means enemy.

The Pathan Way: Pathans follow a rigourous code of behaviour called *pukhtunwali*, the way of the Pathans. For them, it has more force than the law of the land. Not all manage to live up to it, but it is always there as an ideal. In the designated Tribal Areas, life is led almost according to these tribal customs. Pathans call the Tribal Areas *ilaqa ghair* – lawless country. But they are not anarchic. What this means is that the laws of Pakistan do not apply.

First and foremost in this tribal code comes hospitality (*melmastia*). It should be freely offered to all visitors, even enemies, without anticipation of any reward. It is lavish on the occasions of births, deaths and marriages, circumcisions and the resolution of feuds. Since the house is the domain of women, every Pathan village or neighbourhood has a *hujra* (guest house) to entertain casual visitors. It is maintained by contributions from each household. Special guests, entertained in the home, are always given a gift upon leaving.

Revenge (*badal*) is the second rule. Altercations usually begin over *zar zan zamin* (gold, women and land) as the Pathans put it, but the bloodiest quarrels of all centre around women. Pathan women are cherished by their menfolk, whose duty it is to protect them. Any affront to women's honour is resented and retaliation is severe. The slightest illicit approach by a man to a Pathan woman, even lingering to watch her at work in the fields, singing within her earshot or combing his hair in public, invariably leads to the exchange of hot words and often hot lead.

Damkot Hill, where Churchill nearly lost his life.

If the woman has "encouraged" the approach by forgetting to cover her head, failing to go quickly about her business or returning a glance, she will be beaten. Cases involving women's honour are called *tor* (black) and require the payment of *shaam namah* (shame money). If the offence is considered to be serious only bloodshed can wipe out the shame. Ideally, the offenders should be killed by their nearest male relatives – in the case of the woman her own brother – so that a vendetta can be avoided.

This is often a forlorn hope since every insult or injury must be avenged. The smallest of beginnings can eventually lead to feuding between entire tribes. "He is not Pathan who gives a pinch for a blow" so, although the punishment should fit the crime, once started, violence tends to proliferate. A man's throat is cut while he sleeps in Los Angeles today to avenge the abduction of someone's sister by his cousin thirty years earlier, in Charsadda. This was revenge for the bawdy insinuations which her brother had made about his wife ten years before.

Another Pathan saying warns: "Revenge is a dish which tastes better cold."

History of the Frontier: The first mention of the region is in the Rig Veda. One of the 1,028 hymns sings of a victory on the banks of the Suvastu, the Swat river.

From the 6th century B.C. to the 11th century A.D. the Vale of Peshawar was an important centre of the kingdom of Gandhara. The capital, now called Charsadda, is first mentioned in the *Ramayana*, when Bharata conquers Gandharvadesha and names two cities, Taksha (Taxila) and Pushkala after his two sons. In 367 B.C. Alexander the Great marched into Swat and fought four battles there, before crossing the Malakand Pass.

Everyone who has come upon the Pathans, from Alexander the Great onwards, has remarked upon their fierce independence. They have proved almost impossible to conquer. History is mostly concerned with the so-called Settled Areas. After each "conquest"

Tribal lands around Darra Bazaar.

invaders were usually content to secure military and trade routes and left the rest of Pathan country firmly alone.

Kushans, Persians, Huns, Arabs, Mongols and Moghuls have all tried to conquer what is now NWFP and given up in the attempt. The Yusufzai totally destroyed the Moghul Emperor Akbar's army at the Karakar Pass. The Orakzai annihilated a Sikh detachment at Saraghari.

First British contact with the frontier was in 1809 when Mountstuart Elphinstone led a diplomatic mission to Kabul by way of Kohat and Peshawar. He had a picnic on top of the Kohat Pass with Bosti Khel Afridis, neighbours of the Zarghun Khel Afridis who make the guns at Darra Bazaar. In 1849, following the Sikh wars, the frontier lands came under British control for the next hundred years.

British concern over Russian expansionism in the Pathan borderlands fuelled a series of conflicts known as the Afghan wars, during which the British attempted to secure their interest in Kabul. The British were invariably forced to retreat, were massacred, or suffered a combination of both. They established an international frontier, the Durand Line, in 1893.

Throughout the 19th century and well into the 20th century, the British fought the warlike frontier tribesmen, often receiving a severe drubbing. In 1897, the Khyber forts and the Malakand and Chakdarra forts were attacked. No less than 60,000 men had to be put into the field to pacify the frontier.

Just the sound of the names, Ahnai Tangi and Shahur Tangi, caused British soldiers stationed on the Frontier in the 1920s and 1930s to fall into a cold sweat. Entire convoys were trapped there and annihilated.

Yet Pathan soldiers also served in the British forces and fought on the British side in the two World Wars. Their cheerfulness and bravery in such terrible places as Passchendale, Gallipoli and Monte Cassino, in an utterly alien theatre of war, evoked admiration, even amongst their foes.

Side by side.

Love them or fear them, Pathans command respect. Colonel "Buster" Goodwin, stationed for twenty years on the Frontier with locally recruited levies, often quite alone, expresses his feelings about the Pathans this way;

"Our dealing with the Pathans was a gentleman's game. No matter how poor a Pathan was, he might meet the King of England or the Viceroy of India but he'd look him in the eye and shake hands with him as if to say, I'm as good a man as you are."

In the summer of 1947, the frontier tribes voted to join Pakistan. But the territory of the Pathans had been divided by the Durand Line, fuelling periodic demands ever since for an independent Pathan homeland, *Pukhtunistan*. There were disturbances in Mohmand Agency from 1960 to 1962. As in earlier struggles with the British, the Pathans were supported by arms and money from Afghanistan.

In June 1989, the pro-Soviet Afghan Government was again discovered to be distributing arms and money to the trans-border tribes in Pakistan. History repeats itself.

Where and where not: For reasons of security it is not possible to visit certain parts of NWFP. The Tribal Areas of **Mohmand**, **Bajaur**, **Khyber** (but not the famous Pass) **Orakzai**, **Kurram**, and the **North** and **South Waziristan Agencies** are out of bounds to outsiders. This includes non-Pathan Pakistanis. Each area is in the charge of a Political Agent, who has his own law enforcement organisation: the legendary Frontier Corps. Part of his job is to ensure that tribal feuding does not threaten Settled Areas. But as the law of the land does not apply, he is empowered to take action only in the event of crimes actually committed on the highway.

The Tribal Areas are mostly arid, hilly tracts whose economy is based on animal husbandry. No rents or taxes are paid. The people live in widely dispersed, fortified hamlets, each inhabited by a distinct group of kinfolk. There are no sharp divisions of wealth, rank or status. Authority rests with the *kashar* (elders) and when the occasion demands they summon a tribal or intertribal *jirga* (council) to debate issues. Any decisions they take can be enforced, if necessary, by a temporary tribal militia – the *lashkar*. The vast majority of the population are illiterate but there is a strong oral culture of epic poems and legends.

The fact that people are tribal and illiterate does not mean that they are yokels, or in any way lacking. Their homes, even in remote areas, display the most up-to-date examples of modern living, such as video-cassette recorders and other electronic gadgets. One particularly well-known group of Pathans are the Afridis of Darra Bazaar, who are famed for their arms factories, owned and operated by the local tribal people, producing sophisticated weaponry. "Tribal" then, does not mean technologically backward, but simply that certain areas remain outside the jurisdiction of state institutions.

It is possible to travel freely in the Settled Areas, the five Administrative Districts of **Dera Ismail Khan**, **Kohat**, **Bannu**, **Peshawar** and **Hazara**. Here the laws of Pakistan do apply. The territory of the former **Malakand Agency**, which includes **Dir**, **Swat**, and **Chitral** (see page 327) is open to travellers, but they nonetheless should not stray off the highway. Tribal feuding in Kohat Frontier Region and the Khyber sometimes causes through roads to be closed.

The Settled Areas are largely the fertile irrigated plains. Cultivation is organised on great estates owned by Pathan landlords. Tenants, frequently not ethnic Pathans, pay rent to the landlords and taxes to the Government. Differences of wealth, rank and status have thus become pronounced. The population lives in large villages, towns and cities. Political power is controlled by the landlords, known as *Khans* (Chieftains). They are strongly represented on village councils and municipal boards as well as local and central government constituencies, all part of the central administrative system. The literacy rate is still low in these areas. Despite this setback, there is a strong literary tradition, and much admired too.

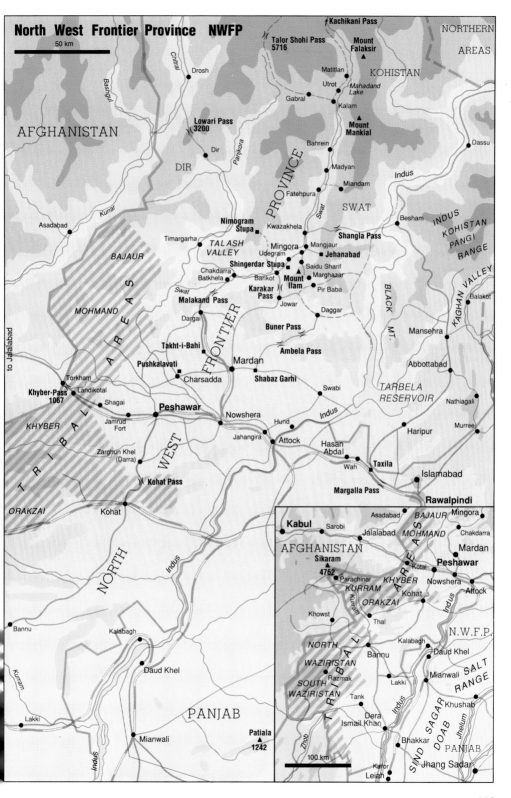

North West Frontier Province NWFP

50 km

NORTHERN AREAS

AFGHANISTAN

Kachikani Pass

Talor Shohi Pass 5716

Mount Falaksir ▲

KOHISTAN

Chitral

Drosh

Matitlan

Utrot

Mahadand Lake

Dassu

Gabral

Kalam

Lowari Pass 3200

Bashgul

Dir

DIR

Bahrein

Mount Mankial ▲

Madyan

Indus

Kunar

Fatehpura

Miandam

SWAT

Besham

INDUS

KOHISTAN PANGI RANGE

Asadabad

Nimogram Stupa ■

Kwazakhela

Shangla Pass

Timargarha

TALASH VALLEY

Mingora

Mangjaur

Jehanabad

BAJAUR

Udegram

Saidu Sharif

Shingerdar Stupa ■

Chakdarra

Barikot

Marghazar

Batkhela

Mount Ilam ▲

Pir Baba

BLACK MT.

KAGHAN VALLEY

MOHMAND

Karakar Pass

Jowar

Daggar

Balakot

Swat

Malakand Pass

TRIBAL AREAS

Dargai

Buner Pass

Mansehra

to Jalalabad

Takht-i-Bahi

Ambela Pass

Abbottabad

Pushkalavati ■

Mardan

FRONTIER

Charsadda

Shabaz Garhi

TARBELA RESERVOIR

Nathiagali

Torkham

Landikotal

Swabi

Khyber-Pass 1067

Shagai

Peshawar

Nowshera

Indus

Haripur

Murree

KHYBER

Jamrud Fort

Hund

WEST

Jahangira

Attock

Hasan Abdal

Zarghun Khel (Darra)

Wah

Taxila

Islamabad

TRIBAL

Kohat Pass

Margalla Pass

Rawalpindi

ORAKZAI

Kohat

Asadabad

BAJAUR

Mingora

NORTH

Kabul

Sarobi

Jalalabad

MOHMAND

Chakdarra

AFGHANISTAN

Sikaram ▲ 4762

Parachinar

KHYBER

Mardan

Peshawar

Indus

Kotal

Bannu

KURRAM

Kohat

Nowshera

Attock

Kalabagh

ORAKZAI

Khowst

Thal

N.W.F.P.

Daud Khel

Kalabagh

NORTH WAZIRISTAN

Bannu

Mianwali

SALT RANGE

Daud Khel

SOUTH WAZIRISTAN

Razmak

Lakki

Khushab

Tank

SIND SAGAR DOAB

Lakki

PANJAB

Kurram

Dera Ismail Khan

Indus

Jhelum

Bhakkar

PANJAB

Mianwali

Patiala ▲ 1242

Zhob

Karor

Jhang Sadar

Leiah

100 km

PESHAWAR AND THE KHYBER PASS

Peshawar is the largest city of NWFP and its capital. Pathans just call it *Shehr*, The City. There are others, but from Turkey to China this is *the* city of Central Asia. Everybody who is anybody has been to Peshawar at some time: Alexander, Marco Polo, the Moghul Emperors Babur and Akbar, Queen Elizabeth II of England (who saw Khattak dancing there and liked it very much) and even Lawrence of Arabia, to mention just a few. The list is endless.

Like the cafes of the Champs Elysees in Paris, if you sit long enough in one of Peshawar Old City's teashops or *chaikanas* the whole world passes by. Trans-frontier Pathan tribesmen in voluminous, green turbans and khaki *partog* (baggy trousers) with bandoliers slung across each shoulder mingle with camera-toting Japanese tourists on a pilgrimage to Gandharan Buddhist sites; Baluchi nomads leading strings of pack camels loaded with brilliantly coloured carpets jostle against Afro-Caribbean "military advisers" and United Nations frontline observers; Italian television crews point out slant-eyed, fur-hatted Turkomen horsemen from beyond the Pamirs, who stare back in equal astonishment, getting in the way of Australian schoolteachers backpacking around the world, lady mountaineers from the north of England and an expedition of Scandinavian botanists.

Peshawar has often been described in the past as a city of intrigue. Today it is still a city of spies, people posing as spies, journalists and people pretending to be journalists, arms dealers, and people pretending to be arms dealers. Throughout the 1980s, there were at least 2,000 Americans involved in one, some or all of these activities. Several so-called aid organisations were known to be offering cross-border assistance of a distinctly non-humanitarian kind, acting as fronts for mercenaries. These too, an international bunch in camouflage battle fatigues and combat boots, added to the atmosphere.

Long gone are the carefree mobs of hippies, though the occasional hashish dazed "middle-aged teenager" still occasionally lurches through Khyber Bazaar, trailing waist-length greasy locks. The Afghan war put a stop to the hippy bus trail through Meshad and Kabul to Peshawar and Delhi. Their purchasing power was never great, but hippies are much missed and not only by the drug dealers. 'Is there a bus in town?' shouts Honest Ali, one time brass coffee potseller to Jacqueline Kennedy Onassis (with a photograph to prove it) spotting a party of young people wandering into the much-fabled Qissa Kahani Bazaar. The surrounding shopkeepers wake up, smile to themselves and flap the dust off their beautiful antique copper chafing dishes.

Peshawar is old, so old that its origins are lost in antiquity. Founded over 2,000 years ago by the Kushan Kings of Gandhara, it has had almost as many names as rulers. When Babur came to Peshawar, he found a city called Begram and rebuilt the fort there, in 1530. His grandson, Akbar, formally gave the city the name Peshawar which means "The Place at the Frontier" and much improved the bazaars and fortifications. Earlier it had been known as the "City of Flowers" and the "City of Grain", names which reflect the fecundity of the great basin of land in which Peshawar is situated, all the more beautiful in contrast with the arid mountain ranges which surround it.

No wonder that in the days of the Kushan kings it was called the Lotus Land. From about the 2nd century A.D., when the dynasty relocated its capital from Charsadda, to about the 7th century, Peshawar was the centre of Buddhist Gandharan civilisation and an important place of pilgrimmage. As Buddhism declined in international importance, Peshawar also fell on hard times. In the 9th century the provincial capital was shifted by the Hindu Shahi kings to Hund on the Indus. After the invasion of Mahmud of Ghazni, all traces of gentle, artistic Gandhara were lost; even the name is unfamiliar to the local inhabitants today. Peshawar did not regain any of its former glories until the advent of the Moghuls in the 16th century.

When Marco Polo visited Peshawar Province (which he Italianises to Bascia) in 1275 or thereabouts, he found a place "the people of which have a peculiar language. They worship idols; are of dark complexion, and have an evil disposition; and are skilled in the art of magic and the invocation of demons, a study to which they continuously apply themselves."

These days the disposition of the inhabitants has improved. Pathan hospitality is legendary, and since conversion to Islam, worshipping idols has ceased. But it is still possible to buy magic spells or love potions in the old bazaars and to get your devils cast out, if you have any. In fact, in Peshawar, it is possible to purchase almost anything money can buy, providing you have got the time. Pathans have a saying, "Wait a year, and then make your mind up."

Purchases or commissions should be made slowly, over several days and many cups of delicious green tea with cardamom and lemon, called *qawa*, whilst discussions of world affairs are mutually savoured. Fixing the price comes at the end. Pathans are much more courteous bargainers than other shopkeepers in South Asia. Many, especially the northern Pathans, will not haggle at all.

A tour through the bazaars of the **Old City** could start at any one of its 16 gates, but the **Jail Bridge** over the railway is a very well known landmark. On one side of the bridge is the Cantonment Area, where Peshawar's international class hotels are situated. On the other side is the **Khyber Bazaar**, which has several decent, inexpensive hotels, as well as a great number of cheaper but less comfortable ones. These range from reasonably acceptable hostelries with room service and air-conditioning, like the **Galaxie Hotel**, to flophouses with half a dozen beds to a room, without food or running water, for only a handful of rupees a night. The better hotels are located just at the foot of the Jail Bridge.

Turning left at the first intersection past the bridge takes the traveller into the Khyber Bazaar itself. This is the terminus for buses to Kabul and the Tribal Agencies and is a good place to pick up a *tonga* or motor rickshaw to avoid the crush of the Old City. It is intensely busy. Shops, the lawyers' and accountants' chambers and artisans' workshops are cheek by jowl along the street and in the maze of alleyways.

As elsewhere in South Asia, businesses specialising in similar lines tend to bunch together. By the bus terminus, there are cafes (in local parlance "hotels") and street stalls selling grilled or fried snacks. Peshawar's speciality is the *chappli kebab* (a spicy beefburger mixed with tomato and eggs) served on *naan* (unleavened bread) which acts as an edible plate.

Barrow boys hawking fruit loiter under lurid billboards displaying larger than life pictures of false teeth or human organs alerting a largely illiterate populace to to the services of dentists and doctors available in the locality. Further **Tea break.**

along are shops selling tin trunks in all sizes from deed box to wardrobe and men's embroidered hats and woollen waistcoats.

The street bends around to arrive at a cross called **Kabuli Gate**. What is left of the ancient gateway to the Khyber Pass can be seen by the police station. To the left and over a slight hill there is the **Lady Reading Hospital**, the walls of which are the remains of the Old City's fortifications.

On the same street is the impressive and forbidding **Bala Hissar Fort**. It is still in use by Pakistan's Armed Forces and therefore is not normally open to visitors. Photography in its vicinity is, strictly speaking, illegal. The present fort was constructed by the Sikhs in 1834 and modified during the British occupation, which commenced in 1849. The fort which the Emperor Babur built was destroyed when Ranjit Singh captured the city, in 1818. His Sikh army burned most of the Old City to the ground. During the 30 years of Sikh rule the population of Peshawar was *halved*.

Across the street from the main entrance of the Lady Reading Hospital a poky entrance through a dark alleyway leads to **Andar Shehr** (the Inner City). On either side of the alley are jewellers shops, some specialising in silver jewellery, some in gold. The goods are displayed in showrooms, dazzlingly bright inside, lights and mirrors making the most of the wares on offer. Unless travellers know what they are doing, the quality of "gold" or "precious" stones purchased may prove disappointing back home and is not reliably guaranteed. It helps to have personal connections to buy from reputable firms.

Consultations take place by appointment in the upper rooms of the tall houses lining this narrow bazaar. Customers with an entrée to a house make their selection from the sacks of precious and semi-precious stones stored there. Designs are made to order and quality is unreservedly guaranteed. Individual families stick with particular jewellers for generations and the amount of shopping around is minimal.

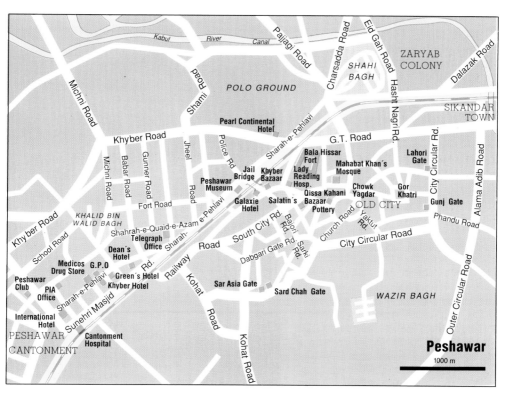

Peshawar

1000 m

Antique and secondhand silver items and semi-precious stones are probably much more interesting and certainly less risky buys for the casual shopper. The shopkeepers dump their wares in large handwoven baskets for the browser to pick through at leisure. Eye-catching bric-a-brac is put out on the street to attract passers-by, but hard sell techniques are notable by their absence. Besides tribal jewellery, there is a fine assortment of historic military memorabilia: regimental badges, buckles and buttons, powder cases and bayonets. Grisly "souvenirs" of the Afghan-Russian conflict, like bloodstained fur hats and tunics, are also displayed.

In the mid-1980s a new shopping arcade opened halfway along the bazaar, called **Shinwari Plaza** after one of the Pathan tribes of the Khyber Agency. This is the place to look for antique silver jewellery from Afghanistan set with ivory, amber, lapis lazuli, cornelian, turquoise or malachite. The silver bangles and lockets from Turkestan are especially fine. The shops in the upper storeys of the plaza also sell Afghan rugs, dresses and embroidery.

Further along Andar Shehr is the **Mosque of Mahabat Khan**, the only Moghul mosque in Peshawar to survive the depredations of the Sikhs. During the Sikh occupation of the city its minarets were used as gallows by General Avitabile, an Italian military adviser to Ranjit Singh. It dates from the 17th century and is named after a man who was governor of Peshawar during the reigns of Shah Jahan and Aurangzeb. Travellers are welcome but should avoid sightseeing during the Friday mid-day prayers, when it tends to be crowded.

Chowk Yagdar (the place of remembrance) is at the end of the Andar Shehr. The monument in the middle of the square, looking rather like an enormous kilt-pin, is a memorial to those who fell in Pakistan's wars with India. Chowk Yagdar is the Speakers' Corner of Peshawar, traditionally the place where rebel-rousers address political meetings. During the struggle for independence, many anti-British demonstrations started out from this square. Across it, bearing right at the **Clock Tower**, a narrow street leads past the **Vegetable Market** to the picturesque if smelly **Leather and Skin Market**. Caps and hats are cut and stitched from curly coated Karakul lamb skins and the cured skins can be purchased direct from the tanners.

Straight across at the next intersection and up another hill leads to the **Moghul Gateway** of a caravanserai known as **Gor Khatri** (warrior's grave). This was built by Shah Jahan's daughter. During the Moghul era, it was common practice throughout the Empire for local notables to construct safe places where wealthy merchants could stay. This was not entirely altruism, since it encouraged long distance trade and increased the revenue uptake from local taxes, customs and excise duties. The merchants and their retinues lodged in the lock-up rooms surrounding the central courtyard of the caravanserai, normally paying a charge for the privilege. The gates were locked from sunset

An old man of Peshawar poses with his jewellery.

to sunrise and the walls manned day and night by armed guards, so that merchants could rest secure in the knowledge that their goods were safe from robbers.

Gor Khatri has been an important place for travellers for thousands of years. In the 2nd century Buddhist pilgrims came to visit the **Tower of Buddha's Bowl** which was located on the site. But today no trace of the tower remains. After the demise of Buddhism, the site became a place of Hindu pilgrimage. The *Ain Akbari* (Institutes of Akbar), which was written by Abul Fazl in the second half of the 16th century remarks, "Here is a temple called Gorekehtery, a place of religious resort, particularly for jowgies."

The Sikhs demolished the mosque built by Shah Jahan's daughter and replaced it with a **Temple to Gorakhnath**, a Sikh deity. This is opposite the main gateway and next to it is the **Nandi Temple**. The bull is a symbol associated with the god Siva in Hindu iconography and stands for the masculine sexuality. Be that as it may, Gor Khatri is now used as government offices and also houses police and fire stations.

Returning down the hill gives a pleasant view of the **Old Merchants Houses**. These tall buildings were built of wood and unbaked brick, in the belief that this would be less hazardous to life and limb during earthquakes. (Peshawar experiences frequent low intensity tremors.) The carved wooden doors of the *havelis* and their overhanging balconies are beautiful examples of the joiner's craft.

Meena Bazaar is the first street on the left at the foot of the hill. This is the women's shopping centre, selling an astonishing profusion of haberdashery: ribbon and lace, buttons and bows, beads and braiding, hair ornaments, the lot. Hand and machine embroidery can be commissioned in gold, silver or coloured thread and wood block printing is done by hand in a nearby side street. Customers bring their own choices of fabric and decide on designs from the made-up patterns on display. *Pur-*

Honest Ali has many important customers for his shiny wares.

dah (veil) of every degree of severity is for sale here. It ranges from the simple *dupatta* (headscarf) and embroidered shawls and *chaddars* (sheets to be wrapped over the head and outer clothing) to buttoned coats with matching attached veils and the all-encompassing *shatelkoq*, which looks exactly like the shuttlecock used in badminton – presumedly named after it.

Meena Bazaar and the Andar Shehr are the two places in the Old City where women sometimes outnumber men. Normally, doing the shopping is men's work in the Frontier.

Turning right at the end of the bazaar takes the traveller along a street of saddlers and gunshops back to Chowk Yadgar. At this end of the square are the banks. Outside them, moneychangers lounge against their cash boxes. Beggars and pickpockets, not usually a great nuisance in Peshawar, can be a pest here, somewhat relentless in their endeavours to relieve customers of the burden of small change weighing down their pockets.

The alleys to the left lead into the **Banjara Bazaar** or gipsy's bazaar. This place sells all kinds of oddments: carved beads of bone and wood, real and false hair, skin and hair colourants and traditional cosmetics like *kajaal* (black eyeliner). In the rooms above, fortunes are told and magical remedies prescribed. Protective tattoos against supernatural attacks by *djinns* and the evil eye can be had. In a side street, off to the right, handmade basketwork and mats from Dera Ismail Khan are sold. Few tourists come to these places and the shopkeepers rarely speak anything but Pushtu or other Frontier tongues. Even Urdu, the national language of Pakistan, is unfamiliar hereabouts.

Pipal Mandi lies beyond the network of alleyways. A *mandi* is a grain market, particularly for the wholesale trade. There is a peepul tree in the quiet square believed to be the tree (or a descendant of it) under which the Buddha preached. The *chaikhanas* from which the dealers and brokers obtain their tea are good places to rest away from the heat and

The vegetable market.

throng and listen to the surprising sound of birdsong right in the heart of the city.

Little streets on the west side lead through to the **Cloth Market**, the other side of which is **Qissa Kahani**, the romantically named "Street of the Storytellers". Much has been written about this place, so appropriately described by Sir H.B. Edwardes (Second British Commissioner in Peshawar) as "the Piccadilly of Central Asia". All human life is here. The name derives from the tall tales of travellers, who have stopped to drink tea and swap yarns in the bazaar from time immemorial.

Honest Ali's shop is just one of many brass and copperware businesses on the Qissa Kahani, but is beyond doubt the best known. It sells both antique and modern pieces and purchases have been reliably forwarded from here to customers all over the world. A side street nearby leads past tinning works to the signposted **Peshawar Pottery**, whose customers include the British Royal Family. The potter upstairs makes china and earthenware goods to order and the forwarding service is again reliable.

Back on the main street and turning left, the first clump of shops display striped handloom blankets from Swat and the Kaghan Valley. Beyond them are the **Bird Market**, selling partridges, quails, parrots, doves and songbirds in miniscule cages and the **Fruit Bazaar**, which swings around the corner into Chowk Yadgar. Turning right and right again is the Khyber Bazaar.

Travellers will now most likely feel like a little spot of something from **Salateen's Hotel** on Cinema Road, famous for its tasty food and general atmosphere. The room upstairs has "family booths" where ladies or men accompanied by ladies are expected to sit and will probably feel more comfortable. The stares downstairs from men unused to seeing unveiled women can be unnerving.

Over the other side of Jail Bridge the **Cantonment Area** is quite different from the Old City, with wide streets, parks and gardens and trees painted white by the Armed Services which inhabit it. Like all cantonments in the

subcontinent, it was originally constructed by the British administration and is a living legacy from that period.

Cantonments were always built to a recognisable pattern: on the outskirts of a native settlement, with regimental barracks and parade grounds, cricket and football fields, a *maidan* for playing polo and holding gymkhanas or flower shows, messes for officers and other ranks, a church or two, armed and civil service bungalows spaciously laid out along roads called "lines" (after the original lines of tents). They possessed their own shopping areas and of course, that hub of British social life in Hindustan, "the club".

When the British Army pitched its tents in Peshawar for the first time, it did so in the remnants of the **Shalimar Gardens** to the north of Bala Hissar Fort. These had been extensive pleasure grounds, laid out like their namesake in Lahore during the Moghul era. The gardens were ransacked by the Sikhs, who felled its ancient groves for firewood. All that is left of it today is the

"Oranges for you, sir?"

Khalid Bin Wali Bagh on the Mall and one or two large trees at the cantonment's heart.

The Peshawar Club on Sir Syed Road, near the Mall, is the former cantonment clubhouse. As in the past, its recruitment policy is still extremely exclusive, where members are mostly high-ranking civil and military officers stationed in the city. There is a reciprocal arrangement for temporary membership with the Rawalpindi, Quetta and Karachi Clubs. One of Peshawar's two swimming pools is here, the morning sessions being reserved for women. A *shamiana* curtains off the ladies until noon, when a bell rings to warn that mixed bathing is imminent.

The library is a trip down memory lane, containing paperback romances and "thrillers" from the 1930s.

Next door to the club is **St. John's Church**, the foundation stone of which dates from 1851, two years after the British forces arrived and evidence of their firm intent to stay. The **Christian Cemetery** is situated on Jamrud Road and is entered by a lichen covered lych gate. One of the gravestones reads:

Here lies
Captain Ernest Bloomfield
Accidently shot by his orderly
March 2nd 1879
'Well done, good and faithful
servant'

Dean's Hotel is on Islamia Road. It is named after Sir Harold Deane, the very first Chief Commissioner of the North West Frontier Province. The hotel, a collection of tin-roofed bungalows with verandas, is set in pretty gardens, overhung by shady trees and secluded from the dusty streets. Afternoon tea on the spreading lawns is a most gracious experience. From within it is hard to believe that Central Asia lies on the other side of those high brick walls.

Jan's Hotel and **Green's Hotel** nearby are also to be recommended. Green's hotel has a tranquil courtyard and pleasant restaurant. Its buffet lunch is excellent and is a good place for

Hidden from the crowd – Dean's Hotel.

264

eavesdropping on current affairs. On the first floor there is an impressive snooker room. The tables were left in Peshawar by the British.

Saddar Bazaar is the shopping area of the cantonment. Wooden furniture inlaid with brass, Pakistani, Persian and Afghan rugs and waxed cloth are things to look out for along the main street. The waxed cloth is a traditional speciality of Peshawar. Stylised designs of birds, chrysanthemums, goldfish and dragons in the Chinese fashion are worked in brightly coloured wax on silk or satin cloth lengths. Little is known about its origins and the technique is a closely guarded trade secret.

Bara Market at the far end of Saddar sells legitimate foreign imports, such as Italian shoes, Japanese electrical goods and Danish china, as well as confiscated contraband items, like Russian snow-boots and vodka. The back streets in between sell everything from guns to water heaters and lawn mowers. Just behind the mosque is another interesting **Meena Bazaar**, manned at both ends by armed policemen to prevent men from entering.

Peshawar Museum is situated between Dean's Hotel and the Old City, about five minutes walk from Jail Bridge and the railway station. The museum was built in 1905 as an assembly hall for cantonment functions, but no one has done the military two step or played bridge there for a long time. It now houses a permanent exhibition of Gandharan art, including many reliefs showing events in the Buddha's life as well as a large number of bodhisattvas. The most prized possession, however, is a superb statue of the Fasting Siddhartha. There are also displays of tribal handicrafts and Islamic treasures.

Peshawar's most luxurious hotel is at the foot of Khyber Road. The **Pearl Continental** boasts the other of Peshawar's two swimming pools, as well as a large bar. It is possible for travellers not staying at the hotel to use the pool, but the pleasure is pricey. Only residents may use the bar. The barbecue in the gardens on summer evenings is

Khyber University.

A DAYTRIP TO DARRA

A Suzuki pickup truck noses through the bustling Saddar Bazaar in Peshawar. In the tarpaulin covered back are eight green turbaned tribesmen from beyond the frontier. The driver finds the Kohat Road and soon the pickup truck is heading through frost covered fields towards the jagged blue-grey peaks becoming visible through the early morning mist. Wintertime in the Frontier.

The tribesmen wrap their khaki shawls tightly against the dawn air. Countryside unrolls through the back of the truck. Sodden

asleep in a gloomy gorge. "Darra Bazaar, Darra Bazaar, Darra Bazaar" shouts the Suzuki-wallah. The tribesmen clumsily alight, stiff from the trip, and head for the nearest teahouse to get warm.

Darra Bazaar is what outsiders call it. The real name of the village where the guns are made is Zarghun Khel (Zarghun's lineage.) This is a branch of the Adam Khel Afridis, in whose territory the pass or *darra* is situated. Zarghun Khel is the only bazaar hereabouts, hence the name Darra Bazaar, "the market in

fields and canals, a haze of green on orchards coming into bud, houses and roadside shops, a police checkpoint trundle past. The truck reaches a smuggler's village, known throughout the Frontier for kidnapping and highway robbery. Nobody speaks.

The irrigated fields of the Vale of Peshawar give way to smaller and smaller terraces as the truck climbs into the foothills. A group of red-dressed girls taking sheep and goats out to graze pull their black chaddars over their heads and turn their backs to the road. Houses are fewer, fortified and have watch towers. About 45 kilometres from Peshawar, the truck enters a long bazaar seemingly still

the pass".

Nobody knows when the Afridis of Zarghun Khel began making guns. When Mountstuart Elphinstine came through here in 1809, on his way to Kabul, he noted that the Frontier Tribes were armed with *jezail* (indigenously manufactured long barelled muskets). The first workshop copying the British Lee Enfield rifles so much esteemed by Pathans was started in 1897. Some say that the British administration "gave the Afridis the right to make guns in exchange for rights of passage through the pass." The strategic route to Peshawar from Kohat was indeed secured, soon after the establishment of a

British military presence in 1849. But the fort on top of the Kohat Pass marked the end of settled territory and the Afridis beyond were free to do as they liked anyway.

Zarghun Khel lies in the narrowest part of the pass and the cliffs on each side are almost vertical. Even at noon it is difficult to see the sun. Gunshops line the highway, which runs through the centre of the bazaar. The workshops lie behind. The drill presses, lathes, grinders and borers used by the gunsmiths are basic in the extreme.

Visitors from the Western World are often astounded to see steel still being cast in sand, crucibles of molten metal hand-held and the rifling done manually. Though the machine tools needed to perform the 1,500 separate operations necessary for the production of one machine gun are elementary, they do work. It has to be said that the quality may not always be as good as internationally known brand-names, but then again they are a good deal cheaper.

The workshops and gunshops are family businesses. Some specialise in making particular parts, like firing mechanisms. Others make finished products, from casting the steel to engraving the stock. A small number of families organise the finance. These are the shops with international direct dialling connections – most telephone calls in Pakistan have to go through the operator.

All kinds of weaponry are on offer, ranging from small hand guns, to custom built rifles that can be disassembled for concealment in a car engine. Allegedly, field artillery is also produced. The most popular item is a still a "Lee Enfield" rifle, prized for sniping. Everything, well almost everything, can be copied. The Afridis joke that they have not yet mastered fighter aircraft, because they cannot replicate the sophisticated electronics. But they are working on it!

Skills are passed on from father to son in the time-honoured way. Pathans believe that children learn best by copying their elders and the sooner the better. At the age of four or five, they start work on simple tasks like sorting screws and washers.

By the time they are 10 or 11 years old they are competent to take charge. In their elders' unavoidable absence they do, handling con-

fidently tens of thousands of rupees. They know the business inside out.

The Main Street is a place to be avoided when guns are being tested and Afridis, like all Pathans, do quarrel amongst themselves. But they swiftly unite against a common threat. If everyone is heavily armed, no one is quick to start anything foolish.

Transactions completed, the tribesmen climb back into the truck and head for Kohat. It has taken the best part of the day to order what they need. They are pleased with their courteous reception, having been entertained to a lunch of mutton pilau as well as innumerable cups of tea. They are also wary of the Afridis' reputation for treachery.

Passing the Handyside Memorial on the edge of tribal territory, at the top of the Kohat Pass, someone remembers he was a Commander of the Frontier Constabulary murdered by local Afridis, who later contributed to the cost of the plaque! Another recalls that Molly Ellis, kidnapped by Afridis, was brought this way into the wild of the Tirah. Her mother's throat was cut by the kidnappers on the veranda of her own bungalow (still standing at No. 26 in the Kohat Cantonment). They pause to say their prayers, then hasten down the last few miles to the city. Heavily armed as they are, no one wants to be caught in these hills after dark.

Left, quality control. **Right**, the long and short of it all: weapons for sale in Darra.

delightful. Sometimes Pathan folk music can be heard there.

Up the Khyber Road is the Airport, which has daily flights to Islamabad, Lahore, Karachi and (weather permitting) Chitral. Beyond that are the golf course and University and, ultimately, the Khyber Pass itself.

Up the Khyber: Up the Khyber is British army rhyming slang. (The rhyme is with "pass".) It means dashed hopes. The Khyber is certainly the most famous pass in the world. Its hold on popular imagination is such that every visitor wants to see it. It still retains its importance in superpower rivalry.

There was no road through until 1586 when Akbar linked Kabul to Delhi by the Grand Trunk Road.

Jamrud is 18 kilometres west of Peshawar where the Pass meets the Vale of Peshawar. The fort at Jamrud was originally built by the Sikhs in 1823 with walls more than three metres thick and great bastions and gates. It is associated with the Sikh hero, Hari Singh Nalwa who was killed here, fighting Afghans.

His cremation took place in the fort. Nowadays the fort is a customs office and visitors have to get permits to proceed further.

There is also an arch, the **Bab-i-Khyber** (gateway to the Khyber) which dates from 1964. There is a viewing platform for visiting dignitaries and information about the pass on a nearby wall. The Khyber Pass has been closed in recent times due to the bitterness of the fighting among the feuding residents. Visitors need to check as to whether it is possible to go up the pass, and need permission from the Ministry of Foreign Affairs and an armed escort to go beyond Jamrud.

The road leads off through some barren hillocks and after a few kilometres, starts to climb. The best viewpoint is 10 kilometres from Jamrud. Looking back toward Peshawar two roads can be distinguished, the top one is the one for vehicles: trucks groan up the incline, all grinding gear changes and choking engines, through the dust. The lower route is the older one, traversed by

Long and winding road up the hill to the Khyber Pass.

people camels and donkeys. A little further on, there is a viewpoint offering a vista of the **Khyber Railway. Shagai** is 30 kilometres from Peshawar. The fort is British-built and is still used as the office of the Khyber Rifles.

Ali Masjid is in the centre of the pass. There is a mosque and there is a tradition that Hazrat Ali visited the place. Hence, the name. It is the narrowest part of the Khyber, said to be only 5 metres wide – so that two fully laden camels could not pass. The road has been widened, but even so is still a one way street. The carriageways and railway are hewn from the rockface above.

There is a fort at Ali Masjid but this is also operational and therefore not open to visitors. Occasional visitors are allowed to the British cemetery – if there is a family connection. The graves of British soliders who died in 1878 are still well maintained.

Zarai Valley lies through the gorge. The inhabitants are Afridis who are given to feuding among themselves. Their houses have high walls around them with gun emplacements and watchtowers. Many gates are made of explosion proof steel. The men take turns doing sentry duty on the roof.

Landi Kotal is at the top of the pass, 1,100 metres above sea level, and is the end of the line and the end of the road for tourists. There is a Central Asian caravanserai and a fort garrisoned by the Khyber Rifles. But the most exciting aspect of the town is the bazaars. All kinds of imported goods are available. One shop sells only clothing with the St. Michael (Marks and Spencer's) brandname. There are all kinds of electrical goods, china and glassware, secondhand cars and parts of cars. The best known of all are the drugs and gun shops. Imports have continued unimpeded by the war in Afghanistan, for the tribesmen are businessmen and "business is business".

The end of the pass is at **Torkham**, which is on the Durand line, the Afghan border. A tourist complex was erected there, but it has not been possible to travel to Torkham in recent times.

Attracting the passer-by: vendor's items in Landi Kotal.

TAKHT-I-BAHI

Of all the Buddhist monasteries built through the length and breadth of Gandhara, Takht-i-Bahi is renowned as the most beautiful. This reputation is based partly on its extraordinarily good state of preservation, carefully blended with its conscientious restoration, and partly on its glorious location. It is situated about three kilometres west of the modern town of Takht-i-Bahi on the Peshawar-Swat road south of the Malakand Pass. The site itself is located on the northern flanks of a rocky spur rising 150 metres above the plains.

The first proper scientific excavations on the site were carried out by D.B. Spooner on behalf of the Archaeological Survey of India between 1907 and 1911 and then by H. Hargreaves between 1910 and 1913. Unfortunately the results were never properly co-ordinated and so no stratigraphical sequence has ever been established for the site. Nevertheless it seems probable that the monastery itself was founded in the 1st century B.C. and flourished during the time of Kanishka by which time the Court of Many Stupas had been added. The Main Stupa and the Assembly Hall are likely to belong to the 3rd and 4th centuries A.D., whilst the Court of Three Stupas, the Low Level Chambers and the Open Courtyard date from the 5th, 6th or even 7th centuries.

Having ascended the steps leading up from the plains, the visitor enters the impressive surrounds of the **Court of Many Stupas**, so called because it contains at least 35 votive stupas. In all likelihood they were dedicated by visiting pilgrims and therefore were constructed at quite different times. Regrettably nothing can now be seen of the stucco plaster and decorative and narrative reliefs which must have once adorned their faces, but in many cases Corinthian pilasters and cornices can still be traced, hinting at the former splendour of the Court.

The Court itself measures some 36 metres by 15 metres and is enclosed to the north, south and east by walls eight to nine metres high against which were built a series of 30 chapels facing inwards. Within these once stood huge statues of the Buddha, perhaps four times life size. Although archaeologists found that all the roofs of the chapels had collapsed, those along the northern side have now been fully restored.

Running from north to south through the Court and between the stupas is a clear paved pathway which links up the Monastery to the north with the Main Stupa to the south, so presenting the visitor with an exciting dilemma as to which way to turn next.

The **Monastery**, entered by ascending five steps, takes the form of a quadrangle around three sides of which are fitted 15 cells, the abodes of the monks. Intriguingly the two cells in the north-west and south-west are substantially larger than the others. The cells look remarkably austere, partly due to their small floor spaces contrasting with the height of their walls which reinforces a sense of isolation once inside.

Furthermore, although in their heyday the walls were apparently plastered and colourfully decorated, today they are totally plain apart from occasional niches for the monks to store the simple necessities of life such as oil lamps and books. The single window was, however, so small and so high it could only have served as a ventilator. The greatest evident luxury today is the watertank lying in the south-east corner of the quadrangle though this may have been filled by hand from the spring below the monastery.

A doorway leads through the eastern wall to two small courts which formed the kitchen and the refectory. From the kitchen, the smaller of the two, leads a flight of nine stairs up to what must have been a second storey. This potentially provided for a further 15 cells, so doubling the capacity of the monastery to at least 30 monks.

Had the visitor turned south from the Court of Many Stupas and headed up a set of 15 stairs, he would have arrived at the **Main Stupa** which stands in a rectangular courtyard measuring about 17 metres by 13.5 metres. Today only the bottom of the square base of the stupa remains intact, having suffered through the centuries at the hands of treasure seekers. According to Sir Alexander Cunningham, who visited the site over 100 years ago, the base of the stupa then comprised of three stages, each one smaller than the last. He records that the uppermost stage was then adorned with pilasters, yet even at this time the body and umbrellas of the stupas had already been destroyed. The 4½ steps leading up to the top of the base, providing access to the monument which the faithful would then perambulate, are the result of careful reconstruction.

Like the Court of Many Stupas, the **Court of the Main Stupa** is surrounded on three sides by chapels. Initially there were five on each side, 15 in all, with spaces between them, and two of these chapels still have their original domed roofing intact. At a later date the spaces were filled through the addition of intervening smaller chapels, possibly to

The Court of Many Stupas.

cope with the increasing number of pilgrims wishing to make dedications to the monastery.

The face of each side wall looking onto the court was adorned with a pilaster, which was surmounted by an elaborate Corinthian capital of *Acanthus* leaves. Within each of these larger chapels were no doubt large statues of the Buddha, while in the smaller chapels would have been images of the saints, kings, votive stupas or even whole scenes in *Alto-Relievo*.

Cunningham reports that he regularly found gold leaf together with statue fragments in this area, strongly suggesting that the statues may have been gilded.

In the north-west corner of the site, just west of the Monastery itself, is the **Assembly Hall** where meetings of the whole community would have been staged – the routine monthly readings of Buddhist texts as well as extraordinary meetings for matters of urgency. The four water tanks sunk into the floor are all modern intrusions.

Domestic quarters scattered over the hill.

Immediately south of the Assembly Hall are the **Low Level Chambers**, the roof of which is level with the Court of Many Stupas. The Chambers, however, are not underground as two arched doorways lead out onto a large open courtyard on its western side. Access is gained via a staircase to the south. It is dark and caverous within, like an old wine cellar. Five rooms open up both to left and right from a central corbel-arched passageway.

Although the rooms vary considerably in size, those to the right are consistently larger. These larger rooms, which also have flat lintelled doorways, have no windows, lending support to the theory that they might have been granaries. However, the smaller rooms, which have arched doorways, are equipped with either doors or windows facing the western courtyard, suggesting rather that they provided an alternative venue for serious meditation and learning. Nowadays they are occupied by thriving communities of bats.

South of here in the south-west corner of the site, is the **Court of Three Stupas**, so called because it originally housed three stupas. Today the chief attraction is probably the array of sculptures collected from the site and on display under the modern roof. Immediately to the south again is the **Wall of Colossi**, over five metres high, named after the discovery of six pairs of giant feet on a low platform at the base of the wall. The feet are thought to be the remains of of standing statues of the Buddha which may once have been six metres high. Other fragments of these statues, among them two heads, were recovered by archaeologists from the debris which filled the court.

There can be no doubting that the monastery at Takht-i-Bahi was a remarkable institution. The final indication of its importance is provided by the spread of stone domestic buildings over the surrounding hill. For the most part two-storied, often with sophisticated staircases, they were originally plastered externally with lime mortar as well as being well decorated internally. Here indeed was a thriving community.

THE SWAT VALLEY

A journey through Swat is without a doubt one of the most beautiful and rewarding trips in the northern valleys and one of the most accessible to travellers. There are daily flights to Mingora from Islamabad and Peshawar, a journey of about 30 minutes by air. By road, it takes about five hours from either city. There are regular buses and flying coaches from both.

The road to Swat turns off the Grand Trunk Road just north of **Nowshera** and leads through **Mardan** and **Takht-i-Bahi** to the **Malakand Pass**. Earlier accounts depict the climb as hair raising, but today, the gradient is gentle and well-guarded. Small rivulets cross the road but present no hazard except for the superannuated trucks topping up their radiators. A stopping place one kilometre below the summit gives a breath taking view of the Takht-i-Bahi mountains and the wild ranges of Mohmand and Bajaur Agencies. From here on it was all downhill for Alexander and his army.

Below the present road the older mule track can be picked out – the journey on that track must have been hair raising. At the summit is a shrine. Handfuls of change are thrown out of buses and trucks to give thanks to the saint for a safe arrival. The shrine's guardians carry water there daily. It is an act of religious merit specifically mentioned in the Holy Koran to provide shelter, water and guidance for people travelling on the road.

The Malakand Fort guards the summit and approaches. Like the **Dargai Fort** below, it played a key role in the Malakand uprising of 1897, an event covered by the young Winston Churchill for the London *Daily Telegraph*.

In June that year the British garrisons throughout the frontier were attacked. The tribes of the newly formed Malakand agency were led by a *Sayyid* (a descendant of the Holy Prophet of Islam) whom the British soldiers dubbed "the Mad Mullah". Actually, his name

was Hajji Shoaib Baba and he resided in the village of Turangzai, near Chardsadda, where his descendants still live today. The Hajji Sahib preached *jihad* (holy war) against the infidels and 10,000 Pathans, mostly Yusufzai, assembled for the attack. Dargai fell but 1,000 Sikhs, commanded by British officers held Malakand until reinforcements could arrive from the Guides Headquarters at Mardan.

Batkhela is the first sizeable settlement the other side of the pass. It is an administrative centre and market town with an interesting cloth market. All kinds of material, both traditional and modern cloth lengths and ready-made outfits are for sale.

The road follows the **Swat River** upstream, past the headworks of the **Swat Canal**, which conveys water to the Malakand Range, through a tunnel, to irrigate the lush and fertile Samah plains as far as Mardan. This part of the valley is a delight to the senses. In springtime the orchards are bright with blossom and in summer the rice fields

Left, terraces above the Swat River. **Right**, peeking through the trees.

are ready to be harvested. The air is scented with a peculiar smell of honey and limejuice.

At **Chakdarra**, the road divides into two. Historically, it is one of the most important crossroads in Pakistan. Over the bridge is the way to Dir and Chitral, via the Lowari Pass. Historians now believe that most of the invasions of the subcontinent came this way, including Alexander the Great in 327 B.C., having crossed the passes of the Hindu Kush from Afghanistan.

Straight on is Mingora, and the Upper Swat Valley. From Khawazakhela in Middle Swat, the Shangla Pass goes over to Besham in the Indus Valley and thence along the Karakoram Highway to Gilgit, Hunza, the Khunjerab Pass and China. This is a part of the historic Silk Road, used by Chinese pilgrims to Swat over a thousand years ago.

For today's travellers, Chakdarra also plays an important role; there is the choice of either remaining in Swat, crossing the Lowari Pass to Chitral, or taking the Shangla Pass to the KKH.

The crossroads are guarded by **Chakdarra Fort**, still operational. The **Churchill Picket** on **Damkot Hill** opposite the Fort was rebuilt in 1896 by the British army on the ruins of the Moghul fortifications. Winston Churchill nearly lost his life on Damkot Hill in a skirmish.

The views from the picket are panoramic and it is easy to see why the location is strategic for military confrontation. No less than seven passes through the mountains are controlled by this strongpoint.

Chakdarra Museum is about half a kilometre along the Dir Road and houses a collection of Buddhist sculptures from nearby sites, Hindu relics and more recent folk art and handicrafts. It is highly praised by visitors.

To the Lowari Pass: For those wishing to visit Chitral (see Karakoram to Hindu Kush) the journey via the Lowari Pass can take as much as fourteen hours from Peshawar.

From the bridge at Chakdarra, the road follows the Adinzai River northwards and then crosses the **Wuch** (or Uch) **River** to enter the **Talash Valley.** The whole region is very pretty and there are Buddhist and Hindu remains, to date unexplored.

The shrine of **Majawar Baba** is located at one of the most beautiful spots. At the western end is the Katgalla Pass, guarded by a fort dating from the 8th or 9th century A.D. It is believed that Alexander the Great fought and won a battle in the vicinity. The Moghul conqueror, Babur, also passed this way and got married here, in January 1519.

The legend is told that there had been ill will between Babur and the Yusufzai, though relations were improved by the start of a friendship between the Yusufzai leader, Malik Ahmad and Babur. Ahmad however, evaded a second invitation to meet Babur and sent his brother, Shah Mansur instead. Babur was disappointed not to see Ahmad: Mansur was speedily dismissed and Babur arrived at the ancestral fort with his army.

Disguised as a *qalandar* (holy man), Babur went inside to see the Yusufzai

In good cheer.

stronghold. It was *Eid-i-qurban*, the feast to commemorate Abraham's sacrifice, and a banquet was spread. Shah Mansur's daughter, Bibi Mubarika was sitting with the other women. Her eyes fell upon Babur, whom she clearly found attractive, and she sent some food to him. Babur asked the servant about his benefactress. He left, but hid the food behind the house.

He was in trouble – in love – and unable either to conquer her home or to retreat without looking foolish. He opened marriage negotiations. They were reluctant, even denying that there was such a daughter. But Babur then told of his visit and asked them to search for the food, in order to substantiate his story. They found the food and agreed to the match. The marriage undoubtedly helped Babur's conquest of Hindustan for Yusufzai soldiers served in the army which defeated Ibrahim Lodi at Panipat in 1526. Many of the details about the country and the people which are written in the *Baburnama* may have been culled from these Yusufzai kin.

Leaving Mingora.

From the Talash Valley the road follows the **Panchkora River** northwards to **Timargarha** (Timolgrah, the locals call it). This is the historic bridging point where the Jandul River leads in from the Bajaur Agency, the way that Babur came to Swat.

Dir is the last settlement of any size before the long haul up to the Lowari Pass. It has been described as a town, but does not provide very respectable facilities for tourists, bad news for those who arrive here in the afternoon, for it is then too late to continue the journey.

An atmosphere of evil pervades the place. Exchanges of gunfire are common. The showdown could take place between any two parties, or a combination, of the following: opium poppy cultivators and drug eradication agents, rival factions of mujahidin, feuding families, truck drivers who do not like the look of each other's faces (Dir is a major stopover) or just local hooligans with nothing better to do.

Automatic weaponry is not unusual. In the summers of 1987 and 1988, Paki-

stani newspapers reported that local political factions were firing rocket launchers at each other's houses. Missiles screamed across the narrow valley for days. The editor of this book was caught inside a downtown hotel on one of these occasions, locked inside his room, apparently for his own safety. The locals are friendly to outsiders.

When the traveller finally escapes from Dir, he is happy to be over the Lowari Pass and steaming down into the bliss of Chitral. But everything depends on the weather.

The **Lowari Pass** is not especially high at 3,200 metres. But after rain or frost the 47 hairpin bends on the Chitral side become impassable, even for four wheel drive vehicles. Some of the hairpins are so tight that they require a great deal of caution forward and even more caution reversing to ever be able to get round the bend at all. This involves backing up towards a chasm with not as much as a rail to mark the edge.

The pass can be traversed from late May till the end of October, when the snows return. Much of the open season coincides with the wet monsoon. Hence, even experienced drivers approach the journey with caution. Foreigners are forbidden to travel after dark.

To Upper Swat: Back at Chakdarra the road to Upper Swat leaves the river, bypassing the town of Thana or Thanra. At Landakai police checkpoint, formerly the border of Swat Princely State, the road starts to climb through terraced fields and orchards. Almost every hill is topped with ruined fortifications of earlier civilisations.

Barikot lies on another historically important route. It is the site of the ancient city of Bazira, where the Karakar Pass to Buner and Ambela and the Mora and Shahkot Passes join the valley. The city was taken with great difficulty by Alexander.

The Buddhist remains of **Shingerdar**, **Gogdara** and **Udegram** are a little further on. At Udegram is the shrine of Pir Kushal Khan Baba, believed to have been the commander of Sultan Mahmud of Ghazni's army, **Up into the hills.**

which brought Islam to Swat in the 11th Century A.D. The commander was killed in the siege of Raja Giri's fortress which stands on the ridge behind.

Mingora (pronounced Min-gow-ra) is about 40 kilometres from Chakdarra and is the biggest town in Swat. Throughout the Frontier, Mingora is just known as Swat. Mingora is a major, long–distance communications centre and has been an important market place for thousands of years.

Buses leave here for destinations all over Pakistan, departing when they are full, and travelling almost non-stop. It takes three days and two nights to get to Karachi from here. The journey is quite an experience – perhaps too much of an experience for most people.

The lower town, near the bus stand caters for low budget travellers and has inexpensive hotels, lodging houses and cafes. This is also the place to buy cheap but delicious snacks like *pakoras* and *samosas*.

Across the river and up the hill is the old town. The bazaars are fascinating.

Mingora is known throughout Pakistan for its men's sandals (suede, decorated with woollen pompoms), woollen waistcoats and caps, handloom blankets and embroidered shawls. Traditional Swati embroidery and old silver jewellery from the tribal areas are sold in the side streets off the main thoroughfare. Curios and antiques can be found in the upper bazaars, silver opium pipes, snuff boxes and old coins, strings of cowrie shells (from the Comoro Islands, off East Africa) once used as currency, coral and freshwater pearls, precious or semi precious stones, cut, uncut or carved with religious inscriptions, loose or set in gold or silver, ornaments and artifacts of bone and horn – a treasure trove for bric-a-brac collectors.

There are several good hotels in the upper town, including the Pameer which is of international standard. Mingora also boasts a splendid golf course, one of just half a dozen or so in the country.

Saidu Sharif is the twin town of

Autumn glow.

Mingora and administrative capital of Swat District. It lies about two kilometres south of Mingora along the Saidu river. Saidu is *sharif* (holy) because of the grave (*mazar*) of Abdul Gaffar, a Sufi Pathan from Jabrai Village in Upper Swat and greatly revered as a religious teacher. After his death at the grand age of 93, a shrine was raised above the grave. It became a popular pilgrimage place, rivalling Pir Baba in nearby Buner District.

Abdul Gaffar is the archetypal messiah figure who arises from time to time in the Frontier and his story is worth telling. Born in 1784 he started life as a shepherd, like his father. One day hearing about a *pir*, a saint, living at Beka on the Indus, he decided to walk there and hear his teachings.

After a few years, he began to teach and wandered throughout the Samah. He was somehow implicated in the death of the Khan of Hund and fled to Gujar Garhi near Mardan and later Torderh, a Khattak Village near Nowshera. Wherever he went, against his will it seems, crowds gathered, calling him "*Akhond*" (teacher).

Hearing of this, the Afghan rulers of Peshawar sought his help in raising *jihad* against the encroaching Sikhs. But the Sikhs won and Abdul Gaffar fled again, to Sam Ranizai below the Malakand Pass, Batkhela and finally Saidu. There he married a Yusufzai woman and had two sons, from whom the rulers of Swat are descended. Yusufzai women rarely marry outside their own lineage, let alone their own tribe. The fact that this happened shows the enormous respect and prestige that he commanded among Pathans.

His obituary in *The Times of London* in 1877 prompted Edward Lear to write the poem which begins :

*Who or why, which or what
Is the Akond (sic) of Swat ?*

Now you know. The old shrine of carved wood has since been replaced by a lurid coloured plaster edifice, but the wooden mosques at Bahrein or Kalam

Spring time.

in Upper Swat give an impression of how it might have looked.

Saidu Sharif is very different from the bustling bazaars of Mingora. The streets are lined by flowering shrubs and buildings, mostly in the Indo-British administrative style, set out in charming lawned gardens.

The **Serena Hotel**, (formerly the Swat Hotel) is an especially gracious building. At one time the residency of the British Representative in Swat, it offers the best cuisine in the valley. The Palace of the Walis of Swat, rulers of the princely state until 1969 (when Swat became absorbed into Pakistan as a district) is nearby. There is also a museum of Gandharan sculpture and local Swati handicrafts.

The **Marghazar Valley** follows the Saidu River back toward its source, with distant views of **Raja Giri's Castle**. Marghazar was the summer residence of the Walis and the entire administration of Swat was moved up to the **Safed Mahal** (White Palace) for the season. Its situation at the head of the valley is idyllic. From the side of the palace, a pleasant footpath leads beside a stream to the summit of **Mount Ilam**, sacred to Hindus and members of allied faiths for thousands of years.

Until 1947 there was an annual pilgrimage up the mountain. This was undertaken on foot, pilgrims thus acquiring religious merit through self-denial and perhaps even freedom from rebirth. The peak is also sacred to Buddhists, since legend has it that in one of his incarnations, Buddha gave up his life here.

From Mingora, the highway runs above the Swat River on a ledge blasted out of the rock face by British engineers, on behalf of the newly recognised Swat State in 1926. Before that travellers had to paddle, scale the heights, or cross the river twice at Mingora and Fatehpura, on what Eric Newby in his book "A Short Walk in the Hindu Kush" aptly calls "suicide bridges". These consist of wooden slats tied together by rope and suspended from rope cables. Coming downstream was relatively easy. Trav-

The main street in Bahrein.

A ROOM WITH A VIEW

Muambhar Khan's "House Rental and Food Shop" is run by four brothers and their father. It is known all over the world and sells everything: cosmetics, toiletries and local medicines; jars of preserves and pickles, packets of sweets and biscuits; imported baby foods, cigarettes and matches; batteries; kerosene; knitting wool and steel wool; dried fruits and nuts; blocks of raw sugar and rock salt; various sorts of grains and flour and whole and ground spices. In the winter, the shop sells the woollen *weskits* (waistcoats) and bright, hand loom woven striped blankets, made in Madyan, for which Swat is famous.

All of the brothers speak good English and have a smattering of other European languages too. One of the brothers went to Sweden a few years ago, hence the family nickname in Madyan: "Scandinavia-wallah!"

But the reason that the shop has become locally and internationally famous is because Madyan (Swat) 89 is the number to telephone for a quiet room with a view. The house is known by word of mouth to low budget travellers throughout the world as an inexpensive but decent place to stay.

Often an anthropologist, ethnomusicologist or sociolinguist is in residence. The research for at least two doctoral theses have been completed

from here – one on Pathan women's laments. American students from Berkeley University's Language Programme in Pakistan have come here every summer for years to get away from the intense heat of the plains, practise their Urdu and maybe learn a little Pushto.

Muambhar Khan started the house rental side of his business accidentally. Before that, the family livelihood was farming. In the late 1960s Swat was invaded by hippies, partly as a result of media features on the valley, partly because it was then a place where cheap drugs could be found and where the local populace were hospitable. At first, they camped on flat land near the river, an area used from time immemorial by travellers. Later, hippies started to sleep more or less anywhere. Muambhar Khan was horrified that young

women should spend the night in the open. With the agreement of his wife and other women of the family, he let them sleep in the compound. The girls offered money in return for the hospitality and so the business was born.

As word spread, it became impossible to house everybody who needed somewhere to stay. Sometimes travellers needed to rest for more than a day or two. So Muambhar Khan took a gamble, sold land near the river and used the money to construct six rooms adjacent to, but outside, the compound, that way ensuring privacy for everyone. He installed running water and a bathroom with a shower and a flush system.

The house is a steep climb from the road and like all traditional Pathan households consists of two parts. Behind the main gate and high mud walls are the guest rooms, then an inner courtyard. This is closed to outsiders so that the women can go about their household duties and have no need to withdraw or veil themselves. Rooms are arranged around the courtyard, shaded by mulberry trees. A ladder leads to the flat roof, where fruits and vegetables are dried in Swat's short summer season.

Every married brother has a room for himself, his wife and children. Before they were married, they were expected to sleep in the guest rooms or with other families. Each sub-family stores its belongings in huge tin trunks and looking after these is women's work. The wives keep the keys to the trunks on chains around their waists.

A shop was located, rented and stocked with things that travellers and local people needed. Business flourished but then luck turned. The wars in Afghanistan, Iran and Iraq in the 1980s reduced the overland tourist trail to a mere trickle. Not only did the demand for rooms dry up, but the shop too experienced difficulties. Today, tourists travel mostly by car and speed through Madyan to Kalam and Upper Swat. But somehow, word got around that Muambhar Khan needed help and money began to arrive, sometimes handfuls of francs or lira, sometimes hundreds of dollars or pounds from former hippies now made good. It is their way of saying thanks to someone who gave them a helping hand when their own luck was low. Here is Pathan hospitality at its best.

ellers floated on rafts of inflated buffalo skins, hoping not to be caught on the rocks.

At **Manglaur**, a new road leads up the mountainside to Malam Jabba ski resort, built with Austrian Aid.

Khwazakhela about 32 kilometres from Saidu was formerly the largest commerical centre in Upper Swat, but has declined since the opening of the Karakoram Highway. The Highway has diverted much through traffic. It is noted for its furniture trade and is a good place to look for antique chairs, beds and chests of carved wood. Turn right here for the **Shangla Pass** and the KKH.

At **Fatehpura**, the fertile farmland and orchards are left behind and the valley narrows into an alpine glen. **Miandam**, a village up one of the loveliest side valleys is reached by a road branching off about two kilometres beyond Fatehpura. At 1,800 metres above sea level, it is an ideal hot weather holiday resort and has several reasonably priced decent hotels. There are easy trails in the pine-clad mountains, the air is a tonic and the sunsets are the best in Pakistan.

Madyan (pronounced, perversely, Mad-ayn) is about eight kilometres along the highway from Fatehpura. It is a busy shopping centre and there are several interesting antique shops, selling all kinds of curiosities. The present writer once bought a set of intricately carved divining bones here! Madyan is the best place in the entire valley to purchase traditional embroideries and handloom shawls. The work is done in the farm houses which perch on the mountain sides around. The embroidery is beautiful, mostly fuchsia pink on black and constitutes former dowry items, now unwanted. These days girls are expected to bring VCRs and refrigerators in their bottom drawers, not counterpanes and bolster covers.

A little embroidery is still done, nothing like the old days, and handloom weaving continues. Formerly the colours were hand made from roots and berries but today, aniline dyes are used. These make the shawls and blankets even more strikingly coloured.

After Madyan, the road crosses to the right bank and proceeds along a gorge to **Bahrein** where the Daral River, joining the main stream, turns it into a torrent. At 1,300 metres above sea level, Bahrein, like Madyan, is cold enough to require a *razai* (cotton-wool filled bedquilt) even in summer and is another very popular holiday resort. The bazaars, especially the side streets, are fun to explore and the shopkeepers are exceptionally cooperative.

Bahrein's speciality is hand-knitted sweaters for men and embroidered dress lengths and shawls for women. The houses are made of wood in the upper town and decorated with intricate wood carvings. Bahrein has two mosques of wood, both delightful examples of traditional architecture.

Beyond Bahrein, the road is often closed by snow from December to April and can be slippery for saloon cars in the summer, after rain. It leads to **Kalam**, an interesting journey of about 40 kilometres sometimes high above the river in the pine trees, sometimes beside the torrent below. Narrow, hanging valleys

permit **Mount Mankial** to come into view from time to time.

Kalam itself is not particularly attractive. On one side of the valley is a huge black glacial moraine, looking like a spoil heap. The numerous government department rest houses, roofed with rusting corrugated iron do not improve it. Only one hotel, the Falakshir, is reasonably clean.

On the other side is the bazaar, a higgeldy-piggeldy mass of damp, smoke-blackened, decaying wood. The wooden mosque is very charming though and well worth seeing. It is carved with scroll patterns which, ethnographers claim, resemble Kailash designs. The streets are wet and dirty. It is cold and always seems to be raining. At times the scene is reminiscent of the last days of the Alaska Gold Rush.

But it is the cold weather and the scenery which bring travellers to upper Swat, to get away from the heat and dust of the plains. The fishing and trekking roundabout are excellent.

At Kalam the white crested **Utrot** and

Ushu streams join together to form the Swat River. Both streams are noted for their excellent fishing reaches. Angling enthusiasts imported Brown and Rainbow Trout eggs from Scotland and the North of England in the early years of this century to improve the sporting stock. **Lake Mahodand**, about 20 kilometres from Kalam, in the upper Ushu Valley, is lauded as some of the best course fishing to be had in Pakistan. Transport from Kalam and overnight stay at **Utrot**, **Gabral** and **Maltitan** can be booked through the PTDC. Travel companies like Lords and Waljis in Islamabad, specialists in adventure holidays, also organise fishing permits and fishing tackle. Anglers with their own equipment can hire jeeps or pickup trucks in the bazaar and apply for a permit through the local PTDC representative at the Falakshir Hotel (when available).

People who don't like fishing can take an enjoyable walk in the forests around Kalam and along the rushing rivers. The Ushu valley is especially pretty, with glimpses of snow clad **Mount Falakshir** through the enormous pine woods.

Treks of differing lengths and degrees of severity can be undertaken from Kalam, but in this rugged, remote region all are foolhardy without a guide, proper equipment and substantial "tough country" experience beforehand. Solitary backpackers camping in undesignated sites put their lives at risk from robbers. Locals blame bears and leopards but unfortunately upper Swat's wildlife has been more or less shot out. Travellers would be lucky to see a hawk or a hedgehog, let alone a markhor or urial today.

Having said this, the trekking is absolutely spectacular. A popular trek leads through the mountains to Gilgit and Chitral following ancient trade tracks. From Lake Mahodand, the **Kachikani Pass** climbs up a glacier and over frost shattered peaks to Laspur on the Gilgit-Chitral road.

High even by Himalayan standards, the Kachikani Pass, at 5,700 metres, is a bit of a gasper.

Left, old man from Kalam. Right, high up in Upper Swat.

THE BUDDHA IN SWAT

Buddhist stupas, monasteries, rock carvings and statuary abound throughout the Swat valley. The more valuable objects of art from this period can be seen in the museums at Chakdarra and Saidu Sharif.

From about the 2nd century B.C. to about the 7th century A.D., Swat was a major religious centre of Gandhara. Though it declined thereafter, practising Buddhists could be found in Swat until the 16th century A.D. At it's height there were more than 1,400 monasteries in Lower Swat alone.

travellers, because they are the most intact.

Butkara Shrine is located behind the Saidu Sharif Museum. There is a central stupa – the *chaitya* or shrine – surrounded by 215 smaller stupas and chapels. The shrine was built to house some of the Buddha's ashes. It is thought to have been constructed by the Emperor Ashoka and dates from the 3rd century B.C. In its heyday throngs of pilgrims visited the shrine to perform perambulation. This meant walking around the stupa a certain number of times in order to acquire

These were internationally influential. Tantric Buddhism was developed in Swat. Many major *tantras* (manuals of magic gestures, sounds and diagrams) were compiled here. Traders, as well as pilgrims and preachers, took Tantric Buddhism along the Silk Road.

There are important Buddhist sites at Damkot Hill, Chat Pat and Andharan Deri (all near Chakdarra); Top Dara, Gumbaruna and Nimogram (near Landakai); Gumbat, Shingerdar, Gogdara and Udegram (near Barikot); Butkara and Mount Ilam (near Saidu Sharif); and Jehanabad (near Manglaur). Butkara, Nimogram, Jehanabad and the Barikot sites are of the greatest interest to

punya, religious merit.

The smaller stupas were built by rich pilgrims, to acquire *punya* through fulfilling a vow. The earliest date from about the 1st century B.C. Over time they grew increasingly more elaborate, acquiring pillars carved with lions, eagles, lillies and lotus flowers, painted and guilded to show the love of living things which is central to Buddhism. The famous **Crouching Lions** near the shrine may once have graced some of these stupas. Others were topped by stone umbrellas, a symbol used throughout South Asia to signify royalty.

About a century later a *vihara* was built,

north of the shrine. It was originally a meeting hall, but was later enlarged into a monastery, replacing the temporary huts built by mendicants during the Buddha's lifetime. Beside this, an entire town grew to house pilgrims. It is, as yet, unexcavated.

The shrine, like the surrounding stupas and monastery, was maintained by pilgrims' donations. It has been rebuilt twice and redecorated at least five times. In the 3rd century A.D. it must have been quite amazing, with great swags of plaster garlands, stone and stucco statues in niches and relief carvings of the Buddha's life, the whole lot gilded and painted in the brightest colours. The path round the shrine was paved with coloured glass, in those days a stupendously expensive commodity. The traditional wooden guard rail had been replaced by a stonewalled passage, decorated by coloured stucco figures of meditating Buddhas and abutting into the smaller stupas around it. Butkara, however, was prone to flooding and, as pilgrimage to Gandhara declined, maintenance also became financially impossible. In the 8th century A.D. the site was finally abandoned.

Up in the Swat Valley beyond Mingora is the **Seated Buddha** at **Jehanabad**. The Buddha itself is a steep climb from the village, situated east of Manglaur on the Malam Jabba Road. The image is carved straight out of the rockface and is four metres high.

The **Barikot** sites are south of Mingora. According to legend, **Shingerdar Stupa** was erected by King Uttarasena, over relics of the Buddha in his safekeeping. It dates from the 3rd century A.D. and resembles Butkara. Archives record that it once had a golden dome. Nearby is the **Elephant Rock**, where Mata, the elephant which transported the Buddha's relics to the site fell dead. Story has it that her body turned to stone, but her spirit was reborn as a human. The rock is mentioned by Hsüan Tsang, the Chinese pilgrim who came to Swat in A.D. 630.

Carved in the cliff face by the Silk Road itself is a huge, if battered, **Relief of the Buddha**. The **Galagai Cave** close by also contains relief carvings. The principle figure, in Central Asian costume, may be one of the Kushan Kings, possibly King Utta-

rasena. **Gogdara** engravings, a little further on, were started by Aryan invaders in about 1000 B.C., but several Buddhist carvings (from the the 6th or 7th century A.D.) can be seen on the rocks. One depicts the *Papmapani* (Lotus Bearer) Bodhisattva, with attendants. At **Udegram** site there were seven reliefs of *Papmapani*, each on a rock.

Gumbat Stupa, off the Pir Baba Road from Barikot, has a square, central cell, surrounded by an enclosed perambulatory passage, both lit by skylights. The cell was used for meditation. Several small stupas and a ruined complex called the **Kanjar Kot** (the prostitute's house) are nearby. The name suggests that this place at times served as a

centre for more worldly pursuits.

Nimogram is the least accessible site, stuck out on the spur of a barren hill about 30 kilometres northwest of Landakai. The track is best negotiated by four wheel drive. The last steep section up can only be ascended on foot, but it is well worth the climb. There are also three main stupas (there is normally only one). One stupa is for the Buddha (the teacher), one for *sanga* (fellowship) and one for *dharma* (principles).

In addition there is a monastery which has not yet been excavated. Nimogram's magnificent sculpture is now dislayed in the Saidu Sharif Museum.

Left, Nimogram monastery and stupa. **Right**, the Buddha meditates above Jehanabad.

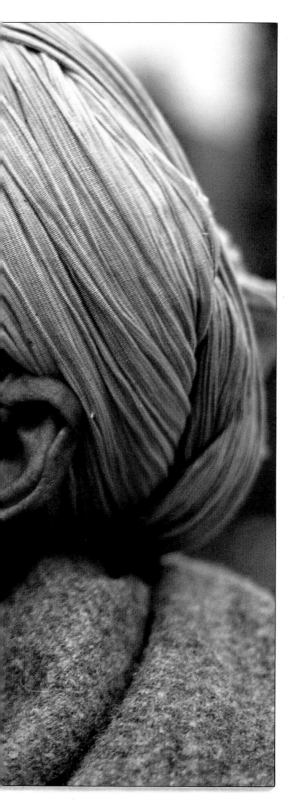

KARAKORAM TO HINDU KUSH

There can be few areas in the world where mountains rise in such awesome splendour as in the Northern Areas of Pakistan. Towering above the Chitral Valley, on the northeastern border of Afghanistan, Tirich Mir reigns as the highest of the majestic peaks of the Hindu Kush. Some 500 kilometres further east, the magnificent pyramid of K2, the second highest mountain in the world, crowns the violent spires of the Inner Karakoram. To the north the remote Pamir Plateau separates South from Central Asia, two continents once joined by the caravan routes of the Old Silk Road which sliced their way across the passes and through the central valley of Hunza. To the south, the huge bulk of Nanga Parbat rises in splendid isolation as the last great bastion of the Himalayan Range, dividing the fertile plains of Kashmir from the forbidding gorges of the Indus.

The high mountain regions of northern Pakistan are very different in character to the neighbouring Himalayas of India and Nepal to the south-east. The Karakoram and Hindu Kush lie beyond the clutches of the monsoon, resulting in a distinct lack of natural vegetation. Precipitation is normally only to be found at altitude, leaving the main valleys as dry as a bone, very hot in summer, and largely dependent on artificial irrigation for the support of crops.

Geology has also played a role in creating a quite unique mountain environment, particularly in the east of the region, in the Karakoram ranges of Baltistan. Whereas in the Himalayas there are gently graded slopes leading to the face of a mountain, here many of the mountains are simply huge monoliths of granite which rise vertically, for thousands of metres, straight out of the valley floors.

The result is a high altitude vertical desert, which may come as a shock for those used to more "Alpine" regions. Above some of the longest glaciers in the world rise some of the highest and

293

most inaccessible mountains, guarding some of the remotest valleys where beneath all the hectic jumble of rock and ice, neat villages cling to their green oases, as if stranded on the very edge of civilisation.

To the first inhabitants of the Karakoram and Hindu Kush, the land must have appeared even more hostile. But who were the people who first decided to settle down in these remote regions? While certain noble rulers of Hunza and Chitral claimed to be the descendants of fairies, many groups of lesser mortals from throughout the north of Pakistan still claim to be descended from the legions of Alexander the Great, Iskander as they call him; that great legendary figure who once came marching in over the Hindu Kush.

The distinctly fair complexion of many local people, particularly in the northern part of the Chitral Valley, may support the theory that indeed some of Alexander's soldiers got sore feet. But this doesn't really suffice as being an explanation of the origins of the multitude of different races and languages which still thrive in the Northern Areas.

The people living in the remotest northern valleys are descended from the combined waves of invasion and emigration which entered the Indian subcontinent from the north; from the first Aryans all the way through to the Huns. There was also influence from the south, particularly following the decline of the Gandhara Civilisation, when waves of emigrants, first Buddhist and then Hindu, pushed northwards from the plains. The original settlers were pushed back further and further into the mountains, into the remotest valleys. While some managed to survive and even thrive, like the Hunzakuts with their ideal position on the caravan routes coming down from the north, other groups such as the Nagar, and the Kho in Chitral became the definite underdogs and became part of the greater Kingdom of Dardistan which had emerged by the 11th century.

In the east, in Baltistan, the people were originally of Aryan stock, though after the Tibetan conquest in the 10th century, their history became interwoven with that of Ladakh. The Tibetans were in a constant state of war with the Dards and both tried to gain supremacy in the area. Islam arrived in Dardistan in the 12th century, but it took another 300 years for Kashmiri missionaries to convert the Baltis.

After the central powers declined, they fragmented into a number of small kingdoms, each with its own powerful ruler. There were, for example, the *Thums* of Hunza, The *Rajas* of Skardu and the *Mehtars* of Chitral. When, in 1846, Maharaja Gulab Singh was granted control of Kashmir by the British, his sphere of influence was extended to control the whole of the Northern Areas. The Muslims resented this Hindu domination, but didn't get rid of Dogra rule until 1948 after the British had left.

The British didn't enter the region in force until the Russian advance in Central Asia started to pose a threat to their power in the subcontinent at the end of the last century. One of the remotest

Preceding pages: **Masherbrum; sunrise on Tirich Mir; herdsman of the Kaghan Valley. Below, welcome to the mountains!**

outposts of the British Empire, the Gilgit Agency became the springboard from which a whole series of expeditions were launched to explore and survey the area.

Men like Francis Younghusband and Sir Martin Conway penetrated into the remotest corners of this forbidding land, providing the first detailed maps of the area as well as information about the obscure roots and folklore of all the peoples living between Karakoram and Hindu Kush.

Today the majority of people in the region are Muslim, divided between the Sunni, Shia and Ismaili sects. Islam, a religion inspired by the clear skies of the desert, has in no way destroyed the natural beliefs of the mountain folk who live here. As far as many locals are concerned, the Northern Areas of Pakistan is still a land of fairies and demons.

But changes are coming, spurred on by the radical opening up of the area to the outside world over the last few years. While its geographical location has made the region a constant spectator and participatant in major developments right through history – the rate of change which it now faces is far more drastic than at any time in the past. Under the British, the different kingdoms continued to enjoy a high degree of autonomy provided their allegiance remained with Kashmir. And local rulers continued to have a fairly free hand until the beginning of the 1970s when the Bhutto regime absolved them of all power. Since then, changes in the Northern Areas have reflected mainstream developments in the whole of Pakistan, modernisation being the key word.

The developments found their greatest physical manifestation with the building of the Karakoram Highway, built along the path of the caravan routes of the Old Silk Road from China. With it, the entire area has been laid open to commerce and tourism and the forces of central government in Islamabad. The resulting "progress" is undoubtedly causing a great deal of change and a certain amount of conflict as tradition tries to hold on.

Jeep travel in the Hindu Kush.

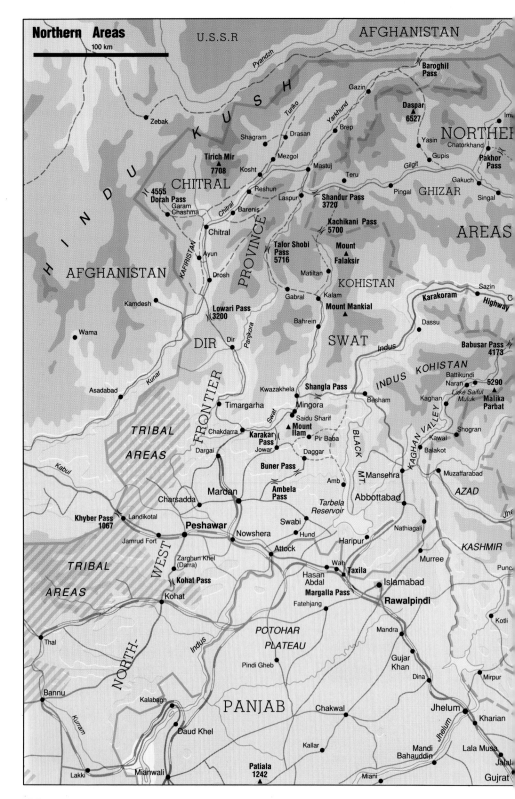

Northern Areas

100 km

U.S.S.R

AFGHANISTAN

Pyandzh

Baroghil
Pass

Zebak

Turiko

Gazin

Daspar
6527

Imi

Shagram

Drasan

Brep

Yarkhund

NORTHER

Mezgol

Yasin

Chatorkhand

Pakhor
Pass

Tirich Mir
7708

Kosht

Mastuj

Gilgit

Gupis

CHITRAL

Reshun

Teru

Pingal

GHIZAR

Gakuch

4555
Dorah Pass

Laspur

Shandur Pass
3720

Singal

Garam
Chashma

Barenis

AREAS

Chitral

Kachikani Pass
5700

Chitral

KAFIRISTAN

Ayun

Talor Shobi
Pass
5716

Mount
Falaksir

PROVINCE

Drosh

Matiltan

KOHISTAN

AFGHANISTAN

Kamdesh

Gabral

Kalam

Karakoram

Sazin

C

Highway

Lowari Pass
3200

Mount Mankial

Dassu

Wama

Bahrein

SWAT

Indus

Babusar Pass
4173

DIR

Dir

Panjkora

INDUS

KOHISTAN

Battikundi

Naran

5290

Asadabad

Kunar

Kwazakhela

Shangla Pass

Besham

Kaghan

Lake Saiful
Muluk

Malika
Parbat

TRIBAL

Timargarha

Mingora

KAGHAN VALLEY

Shogran

FRONTIER

Swat

Saidu Sharif

Mount
Ilam

Kawal

AREAS

Chakdarra

Karakar
Pass

Pir Baba

Balakot

Kabul

Dargai

Jowar

Daggar

BLACK

Muzaffarabad

Buner Pass

Amb

Mansehra

AZAD

Charsadda

Mardan

Ambela
Pass

MT.

Abbottabad

Tarbela
Reservoir

Khyber Pass
1067

Landikotal

Swabi

Nathiagali

KASHMIR

Jhe

Peshawar

Nowshera

Hund

Haripur

Murree

Jamrud Fort

Attock

Punc.

WEST

Zarghun Khel
(Darra)

Wah

Hasan
Abdal

Taxila

Islamabad

Kotli

TRIBAL

Kohat Pass

Margalla Pass

Rawalpindi

AREAS

Kohat

Fatehjang

Thal

NORTH-

Indus

POTOHAR

PLATEAU

Mandra

Gujar
Khan

Dina

Mirpur

Pindi Gheb

Bannu

Kalabagh

Kuram

PANJAB

Chakwal

Jhelum

Kharian

Daud Khel

Kallar

Mandi
Bahauddin

Lala Musa

Lakki

Mianwali

Patiala
1242

Miani

Jalal

Gujrat

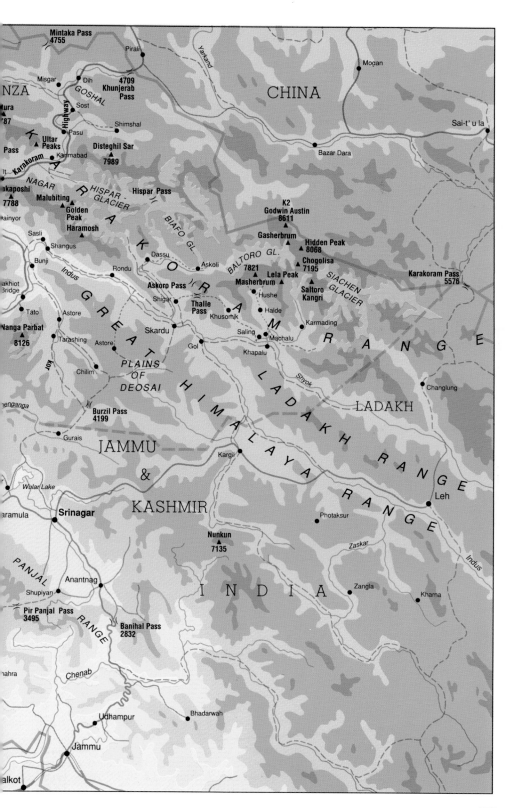

NZA

Mintaka Pass
4755

Pirali

Misgar   Dih

GOSHAL   4709
Khunjerab
Pass

ura
87   Sost

Pasu   Shimshal

Ultar
Peaks   Karimabad

Pass

It

Karakoram

NAGAR

akaposhi
7788   Malubiting

Golden
Peak   Haramosh

ainyor

Sasli

Shangus

Bunji

akhiot
3ridge

Tato   Astore

Nanga Parbat
8126   Tarashing
Astore

Chilim

enganga

Burzil Pass
4199

Gurais

JAMMU

&

KASHMIR

aramula   Srinagar

PANJAL

Anantnag

Shupiyan

Pir Panjal Pass
3495

Banihal Pass
2832

nahra   Chenab

Udhampur   Bhadarwah

Jammu

alkot

Highway

KARAKORAM

HISPAR
GLACIER   Hispar Pass

Disteghil Sar
7989

BIAFO GL.

Dassu

Rondu   Askoli

BALTORO GL.

K2
Godwin Austin
8611

Gasherbrum

Hidden Peak
8068

Chogolisa
7195

Lela Peak

Masherbrum
7821

Saltoro
Kangri

SIACHEN
GLACIER

Karakoram Pass
5576

Askoro Pass

Shigar

Thalle
Pass

Khusomik

Halde

Hushe

Machalu

Karmading

Skardu

Gol

Khapalu

Saling

Khalu

Shyok

Changlung

LADAKH

Leh

Photaksur

Zaskar

Zangla

Kharna

Indus

Indus

GREAT   HIMALAYA   RANGE

LADAKH   RANGE

PLAINS
OF
DEOSAI

Kargil

Nunkun
7135

INDIA

CHINA

Yarkand

Mogan

Sai-t' u la

Bazar Dara

Wular Lake

297

SLOWLY INTO THE MOUNTAINS

The Kaghan Valley: Prior to the building of the Karakoram Highway, the main route northwards from the plains of Hazara did not follow the River Indus, but crossed the mountains by a more direct route from Abbottabad in NWFP. Following the **Kunhar River** along the Kaghan Valley to **Babusar Pass** (4,150 metres), it joined the Indus near Chilas. While the scenery here contrasts with the high Karakoram, the journey up the Kaghan Valley provides a gradual and sober introduction to the mountains of Northern Pakistan.

At the northern edge of the monsoon belt, Kaghan supports an abundance of vegetation. The lower slopes are well cultivated with spectacular terraces. Higher up, the mountains are clothed in forests of Himalayan pine and fir which then give way to spectacular snow-covered mountain peaks. The general lushness of the environment makes the

region very similar to Kashmir to the east; a Himalayan hideaway left behind by the rush of traffic plying the KKH.

At 900 metres, the small town of **Balakot** provides the gateway to the 150-kilometre long valley. During the summer months the town is fairly quiet, with the majority of the population involved in farming or tourism up in the valley. From Balakot the road snakes its way steeply up into the confines of the narrow valley, defying precipitous drops down to the Kunhar River below.

Shortly after the village of Kawai a rugged road leads steeply off to the right up to the plateau of **Shogran** which at 2,500 metres lies in a cirque surrounded by stunningly beautiful mountains rising to over 4,500 metres. Shogran literally means the "forest in the sky", and the area offers marvellous possibilities for trekking and mountaineering. Returning to the "main road", the route continues its ascent.

Above the dense forests, isolated homesteads cling to precipitous spurs, defying any logical reason for their presence. But most human settlement is at the base of the valley, on the river, where there is enough flat ground for worthwhile cultivation. In summer the populations of the villages swell with the influx of tourists, up here from the plains to catch a taste of this distinctly Alpine environment.

The centre of activity in the Kaghan is undoubtedly the village of **Naran** about three quarters of the way up. There is one simple bazaar where all the shops are situated, typical for any small settlement in this part of the world, though in the winter months the majority of the population descends to the warmer climes of Balakot.

It is a hive of activity, with tea stalls and simple restaurants offering basic meals. There are hairdressing salons and showers and hardware shops selling anything from cigarettes to kerosene. There are also a number of stores offering local handicrafts, including fine woodcarving for which the valley is famous. Jeeps, Toyotas and Suzukis, arriving or departing with their cargos of people all add to the general atmos-

Alpine feeling in the Kaghan Valley; Lalazar Plateau.

phere. Fishing, for which a license is required, is a particularly popular activity in this part of the valley. At this stage the Kunhar river abounds with trout, said to be some of the best in the entire subcontinent.

And there are numerous possibilities for trekking. Along a side valley to the east of Naran, a jeep track leads up to the fabled **Lake Saiful Muluk**, the walk taking about half a day. The jeep takes about half an hour.

At over 3,000 metres the lake is surrounded by impressive snow-capped mountains, crowned by the summit of **Malika Parbat** (Queen of the Mountains) which at over 5,000 metres is the highest mountain in Kaghan. Apparently the lake is inhabited by fairies and legend has it that Prince Saiful Muluk, a poet and philosopher, fell madly in love with one.

It is difficult to imagine a more silent and eerie place than Lake Saiful Muluk. From Saiful Muluk it is also possible for experienced trekkers to ascend a precipitous track to the north of the lake.

Saiful Muluk can look very eerie.

It can be a bit dicy due to sporadic rockfall and it is advisable to take a guide. But the rewards at the other side of the pass are worth the toil. A long but gradual descent leads to the plateau of **Lalazar** where there is an extremely picturesque village in the dappled shade of woodland among pastures choked with an amazing variety of wild flowers. Life in the village seems to go on as it has always done, with scruffy and smiling children and women in their local embroidered costumes.

A further descent leads down to the village of **Battikundi**, back on the Kunhar river and the main route up the valley. (Lalazar is most easily reached this way). A series of wooden shacks selling the most basic of provisions forms the main bazaar. There is a tributary to the Kunhar River here whose valley, leading east towards Azad Kashmir, is well worth exploring.

The whole region, a jagged mountain wilderness, is incised with a myriad of ancient trails and pony tracks, the legacy of a flourishing Kashmir trade of a

bygone age. Activity inevitably declined after partition, but the tracks are still used by locals as well as Afghan refugees seeking new pastures for their sheep. The region is a potential paradise for trekkers especially with the prospect of being offered a cup of tea and delicious *dahi* (yoghurt) with *roti* by a local shepherd. Further up the valley, the headwaters of the Kunhar river are to be found at **Lalusar Lake**, a short distance from the village of Gittidas. Beyond, the road, which is now only a jeepable track, makes a final steep ascent to the Babusar Pass. The pass is normally open for jeep traffic during the summer, allowing direct access to Chilas on the Karakoram Highway.

Trekking all the way over the Pass without a guide is not advised as the Kohistanis living on the other side are not generally very hospitable to outsiders. Some travellers will choose to return to Balakot and join the highway at the town of Mansehra. From here it is an 18-hour bus ride to Gilgit, along the Indus. A different world lies ahead.

UP THE KARAKORAM HIGHWAY

Having left the plains of Hazara behind, the **Karakoram Highway** arrives in the small town of **Besham**, whose long and tatty bazaar provides a break in the journey for traffic heading north. From here on, the traveller is soon made aware of the forbidding nature of the region he has just entered. The **River Indus** gushes below and gaunt cliffs of bare rock soar above, as the KKH begins to cut its way through the arid Indus Gorge of **Kohistan**. It is one of the most isolated regions in the Northern Areas where mountain folk must walk for days to obtain provisions. It is difficult to imagine that traffic has been plying this same route for thousands of years.

Kohistan straddles the zone of collision between the Indian and Eurasian continental plates. Continually beset by rockfalls caused by earth tremours, constant repair jobs have to be carried out on the highway. But nothing can

Nanga Parbat lies unusually placid above Fairytale Meadow.

compare with the disaster that occured in the summer of 1987 when torrential rains caused landslides which washed long sections of the road down into the Indus. The damage took months to repair and tourists had to be airlifted out of Gilgit. Whatever the engineeers do, how long their work lasts in in this part of the world is entirely dictated by the whims of nature.

The KKH emerges from the gorge at the town of **Chilas**, which is situated on a desert plain about 1,200 metres above sea level. Well camouflaged by the blank tones of this barren wasteland, all around, on the rocks above the Indus, rockcarvings and inscriptions bear witness to the waves of civilisation which either chose to stay here, or simply passed through. Today, among the local population, there are few descendants of the distant past. Locals are now the descendants of brigands seeking last refuge in the anonymity this featureless land provides. Over the centuries this part of Kohistan has always been a stumbling block to peaceful progress up the Indus, particularly for the British whose supply line from the south had to pass through this territory. But they were not the only people to complain of being persistantly attacked and robbed, and worse, by the dreaded Chilasis. Other tribes would avoid the place at all costs. Today the area still has a reputation for its singularly hostile attitude towards outsiders. Don't worry! The problem is now by no means as bad as it used to be.

The Killer Mountain: In summer the gorge becomes an inferno because of the lack of vegetation to diffuse the heat. Temperatures can rise to over 50 degrees centigrade. The westwards flow of the Indus at this stage is the result of a huge mountain blocking its progress to the south; the summit of **Nanga Parbat** rises to the southeast, 7,000 metres above the river. At 8,125 metres, the awesome dimensions of this mountain confirm that while not being quite the highest mountain in the world it is undoubtedly the largest. Standing at the very edge of the monsoon belt, Nanga Parbat always receives the final onslaught of the storm, despite the fact that the shape of the sleeping woman lying along its summits induces an impression of absolute tranquility. But it is the snow, the avalanches, the collapse of ice and the yawning crevasses on its faces which have led to the mountain being renamed the Killer Mountain. Expeditions which have tried to climb it have often ended in disaster; on one German expedition in the 1930s no less than seventeen people lost their lives as a result of the collapse of a huge ice wall. The summit was first reached by Hermann Buhl in 1953. His solo push to the top, climbing the last 1,700 metres in one day, is one of the greatest mountaineering feats of all time.

The Fairytale Meadow: To the immediate north of the mountain at **Rakhiot Bridge**, where the Indus turns west, a trail leaves the road, accompanying the **Daimar Valley** as it climbs to the northern flanks. Before the village of **Tato**, it is a steep ascent on a narrow precipitous trail, every bit as arid as the Indus gorge below. Beyond Tato, the heat

The river: a constant companion on the Karakoram Highway.

BEYOND GANDHARA

The construction of the Karakoram Highway, cutting through Kohistan, Gilgit and Hunza, has opened up an area of Pakistan which was previously inaccessible to all but the hardiest of travellers. The very meaning of the word Karakoram – "black mountain" – conjures up an image of the precarious nature of a journey through this land. Yet even from the 2nd century B.C. a major branch of the Silk Road wound its way through here enticing merchants to head both east and west. Buddhist missionaries too were sent

quantity of circles, mounted horsemen, battleaxes, ibexes and markhors which make Chilas important, but the occurrence of a number of quite special scenes, only a few of which can be described here. One such is the carving close by the riverside below Chilas of a man on a high seat whose soldiers in Scythian attire bring him to a fat chained prisoner. The seated man is named as *Moga Raja*, i.e. the Scythian ruler Maues. The prisoner is named as *Gopadasa* and the whole scene is a pictorial affirmation of the

out from all areas of Gandhara, including Swat, and Chinese pilgrims were gratefully received, among them Fa-Hian in the 5th century, Sung-yun in the 6th and Hsüan Tsang in the 7th century.

Remarkably, the mark of Man from almost every age, in the form of rock carvings and inscriptions is manifest along virtually the whole route, showing that this most harsh and bleak of passages has constantly been a cultural artery through Pakistan.

Chilas: Along the whole length of the Karakoram Highway by far the greatest concentration of rock carvings is to be found around Chilas. However, it is not just the

conquest of this region by the Scythians.

To the right is a carving of a Buddhist monk named *Buddharakshita* holding an incense burner on his way to worship at a stupa. Above him is the carving of another pilgrim holding a water jar with a load suspended from a stick over his shoulder; it is a reminder that pilgrims from Central Asia also came to these parts.

Some of the carvings refer to legendary tales. Following the Karakoram Highway eastwards over the Butogah stream, a series

Above, signs of Buddhism on the Silk Road – petroglyphs from 3rd century.

of carvings are found on the left hand side, among them a remarkable representation of the story of the self sacrifice of the Bodhisattva *Mahasattva*. To the right of a tall stupa, either side of which a worshipper is praying, the Bodhisattva has lain down and offered his body to a lioness which, along with her cubs, is devouring his flesh. The inscription to the top right explains this as *Vyaghrani Dharma Nyayam* or "the principle of duty to tigers".

Across the Talpan Bridge and about 100 metres to the east is found the "Rock of the First sermon", so called because upon it is represented the story of the Buddha's first sermon at Sarnath. The Buddha himself is shown seated and surrounded by his five disciples. Below him on a pillar is the wheel of a law with a deer on either side. This is all orthodox enough, but the reminder that the Buddhism with which we are familiar today emerged only slowly is provided by the "Altar Rock", further still to the west. The Buddha himself appears without halo, yet around him is not only *Maitreya* but also *Avalokitesvara* and *Manju Sri*, two Bodhisattvas, all of whom are shown with halos. Furthermore there is the curious inscription *Vicharati Devadata Sabodhapati* or "Devadatta, Lord of Knowledge, preaches" – Devadatta being the rival cousin of Buddha.

The Sacred Rock of Hunza: Up in the Hunza Valley, two kilometres beyond Ganesh and lying directly on the left hand side of the Karakoram Highway as it winds its way up towards the Khunjerab Pass, between the Indus and the road itself, lies the Sacred Rock of Hunza. The rock, more accurately four rocks, is covered in carvings and inscriptions from earliest times through to the historic period possibly the most recent of which relates to the time of the Tibetan conquest of this area in the 8th century A.D. It is known locally as *Haldeikish* or "the place of the male ibexes". Indeed, dominant among the images inscribed upon it is the ibex, testimony to the immemorial local tradition of *thuma saling* or ceremonial ibex hunting which appears to have been linked to a fertility cult.

Some of the later ibexes have short horns, some have curved horns, some have angular, some semi-circular, others even dotted horns. The shape and size of their bodies change too.

Human forms too appear regularly, sometimes hunting, sometimes dancing, sometimes on horseback. Trees are occasionally to be found, as are stupas, swastikas, daggers, ropes, goats and tridents. There is a small bird, a spider and the occasional phallus. Among the written inscriptions appear Karosthi inscriptions, some carrying Buddhist messages, and later Gupta Brahmi inscriptions too can be traced, some of which have been closely dated to the 5th century A.D. On rock No. 2 a Chinese inscription, distinctively written from top to bottom, tells of a visit of a Chinese ambassador from the Ta-Wei dynasty which may date from the 6th century. Perhaps most intriguing of all, however, is the carving on rock No. 1 of a man in a long robe and a cap, typically Kushan dress, and bearing a striking resemblance to the image of the Kushan emperors who appeared on the coinage from the time of the Emperor Kanishka onwards. On his left an elephant can be made out.

The Satpara and Gilgit Buddhas: The northern mountains of Pakistan are home to two remarkable rock carvings of the Buddha which have been dated to the 8th or 9th centuries A.D. They demonstrate Tibetan influences in the region and are thus testimony of the enduring vitality of Buddhism in the Northern Areas long after the Gandharan school had gone into decline.

The first, the **Satpara Buddha**, is to be found just on the southern outskirts of Skardu on the way up to Satpara Lake. Following the jeep track up, it is located on the far western bank of the Hargissa Nullah. The Buddha forms the centrepiece of a series of carvings etched into a large isolated boulder which is about six metres high. The Buddha is seated in the attitude of meditation or *Dhyana-Mudra*. Towering over him on both sides are standing figures of *Maitreya*, the future Buddha.

The **Gilgit Buddha** is found about six kilometres west of Gilgit along the road to Punial, and then to the left up a track leading to the Kargah Valley. Carved into the rock face about three metres tall and about 10 metres above the ground, the commanding figure has his right hand raised before his chest in fearless pose or *Abhaya-Mudra*. A series of 13 holes spaced symmetrically around the figure suggest that the Buddha was originally contained in a wooden shrine.

begins to subside as the greenery begins and occasional glimpses of the upper reaches of Daimar face can be seen. But it isn't until the valley opens out into the broad pastures of **Fairytale Meadow** that the whole of the North face confronts the senses in a scene of unrivalled grandeur. The valley here is of a lushness which is still Kashmir. Streams trickle down through the meadows amidst a profusion of wild flowers; the forests of fir giving out to dwarf pine and higher up, towards the base of the mountain, silver birch. For the experienced trekker, the flanks of Nanga Parbat provide unequalled possibilities. At 5,400 metres, the **Mazeno Pass** gives access to the southern part of the mountain and the **Rupal Valley**, above which a sheer rock face soars an awesome 4,500 metres to the summit.

Escaping the heat: Back down on the Indus, the KKH also begins to ascend out of the heat, now turning northwards. From the village of Bunji a look back to the south sees the whole of Nanga Parbat, looming above the gorge. Ahead,

the summits of **Rakaposhi** and **Haramosh** peep out from behind the guardian ramparts of the Karakoram, beneath which, in a broad valley to the west of the highway, lies the central administrative town of **Gilgit**.

Situated at an altitude of 1,500 metres Gilgit is and always has been a prosperous market town. With the establishment of links to China around 2,000 years ago, Gilgit was strategically placed and became an important trading centre along the Old Silk Road. Today it remains the focal point for the northern region of Pakistan, where the tradesmen of Central Asia and the plains to the south still meet. Since the opening of the Karakoram Highway the volume of goods and people passing through has increased dramatically; the single **Cinema Bazaar** snaking through the town offers an incredible variety of products, from the basic essentials like *ghee* used for cooking to more luxury items including fine silks from China.

In the summer, after the apricot harvest, mountains of this fruit arrive at the bazaar to be shovelled into plastic bags and laden onto the shelves of groceries, bakeries, hardware shops, bookshops, and sweet, cigarette and drink stalls. Restaurants selling an amazing variety of food are strategically located.

With the influx of tourists in recent years, there are also shops to cater for their needs, selling everything from dark glasses to ice-axes to freeze-dried mountaineering rations.

Polo: The Mosque has just been restored to its former glory and the sound of the call to prayer has a strange echo in this mountain environment as do the drums and clarinets of the local band attending the afternoon polo game. The game of polo actually originated in Central Asia and was developed into a competitive sport by the Persians. It spread to southwest Europe where it died a death and also east to the north of the Indian subcontinent which is where the British rediscovered it.

Polo in the Northern Areas has assumed its wildest and most untethered form. The unbelieveably daredevil horsemanship of the players is almost

The Cinema Bazaar snakes all the way through Gilgit.

matched by the bravery of the spectators who line the ground atop a low wall from which the ball, hit around at amazing speeds, rebounds into play. The pace of the game is controlled by the music which, incredibly, actually increases in pitch as the contest continues. The horses have got to be admired for staying the pace. This could be explained by their diet which consists of walnuts and mulberries.

The game used to be played all over the Northern Areas, but can now only be seen in those areas still wealthy enough to scrape a team together. It is still played in Gilgit and Chitral and some parts of Baltistan. While owning a horse was always a matter of social prestige, and beyond the means of everyone but the local nobility, numbers today are made up by the local police and the military. The only rule seems to be that there are six players to each side, though even this seems to be overlooked on occasions.

The first game of the season always comes with the Spring Festival towards the end of March. The old practice of sacrificing a goat and using the head as the ball has all but died out, but judging by the way the ball is hit around the ground it seems that it may still symbolise the skull of the devil.

The area around Gilgit gives the first hint that no civilisation would be possible in the area without the use of irrigation. In this essentially desert environment there is not enough rainfall for natural watering of the crops. Instead, water has to be channelled from the rivers and glaciers. Areas for cultivation commonly utilise the rich alluvial fans down near the rivers; oases of green among the greys and browns of the desert.

Gilgit is the central hub for travel by land throughout the Northern Areas. While regular bus and minibus services ply the Karakoram Highway, and the route eastwards through the Indus Gorge to Baltistan, the remainder of the roads disecting the region can only be negotiated by four-wheel drive. For the adventurer who wants to go beyond

A fine display of horsemanship in Gilgit.

these to really explore the mountains, there is a highly developed system of trails, built up over thousands of years by tradesmen, nomads and herdsmen, all granting access to some of the most magnificent mountain scenery on earth.

To Hunza: The northern edge of the town of Gilgit is bordered by the Gilgit River which is fed by the meltwaters of the **Hindu Raj** to the West. It is spanned by an impressive 180-metre long suspension bridge, built by the British, reputed to be the longest in Asia. Now it is possible to travel up to Hunza in 2½ hours on the KKH, but before this was completed the route north crossed the Gilgit River here and followed the right bank of the Hunza River.

This route passes through the village of **Nomal**, from where another jeep track follows the precipitous Naltar Nullah up into the hidden sanctuary of the **Naltar Valley**. Surrounded by 6,000 metre peaks, the lower reaches of Naltar are furnished with pine forests. A trail leads along the valley to the north, through villages and hamlets to arrive at the Naltar Lakes, a paradise of deep tourquoise pools surrounded by birch and willow, choked with fish. Higher up, the valley broadens to a huge glacial outwash plain, seemingly hemmed in by mountains on all sides.

But for the experienced and adventurous, Upper Naltar provides access to some fantastic trekking. Via the **Pakhor Pass** to the northwest, a trail leads over the passes and between the valleys of the Hindu Raj, to Chitral and the Hindu Kush. This route is covered in about two weeks. To the northeast, the 5,000-metre **Diantar Pass** provides a back door approach to Hunza and access to some of the remotest valleys of the Karakoram. The top of the pass is saddled with snow all the year round and there is a precipitous descent at the other side. But the view from the summit is spellbinding.

From the towering Hindu Raj in the west to the Batura Peaks due north and to the peaks of Hunza in the east, great monoliths of rock, thousands of metres high, march towards the horizon.

The Naltar Lakes.

From Diantar it is a long descent to the Hunza Valley. The route passes through villages which appear deserted. Not a soul in sight; just the creaking of doors and the trickle of water flowing along the irrigation channels. Occasionally a young boy on a pony or an old shepherd offering all the tea and *dahi* he can provide, but nobody else; the crops are not yet ready for harvest and apart from herding, there is no reason for anyone to be here.

Further down, the village of **Das** provides the first permanent settlement, and from here there is a track up to **Baltar Meadows** beneath the southern flanks of the **Batura Massif**. Towards the southeast the huge spire of Rakaposhi looms into view and a jeep track winds down in the same direction to the village of **Chalt** just above the Hunza River and the KKH which has now fought its way through the outer defences of the Karakoram.

Fair lads with happy (and sad) faces.

The jeeps and the brightly painted trucks and buses, swerving round the corners at breakneck speed are now over half way from Gilgit to Hunza. The walk over the mountains has taken a full four days.

At the end of the last century the British used Chalt as an important outpost of the Gilgit Agency. The permanent garrison here provided support for expeditionary forces visiting the Thums of Hunza and Nagar in a bid to gain allegiances in the face of the much feared advance of the Russians over the Hindu kush. The neighbouring village of Nilt was the scene of the final battle in 1891, by which all resistance to the British presence was crushed. To the east, beyond Chalt, lie the ex-kingdoms of **Hunza** and **Nagar**, Hunza lying to the north of the river, Nagar to the south, where **Mt Rakaposhi** now rises steeply from the river bed.

It is the only mountain in the world to rise uninterrupted from river valley to summit; nearly 6,000 metres from top to bottom. The road goes so close to its base that it is hidden for most of the way behind lesser spurs. Despite the occasional awesome view of the whole

mountain from here, it is best viewed from more of a distance further up the valley, from the Hunza side.

Villages cling precariously to loose conglomerate spurs rising above the river as the KKH continues on the Nagar side for about 35 kilometres before crossing over to the northern bank via a solid concrete bridge of Chinese design, with the usual lions standing guard.

Before modern bridges started to span the rivers of the Northern Areas, the traditional form of crossing was made of cables of twisted birch twigs arranged in a triangular fashion whereby the lower vortex was used to walk on while the other two were used as handrails. This type of bridge is still to be found in the more remote parts of the Northern Areas, and crossing them can be a dicy experience, particularly when a strong wind is blowing.

A few miles further on, the valley opens out into a scene of unparalleled beauty. To the immediate north, **Ultar Mountain** (7,388 metres) towers above Hunza, while to the south, Rakaposhi (7,780 metres) dominates the territory of Nagar on the other side of the river.

A long time ago it appears that Nagar and Hunza were ruled collectively by the same chief or *Thum*, until the ruler of the day decided to divide the territory between his two twin sons. They turned out to be deadly enemies; the new ruler on the Hunza side had only one daughter before he was savagely murdered by one of his brother's followers. The problem of finding a male heir for Hunza was solved by this daughter falling in love with her cousin on the other side of the river. He swam across to her every night. The subsequent line of Hunza rulers thus produced was called *Ayeshe* or 'heaven-sent', the exotic Persian title intending to infer just that.

Hunza is actually divided into two separate regions, a northern and a southern, which are clearly defined by the ethnic background of the people living here. This southern part, known as **Kanjut**, is thought to have been originally settled by Indo-Germanic Aryan herdsmen, though there is bound to have been influence from the later waves of settlers coming up from the south. The language spoken is *Burushaski* which doesn't appear to be related to any modern tongue. Much like the Basque language, its roots remain a mystery.

Less of a problem is the descent of the people of northern Hunza, **Gojhal**, a region which occupies both sides of the river after the village of **Gulmit**, and continues right up to the borders of Xinjiang to occupy the passes over the Pamir. Here the inhabitants are descendants from emigrants from Wakhan at the other side of the Pamir, and the language spoken is *Wakhi*.

Brigands: Hunza was never totally independant, acknowledging suzerainty to the greater powers of China to the north and Gilgit to the south, and later on to the Dogra regime of Kashmir. However, with the possession of the passes, Hunza was always strategically placed to derive a great deal of power and wealth of its own. It basically had the tradesmen at its mercy, as it plundered and looted the caravans on their

way from Turkestan and Central Asia to the subcontinent.

The names of Hunza's rulers bred terror in the hearts of the peaceful merchants, to such an extent that certain routes were completely abandoned leading to depopulation of much of the country north of the passes. Hunza became even richer by becoming the centre of the slave trade, supplying whoever could afford the price; the merchants of Badakstan would regularly come here to replenish their stocks.

This all enabled the people of Hunza to live a life of relative autonomy, sitting fast in their mountain citadel, dictating the score to anyone with the nerve to pass through. It was a great position to be in, particularly for the autocratic *Thums*. And it wasn't only outsiders who were at their mercy; The lowly inhabitants lived in equal fear of being killed or at least forced to join the slave caravans.

The *Thums* demanded complete loyalty, but in times when Hunza was under threat, they would only offer protection in return for sizeable dues which were used to line the coffers still further. And even the history of the nobility itself is one of intrigue, murder and vengeance.

Hemmed in by the Rakaposhi massif to the south and the river to the north, Nagar never possessed the strategic luxury enjoyed by its neighbour. Its only real outlet was down the valley to Gilgit on which it became dependant for luxuries such as sugar, salt and cloth. For other more valuable products, those of Central Asia, Nagar was totally dependant on Hunza, though in times of peace between the two sides, they would join forces to attack the caravans.

Oasis: Viewed from above, the whole valley's only life support, apart from the KKH, is tenuous ribbon of green closely following either bank of the Hunza river, occasionally spilling up onto the mountain sides.

The intricate terraced fields, held in place by dry-stone retaining walls, and the complex system of irrigation channels leading down from the glaciers above, are testimony to the skilled and patient labour required to keep this land from returning to the glacial desert of the Karakoram.

The horizontal lines of the terraces are broken in places by tall avenues of poplar trees and birch used as windbreaks to protect the crops. Orchards of mulberry, walnut and apricot abound. After harvest, on the flat rooftops of the squat stonebuilt houses, the crops are dried to preserve them for the coming winter. In late summer, when the sun converts the valley to burnished gold with its backdrop of white peaks, the setting is particularly idyllic.

There is nothing at all to suggest that history in this part of the world has witnessed anything other than total peace and tranquility.

The east-west axis of the valley at this stage means that the southfacing slopes to the north of the river receive far more sunlight than the precipitous flanks of the mountains to the south. Again, Nagar appears to have drawn the short straw, with several of its villages receiving absolutely no sunlight at all in the winter months. A reason, perhaps, why the people of Nagar have extended their cultivation and grazing areas right up to the edges of the glaciers where it is not until late afternoon that the long shadows of Rakaposhi cut out the sunlight.

Land available for cultivation on the Hunza side of the valley is much more limited and is centred around Hunza's 'capital', the village of **Karimabad**, which is nestled a kilometre above the KKH beneath the towering ramparts of the still unclimbed Ultar peaks. Land is so scarce here that there is little room for the grazing of animals. The local economy revolves around various crops such as wheat and maize which can be grown on the available space as well as the abundance of fruit.

Hunza is particularly well known for its delicious apricots, of which the traditional summer diet almost entirely consists. Apricots are also dried for consumption during the long winter months, by the end of which, in early spring, stocks of all rations have just about run out. This is a vulnerable time of year for the people of Hunza, when the rate of infant mortality has always been at its highest.

Nothing in Hunza is wasted; the apricot stone is ground to pulp to use as fodder for the animals and the kernel is made into oil used for heating and as protection for the skin. As a result of their diet, the people of Hunza have a reputation for longevity. While it is to be doubted whether they live much longer than anyone else in the Northern Areas, the good air and all the fruit in the staple diet must contribute to good health. This in conjunction with the local glacier water whose muddy colour would suggest that it contains all kinds of invaluable minerals!

The outdoor tasks in Hunza are shared by men and women alike. Women go around without the veil, the result of the fact that the people here are Ismailis. In the early 19th century, the then *Thum* of Hunza visited the Aga Khan in Afghanistan and the people here have been his follower ever since.

The present Aga Khan ensures that the local people retain allegiance to his sect by lending the necessary financial support to schemes for the improvement of agriculture and education. Almost every new project carries the banner of the Aga Khan and his minions turn up in smart white jeeps to oversee the developments.

The women also get involved in producing the local handicrafts of the area, including the white woollen outer robes or *chogas* worn traditionally by the men. It is interesting to note that in imperial France before the revolution, those who could afford it wore woollen shawls produced in Hunza, exported in direct competition to the better known variety from Kashmir.

There is hardly any aspect of life in Hunza which has not been affected by its continuous interaction with the outside world, though change has undoubtedly occurred much more quickly in recent years. Much of the food and clothing is now imported from the plains via the KKH. Costume has become a mixture of traditional hats and training shoes. New hotels to accom-

Looking across to Nagar, the valley is dominated by Diran and Rakaposhi.

modate tourists replace valuable land with their promise of higher income.

Less has changed over in Nagar. The people here are still Shia Muslims which they have been ever since Islam first reached the area in the 12th century. Down at the other side of the KKH black Shia prayer flags nod suggestively at the Ismailis on the hill.

Despite the developments, many festivals are still celebrated in Hunza, including one to mark the planting of the crops and the *Nauroz* festival to signal the beginning of spring. There is also a festival in autumn which celebrates the return of the herdsmen from the higher pastures.

Occasionally a Sword Dance is held: a reminder of the fact that in the brigand days of Hunza, the locals were feared for their masterly swordsmanship. Most interesting of all, however, are the ceremonies carried out by the **Bitans**, the local shamans.

In former times survival of the feudal regimes of Hunza was ensured by the impressive fort at **Baltit**, just above Karimabad. The architecture is a clear indication of Tibetan influence in the area at the time it was built about 400 years ago. The story goes that a princess from Baltistan married the local Thum and imported master Balti craftsmen to do the job as part of her dowry.

But even before the fort is reached, the old cobbled streets of Baltit spanned by easily defensible archways seem to provide enough of a deterent to all but the boldest of intruders. Within the fort itself, narrow stairs with a small opening into the living quarters on the first floor are features which must have helped ensure that the ruling Thum stayed out of harm's way.

While there is a splendid view of Hunza from the Thum's balcony on the first floor, the best view is from the roof which is gained after an equally well-guarded ascent. The Thum vacated this fort as late as 1960, and his new palace can be clearly seen down the hill in Karimabad, as can the older **Altit Fort** perched on a knoll 300 metres above the Hunza river, in a position even more inaccessible than Baltit.

Irrigation Channels: Emerging from the gorge of the Ultar Nullah immediately behind Baltit is an irrigation channel which provides Hunza with all its water needs. So marginal is the gradient that it is sometimes difficult to tell in which direction the water is flowing. Passing on between the vertical rock faces of the nullah, following the line of the channel, it becomes apparent that skilled, precise and ingenious engineering was required to guide the water down from the **Ultar Glacier** above. In some places it is carried across the face of a vertical cliff. Corners are dodged by using tunnels and where the cliff is too steep, timber troughs are used. At regular intervals, carefully constructed pools act as valves to control the flow of water which must remain constant to ensure that the system in the villages below does not flood.

About three kilometres up the *nullah*, the ravine opens out into a broader valley which is blocked at its head by the 4,000-metre wall of Ultar 1, 2 and 3. Up to the left, a vertical granite spire known

Stopping for a chat.

locally as **Ladyfinger Peak** completes this amphitheatre of rock and ice. From a shepherd's hut a steep trail leads up towards this 2,000-metre monolith, and from a shoulder 1,500 metres above, the view over Hunza and Nagar is certainly breathtaking.

Rakaposhi and Diran to the South, with the karakoram Highway weaving its way between the green settlements on the banks of the Hunza River. Arching around towards the east above Nagar are Malubiting and then Golden Peak at the head of the Barpu Glacier, its giant West Face remaining one of the great mountaineering challenges in the Karakoram.

To the north the **Hispar Glacier** rises behind the Hispar Wall, into a land of silent mystery. This river of ice connects the Central Karakoram with Baltistan via the Hispar Pass and the Biafo Glacier. While Eric Shipton completed the route in 1937, exactly fifty years after Francis Younghusband, it appears to have been used for centuries by the Hunzakuts and the Baltis. For the well-acclimatised and experienced trekker, the Hispar Glacier undoubtedly provides the most direct and spectacular entry into the former kingdom of Little Tibet. Days and days of icy wilderness, snow lakes and magnificent views of breathtaking mountains.

The KKH sweeps round to the north, now out of sight, squeezing between the huge **Disteghil Sar** (7,900 metres) to the east and the impressive **Batura Peaks** (7,784 metres) back to the west on its way towards the Khunjerab Pass.

The village of **Gulmit** provides the most extensive agriculture in Hunza, the impressive **Pasu Peaks** providing a wonderful backdrop to the acres of terraced fields.

Apart from the well known trail along the Batura Glacier towards the Batura and Pasu Peaks, the region of Gojhal provides a wealth of adventure for those who want to get lost within the confines of the remote **Shimsal Valley** or the nooks and crannies of the even remoter **Pamir Plateau** which straddles the border regions to Xinjiang.

SHAMANS

High up in the mountains, where the eternal ice of the glaciers ends with the first blades of grass of the summer and where, untouched by human hand, delicate plants bloom after the winter snows have gone, there is a zone of such amazing purity that it lies beyond the limited perception of lesser mortals. It is said that this is where the fairies live, and where they build their castles.

Hikers and all would-be intruders beware! The fairies are sensitive creatures, and despite their handicap of toes pointing backwards and heels to the front, they are perfectly capable of protecting their domain. The slightest turn of a boulder or throw of a stone can shake them from their peaceful state and actually make them quite aggressive. Indeed the roar of an avalanche down the mountainside or a sudden crack of thunder are signs that in this part of the world the fairies rule. While trekkers from the West may have their own ideas about the cause of such natural occurrences, locals know that these are signs of wrath and that it pays to be friendly with the mountain ghosts.

The local inhabitants who occasionally have to encroach offer them sacrifices to calm them down. But even this isn't always effective and an intermediary who understands all the ins and outs of their complex minds has to be employed.

This is the shaman. The shaman works as an agent between villagers and the fairies, and as well as calming them down, he is also capable of extricating from them what the future might bring. And the shaman's great knowledge in herbal medicine is backed up by the advice he gets from the fairies in how best to heal the ill.

It is impossible to train as a shaman, or even to consciously decide to follow this vocation. Either the gift is inherited or a likely candidate is chosen by a fairy. It is usually when a man is high up in the mountains, maybe tending his goats, that the fairy appears in a dream to reveal to him the secrets of shamanism. An intimate mother-child relationship forms, or occasionally the union may even be of a sexual nature.

But it is only after the initiation ceremony, which all the villagers attend, that he is allowed to take up his work as a shaman. His daily life will hardly be affected by his new profession; he is only called upon when needed; for predicting the future at annual festivals or when somebody sets out on a long journey, or for healing the sick.

To make contact with the fairy, the shaman must follow a certain procedure. Surrounded by villagers, he first inhales the smoke of burning juniper bushes and other narcotic herbs until he is completely stupefied. Then the drums and the flutes start to play and the shaman starts to dance. The beat gets faster and faster, as does the dance of the shaman as he fixes his gaze on the distant mountain peaks where the fairies live. A crescendo is reached where he whirls himself around the square while jumping in the air.

Then the drums and the flutes suddenly slow, and the shaman stops, as he listens in his ecstasy to soft sounds of the music; almost as if it were a language that only he understands. It is the fairies who are transmitting their messages through the tune. Then the shaman responds and starts singing in a loud voice, translating the prophesies of the fairies to the expectant crowd. Sometimes his soul leaves his body during these sessions, and travels far and wide; his songs tell of what his inner eyes can see. It used to be that shaman songs had political contents. Being allowed total free speech in his ecstasy, the shaman could get away with saying almost anything, including telling the ruler what the villagers thought of him.

On special occasions a goat is slaughtered and its bloody head is offered to the shaman while he is still dancing. He sucks the blood thinking it to be the milk of the fairies.

Shamanism was once a common belief shared by many societies all over the world. Because the belief in fairies is still quite strong amongst the mountain people of Northern Pakistan, even today the shaman plays an important role in village life. There is only one aspect in which the influence of Islam is noticeable: in former times women were also allowed to practise as shamans, nowadays it is a profession which is solely reserved for the men.

TO BALTISTAN

From Hunza the main chain of the Karakoram now sweeps eastwards towards its apex and its very heart; the thundering, towering rock and ice spires of Baltistan.

Access is most easily gained by following the road along the Indus as it recedes eastwards from the KKH just south of Gilgit, funnelled between the **Haramosh Range** to the north and the sprawling Deosai Plateau to the south. The road appears even more vulnerable than the KKH as it slices its way beneath the overhanging rock walls which tower above it. A vertical, dizzying landscape beyond which the greater peaks remain obscured from view. It isn't until the gorge emerges onto the broad sandy plains of the **Skardu** Valley that the vista opens out.

However, while the lines of peaks surrounding the valley are impressive, they are only the first lines of defence to the inner sanctuary of the Karakoram; K2, Gasherbrum and Broad Peak are more than 100 kilometres away.

The region of Baltistan can be divided into three main areas; The administrative centre of Skardu with its hinterland leading up onto the Deosai Plateau connecting it with Kashmir to the South. Then there is the region north and east of Skardu, centred round the town of Shigar whose valley continues through the settlements of Dassu and Askole before reaching the Baltoro Glacier. The third area constitutes the region surrounding the valley of the Shyok River, from where it crosses the Ladakh border to its confluence with the Indus river near Humayun Bridge some 40 kilometres east of Skardu. This is centred around the administrative town of Khapalu. To the south of the Indus are the additional regions of Kharmang and Rondu.

Despite the remoteness of the region, it appears it has been settled by numerous nationalities arriving from all points of the compass. Aryan herdsmen ar-

rived from the north. Buddhists came via the Silk Road up the Indus. There were adventurers from Hunza and Nagar who presumably made their way via the Hispar glacier; Tibetans entered the country from Ladakh via the Shyok and Indus Rivers. There is even evidence to suggest that there was once a direct road linking Kashgar with Baltistan via the Pamir Plateau and the Saltoro Pass to the east of K2. While the British were anxious that this might provide yet another means of approach for the Russians, this route was closed to traffic for many years, the result of the rapid advance of the glaciers.

Whoever the original inhabitants of the area were, it seems that until the coming of Islam in the 15th and 16th centuries, it was the Tibetans who had the greatest influence on the area, an influence which still thrives, particularly near the borders of Ladakh in the east. Many of the people are of stocky build and possess distinctly Tibetan features. Much of the vernacular architecture is also Tibetan in style. Great

A dust storm kicks up.

herds of yaks also confirm a great deal of influence from the great plateau to the east. The Balti language is also closely related to Tibetan. The Baltis are a friendly, happy people.

But apart from the Buddhist petroglyphs near Skardu, there is very little history which has actually been written down. One story tells of a mountain near Skardu breaking away and crashing down into the Indus. The debris rose to the level of the surrounding mountains resulting in a huge lake stretching as far as Karghil. Indeed, this kind of catastrophe has happened on several occasions, the most recent being in the middle of the last century when the Skardu Valley was flooded as a result of a landslide further down the river, near Gilgit.

Dust and dunes: But nowadays, the size of the valley at Skardu, about 40 kilometres long by about eight kilometres wide, is disproportionate to the amount of water flowing through it. The Indus plies its way slowly between huge expanses of sand dunes, often leaving calm blue lakes behind it.

Above the town, on a cliff to the north, is the impressive **Kharpoche Fort** built by the last of the Buddhist rulers Maqpon Bokha, the founder of the kingdom of Skardu, at the end of the 15th century. It is in a seemingly impregnable position, guarded by cliffs to the west and the Indus to the east and north. With the subsequent tide of Islam into the area, the fort became the focal point for migrations from the outside, with settlers arriving from Kashmir. Baltistan gradually became crystallised into one state and while fending off threats from the Chilasis, amongst others, from the west, the rulers of Skardu began to impose their influence further east, with Shigar and Khapalu coming under their domain.

The great ruler Ali Sher Khan extended the boundaries of Baltistan in the late 16th century by attacking Ladakh in the east as well as Dardistan in the west, even penetrating as far as Chitral. His military achievements are legendary and are still part of popular folklore throughout much of the Northern Areas. Ali Sher Khan came into contact with the Moghul Court when Akbar conquered Kashmir in 1586, and proceeded to marry the Moghul princess Gul Khatoon.

While her husband was away campaigning, the princess grew weary of the bland dusty, windswept environment and decided to build a palace, the **Mindoq Khar**. Immediately below, she laid out beautiful terraced gardens with marble fountains. The problem of water supply on the hill was solved by diverting water from the Sat stream along an impressive aquaduct. Sadly, very little of the princess's achievements remain today, her palace having been destroyed by the Sikhs in 1840.

The town of Skardu itself is still rather a dusty place and strong winds funnelling through the valley are quite common. There is a small bazaar which comes alive during the month of Muharram when the Shia population all get very involved in the ceremonies.

Deosai: But surrounding the town the mountains beckon, hiding the secrets of

Traditional threshing.

the magnificent landscape which lies beyond. To the south-west is the sprawling **Deosai Plateau** to which access can be gained via **Satpara Lake** eight kilometres away. About 70 kilometres across and averaging 3,500 metres in height, Deosai connects Baltistan with the **Astor Valley** to the east of Nanga Parbat.

There is a jeep track which leads over the top, but actually walking it provides a wilderness experience which is hard to beat. This is the real outback of Northern Pakistan, out of the confines of the valleys to enjoy the broad open spaces and the views that the plateau provides, particularly from at its southern fringe, as Nanga Parbat soars above the horizon. The plateau is dissected by a myriad of small streams in shallow valleys divided by smooth rounded hills, the happy home of multitudes of marmots.

To the back and beyond: But it is to the north and east of Skardu that the Karakoram Mountains assume their most impressive and unyielding character. It takes two hours by jeep to reach the gateway to it all; the ancient village of **Shigar** tucked away in a lush green valley containing an abundance of fruit including apples and apricots for which the whole of Baltistan is renowned. To the north, the valley follows the **Braldu River** and arches round to the east as the land becomes more desolate and the fortresses of the inner Karakoram come within reach. Beyond the village of **Askole**, the forbidding Braldu Gorge is the last key to open the secrets of the Baltoro Glacier which lies beyond.

Of the world's fourteen peaks over 8,000 metres, four are to be found here at the head of the Baltoro, including **K2**, the second highest mountain in the world, at 8,611 metres. The Glacier itself is a tumbling mass of ice transporting the debris of millennia. From the camp at Urdukas there is absolutely no vegetation at all. The trek up the glacier would be pure drudgery were it not for the spectacular mountains of granite and ice that surround it. A barren frozen wasteland whose only outlet are the peaks soaring above; their shapes, sizes

and colours providing a scene beyond description. Among the most beautiful mountains are the giant wedge of **Gasherbrum 2** and the sky-cleaving monoliths of the **Trango Towers** as well as the perfectly shaped **Paiyu**.

The title of Gallen Rowell's book "In the Throne Room of the Mountain Gods" is a perfectly apt description for the awesome crags surrounding the Baltoro. But unless you are a mountaineer, this glacial wonderland actually offers very little except the stunning gaze at peaks beyond reach. For a look at Baltistan itself, it is perhaps better to return to Shigar and observe this fascinating land from another angle.

Transhumance: Beyond the remains of **Shigar Fort** on a rocky plateau to the east of the village, a narrow valley ascends towards the northeast accompanied by a well used trail. This route up to the **Thalle La** is an example of the well established system of communication between the different isolated valleys of Baltistan. The pass connects the Shigar valley to the Shyok River east of

Ferryman plies the Shyok River.

Skardu, and the route takes three or four days on foot. For the well-acclimatised trekker it provides a relatively easy amble into the heart of Baltistan.

In summer, the goats, cattle and their herdsmen shift to high altitude, above 3,000 metres where there is enough precipitation to provide adequate grazing. Villages, abandoned during the winter, come to life, and the locals live off the cheese and curd that their herds provide as well as the supplies of flour and ghee brought up from the valley for the endless production of *roti*. They also brew wonderful tea strongly flavoured with pepper. Fuel is supplied by the dung of the animals and by local deadwood. It is a common sight to see old but sturdy-looking men racing across the hillside to stack their wood in huge bundles which they strap to a frame on their backs.

Back at the village, smoke issues from the roofs of the simple huts and as evening comes, the cold sets in and the herds all gather round.

The Thalle Pass itself is surrounded by jagged 6,000-metre peaks. Although it is almost 5,000 metres high, in late summer snow only drapes the final 200 metres or so and the final ascent is fairly shallow. Beyond, great rock walls glimmering red in the evening light obstruct a view of the even higher Baltoro peaks further to the east. It is a long descent into the Thalle valley at the other side, but quite idyllic. High altitude meadows are flushed with the bubble of streams and springs. Further down, as the mountain slopes turn to grey, even darker specks can be seen clinging to the barren slopes; the indigenous yaks will go anywhere in search of nourishment. Lower still come the first signs of cultivation and the distribution of villages becomes more dense.

Harvest time: By mid-September the bed of the valley is full of maize and wheat awaiting harvest. The crops at higher altitude naturally ripen last and so the process of harvesting begins at the bottom. It is an activity in which all able hands are employed, and a great team of men, women, children, indeed **The Thalle Valley.**

whole villages, with their animals and machinery, gradually move up the valley to complete the task. Half way down, where the harvest is half complete, tapestries of browns and gold brush the hillside.

Further on the threshing has already begun. Livestock yoked to a vertical pole in the middle of a large circle slowly move round and trample the freshly havested crop under foot. This method of threshing seems first to have been used in ancient Egypt and Babylon, later spreading into Central Asia. While in Baltistan the task is generally carried out by the yaks or oxen, occasionally the particularly rare practice of mixing these with horses can be seen.

Below the village of **Khusomik**, the settlements are more permanent. After harvest, all but the herdsmen return to start on the tasks that the long isolated winter months require. In between spinning wool and making it into rugs and clothes on their looms, the old men start telling the same old stories and legends which their fathers once handed down.

Left, young mother with child in Hushe. Right, Lela Peak.

The Garden of Eden: The trail occasionally becomes absorbed into thick orchards of apple and luscious apricots and wanders between the hamlets and a myriad of irrigation channels. At just over 2,000 metres, the **Shyok River** is reached, and with it the main road from which the drone of civilisation occasionally reaches the ears; the jeeps have only taken six hours to come up from Skardu.

The valley to the east lives up to the list of superlatives which have been used to describe it by various travellers who have passed through ever since the Earl of Dunmore first explored the region at the end of the last century. The locals look upon it as the Garden of Eden, the blue Shyok, bordered by richly cultivated land dappled by picturesque Tibetan-looking villages and enclosed by vertical granite thousands of metres high.

The road leads to the east along the north bank of the river, between the villages snaking its way around rock shelves jutting out above the water.

A short distance before the village of **Saling**, there is a ferry service which operates between the north bank and the small town of Khapalu across the other side. The same type of ferry has been operating for hundreds of years and it consists of a wooden lattice bound together with rope. The contraption floats on a series of inflated goatskins on which the passengers also sit. Using long poles, the local Balti ferrymen steer the ferry to the other side, arriving at the opposite bank somewhat further downstream.

Khapalu is the principal town of the Shyok Valley, a sprawl of Tibetan style houses encroaching up into the mountains above the river. Overlooking the whole valley is the Palace of the former Rajas of Khapalu through whose present descendant the traditions of the past are still kept alive. The annual Spring Festival, held throughout the northern areas, lasts for three days here. The 'Raja' invites the local band to the Palace and the song and dance begins. A sideline is the polo competition held on

the ground just below the palace in which local teams from neighbouring villages participate. From the wooded hillsides above the town, there are marvellous views of the perpendicular mountains to the north, access to which is gained by re-crossing the river and and entering the confines of the beautiful **Hushe Valley** via the village of **Machalu**.

Hushe: The valley runs due north for about 30 kilometres until it stops at the massive bulk of **Masherbrum** (7,821 metres), its giant southern flanks standing out above the greens of the valley, which is one of the most fertile in the entire Karakoram. Here orchards of walnut, apple and apricot abound amidst a patchwork quilt of tiny fields producing a great diversity of crops, all carefully irrigated by channels emanating from further up the valley.

Brightly dressed children peer from behind the security of old stone doorways and then come running. Women look down from the flat rooftops where they are busy laying out the corn, the apricots, and a multitude of other products to dry.

Despite the bliss of it all the valley does have its problems, not least of which is that a disturbingly large proportion of the population suffer from goitre, the result of a deficiency of iodine in the diet.

Before land communications between Shigar and Askhole were improved, the Hushe Valley used to provide a more direct route to the Baltoro Glacier via the **Masherbrum La**. The village of Hushe itself always provided the manpower for the expeditions that passed through, and still today the majority of high altitude guides and porters hail from this village. This is the home of the unsung heros of mountaineering expeditions, of legendary figures like Abdul Karim who has spent more time above 8,000 metres than most of the better known western climbers.

The village itself is a collection of squat stone houses lost among fields of maize and wheat divided from each other by a maze of dry stone walls. In the presence of the soaring south face of

Abdul Karim, one of the several popular high-altitude guides in the Karakoram.

Masherbrum, the village is particularly inconspicuous.

To the east of the great mountain the possibilities for trekking are some of the best in the entire Northern Areas. An absolute delight compared to Baltoro for here, to counterbalance the ice and rock of the glacier, is enough green to make walking along the morraines of the thunderous glaciers a real pleasure.

The hub of the whole area is a broad valley to the east of Hushe whose name translates into **Rosehip Valley** which in springtime is a profusion of wild roses. Due east of this, is the snout of a huge glacier emanating from the magnificent spires of **K6** and **K7** looming in the distance. When the first reconnaisances of this country were made, where a local name for a mountain was not assumed to exist it was simply tagged with a number. And for the cartographers an abbreviation was much easier to cope with. Karakoram Six has remained K6.

To the north the great serpentine **Chondogoro Glacier** rises past the eastern flanks of Masherbrum. On a broad plateau above the glacier a collection of stone huts marks the limit of civilisation, except for a shepherd who lives with his family a little further up, at **Dalsam**. In late September all the villagers from below ascend to gather their goats and sheep and cattle which have spent the summer roaming the mountainsides. The winter arrives quickly and the beasts must be brought down to the confines of the valley. But there are no dogs to assist the shepherds. Instead, nimble boys leap from rock to rock, throwing stones at the animals with incredible accuracy.

The glacier winds round to the northeast and finishes at a large green meadow below a 5,500-metre ridge, the watershed to Baltoro to the north. To the south, shaped just like a pencil tip, the magnificent **Lela Peak** pierces the skies. For the trekker with ice axe and crampons, the challenging steep ascent to the summit of **Gondoro Peak** (5,700 metres) is well rewarded by superb views of the magnificent peaks of the Upper Baltoro Glacier.

The majestic K2 seen from Condordia.

TO THE HINDU KUSH

About 400 kilometres away to the west of K2 lies the obstacle which has either made or broke millennia of potential invasions; the towering Hindu Kush looms above the last outpost of the north of Pakistan, the valley of Chitral. The town of Chitral can be reached by one of two possible land routes. The first one involves returning to Gilgit and retracing the Karakoram Highway down as far as the town of **Besham**, then crossing the scenic **Shangla Pass** into Lower Swat with further connections up to Dir and the **Lowari Pass**.

A rough ride: The second route is more direct; from Gilgit a two day helter-skelter following the **Gilgit River** through the Hindu Raj to Shandur Pass and to the northern reaches of the Chitral Valley via Mastuj. Beyond the village of Gakuch, this route is particularly rough, often clinging to precipitous, almost vertical slopes hundreds of metres above the river.

But apparently, it is not as rough as it used to be when the journey was negotiated by horse, as indicated by Algneron Durand who traversed this route several times at the end of the last century and wrote:

"...still, however bad the track, so long as a man stuck to the riding road he generally stuck to his horse; nowhere in the world, I should think, do men habitually ride over such awful ground, and yet the Chitrali is no horseman, but then he has no nerves."

Despite the fact that the riding road has now been converted into a track wide enough for a jeep, nerves are still required. A passenger must also cling on for dear life, especially if perched on the top of a cargo jeep, wheels barely touching the ground, the torrent below. Occasionally the route passes through narrow bazaars of small villages, too narrow for anything wider than a jeep.

The stretch between **Gakutch** and **Gupis**, a deep gorge, is particularly rough going. But then the valley opens out into a broad plain surrounded by farmland and meadows. The river slowly meanders through, and the trout, which are here in abundance, fall easy prey to local boys who pluck them from the water and fry them for breakfast. Here too, many of the local population are Ismaili, and the projects of the Aga Khan are numerous. There are new roads, schools, fish farms and canals.

Beyond **Phander** the landscape gets more desolate once again and the terrain flattens out at **Shandur Pass**, which at 3,720 metres is the home of the highest polo ground in the world, scene of summer polo competitions between Chitral and Gilgit.

Then the route drops down via the Laspur Valley to **Mastuj** where the **Yarkund River** emerges from the north, from the direction of the **Baroghil Pass**, one of the most strategic and historically important passes in the entire Hindu Kush. There is an old fort at Mastuj. Not too much else. It is a barren windswept place. But away to the west, **Tirich Mir** (7,708 metres) can be seen standing clearly above all other

Left, Tirich Mir looms large from the valley. Right, a girl peeps from behind a door in Chitral.

ridges and the road continues to follow the **Mastuj River** into the upper reaches of the Chitral.

The **Chitral Valley** is perhaps the least developed corner of the Northern Areas. It is hemmed in by the Hindu Kush to the north and west and by the mountains of the Hindu Raj to the east, and by the Pathan tribal areas beyond the Lowari pass to the south. During the long winter months, except for the lifeline provided by the daily but often cancelled flight from Peshawar, the Chitral Valley is completely cut off from the outside world.

Few corners of the world can have witnessed so many waves of invasion as the Hindu Kush. Over the mountains and into the valley came the Aryans, Alexander, the hordes of Ghengiz Khan as well as many more invaders, emigrants and innocent herdsmen. It is therefore hardly surprising then that the precise origins of the Chitralis remain unclear. The earliest inhabitants in the north are known collectively as the Kho, and the language they speak, Khowari is a combination of the multitude of different dialects spoken throughout the region. In medieval times, many of the Kho led an isolated existence, cut off from developments in the outside world by the remote valleys of the Hindu Kush, particularly of Nuristan and Lower Chitral.

When Islam became entrenched in the main valleys, the Muslims named this mysterious folk *kafirs*, or pagans. They gradually became the lowest, most downtrodden class. They were sold to slavery and their numbers dwindled. Many converted to Islam. Today, the Kailash (black dresses) people of "Kafiristan" only exist in three remote valleys to the south west of the town of Chitral in the southern part of the valley.

Where the rivers are young: All the younger rivers draining the Hindu Kush are, except in time of flood, bright blue in colour. As the route continues from Mastuj the river here provides a marvellous contrast to the snow peaks soaring above the greens and browns of its

Autumn is a good time to see Chitral.

banks. Upper Chitral posseses miles of splendid cultivation supported by a rich alluvial soil. In the autumn, as the leaves of the willow and birch turn orange and gold, the valleys and the isolated settlements on the mountainsides above are a blaze of colour.

At the village of **Kosht**, the Mastuj River merges with the **Turikho River** flowing down from the north. The road branches off here, up the valley of the latter through the village of **Mezgol** and on towards **Drasan**. The mountainsides above provide fantastic possibilities for wandering from village to village to discover the people and the places that Alexander the Great and the others left behind.

It is a journey back in time. On approaching a village, surrounded by orchards, hay drying on the mudded rooftops of the earthen houses, a man and his oxen ploughing a harvested field, women and children disappear behind the secure walls of their houses. Silence until a headman approaches and beckons a closer approach. Its a man with bright ginger hair and fair skin. The children dare come out, some dark and some blond, with bright blue dazzling eyes. One of them offers a huge rosy apple and the barriers are down.

The apples in this area must be the best in the entire north of Pakistan. Then the call to prayer comes over the loud speaker attached to the simple mosque. The men all disappear.

Within the village, water trickles along a system of channels which are not only used for irrigation, as in the rest of Northern Areas, but for the powering of elaborate mills used for grinding the grain to flour. The mills are arranged in series at points where they can best serve the needs of the villagers, and the channels, having completed their task in one village, then snake down through the fields to guide the water into the mills of the next. The whole process continues right down the mountainside for thousands of metres serving the needs of everyone and enabling the communities to have a booming self-sufficiency.

The abode of fairies: The ridgeline above blocks out any view of Tirich Mir, though it can be ascended via the **Zani Pass** revealing the mountain in all its glory. The track continues on through **Shagram** and **Tirich Mir Village**, eventually ceasing at the snout of the **Barum Glacier** beneath the south face of the mountain. Local folklore holds that Tirich Mir is the abode of the local fairies. Fairies from all over the Hindu Kush come here for special meetings held on Friday nights. It is said that beside a lake at the base of the mountain the fairies use large flat stones for their washboards and potholes for grinding their rice.

The siege: A little further down the main valley is the village of **Reshun**. Here is a house which in 1895 provided a prison for two British Officers during the famous siege of Chitral. This brings to light a whole saga which unravelled after the British first established contact with the ruling *Mehtar* in 1889 in a bid to ensure stability in this, one of the most strategically important areas of the whole frontier.

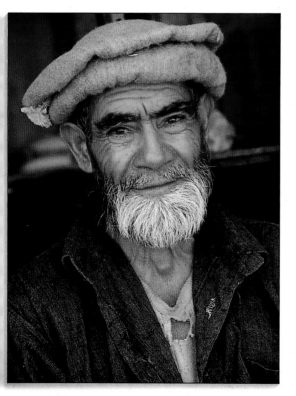

An old Chitrali gentleman.

The British had an amicable relationship with the said *Mehtar*, Aman-ul-Mulk, who was one of a long line which had ruled the region for about 350 years, latterly at odds with the Afghans on the one side as well as the Pathans on the other. The alliance promoted mutual stability and it was only when the old man died that a battle for succession ensued.

There was treachery, murder and vengeance, intrigue and deceit. Most of the Mehtar's heirs gradually wiped each other out and the whole valley was finally laid open to a two-pronged attack from Afghanistan and from the Pathans, the remaining Chitrali nobility joining in, in a bid to drive out the British. What saved the day were the heroic efforts of Colonel Kelly who had humped two heavy cannon all the way over from Gilgit and the forces of General Low mounting a rearguard action via the Lowari Pass (named after the General). Peace was restored and apart fom a few days' involvement in the Third Afghan war of 1919, the Chitralis have lived in peace ever since.

Boom town: Further down the valley is the main administrative town of **Chitral**. By the banks of the river is the old fort and palace of the *Mehtar*. Neatly lined up outside its walls is a series of cannon, testimony to the presence of the British garrison, originally numbering 419 men, which suffered heavy casualties at the time of the siege.

But there is very little action now to be seen in the vicinity of the fort and while just above it there is a large mosque providing an impressive foreground to the far more impressive Tirich Mir looming to the north, most activity in Chitral is now to be found along the main **Shahi Bazaar**.

Since the Russian invasion of Afghanistan, the population of the town, and for that matter the whole southern part of the valley, has increased dramatically. While many of the refugees live in tent accommodation along the valley floor, others have integrated themselves into the town life. The bazaar provides an interesting mix of local people and Afghans, the latter now actively involved in the local economy, many even running their own businesses. It could even be said that since the arrival of the Afghans, Chitral has become a boom town. The Afghans are busy selling their precious stones and other wares which they have managed to smuggle in from their homeland.

The bazaar is lined with general stores, food stalls, biscuit shops and tea houses. Toyotas and jeeps arrive in a continuous flow from north and south and the street is clogged with vehicles and people. Local shops also include makers and vendors of the famous Chitrali hat, the *pakol*, among other garments including *chogas* and socks. All these items are made out of the same fine wool known as *puttee* which is largely produced in the Turikho Valley. The region produces so much of this material that it also exports it to the markets of Peshawar and beyond. The pakol has found favour among locals and foreigners throughout the Northern Areas and beyond.

Into the Hindu Kush: From Chitral it is

Shahi Bazaar in the heat of the day.

possible to make a number of treks in a westward direction towards the border ridges. Afghanistan is not far away. An interesting route is along the **Ludkho River**, which follows a narrow valley to the north of the town, right into the heart of the Hindu Kush.

It is a delightful trek along the bubbling river, leading to the village of **Garam Chasma** (Hot Springs). The journey takes about two hours by jeep or Toyota. Most of the springs themselves are now surrounded by bath houses as the healing properties of the water are known throughout the region.

Continuing up the valley, a track leads northeast over the **Dorah Pass**, route of many an invader and the main trading route between Chitral and Badakstan. More recently the pass has been used by the mujahidin for ferrying their weapons and supplies into Afghanistan from their camp in Garam Chasma.

Somewhere to the north, again, lies Tirich Mir. However, because the fairies don't like to be disturbed too much,

Rice fields.

trekking right into their domain should perhaps only be left to those who don't mind incurring their wrath.

The Kailash Valleys: The valleys of **Bumburet**, **Rumbur** and **Birir**, where the Kailash still live, lie to the south of here and are accessible from Garam Chasma via the **Utak La**. For those who have sore feet, however, access is most easily gained by returning to Chitral and taking a jeep.

Here is all that remains of the so-called pagan cultures in the Hindu Kush, and their existence is under threat. Significant improvements in communications have resulted in easier access for those who wish to change their way of life; Islam is marching inexorably into their domain. The call to prayer blares out from loudspeakers attached to new Islamic schools and the sound of Islam echoes through the valleys, bringing an ever-increasing pressure on the local people to transform their faith. Many have already converted. For the remaining "pagans", time is running out.

THE KAILASH

Surrounded by the mountains of the Hindu Kush live a small group of people (about 3,000) called the Kafir Kailash.

They have their own language, religion and dress. Their religion has little in common with Islam and it is thought that it may have roots in early Vedic religion. There is one creator God and several other Gods. Ceremonies at which animals are sacrificed seem to be central to their customs.

Theories abound as to how the Kailash came to inhabit their lofty valleys. Some say that they are the descendants of tribes who intermarried with followers of Alexander the Great, but there isn't any evidence that he passed this way. Some people discern traces of Greek civilisation and physical characteristics among the Kailash. As in other parts of the Hindu Kush the Kailash are fair in complexion and rosy cheeked. Some people are blonde and blue-eyed. Whatever their origins, here is a little island of "pagans" in a Muslim world.

The women wear a striking costume, consisting of long black robes - frocks caught up into a blouson effect with girdles embroidered with cowrie shells, and voluminous skirts. They also sport striking headgear, caps with huge pompoms and a train at the back of the head, these are also richly decorated with cowrie shells. The cowries were once a small unit of currency in Northern India, a headdress and girdle encrusted with them must have denoted great wealth.

Kailash women used to wear lots of necklaces, made from coral, beads of ivory, and fresh and saltwater pearls. But of latter years a lot of these seem to have vanished. Presumably they have been sold off, because they appear again in tourist shops in Swat and even as far away as Peshawar. Another indication of recent poverty is the fact that many women have had no new dresses for a very long time, and many dresses are also on sale in tourist centres. In the old days Kailash women used to wear shoes but nowadays they go barefoot or wear sandals brought up from Chitral. No doubt Kailash men once had their own costume too, but with greater exposure to the outside world, they have now adopted the *salwar kameez*.

The Kailash are famous for music and especially dancing, which takes place at the time of major festivals. There are four festivals: one in spring, one in mid-July to mark the harvest and another in autumn to celebrate the grape and walnut harvests, and the last festival – on Christmas day, is a new year's celebration. There are dances on the occasions of births, deaths and marriages.

Women dance by themselves; a spectacle which attracts huge crowds because the sight of women dancing appears to provide a great

attraction, also for those unaccustomed to seeing many women not in *purdah*. The Kailash make wine, but only in small quantities. It is not strong but sweet, sticky and thick. The Kailash dilute it with water.

The economy revolves around sheep and goats. Nowadays, Kailash people also keep chickens to sell birds and eggs to tourists. They do not eat them themselves. They grow walnuts, and walnuts were a big source of income, being exported home and abroad. But with increasing poverty, the Kailash have mortgaged their land and trees to settlers in the valleys. They have lost their rights. They did not know what they were signing away and now the Government is attempting to restore the trees to the rightful owners. The growing season is very short, but they manage to grow vegetables, maize, wheat, millet, cabbages, potatoes, carrots etc., and many fruit trees are cultivated, especially mulberry, apricot, apples, pears and plums. Hitherto these were also exported by the Kailash but nowadays the trade has also been lost to them. There is a limited amount of hill rice grown. As in Hunza and Upper Chitral, irrigation is provided by ingenious artificial channels.

To economise on land use on the valley basin, which is suitable for farming, the Kailash houses are carefully stacked one on

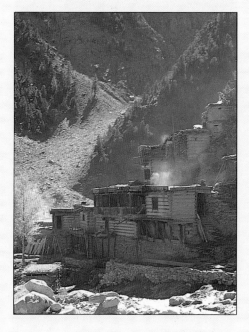

top of the other going up the hill. The roof of one house forms the veranda to another home above. The roof is a convenient place to lay out the fruit to dry. The homes are decorated with carvings, especially the doors and lintels. The designs are presumably very ancient. Sometimes designs are carved and sometimes they come in poker work. The shapes used are curvilinear, going in and out like snail shells.

The insides of the Kailash homes are dark with floors of packed earth. Cooking is done

Left, a headdress of cowrie shells. **Above**, an existence is threatened.

on an open hearth and the walls are blackened by the soot.

There is a part of the village which is reserved for menfolk only. A stone juts from the hillside and there is a ram's skull with huge horns and a rampart of sheep bones. Here animals are sacrificed. Goats are sacrificed to gods and ancestors and every man makes a sacrifice at least once a year. Women are strictly excluded from all this and they are not allowed near sacrificial sites or sacred places. Women may not eat the meat of sacrifices, especially the meat of male goats. They may not go to the pastures or enter goathouses. Animal husbandry is a male occupation and crops are tended by women. They may not eat Kailash honey because it is believed that bees are male and that the all-male beehive is the perfect masculine world. In common with many other cultures, strict notions of purity control women's everyday lives, limiting their mobility, diet and even labour.

Birth and menstruation are particularly impure: There is a hut called the *bashali*, beside the river. It has a stone floor and some utensils are kept there. At the time of menstruation, women retreat to the *bashali* for five days, after which they emerge, bathe, change clothes, and wash and rebraid their hair. Hair braiding and combing is also regarded as impure and combs are also kept beside the river.

Marriages are arranged during childhood. A fee is paid by the bridegroom to the bride's family. The bride also receives a dowry which is her own property, though this dowry tends to be handed over after a decade of marriage when things seem well settled. If the wife is unhappy over her marriage, she may elope with her lover and then negotiate with her husband for a divorce.

When death comes to the Kailash, it is viewed as a release and the deceased are given a good send off. Formerly, carved walnut coffins were prepared. A Kailash graveyard has the coffins above ground and wealthy people had wooden effigies made to stand by the coffins. Nowadays, unfeeling people desecrate the Kailash graves, knock the lids off the coffins and remove the skulls for photographs. Coffins are not left *in situ* these days. And while some Kailash convert gladly to Islam, many are depressed because they feel that their culture is vanishing.

RAILWAY TRACKS

The origin of railways in what was to become Pakistan is unusual in that very few railway lines were built primarily for the commercial purpose of linking centres of population and trade: the first railway line was constructed to reduce the journey time on the final stage of the long haul from Britain to Delhi and Calcutta. Many of the later lines were built for military reasons.

The journey out to India was an endurance test of boredom and discomfort, and many dreamed of the day when through railway carriages might run from Calais to Calcutta. In 1842, when the first P & O steamer took the route round the Cape of Good Hope on its voyage from Southampton to Calcutta, it took 91 days to reach the Indian capital, of which 28 were spent in port taking on coal. International politics prevented European railways being extended through the Middle East, and the hardships of the route from Alexandria made attractive the prospect of taking the steamer to Karachi and a train on to Delhi or Calcutta.

Up the Indus: The first part of the railway route was begun in 1855 when the Scinde Railway Company was established in London to build a 174-kilometre line along the right bank of the River Indus as far as Kotri. It was to be another 34 years before the final link in the 1,982 kilometres to Delhi was completed when the Lansdowne Bridge across the Indus between Sukkur and Rohri was opened. (Delhi and Calcutta had been joined by rail in 1864.)

The long delay in completing the principal railway route through the Sind and Punjab reflects some of the problems that railway builders faced in this part of the Raj. Though construction across the arid flatlands to the north and east of Karachi was straightforward, the Indus posed a major obstacle; not only did the viaducts across it have to be designed for huge increases in the water flow, but the railway across the desert was

liable to inundation when the Indus burst its banks.

The first section of railway from Karachi was opened to Kotri in 1861 and one of the railway's engineers, John Brunton, described the reaction of the locals to the awesome manifestation of power represented by the first steam locomotive: "The natives of Scinde had never seen a Locomotive Engine. They had heard of them as dragging great loads on the lines by some hidden power they could not understand, therefore they feared

them, and supposing that they moved by some diabolical agency, they called them *Shaitan* (or Satan). During the Mutiny the mutineers got possession of one of the East India Line Stations where several engines stood. They did not dare approach them but stood a good distance away throwing stones at them.

"When I got out my Locomotive for trial the Karachi natives were astounded... I drove the Engine myself of course at a slow speed – the natives thronging all round, I was fearful of some accident. At last I thought I would frighten them away, so I blew the engine steam whistle loudly. Instantly they

Preceding pages: train built in Manchester, 1912; Khojak Tunnel in Baluchistan. **Left**, Louise Margaret Bridge – a bold feat of engineering which no longer exists. **Above**, a proud emblem.

all rushed back from the "Demon" - falling over one another."

The railway was a great boon, for it paralleled the most dangerous part of the Indus where the water in the delta was tidal. Previously passengers had taken one of the boats built in Birkenhead and London that formed the Indus Steam Flotilla. Travelling the 965 kilometres up river to Multan could take five weeks, partly because the river's ill-defined channels were much too treacherous to negotiate at night.

After the opening of the Scinde Railway, the next section to open was Lahore to Amritsar in 1862, part of the Panjab Railway which was responsible for building the 409

of the Indus Valley State Railway. The principal reason for the delay was the need to bridge the Sutlej and Beas rivers by the Empress Bridge, to which Queen Victoria gave her name in a telegram congratulating the Government of India on the bridge's completion. It had taken a total of 6,000 workers to construct it, housed in a new town built at Adamwahan where pestilence had sometimes confined three out of four men to their beds.

Even the opening of this section left the crossing of the Indus between Sukkur and Rohri in the hands of a ferry that carried across wagons and passengers. Through running of trains between Karachi and Cal-

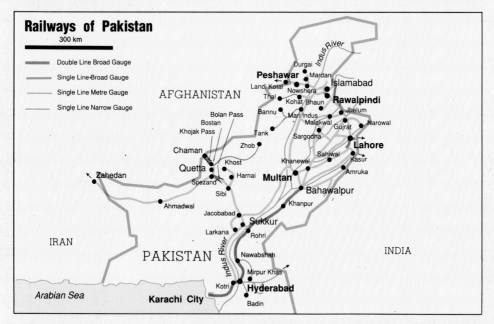

Railways of Pakistan

300 km

- Double Line Broad Gauge
- Single Line-Broad Gauge
- Single Line Metre Gauge
- Single Line Narrow Gauge

AFGHANISTAN

Indus River

Durgai

Peshawar • Mardan
Landi Kotal • Nowshera • Islamabad
Thal • Kohat Bhaun • Rawalpindi
Bolan Pass • Bannu • Mari Indus • Jhelum
Bostan • Malakwal • Gujrat • Narowal
Khojak Pass • Tank • Sargodha
Chaman • Zhob • Sahiwal • Lahore
Khost • Khanewal • Kasur
Quetta • Harnai • Multan • Amruka
Zahedan • Spezand • Bahawalpur
Sibi • Khanpur
Ahmadwal • Jacobabad • Khanpur
Larkana • Sukkur
IRAN • Rohri
PAKISTAN • Indus River • Nawabshah • INDIA
Mirpur Khas
Kotri • Hyderabad
Arabian Sea • Karachi City • Badin

kilometres between Multan and Amritsar, where it connected with the Delhi Railway's 483-kilometre line on to the future capital of India which opened in 1865. Trains ran into a terminal station at Lahore and reversed out, but provision was made for through running in the realisation that the railway would in due course be built on towards Rawalpindi and Peshawar. The main line was constructed south to Multan and opened in 1865, still leaving the 917 kilometres between Kotri and Multan to be linked by the Indus Steam Flotilla.

It was another 13 years before the steamers were finally made redundant by the opening

cutta was at last made possible by the completion of the Lansdowne Bridge in 1889, then the longest cantilever bridge in the world. Despite its claim to fame on account of its size, professional opinion was scathing: The Engineer criticised "the monstrosity of the general design" and concluded that it was "not engineering, nor is it architecture". This was very much the exception amongst bridges on the North Western Railway (as the amalgamated railways became known from 1886); the majority were brilliantly engineered and, with selective strengthening to cope with heavier loadings, have given over a century's service.

Inevitably almost all the locomotives until Partition were built in Britain, mostly in Glasgow and Manchester, though the locomotive workshops at Moghalpura near Lahore undertook major rebuilds. Fuel was a problem, since the reserves of coal in the region were neither large nor of good quality. The first locomotives were fuelled with coal shipped out from South Wales, though the extensive forests around Changa Manga to the south-west of Lahore provided wood for the first locomotives operating up country. Subsequently coal had to be railed from the mines situated on the East India Railway, entailing a haul of between 1,450 and 2,000 kilometres. With a daily consumption of

Russian intentions beyond the borders of the Empire and the unsettled state of the tribal areas along the frontier with Afghanistan; between 1858 and 1902 over forty British expeditions had to take the field against the Pathans. Called the Panjab Northern State Railway until 1886, the line was gradually extended north westwards, entailing the bridging of the Ravi, Chenab and Jhelum rivers. All were bridged between 1871 and 1876, but it was another five years before the superb bridge over the Indus at Attock was opened, enabling trains to run from Peshawar to Bombay and Calcutta. Some idea of the challenge these rivers gave to bridge engineers is provided by the ability of the

3,500 tons, it was no wonder that locomotives in the south were converted to run on oil imported from the Persian Gulf. The steam locomotives that survive into the 1990s are all oil-fired. Another problem for the locomotive power department was the supply of water, often entailing the laying of miles of pipe to bring water from mountain streams to a tank beside the line.

Strategic lines: To the west of Lahore the railway was built by the government as a strategic line, prompted by concern over

Chenab River to widen from 456 metres in winter to five and a half kilometres in summer and to rise by three metres.

The railway between Karachi and Peshawar affords access to a number of tourist sites as well as the intermediate cities of Lahore, Rawalpindi and Islamabad. The most southerly, however, requires a deviation along the line between Kotri and Sukkur on the west bank of the Indus; Mohenjo-daro, one of the great cities of the Indus Valley civilisation, can be reached by the station of the same name, though as Geoffrey Moorhouse related in "To The Frontier", there is unlikely to be more than a tonga

Above, chugging up the Bolan Pass.

waiting for passengers. Alternatively, one can alight at Larkana and take a taxi for the 28-kilometre journey to the city. Another of the Indus Valley civilisation sites, Harappa, can be reached from Sahiwal station between Khanewal and Lahore, while the cities at Taxila, 35 kilometres north east of Rawalpindi, are very close to Taxila station.

Steam engines: For those in search of steam locomotives, probably the best remaining centre lies on a direct line between Peshawar and Lahore, though 70 kilometres to the west of the main line junction of Lala Musa: Malakwal has become a mecca for steam locomotive aficionados from all over the world. The small community is of little importance

except as a railway junction, and accommodation is limited and decidedly spartan; but based at the locomotive shed are the world's last working 4-4-0s (a four-wheel bogie followed by four driving wheels powered by cylinders mounted on the inside of the locomotive's frames).

These stately products of such long-deceased manufacturers as Beyer Peacock, North British and Vulcan Foundry haul passenger trains over a network of secondary routes. Many were working trains before World War I and seem likely to give a few more years' service before succumbing to dieselisation.

To the Frontier: There are few lines in the Indian subcontinent that can rival those stretching to the border with Afghanistan for the number and size of tunnels, viaducts and bridges. They are major engineering achievements; in the barren, mountainous lands of the North West Frontier and Baluchistan, the lives of railway engineers and contractors were accompanied by a constant battle against the elements.

Sudden downpours or melting snow turned tiny mountain streams into torrents. Structures had to be built to withstand earthquakes. Equipment and ironwork had to be ordered from Britain. There was a shortage of skilled labour and the workforce constantly suffered from disease and dehydration. A measure of the extremes of temperature is given by the death from heat-stroke of 32 ill-prepared British soldiers during the crossing of the Sind desert in a troop train in 1915, while less than 500 kilometres away passengers on the Bostan to Fort Sandeman (Zhob) line suffered frostbite when their train was caught in a snowdrift.

Gauges: One of the consequences of the difficulty of building railways through such country, was the use for some lines of smaller gauges, which were cheaper to build and could negotiate sharper curves. The strong winds that could blow throughout the subcontinent also influenced the choice of a wider gauge for the main routes so that trains would be more stable. Even today some carriage compartments, especially on the narrow gauge, bear notices warning passengers to open windows when there is a storm, thereby reducing wind resistance.

Instead of the European standard gauge of 4ft 8½ in, the gauge of 5ft 6in had originally been chosen as the "standard" gauge for the subcontinent by Lord Dalhousie, Governor General of India between 1848 and 1856. When the first railways were being planned, he was determined that the problems which arose from mixed gauges should not happen in India. His successor, Lord Mayo, thought differently: "When we have an elephant's load, we may use an elephant, but when we have only a donkey's load, we have to use a donkey".

The Khyber Pass Railway: Sadly one of the most impressive railway journeys of the whole subcontinent – the line up the Khyber Pass – is no longer possible. By the early

1980s, it was theoretically prohibited for foreigners, and in December 1984 the service was suspended for the duration of military operations against local tribes; it is believed that some bridges have since been sabotaged.

As there had only been one return train a week over the line for many years, it is unlikely that the line will be reopened. Some idea of the loss this represents may be gained from statistics: in 40 km there are 92 bridges, 34 tunnels with an aggregate length of 5 kilometres, and four reversing stations where the train zig-zagged its way up the mountain sides. It was the last and arguably the greatest construction on the North West

guarded the mouth of the pass. The heavy fighting with Afghanistan in 1919 prompted a new survey by Colonel (later Sir Gordon) Hearn which dismissed the idea that it would be impossible to force a 5ft 6in gauge line up the pass.

In the following year, construction began. One of the engineers on the line, Victor Bayley, wrote an account of his work relating the difficulties he encountered in persuading the tribes to allow the railway to be built; though the pass was guarded by frequent blockhouses and the Brigade Headquarters at Landi Kotal, it would have been impossible to build the railway had the tribes been determined to prevent it.

Frontier during the Raj.

The first proposal to build a railway through the Khyber was made during the Second Afghan War (1878-79), at which time the Indus had still not been crossed at Attock. Several surveys for a narrow or metre gauge line revealed only the difficulties the engineers would face, and by 1901 nothing more had been done than extend the NWR by 14 kilometres from Peshawar Cantonment to the old Sikh fort at Jamrud, which

In conversation with one of the tribal chiefs, who had been in the Indian Army, he used a Rabelaisian sense of humour to suggest that the Pathans' tradition of raiding caravans might not have to cease simply because of the railway: "But, Subehdar Sahib, this will be no ordinary railway. The gradient will be steep and the trains will travel slowly. They will be carrying rich merchandise and will pass close to your doors. The Sultan Khel are notorious robbers and raiders. Think of the opportunities for looting the trains!"

The tribes were persuaded not only to accept the railway but to help build it, though

Left, a pointsman at Bostan Junction. **Above**, getting up steam.

the enmity between the tribes which worked on the line was palpable, and Bayley wrote in dismay of the degree of hatred and cruelty which feuds engendered. He somehow managed to insist that the railway workings were a strife-free zone.

By 1925 the line up to the summit at Landi Kotal was complete; the extensive sidings and platforms provided there were an anachronism for the three-coach train that plied the railway once a week in its final years. But in 1929 the fort held one British and three Indian infantry battalions, an Indian mountain battery, a section of 18-pounder guns and a Brigade signal section. Between 1926 and 1932 two trains a week dropped down to Landi Khana, three kilometres short of the border, though earthworks were prepared for an extension to Torkham in the event of the railway being extended into Afghanistan.

For the last decade before suspension of services, the Khyber railway was a tourist attraction. The Hotel Khyber Inter-Continental even advertised a special two-day package tour featuring a journey up the line (erroneously describing it in the promotional literature as a metre gauge railway), lunch at the Pakistan Tourist Development Corporation restaurant at Torkham and a visit to one of the typical fortified tribal houses that pepper the pass. Landi Kotal's reputation as an open market for drugs, and war in Afghanistan, put an end to tourist visits.

Although lacking the spectacular scenery of the Khyber Pass, the branch line from Nowshera (40 kilometres east of Peshawar) to Durgai affords a flavour of the military railway. The station at the terminus is surrounded by a defensive wall with metal gates, which can be closed across the tracks, and protected by a blockhouse on the platform and by a large fort bristling with metal-plated gun slits. (A reminder of the precariousness of life on the North West Frontier is provided by a plaque in Holy Trinity Church at Murree, commemorating an action at Durgai, in which Major Richard Dyneley Jennings-Bramly of the 1st Battalion, Gordon Highlanders, fell on St. Lukes Day, 18 October 1897.) The train stops at Takht-i-Bahi and so is also of interest to those wishing to visit the Buddhist remains.

Baluchistan tracks: Steam locomotives long since gave way to diesels on what is probably the most awe-inspiring journey on the 5ft 6in

gauge: what began as the Kandahar State Railway runs from Ruk Junction (30 kilometres north west of Sukkur on the Karachi-Lahore line) to Sibi and Quetta. The late historian of the North Western Railway, P.S.A. Berridge, gives it pride of place in the pantheon of Indian railways: "The story of its construction has no parallel in the whole of the history of the railways of India. It is a tale of appalling muddle in the beginning, of extreme privations in the face of terrible heat and freezing cold, and of success achieved through sheer grit and determination to win a route through forbidding and inhospitable desert and mountainous country...the line kept open today is evidence of a quality of

engineering endeavour unsurpassed anywhere else in the world."

Quetta had become a military outpost since the Treaty of Jacobabad was signed with the Khan of Kalat in 1876, and it developed into the most important military cantonment in Baluchistan. Construction of the railway was motivated by the recurrent fear of Russian invasion of India through Afghanistan and the appalling toll of life in crossing the Kacchi Plain between Jacobabad and Sibi. Work began in 1879, and the 215 kilometres across the barren, treeless flat land between Ruk and Sibi were completed in just 101 days.

The plain section had been simplicity itself, but the passage through the mountains to Quetta were to prove a very different matter. The railway had to climb from 140 metres above sea level at Sibi to a summit of 1,780 metres, passing through a tangle of valleys. The route of the first line to Quetta, the Sind Peshin State Railway (SPS) from Sibi to Quetta via Khost and Bostan, was chosen because of the Chappar Rift Valley, an extraordinary freak of nature caused by a mountain splitting in two and so creating a defile through which the railway could pass. Over 15,000 men and even elephants laboured on the railway between 1883 and 1887, often under attack from local tribesmen.

hospitable place, reached now only by a bumpy dirt road which has a total disregard for the life of vehicle springs. There is hardly a community *en route* large enough to call a village, so desolate and isolated is the terrain.

Amongst the bleakest spots on the line is Mudgorge where the line was continually slipping down the hillside after rain or snow. The SPS beyond Khost was abandoned in 1942 after a section of line in the Chappar Rift Valley was swept away, and few trains venture up to Khost where coal is still occasionally extracted.

Over the Bolan Pass: The second route to Quetta and the main line from Karachi was begun in 1885, though the present alignment

Finally in March 1887 the first train ran through to Quetta, and at the opening of the railway the bridge at the entrance to the Chappar Rift Valley was named the Louise Margaret Bridge after HRH The Duchess of Connaught who visited it on 27 March 1887. Looking at the abandoned piers of the viaduct, it is difficult to imagine a member of the royal family visiting such a remote and in-

Left, easing out. **Above**, three of these locomotives were used to draw the heavy Karachi to Quetta express trains up the fearsome gradients of the Bolan Pass.

is the result of the third attempt to build an all-weather railway through the Bolan Pass. The first railway was merely laid on the stony bed of the pass and was destroyed by floods after two years; floods also put paid to the second route, though the remains of tunnels and bridges at a lower level than the present line can still be seen. It was the final alignment that justified Berridge's praise: the structures were so well built that even a severe earthquake in 1931, four years before the catastrophic earthquake in Quetta, did little damage to the route.

Through the Dozan Gorge, the line crosses the ravine nine times in six and a half kilometres, but it is the steepness of the climb that made it such an impressive line in steam days. Four big locomotives – two at the front and two at the back – were needed to take nine coaches up the eight kilometres of 1 in 25; at Mach station there was a notice warning passengers not to try the customary practice of boarding the train once it had begun to move, so rapid was the acceleration produced by the three or four locomotives. Though diesels have growled up the pass since 1966, the line still offers one of the finest railway journeys in the world.

To the border: The line through the Bolan Pass and the SPS met at Bostan, an isolated junction amidst barren hills, and from here

five other tunnels to be built, one of which – the elaborately portalled Shelabagh Tunnel – appears on a Pakistan bank note.

The line stopped short of the Afghan border at Chaman where a huge dump of permanent way materials was created in the event that the extension to Kandahar proved necessary. Though primarily a strategic railway, it was the means before Partition of conveying a daily train load of Afghan fruit, mostly nectarines, peaches and grapes, destined for cities such as Madras and Calcutta.

The last 5ft 6in gauge line to be built – the Nushki Extension Railway to Persia – has the doubtful distinction of being one of the loneliest railways in the world. Built to sup-

the final section of the line to the Afghan border branches off. By the time work began in 1888, the idea of building the line to Kandahar had been dropped, so the project was renamed the Chaman Extension Railway. If anything it was an even more taxing line to build than the Bolan route: it required the recruitment of 65 Welsh miners (who had had experience building the Severn Tunnel through treacherous water-bearing strata) to help with the 3,912-metre Khojak Tunnel, the longest in India; workers suffered high mortality in winter from pneumonia and typhus; 19 million bricks to line the Khojak Tunnel had to be burnt on site; and there were

ply the troops maintaining the East Persia cordon during World War I, the line passes through such arid country that several extra water tanks had to be attached to each steam locomotive.

The weekly train was for years advertised to carry a "buffet car" which was in fact a 4-wheel covered goods wagon dispensing curry and *chapatis*; it was a precaution against the possibility of the train breaking down in the wilderness and being without assistance for some time.

Running through an endless terrain of black stones punctuated by patches of clay and sand, the railway could assume new importance if international relations ever allowed the short section in Iran to be linked to the rest of the Iranian railway system, as suggested in moments when diplomatic relations improve.

Miscellaneous tracks: Though some railways were built to metre gauge, all were converted to 5ft 6in gauge except the network of metre gauge lines whose western terminus is now at Mirpur Khas, east of Hyderabad, in the Sind. It used to be such an extensive network that the traveller could reach Delhi, the cities of Rajasthan and even Bombay, but Partition put an end to such through workings, and today the entirely steam-worked lines serve communities in

metre Bostan Junction to Zhob railway, passenger trains have been suspended, leaving only the freight trains of chrome ore from Muslimbagh. An easing of political tension along the border may permit the line to be reopened, enabling travellers to savour the esoteric pleasures of riding a narrow gauge train through landscapes that vary from orchards of fruit trees to impressive snow-capped mountains.

Further north a line from Mari Indus divides at Laki Marwat, one branch going to Bannu, the other climbing over a ghat section to Tank. The most northerly of the narrow gauge lines links the 5ft 6in gauge terminus at the military cantonment of Kohat

the Sind up to Nawabshah and as far east as remote Khokhropar near the Indian border.

Intrepid travellers in search of the unusual may be attracted by the three remaining narrow gauge railways, which were all built to serve military purposes along the border with Afghanistan. None touches a tourist "route", but they pass through impressive scenery and all three are worked by steam engines. The service on the lines is sparse, and in the case of the longest, the 297-kilo-

with Thal, where M.M. Kaye, author of *The Far Pavilions*, lived. Thal is a prohibited area so foreigners have to leave the train at the preceding station; those who do not will almost certainly be detained by the Thal Scouts as the terminal station is situated inside their compound.

Travelling by rail is one of the best ways of seeing Pakistan and besides the often spectacular scenery that can be enjoyed from the window of a train, railway travel offers a great opportunity to meet people. As Paul Theroux comments at the beginning of The Great Railway Bazaar: "I sought trains; I found passengers."

<u>Left</u>, diesel trains are now in more common use. <u>Above</u>, patience is still required.

TRAVEL TIPS

GETTING THERE

BY AIR

Flying time to Karachi from: New York 17+ hours; Tokyo 10+ hours; Hong Kong 5+ hours; London 8 hours; Jeddah 3¾ hours; Abu Dhabi 1¾ hours.

There are many flights into Karachi on a variety of international airlines. Pakistan International Airlines fly to Pakistan from a number of major capitals and operate a domestic network. Only PIA and British Airways have direct flights from London to Islamabad. It is possible to book through some other airlines flying to Islamabad, though the journey involves changing planes. It is also possible to change planes and come into Lahore.

Travellers cheques can be exchanged at airports. Retain receipts for leaving.

BY SEA

There are some sailings around the Gulf area to Karachi, but sea routes are probably not feasible for most people. The boats are operated by the British Indian Navigation Company and McKinnon and McKenzie.

BY RAIL

Unless the situation changes with regard to Iran and Afghanistan, probably the only feasible route for most travellers is from India. (A very small number of people do come via Iran.)

BY ROAD

You may bring your own car to Pakistan. A tourist may import duty-free a motor vehicle under a *Carnet de passage en Douanne*, for a period of three months, provided he/she gives an undertaking before the customs officers that he will not transfer in any manner the ownership of the vehicle during his stay in Pakistan.

Unless there are radical changes, however, few travellers would approach from Iran and Afghanistan. There are crossing points at Torkham, and down the Khyber to Peshawar, but Torkham has been closed for a decade. There is a route through the Khojak Pass, via Chaman to Quetta and a direct route from Iran via Taftan.

A more frequented point of entry is Wagah on the Indian border, only 27 km from Lahore. This has been open more frequently in recent times as the political climate between India and Pakistan has improved. The border is also affected by unrest in the Indian Panjab.

The other route which has been increasingly used is the Karakoram Highway, from China. This is open between May and November from 11.00 a.m. to 4.00 p.m. It takes about 5 hours to travel from Taxkurgan (the last town in China) to Sost (the first village in Pakistan) – not including the time taken for the formalities at the border. The area is high, and can be cold and is not for the faint-hearted. It is best to check on the possibilities of crossing borders near the time of the intended journey.

TRAVEL ESSENTIALS

VISAS & PASSPORTS

All visitors require a valid passport. All visitors except the nationals of Tanzania, Malaysia, Zambia, Uganda, Trinidad, Tobago, and Singapore require visas to enter Pakistan.

Nationals of other countries having visa abolition agreements, or who allow Pakistan nationals into their countries without visas are also allowed entry for specified periods of between one and three months. South Africans are not admitted to Pakistan.

Single entry visas are valid for up to three

months, unless otherwise stated. Multiple journey visas are valid for a five-month stay. Any number of journeys (usually six) during a specified period, not exceeding one year, are normally allowed on such a visa. Visas can normally be used within six months from the date of issue or as provided for.

Foreigners entering different provinces do not have to obtain a new visa but special permission is required to visit restricted tribal areas, such as those in the provinces of NWFP and Baluchistan. Such permission is rarely given.

Some nationals (e.g. Indian and Afghan) are required to register with the Police within 24 hours of their arrival.

MONEY MATTERS

The unit of currency is the Rupee, with 100 paise to a rupee. There are 5, 10, 25, 50 paisa coins and 1, 2, 5, 10, 50, 100, 500 and 1,000 rupee notes.

BANKS

The State Bank of Pakistan is the Central Bank. There are some domestic commercial banks: Allied Bank of Pakistan, Habib Bank, Muslim Commercial Bank, and several others. There are also some foreign Banks, American Express, Grindlay's, Bank of Credit and Commerce International, etc. These are especially common in Islamabad, Karachi and other major cities.

TRAVELLER'S CHEQUES

Money is best transported as traveller's cheques or as bank drafts. It is quicker getting a bank draft sent by registered mail than having money transferred from bank to bank. Telex service is very slow indeed. Traveller's cheques are acceptable in Sterling, German Marks or Dollars.

Other methods, such as telegraphing money transfers, takes time. It is also possible to send money through the Post Office Giro System.

It is quite easy to encash traveller's cheques, even in some unlikely places. (However, there are Banks in Islamabad where it is apparently impossible.) Areas where there are high emigrant populations help facilitate the use of traveller's cheques.

CREDIT CARDS

Credit cards are acceptable at some of the hotels in major cities. It is also possible to get a Habib Bank Card in Pakistan.

Account holders with banks like the Royal Bank of Scotland, which have a close relationship with Grindlay's, may find that Grindlay's will be willing to oblige and credit money, so long as the account holder has a good credit record at his own bank. However, this service is only available in cases of emergency.

EXCHANGE RATES

The exchange rate is tied to the US Dollar and exchange rates applicable to important currencies are announced every day by the State Bank.

There is no limit on the amount of foreign currency or cheques brought in to Pakistan, but only Rs 100 in cash may be taken out, and only Rs 500 can be exchanged back into foreign currency. Save the encashment slips; they may be required upon leaving.

CUSTOMS

Tourists are allowed to take in personal belongings, and duty-free items usually including 200 cigarettes, 50 cigars or a half pound of tobacco. However, the import of liquor is not permitted. If a traveller has some, they should be left with the customs officers who should issue a receipt so that the traveller could claim them when he leaves the country. Bags are often searched and alcohol will be impounded if not handed in. Officially, visitors can also bring in half a pint of perfume, a camera, tape recorder and typewriter.

Imports and exports: The Chief Controller of Imports and Exports is responsible for issuing licences and permits and implementing policies in that area of activity.

PORTER SERVICES

There are porters in brown overalls at airports and in red overalls at railway stations. The tip required is embroidered on their overalls. There are also trolleys.

There are meet-and-assist services at Karachi Airport.

WHEN TO GO

When to go depends on the destinations the tourist has in mind. The primary considerations of most people would be to avoid extremes of hot and cold. For those visiting the plains, the winter and spring months are recommended. Those heading for Mohenjodaro, the Thar Desert or across to the western frontier in summer would feel uncomfortable. Summer, however, is the best time of year for visiting the Northern Mountains, although the heat in the valleys can still be oppressive. North of Nanga Parbat, the monsoon is of no consideration, and the season for visiting the mountains is potentially very long, depending on how long one can withstand the cold. Certainly trekking is possible, and even advisable up to October-November. The autumn is a beautiful time of year in the mountains.

HEALTH

Cholera and yellow fever vaccination certificates are required for travellers from infected areas. Immunisation against typhoid, tetanus and polio is advisable. Some doctors recommend an injection of gamma globulin before travelling as a precaution against hepatitis – fashions change on this one. Precautions should be taken against malaria, and these (pills for adults, syrup for young children) need to be heeded before travelling. Some people also take protection against rabies whilst others aver that this is of doubtful value. Travellers should also be aware of the dangers of AIDS and take sensible precautions.

MEDICINE

There are excellent doctors in the towns. Doctors in big cities are usually Western-trained and have their degrees to prove it. They will normally see patients quickly, and do many tests immediately in their own surgeries. Their charges are very reasonable indeed. They will even perform minor surgery on the spot! If patients are sent to a hospital or polyclinic, attention is fairly speedy and efficient.

Most familiar medicines are available from pharmacies, many on demand, with no prescription necessary. However, if a patient has some particular medicine taken on a regular basis it is wiser to take a supply, as it may not be possible to obtain precisely the same item.

Common medicines used for children are available – calpol syrup, ventolin is available without prescription. There is a syrup for children as a precaution against malaria. Some children seem to find the syrup acceptable. Oral rehydration salts are available and should be kept in readiness.

If travelling up-country and staying down-market, a de-lousing shampoo may not be a bad idea. Caladryl is available in Pakistan. *Keating's Powder* is handy for fleas. And prickly heat powder is a good idea for sweaty journeys.

People travelling much on the roads would find it wise to have a good, emergency first-aid kit and should also learn how to use it.

One of the most common minor problems is stomach upset. One can take some *Arrets* along, though there is a wide range of medicines for tummy upsets on sale. If the problem persists, consult a doctor. He will rapidly diagnose the cause of the problem, and in the case of some of the nastier bugs – amoebic or bacilliary dysentery – will prescribe suitable medicaments.

Another problem which should be guarded against is heat exhaustion, sunstrokes and sunburn. Even those who are used to the sun should take care. Special care should be taken in the northern mountains where the sun is stronger than most people realise. Take factor 8 or 10 to avoid problems. Calamine or other lotion for burns is handy.

HAIRDRESSING

There are many excellent hairdressers in the cities. Chinese practitioners are much admired. Many beauticians are well trained; some trained abroad. Some will be found at hotels and there are beauty parlours.

WHAT TO WEAR

Most discussions of what to wear start from the viewpoint that Pakistan is an Islamic State and therefore ideas of what constitutes respectably covered diverge considerably from what might be acceptable in the west. This is undoubtedly true, though in the major cities, it is acceptable for women to wear skirts and dresses. One can buy western style frocks in Karachi and Islamabad. Many people feel more comfortable, even in western dress, to have sleeves (at least elbow-length ones) and a scarf – just like people in Roman Catholic countries.

It is most important to feel comfortable and dress for the climate and conditions. Don't wear tight garments at all.

Pakistani women usually wear a *salwar kameez*, which is a suit of long shirt or frock and baggy trousers. The costume is complete with a *chunni* or *dupatta*, a chiffon scarf. It is possible to buy ready-made sets, and it is also possible to buy cloth and have a tailor make some up. An average *salwar kameez* takes about four metres (ask for *char gaz*) of cloth and the shopkeepers have plenty of choice of materials, and will explain what is in fashion and what comes in the fabric weight appropriate for the season. The tailors are inexpensive and quick. Ready-made is available in the major towns. Karachi offers the widest choice.

The outfit is cool and convenient. The *chunni* is handy to cover the head and keep the sun off! Very useful for shading the face.

The Pakistani cut of *salwars* is more flattering and easier to wear than some other kinds. Pakistani tailors cleverly pleat the voluminous legs onto a band which fits snugly about the waist and hips, and does it up with a hook. This is far more comfortable and manageable than the old-fashioned cord type with several yards of bulky cloth gathered about the abdomen. Those who cannot forsake western clothes could wear a long-sleeved shirt and loose baggy trousers (tight ones would be rather sweaty) and it would amount to much the same effect.

Although many Pakistani men now favour western styles of dressing, the most popular male garment is still a plainer version of the *salwar kameez,* or a *kurta* and *salwars*. The *kurta* is a long, loose shirt which can again be bought ready made or can be tailored. For men too, as a practical travelling garment in a hot country, the *salwar kameez* is hard to beat.

Children will undoubtedly want to have new clothes. Children's wear can be bought ready-made or they can be made-to-order, though the latter are not entertained by some tailors in Islamabad. Pakistani mothers sew children's clothes.

Clothes for girls often come beautifully decorated. The colours are wonderful. Washing can be a problem as fabrics are not usually colourfast. Suits for boys can have exotic brandnames ("Leeds" might sound romantic to a Rawalpindi resident.) It is also possible to get colourful embroidered Afghan outfits from shops like Threadlines, and western dresses.

Hats are essential. Buy some of the assorted embroidered ones, Sindi caps, embroidered with mirrors in amazing colour combinations, appear very dashing. Chitrali caps, the medieval looking, rolled woollen hats in fawn, brownish tones, are sported by the men of the north and the mujahidin.

The kind of shoes worn depends on the activity. In the towns, sandals are probably best, and are available at very modest prices. For women, there are various styles, the "v" between the toes, or western styles.

Men usually wear the Peshawari sandal, which is a stout leather sandal in a design which crosses over at the front with a peep-toe. It is possible to purchase embroidered slippers, sandals and all kinds of fancy footwear. Some are embroidered with gold and silver thread and have decorative woolly pompoms (these are available for men too!). Small girls will doubtlessly crave the fancy, high-heeled slippers.

Conventional shoes are available. Bata shops and other shoe chains are everywhere. They sell shoes with good value for money, especially "trainers", though large sizes can be a problem.

For walks in the countryside, low-heeled shoes are advisable. Sweaters and winter coats, gloves, woolly hats and scarves are useful during winter and on visits to the hills.

It is possible to buy woollen waistcoats (*weskits*) and *chogas*, the large woollen coats on which western dressing gowns are modelled. Blankets are also available and there is evidence of handknitting. Many Pakistani men sport pullovers and slipovers in bright colours and patterns.

WHAT TO BRING

Bring along a swimsuit if you are staying upmarket and wish to swim in the pool of the luxury-class hotel.

It is wise to carry soap and a small towel (you can buy them in Pakistan). Many small hotels do not provide them. Sometimes, a sink plug is handy, too, as well as your own sheet and pillowcase or sleeping bag.

All kinds of shampoo, cosmetics, and toiletries are available in cities (including well-known western brands).

Suntan lotions are more of a problem. It is best to go well provided.

If women prefer tampons, they should take their own supply along as these are rare or may not be available at all in Pakistan. Sanitary towels are readily available and can be bought from utility stores and other general shops, not necessarily chemists. As utility stores work on a self selection system, this spares embarrassment (unless they don't have any in stock,) as all the shop assistants and checkout operators are men.

Nailfiles, cotton buds and safety pins are hard to come by.

EXTENSION OF STAY

A maximum of three months is allowed on a tourist visa. Short extensions of stay may be obtained from the respective Passport Offices in Islamabad, Karachi, Lahore, Peshawar and Quetta. The length of extension is at the discretion of the officer in charge. Some officers tend to be more generous than others.

ON DEPARTURE

There are airport departure taxes. Rs 100 for international travel and Rs 10 for domestic travel. There is also a foreign travel tax of Rs 250 levied on all passengers leaving Pakistan.

GETTING ACQUAINTED

GOVERNMENT

Pakistan is an Islamic Republic. The capital city is Islamabad. Karachi was the capital from 1947-1959.

There are four provinces: Baluchistan, the North West Frontier Province, Panjab and Sind. Their respective capitals are Quetta, Peshawar, Lahore and Karachi. In addition to the four provinces are the Northern Areas which include parts of Kashmir which acceded to Pakistan just after independence. The Northern Areas are divided into the administrative districts of Daimer (Indus Kohistan), Gilgit (including Hunza and other old mountain kingdoms) and Baltistan (including Skardu, Shigar, Khapalu, Karmang and Rondu). The Chitral Valley is administratively part of NWFP. Since 1974 the Northern Areas have been governed directly under Islamabad.

There are also seven political agencies – federally administered Tribal Areas, within which the laws of Pakistan do not apply. The Pakistan Government, like the British administration before it, leaves these areas to govern themselves. Tourists are not permitted to enter.

For administrative purposes the provinces are divided into a number of commissioner's divisions, and each division is divided into districts and each district is further subdivided into tehsils.

The country has a federal structure. There is a Parliament, consisting of two houses. The lower house is called the National Assembly and members are elected directly by the people. The term of office is five years.

The National Assembly determines the major policy issues, agrees on the budget, passes legislation. It also elects the Prime Minister from among its members. The Prime Minister selects Ministers from among the members of the Assembly.

The Upper House is called the Senate. The majority of members are elected by the Provincial Assemblies. The Provinces also have their own elected legislative assemblies and Chief Ministers.

ECONOMY

Pakistan's economy is largely dependant on agriculture. The main food crop is wheat, followed by rice, maize, millet, barley and pulses, sugar-cane, oilseeds, tobacco, fruits and vegetables. Large scale irrigation has made the cultivation of such a variety possible, carried out mainly on the Indus Plain and its tributaries in the Panjab.

Cotton is another very important crop, and textile manufacture is Pakistan's most important industry. But other industries involving anything from food processing to heavy engineering are developing rapidly, and in some areas quite spectacularly.

All of Pakistan's exports combined do not earn as much foreign exchange as the remittances sent home by Pakistanis working abroad, notably in the Gulf. There is hope that the need to rebuild the devastation in Iran and Iraq will continue to demand Pakistani labour, as many Pakistani families at the lower end of the scale are reliant on the money their menfolk send home from abroad.

GEOGRAPHY

Pakistan occupies the north-western part of the subcontinent of Indo-Pakistan. It is in the Northern Hemisphere at a longitude between 23°E and 38°E. The total area is 891,940 square kilometres, including the Northern Areas which make up approximately 88,000 square kilometres.

Pakistan lies between Iran to the West, Afghanistan to the north west, India to the east and China to the north east. The distances involved are immense: The border with Afghanistan is the Durand line which is 2,240 kilometres long. The Indo-Pakistan border is 1,600 kilometres. Pakistan is over three times the size of Great Britain.

Geographically, the country presents some startling contrasts.

1. The northern mountains and western offshoots of the Himalayas. The four mountain ranges, the Karakorams, Pamirs, Hima-

layas and Hindu Kush meet in the north and here, within a radius of 180 kilometres, is a dense cluster of the world's highest mountains. The ranges boast of no less than 82 peaks above 7,000 metres. Found here are also some of the longest glaciers in the world, outside the polar regions. Several valleys running in a north-south direction connect the high mountains with the foothills. The most notable are the Swat and Kaghan valleys.

2. The foothills provide the relaxing hill stations where people go to escape summer in the plains. The "hills" are more like mountains. As the mountains in this region are the world's highest, the scenic views the hills offer can be spectacular.

3. There are also several ranges of mountains in NWFP, particularly the Safed Koh and Sulaiman ranges.

4. Beyond these lies the Baluchistan Plateau, somewhat bleak and barren with huge boulders and desert and the occasional green, fruit growing valley.

5. The Potohar Plateau lies south of the northern mountains, an area of strange and eroded scenery.

6. Just south lie the rugged hills of the Salt Range.

7. Past Jhelum, the Panjab Plain and canal colonies lie ahead. These areas are heavily populated due to extensive irrigation and colonisation projects initiated by the British. The land between the Jhelum and Sutlej is irrigated and there are many villages and towns which have been developed recently.

8. In the Lower Indus Plain, in Sind, the river has moved very sluggishly, depositing alluvium for centuries so that the level of the water has become higher than the level of the surrounding lands of the plain. The land slopes away from the river, causing disaster when it floods. Defences have been built.

9. Where the land is not irrigated, it is desert. The Thar desert (called the Cholistan Desert in Bahawalpur) is wind-blown sand dunes. It extends south-east into India.

CLIMATE

With the occasional exception of parts of Sind, the only area in Pakistan to be greatly affected by the monsoon rains is the central and northern part of the Panjab, stretching up to Himalayan foothills of Murree, Kaghan and Swat, with a northern limit marked by that last great bastion of the Himalayas, Nanga Parbat. There is very little rainfall in the rest of the country, with over 75 percent of the land area receiving less than 250 millimetres of rain annually. The far north, the west and the south of the country are therefore largely desert where irrigation is necessary for agriculture. The plains of Panjab and Sind make up the largest single area of artificial irrigation in the world.

The hottest months are June and July when the Lower Indus Plain and areas of Baluchistan can see temperatures exceeding 50°C. Sibi in the Kacchi Plain is known as the hottest place on earth. Elsewhere, summer temperatures do not sink much below 35-40°C, apart from in the northern valleys of Swat and Kaghan where heat is tempered by a greater amount of rain. In the Karakoram summer tempertatures can rise locally as high as any on the plains, the scorching sun radiating from the barren desert landscape. In the Indus gorge 45°C is not uncommon. Above 2,500 metres, the heat begins to subside.

Wintertime is a lot cooler on the plains, with daytime temperatures often falling to the 20°C mark or thereabouts, and in the more hilly regions it can get very crisp. In the northern mountains temperatures sink very low indeed, to around minus 20°C in the valleys of Hunza and Baltistan.

CULTURE & CUSTOMS

Pakistan is an Islamic country and this fact influences social behaviour.

The Masjid (Mosque) is a place of worship. Shoes should be removed before entering. This should not be unfamiliar – there is the injunction in the Bible telling one to remove one's shoes before standing on holy ground. If it is a large, historic Masjid, there will be a place set aside with niches for storing shoes and with attendants to oversee their safekeeping.

Friday is the special day of worship and for that reason, it is perhaps better to choose other days for visiting.

Travelling is perhaps rather more difficult for women than men. Women with children are safer than others. Mothers are figures to be respected and children offer an entree like nothing else. Women travelling alone have

to act with circumspection. Take care and think ahead – especially in the Frontier area: Anticipate difficult situations and try to avoid them.

Pakistani women rarely travel alone: It strikes people as peculiar and immodest for a woman to do so. Often, men in other parts of the world get some curious ideas about western women and their "freedom". Western women are supposed to have gargantuan sexual appetites and fancy practically any man they see. Some men think that making a pass is expected, and that indeed, not to do so might almost be seen as an insult. The situation has not been helped by the existence of many videos in the Frontier villages and a plentiful supply of pornographic video films.

On meeting one another, people often shake hands. Sometimes, women shake hands too: if someone is respectable and trustworthy enough to meet, it is possible to shake hands with them. Some people greet by embracing one another. Men often hold hands with other men, especially whilst engaged in conversation. This does not necessarily indicate anything other than friendship. Women also hold hands. The elite (Super Paks!) are very familiar indeed with British habits, usages and social mores. Sometimes the Super Paks mix freely, but the middle class and the lower orders of society maintain their distances. Very religious people will often refuse to meet women at all. If they do, they don't shake hands.

There is a tendency to segregate the sexes even in the home. Women in one room, men in another.

On social occasions, such as dinner, the food is normally served very late – 11.00 p.m. or midnight. Don't anticipate an early meal – have a snack before setting out. The meal is usually a buffet and guests help themselves. After eating, guests leave almost immediately. There is no hanging around for after-dinner chat. The meal indicates the end of the evening.

Pakistan varies considerably from many other countries in Asia in that there are not many beggars about. In some areas the few that beg have become familiar as individuals – one gets to know them. They are so seriously disabled that they could not possibly do anything else and no one would resent giving them money. In this case, the question of whether to give to beggars can be answered easily - Yes, surely.

There are more beggars in certain areas, e.g. Multan, which is proverbially known for it, but they are not in vast numbers. The worst are those on trains.

On the whole, people in Pakistan are not as greedy or grasping as people in some other Asian countries. It is uncommon to find a visitor being harrassed into "changing money", for example. The local folk generally leave visitors alone, but if approached are usually only too willing to go well out of their way to help – they will quite literally accompany a stranger for miles to ensure that he reaches his destination safely.

TIME ZONE

Pakistan Standard time is GMT plus 5 hours. It gets dark at about 5.00 p.m. in winter and 7.30 p.m. in summer.

WEIGHTS & MEASURES

The weights and measures used are a quaint mixture of some antiquated measures used in the hoary past of the subcontinent, some old British units of measurement, and the decimal system as known internationally. Most commonplace shopping – fruits, vegetables etc., comes in kilograms, or fractions thereof.

It is not always clear in linear measurement whether people mean miles or kilometres. It is not clear at all whether the figures on the signboards mean miles or kilometres either. If consulted about distances, people are also somewhat prone to talk in furlongs (of which there are eight to a mile). This book uses kilometres for distances and metres for heights. There are 1.6 kilometres to 1 mile and there are approximately 3.3 feet to 1 metre.

Most of the ancient measures of Indo-Pakistan are not terribly essential and would probably only add confusion. The most important of them are *crores* and *lakhs*, which are still used when discussing very financial or demographic statistics. A *lakh* is 100,000, and 100 *lakhs* are a *crore*.

In purchasing cloth, *gaz* means a yard. *Char gaz* (four yards) is what is required for an average *salwar kameez* for a lady.

Shoe sizes are as English sizes.

ELECTRICITY

The electricity supply is similar to that in the United Kingdom: A.C. 220-240 volts.

Supplies can be erratic with power cuts. Hotels will usually supply candles or paraffin lamps. Don't forget to bring a box of matches. Plugs can be a problem so bring a portable plug, and if you intend to use any sophisticated electrical equipment during your visit, a voltage stabiliser is also necessary. Batteries are easily available. Buy only in sealed packs. Check the "use by" date.

BUSINESS HOURS

Friday is the weekly day off when all the shops and offices are closed. Many offices close on Saturday as well. Official hours are usually 8.30 a.m.–2.00 p.m. in summer and 9.00 a.m.–2.30 p.m. in winter. Most businesses are open 7.30 a.m.–2.30 p.m. in summer and 9.00 a.m.–4.00 p.m. in winter.

Banks are usually open 9.00 a.m.–1.00 p.m. Mondays–Thursdays and 9.00 a.m–11.00 p.m. Saturdays and Sundays. They close on Fridays. Special time schedules may be observed during Ramadan and other festivals. The opening hours may also vary between summer and winter months.

Shops tend to vary in their opening hours. They usually open at about 9.00 a.m., though in summer they open as early as 7.00 a.m. and usually shut their doors during the heat of the day. They then open again until closing time at 8.00 p.m.

HOLIDAYS

There are two kinds: Islamic holidays and holidays commemorating events in the life of the Quaid-i-Azam and historical events in the life of Pakistan. There are also Bank Holidays. On these, the Banks are closed but other businesses unaffected.

MUSLIM HOLIDAYS

Muslim holidays are based on the Muslim calendar. The months are lunar months so the year is 13 days shorter than the western calendar. Thus dates of certain holidays may vary from year to year. It is best to find out whether any of these dates fall within the time period of the projected visit.

Muharram is the first month of the Islamic year and marks the death of Imam Hussain. It is a period of very intense mourning by the Shia Muslims. On *ashura* (the 10th day) the festival culminates in massive processions marching through the cities. Occasionally, flagellation takes place with sharp blades attached to chains. The visitor is advised to avoid getting too involved in muharram, as it can get a trifle xenophobic, particularly in Peshawar and Skardu.

Ramadan is the month of the fast. The fasting relives the 30 days during which the Holy Prophet of Islam spent his days meditating in a cave and the feast celebrates the divine inspiration he received in reward for his devotion. No food or drink is sold in the day except in the dining rooms of large hotels and some restaurants. Travel is difficult. Visitors should be careful not to eat, drink or smoke in public. Visitors may also be asked to wait so that Muslims may be served first, when day is done.

Shops are closed during the Eid ul Fitr, a holiday marking the end of Ramadan.

The Eid-ul-Zuha celebrates Abraham's willingness to sacrifice his son Isaac to God. The symbolic slaughter of a sheep or goat is the main ritual of the feast. The meat of slaughtered animals is exchanged among friends and relatives and given away as alms or rewards to the underprivileged.

Food, sweets, clothes and money are distributed to the poor on both occasions and the populace assembles in vast numbers to pray collectively at various prayer grounds, dressed in festive and colourful clothes. Following prayers, all those present embrace and greet one another with "Eid Mubarak" ("An Auspicious Eid to You"). The rest of the day – as well as the following day – is spent visiting friends and relatives.

The Eid ul Azha – marks the end of the *haj* (pilgrimage) to Mecca. It is the goal of every Muslim to visit Mecca. This is some distance away for Pakistanis and PIA arranges special haj flights during this time. Thousands of Muslims are catered for annually, with the result that most major airports are bursting at the seams and that flights are often delayed.

The Eid i Milad un Nabi marks the anniversary of the birth of the Prophet Muhammad (Peace be upon Him).

Shab i Mairaj celebrates the night of the ascension of the Prophet into heaven.

Shab i Barat is rather similar to "All Souls Day", and is observed in rememberance of the dead.

NATIONAL HOLIDAYS

March 23 – Pakistan Day commemorates the Pakistan Resolution passed at Lahore in 1940. The resolution advocated a separate state for Muslims.

May 1 – Labour Day

July 1 – Bank Holiday

August 14 – Independence Day commemorating the founding of Pakistan, 1947

September 6 – Defence of Pakistan Day commemorating the Indo-Pakistan War of 1965

September 11 – Anniversary of the death of the Quaid-i-Azam, M.A. Jinnah

November 9 – Iqbal Day is the anniversary of the Birth of Allama Iqbal

December 25 – Anniversary of the birth of Quaid-i-Azam

December 31 – Bank Holiday.

COMMUNICATIONS

MEDIA

Newspapers: There are many Urdu publications, and also publications in regional languages.

The major newspapers are *Nawa-i-waqt, Jang, Mashriq, Imroz* and *Wafaq*.

International newspapers and news magazines are available in the cities – at the bookshops, and in the lobbies of high class hotels.

English language newspapers are also published in all the major cities in Pakistan.

There are half a dozen newspapers published in Karachi: *Dawn, Morning News* and *Business Recorder* are morning papers and *The Daily News, Star* and *Leader* are evening papers.

In Lahore, the *Nation* and the *Leader* are morning papers.

The Pakistan Times is published from Rawalpindi, *The Muslim* from Islamabad, *The Khyber Mail* and *Frontier Post* from Peshawar, and *The Baluchistan Times* from Quetta.

There are also some good news magazines and many magazines covering special interests. These come in English and the other languages. All cities contain a good selection of bookshops from which such publications can be obtained, as well as a lot of other material including many a fascinating history of the region. Indeed, for those with any space in their luggage, such masterpieces as *The Tribes of the Hindu Koosh* or *The Making of the Frontier* can be purchased a lot cheaper in Peshawar than in London.

Television: There is a television service which broadcasts in colour. Transmissions are normally between 5.00 p.m. and 11.00 p.m. The English language news is transmitted at 7.00 p.m. Urdu news is at 9.00 p.m. and at 6.05 p.m. there is news in Arabic.

The rest of the schedules contain very much standard fare – popular quiz programmes with modest prizes given by local businessmen, and there are dramas and Pakistani soaps, as well as some elderly films and television series in English. There are also some serious discussion programmes, with talking heads and programmes featuring good Pakistani musicians.

Radio: Radio Pakistan transmits programmes most of the day, from early morning until 11.00 p.m. Apart from Urdu transmissions, there is a world service broadcasting in 14 international languages. The main news bulletins in English are at 8.00 a.m. and 10.00 p.m.

POSTAL SERVICES

There are several post offices, letter boxes, and 310 Telegraph Offices in the country. It is best to register letters, except those airmailed at GPOs in major cities.

There is a Datapost service to the U.K., Netherlands, West Germany, Turkey, UAE, Japan, Egypt, New Zealand, Oman, Sweden, Greece, Qatar, Norway, France, Kuwait, USA, and Bangladesh. All items sent by this service are registered and covered against loss.

There is an overnight delivery service for letters and parcels up to 10 kg. The service is called "Airex". It connects Rawalpindi, Islamabad, Lahore, Peshawar, Faisalabad, Multan, Sukkur, Quetta, and Karachi.

The local packet and parcel service covers the same towns and offers same day delivery. There is an Urgent Mail Service covering the 57 major towns in Pakistan, and it is a very efficient service, too.

TELEPHONE & TELEX

There are STD facilities and telephone connections to some fairly remote places. Direct dialling can connect you to a fair number of cities in Pakistan and there are many facilities for dialling overseas countries. Every major city has a Public Call Office (PCO) and Telegraph Service. These may, but not necessarily, be located near the GPO. Some of them (e.g. Islamabad) are open 24 hours. In places like Gilgit, where the PCO is run by the army, be prepared to wait a long while. Calls have to be made through Islamabad. It can take hours. The PCO in Chitral, a much smaller town, seems to be run much more efficiently.

EMERGENCIES

SECURITY & CRIME

Pakistan is security mad. In some places, there is too much of it. (e.g. When an ignorant security officer keeps demanding that a camera flash-gun be opened when there isn't anything to open!)

Banks, airports and various other institutions are guarded by armed men, lots of security. Some areas – like the diplomatic enclave has plenty of guards. Sometimes, the security is obsessive, particularly near bridges and army installations (which include medieval forts). It is also obsessive on the roads around Kahuta where the nuclear research institution is located. Unfortunately, there isn't much to tell people to keep out. There are no-go areas and for safety reasons it is best to stay out.

In Pakistan, the visitor is safe – much less liable to get "mugged" than in London or New York.

As far as personal valuables are concerned, either keep them safely on your person or lock them in the hotel safe. Most Pakistanis are honest, but nevertheless, it isn't safe to leave a handbag lying about. There are no facilities for left luggage. If you should lose any personal belonging, contact the Police.

Emergencies: There isn't an emergency "999" service as in U.K. You have to look up the number of the local police to call them. The Central Police will not turn up; only the local police will respond. Some helpful numbers for emergencies:

Karachi

Hospital	729719
Police	222222
Emergency	224400
Reporting an accident	233331
Ambulance	536281
Fire Brigade	724981

Lahore

Hospital	60822
Police	54444
Reporting an accident	53333
Ambulance	52070
Fire Brigade	310354

Islamabad

Hospital	840381
Police	823333
Emergency	63333
Reporting an accident	63333
Ambulance	63031
Fire Brigade	62545

Peshawar

Hospital	76211
Police	64213
Emergency	73333
Reporting an accident	75222
Fire Brigade	75666

Quetta

Hospital	73053
Police	70554
Emergency	73333
Reporting an accident	70666
Ambulance	75666, 71087, 683432, 225225

In all five cities:

Telephone enquiries	Dial 17
Telephone complaints	Dial 18
Trunk booking	Dial 109
Trunk enquiries	Dial 108

Note: All **embassies** are located in Islamabad.

GETTING AROUND

MAPS

Maps can be obtained from bookstores and the foyers of major hotels in the major cities. Maps of the provinces of Pakistan and also detailed street maps of the big cities are available. They are printed from various sources and are based on the Government of Pakistan maps produced by the Surveyor General.

The Survey General of Pakistan has offices in Murree Road, Faizabad – on the road from Islamabad to Rawalpindi – where maps may also be purchased.

The Pakistan Tourist Development Corporation also has some maps (as well as tourist information brochures) on the major cities. These maps are less detailed and are intended only to cover the major thoroughfares and popular local sights and amenities.

(It is also possible to buy maps before making the trip. Bartholomew's road map of the subcontinent is recommended.)

The visitor is bound to have a few problems finding his/her way about in a strange city. Even if a good map is available, there are not a great many directional signs. Where signs exist they are often in Urdu. Try asking a policeman. The Pakistani policemen are extremely helpful. They will give directions. Some will even go the extent of finding you a suitable conveyance – hailing a tonga or rickshaw, then instructing the driver to your destination. If you enquire at a police station, the senior officer there might even assign a constable to guide you safely to where you want to go. Incidentally, Pakistan has many handsome and smart policemen!

DOMESTIC TRAVEL

In Pakistan, the visitor can experience various modes of transport: by air, by rail and by road. There are buses of different types, as well as Toyotas and Jeeps. In the cities, there are scooter-rickshaws and Suzuki pickups and tongas. Transport used depends on where one wants to travel and how quickly and safely (and cheaply) one wants to get there.

BY AIR

There are airports in Bannu, Bhagtanwala, Chitral, Dera Ismail Khan, Faisalabad, Gwadar, Gilgit, Hyderabad, Islamabad, Jacobabad, Jiwani, Karachi, Kohat, Lahore, Mianwali, Mohenjo-daro, Multan, Nawabshah, Pasni, Peshawar, Punjgur, Quetta, Rahim Yar Khan, Saidu Sharif, Skardu, Sukkur, Talhar and Zhob. Several more airports are being planned.

Flights to the Northern Areas (to Gilgit, Skardu and Chitral) present difficulties sometimes, as they can be subject to delays caused by the weather. There can be cancellations for days on end and it is unwise to plan a trip to the area at short notice, especially on the day of departure from Pakistan. It is possible to get stuck!

Flying within Pakistan is a quick way of getting around the country, and often very cheap. Shorter journeys are subsidised by the government, so a flight to Gilgit or Skardu is not that much more expensive than taking the bus. The views are impressive too, with mountains above and below.

There is an aiport tax of Rs. 10 for all internal flights.

BY RAIL

The trains tend to follow the course of the river. Though slow, the railways are a convenient means of travel, because they serve all major towns and sites of interest. Many of the railways are feats of engineering, rising through hilly, difficult terrain and crossing mighty rivers or long bridges.

Train buffs will be excited upon seeing the steam engines – these are very common. Permission can be obtained to visit the engine sheds, either from the local Divisional Superintendents or from the Chief Mechanical Officer, General Manager, Pakistan Railways, Headquarters Office in Lahore.

There are various classes of berth available: Air-conditioned, First and Second.

The Air-conditioned Class is preferable during summer. The trains can get very crowded, so it is best to make reservations several days in advance. Seats and sleeping compartments must be reserved in advance and bedding can be provided if requested.

Passengers on First Class provide their own bedding. Note, however, that booking a First Class does not mean that the sleeper is automatically provided. A sleeper has to be booked separately and it is wise to ensure that this is complied with.

In all classes, passengers should take along an adequate selection of food and drink to last the journey. There is food on trains but it tends to be expensive and not very good – except for the "afternoon tea" service, which is excellent.

First Class Tourist Cars are also available. The Tourist Cars have self contained units with kitchens, bedrooms and bathrooms. These cars can be detached at any railway station for any period desired, and thereafter moved on. Pakistan Railways arrange tour programmes by train, and also run some special excursions. The Chief Marketing Manager can furnish interested parties with more information and details.

Concessionary fares are also available for various types of travellers, including students, groups on study tours, tourists, sports groups, youth organisations (Guides and Scouts) etc. As the fares are, by western standards, extremely low, further concessions seem almost too ridiculous.

BY ROAD

It seems fashionable to discount the bus services of Pakistan and say that they are dangerous and grim. There are many types of buses in Pakistan.

Buses: The provincial governments have Road Transport Corporations, which run regular services between the major cities. The buses start from G.T.S. Depots. Some services are more frequent than others, depending on the volume of traffic along the route. Generally, these buses are fast, regular and reliable. There are fare concessions for students. The fares are generally very low and vary according to the kind of buses and mini-buses. In Baluchistan they also vary according to terrain with scales of fares for metalled roads, *kachha* and single roads, hilly roads, and desert tracks. NATCO (Northern Areas Travel Company) runs buses up to Gilgit.

Flying Coaches: Apart from official services, there are a number of private services, some of which are grim and others like the "flying coaches" are excellent. These are small air-conditioned coaches. They depart from different depots (not the ones used by the other buses). The fares are higher but still inexpensive by western standards. The flying coaches do move speedily. Long-distance buses stop regularly at decent restaurants with toilets so travellers can stretch their legs and buy drinks. Still, it is best to board equipped with fruit and water.

Transit Vans: There are now thousands of Ford Transit vans operating in the cities and plying in between. These can seat up to fourteen people and serve as a poor man's flying coach. The Transit van alternative is available at most private bus terminals. There are also other types of mini-buses in Pakistan.

Scooter-rickshaws: These are actually three-wheeled scooter buggies. Most of them have meters which, unfortunately, don't seem to work. The charges can thus amount to something quite unrelated to the distance. It is best to negotiate a fare before starting off. If it seems excessive to you, try another driver. Several drivers will approach you and offer assorted fares. Try to pick someone reasonable. It is possible (though not exactly sane or comfortable) for a European family (parents plus two kids) to get into a scooter rickshaw.

Often, the scooter rickshaw is the only transport which seems to be readily available when one gets lost in the backstreets of a town. Roads rarely seem to have clear signs and scooter drivers are deft at sorting out destinations.

Tactful drivers normally let passengers alight a short walk away from the luxury hotel they stay in; tactless ones bring them to

the entrance and make them scramble on the steps, in embarrassment and in full view of the hotel guests. It is therefore advisable to direct the driver to a road or a landmark near the hotel!

Suzukis: Since the Japanese built their Suzuki plant in Karachi, the Suzuki Pickup has become one of the most popular means of transport around the city, and is even used to cover short distances between settlements. Designed to take eight people, with people clinging on at the back, the number can sometimes increase to 10 or even twelve. Suzukis are very reasonably priced indeed, a journey across town costing generally no more than Rs 2.

Tongas are two-wheeled horse-drawn carriages. Again, it is advisable to negotiate the fare before you board. They are called "Victorias" in Karachi.

Taxis: Taxi meters rarely seem to be functioning. So again, it is best to negotiate a fare before setting off.

Jeeps and Cargo Jeeps: These run in the Northern Areas, where the roads are too narrow for buses. The jeeps are neither inexpensive, nor comfortable and do not run to a timetable. Passengers and baggage jam onto the vehicle as best they can and hang on for dear life. Watch out for "hitchhikers"; they may be robbers. Board a private jeep if you value safety, but the fare will obviously be much higher. "Public" means that anyone can get on, at any time.

DRIVING

There are cars available for hire and self-drive in Karachi. Elsewhere, self-drive is probably just about impossible; the cars can be hired, but they come with a driver. It is possible to make arrangements and rent the car and driver for a period – a day or longer. Agree on the terms first and check whether the sum agreed includes petrol consumption. When facing difficulties with any of these negotiations, ask a policeman for help or advice. Pakistani policemen are inevitably helpful.

If one does get behind the wheel, do note the following tips because driving in Pakistan can be a different experience! This information is also useful to the passenger, making him/her aware of the right course of action to take, even if it only means covering the eyes! Usually, Pakistanis do not drive fast, only dangerously. You may be safe on the North Circular, M 25, or even on Highway 66, but don't take the GT Road. If you must drive, spend a few days observing points. There is a kind of rhythm – like the tango.

There isn't much lane discipline and hardly anyone uses the mirror. Signboards are mostly in Urdu, although some are in English. Distances are quoted sometimes in miles and sometimes in kilometres.

In towns, it is the general opinion that cars should move at 30 mph/50 kph. In some cities (e.g. Islamabad), it is expected that cars will turn left at a red traffic light if the way is clear. (In fact, failure to do so will cause much hooting behind). Elsewhere (e.g Lahore) turning left against a red traffic light is not allowed. The police will haul up drivers who fail to stop.

Beware of traps on the road. They include "sleeping policemen" (speedbreakers), which are constructed of hard rocks and can scrape the bottom of the vehicle (a horrible experience!). They can also jolt the vehicle and its passengers if hit at speed and cause serious injuries.

There are also low walls which often appear suddenly in the middle of the road and are intended to divide traffic. Watch out for them whilst overtaking; they can be terrifying. Sometimes the roads take sudden sharp corners, where the camber of the road leaves much to be desired. Other hazards include railway lines. Some level crossings are not as level as they should be, and the roads may be in bad shape. Only a minority seem bothered about seat belts.

Driving at night is especially risky. This is because of dangerous roads and/or bandits. Many vehicles do not have rear lights which work. (Bullock carts lack everything!) Drivers drive on full beam headlamps most of the time. There are sometimes no road markings, which makes it difficult for the driver to see the road at all in the wind, rain and mud. Foreigners are forbidden to travel after dark outside major cities.

Driving in the hills requires a special skill. Engage a low gear and go slow. The roads on the slopes are often dangerous. The gradients can be difficult, the hairpin bends are so acute that a vehicle will not get around on the first try. It is often necessary to forward and reverse cautiously, to get around. Some car engines do not function well at high altitudes. In such a case, there are alarming moments when the engine stalls suddenly on steep slopes.

Above all, remember: Flashing the headlamps does not mean a courteous "after you". It means "I am coming, I am not about to back down. My foot is down on the accelerator. Get out of my way as soon as possible!" The use of the indicator is highly idiosyncratic. When a driver flashes the indicator, it might mean that his vehicle is about to pull over or turn right. It might also mean that he is about to pull to the left and let you past.

In any event, misreading his intentions could well prove fatal.

Bridges on major rivers usually collect toll. Have a rupee or two ready.

PUBLIC LAVATORIES

Life is always easier for men than women: It is in this case, too! Pakistani men wearing capacious *salwars* and flowing *kurtas* just tend to squat in a suitable place.

This option is not normally open to women. There are not many public lavatories about. In towns, the best bet is a hotel, restaurant or a public building. People in offices will often direct one to a place: but it may not be a very pleasant place.

Most toilets likely to be encountered on the road and in many hotels are the "squatting" variety. They are usually equipped with a tap and a jug of water. Here water is used with the left hand. (This hand should not be used for eating with.)

In the countryside, nature's call can be a problem. Truck-drivers usually wander off into the farmland, somewhere beyond the *dabba* and squat. Western women can look for possible fields or bushes; sugarcane or orchards are good news. Otherwise one just has to look for somewhere a little out of the way.

Nowadays, there are many new modern filling stations going up along the roads. These appear to be provided with suitable facilities. Alternatively there are hotels and cafes and these have a facility of some kind.

WHERE TO STAY

There are many hotels in Pakistan, and together they make up an enormously varied collection of institutions! Some are ancient, historic buildings, where the shades of long-gone imperial officers seem to linger over chops, boiled greens and plum puddings; others are modern, five-star, international class. Some hotels located in the hills bring back pleasant memories of tea dances in the 1930s. Some may appear to be unhygienic, while others charge reasonably low rates and offer good value for money.

The only way to pick a hotel is to take a look at the facilities and judge for yourself. Hotels also change with time – what was once a friendly, clean place a short time ago may be closed now, or taken over, or deteriorated beyond recognition.

PTDC HOTELS/MOTELS

The Pakistan Tourism Development Corporation (PTDC) have hotels and motels dotted around the most popular tourist centres. It also runs luxury cabanas and VIP cottages. Bookings can be made for PTDC facilities in the north from Room No. 30, Flashman's Hotel, The Mall, Rawalpindi. Tel 66231, 68776, 64811. Bookings for facilities in the south are made via Room No. 2221, 263, 268, Hotel Metropole, Abdullah Haroon Road, Karachi. Tel 516151, 510301.

There are also a few camp sites in Pakistan. Advice on where camping is possible may also be obtained from the PTDC.

HOTELS

The Ministry of Culture, Sports and Tourism publishes a Hotel Directory annually. A complete list of all Pakistan's hotels is contained therein.

Here is a province-by-province list of the best-known hotels in the most likely places:

SIND

Hyderabad
   City Gate Hotel, opposite Central Jail. Tel 31677, 31744, 31198, 31707.
   Fataz Hotel, Thandi Sarak. Tel 24425-9.
   New Indus Hotel, Thandi Sarak. Tel 25276, 23997.

Jacobabad
   Mehran Hotel, Tower, Jacobabad. Tel 2366.

Karachi
• Luxury hotels (Rs 1,000–6,000):
   Avari Towers Hotel, Fatima Jinnah Road, Tel 525261.
   Holiday Inn, 9 Abdullah Haroon Road, P.O. Box 10444. Tel 520111, 522011.
   Hotel Taj Mahal, Sharah-e-Faisal. Tel 520211.
   Karachi Sheraton Hotel, Club Road. Tel 521021.
   Pearl Continental Hotel, Club Road. Tel 515021.
• Moderate hotels (Rs 500–1,000):
   Hotel Metropole, Club Road. Tel 512051
   Hotel Midway House, Karachi Airport. Tel 480371.
   Plaza International Hotel, Dr. Daud Pota Road. Tel 520351-70.
   Beach Luxury Hotel, Moulvi Tamizuddin Khan Road. Tel 551931-7.
• Inexpensive hotels:
   Hotel Mehran, Shahrah-e-Faisal. Tel 511387.
   Hotel Sarah, Para Street, Saddar. Tel 527160-2, 525318-19.

Larkana
   Mehran Hotel, New Station Road. Tel 23274.
   Mohenjo-daro Tourist Inn, Old Station Road. Tel 22482.

Sukkur
   Inter Pak Inn, Sukkur Barrage. Tel 83051.

PANJAB

Attock
   Indus View, G.T. Road, Attock Khurd.

Bahawalpur
   Erum Hotel, The Mall, Circular Road. Tel 4291, 4730.

The Bank Who Cares for your business.

BANK DAGANG NEGARA
(STATE COMMERCIAL BANK)

HEAD OFFICE : Jl. M.H. Thamrin No. 5, Jakarta   Phone : 321707, 3800800,
P.O. Box : 338/JKT Jakarta 10002, INDONESIA
Telex : 61628 BDNULN IA, 61649 BDNULN IA, 61621 BDNLN JKT, 61640 BDN FX IA.

OVERSEAS OFFICES :

NEW YORK (AGENCY) &
CAYMAN ISLANDS (BRANCH)
45 Broadway Atrium 30th floor
New York, N.Y. 10006,
USA
Telex :   226698 BDN NYUR
          226690 BDN NYUR

LOS ANGELES (AGENCY)
3457 Wilshire Boulevard
Los Angeles, C.A. 90010
USA
Telex :   3716724 BDN LA USAG
          3716705 BDN LA USAG

HONG KONG (REPRESENTATIVE) &
STACO INTERNATIONAL FINANCE LTD
6/F Admiralty Centre Tower II
Queensway, Victoria
Hong Kong
Telex :   60322 BDN – HX
          60323 BDN FX – HX

SINGAPORE (REPRESENTATIVE)
50 Raffles Place 13-05
Shell Tower, Singapore 0104
Telex : DAGANG RS 24939

THE PROBLEMS OF A

HEAVY TRAFFIC.

You'll come across massive Thai jumbos at work and play in their natural habitat. In Thailand, elephants are part of everyday rural life.

FALLING MASONRY.

A visit to the ruined cities of Sukhothai or Ayutthaya will remind you of the country's long and event-filled history.

EYESTRAIN.

A problem everyone seems to enjoy. The beauty of our exotic land is only matched by the beauty and gentle nature of the Thai people.

GETTING LOST.

From the palm-fringed beaches of Phuket to the highlands of Chiang Mai there are numerous places to get away from it all.

OLIDAY IN THAILAND.

GETTING TRAPPED.

In bunkers mostly. The fairways, superb club houses and helpful caddies make a golf trap for players of all standards.

HIGH DRAMA.

A performance of the 'Khon' drama, with gods and demons acting out a never-ending battle between good and evil, should not be missed.

EXCESS BAGGAGE.

Thai food is so delicious you'll want to eat more and more of it. Of course, on Thai there's no charge for extra kilos in this area.

MISSING YOUR FLIGHT.

In Thailand, this isn't a problem. Talk to us or your local travel agent about Royal Orchid Holidays in Thailand.

Thai
We reach for the sky.

Among the Great Hotels in Pakistan two stand out.

AVARI TOWERS

AVARI LAHORE

Unparalleled in comfort and luxury. Friendly efficient service blends with international hospitality to make Avari the perfect choice for the world traveller at the gateways to Pakistan.

Owned & Operated by:

AVARI HOTELS

AVARI TOWERS
Phone 525261   Karachi
TELEX 24400 AVARI PK
FAX   (021) 510310

AVARI LAHORE
Phone : 69971 - 310281 - 62294
TELEX : 44678 AVARI PK
FAX   (042) 58165

RAMADA RENAISSANCE HOTEL KARACHI LAHORE

AVARI SWAT   Opening summer 1990.

Humera Hotel, Multan Road. Tel 5959.

Dera Ghazi Khan
Shalimar Hotel, Fareedi Bazaar. Tel 2104-5.

Faisalabad
Faisalabad Serena Hotel, Club Road, Faisalabad. Tel 30972, 32023.
Hotel Midway, P-35 Midway Street, Kutchery Bazaar. Tel 24595, 34125.
Rays Hotel, Allama Iqbal Road, close to Flying Coach stop. Tel 24006.
Ripple Hotel, 18A People's Colony. Tel 49973, 41909.

Gujranwala
Gujranwala Hotel, Gondalanwala, Adda Gujranwala. Tel 84679, 84631, 82992.

Gujrat
Faisal Hotel, GT Road. Tel 3088.
Melody Road, Railway Road. Tel 3751, 4651-2..

Islamabad
• Luxury Hotels (Rs 1,000–4,000):
Holiday Inn, Aga Khan Road, Shalimar 5. Tel 826121-35.
Islamabad Hotel, Municipal Road, Civic Centre Ramna 6. Tel 827311.
• Moderate Hotels (Rs 400-1,000):
Ambassador, Shahrah-i-Suhrawardy. Tel 824011.
Dreamland Hotel, Peshawar Mor, I &T Centre, G-9/4.
Margalla Motel, 1, Kashmir Road. Tel 813345-49.
• Inexpensive Hotels:
East West Motel, Near Rawal Dam. Tel 826143, 826983.
Blue Star Hotel, T &T Colony. Tel 852810, 852717.

Lahore
• Luxury Hotels (Rs 1,000–4,000):
Pearl Continental, Shahrah-i-Quaid-i-Azam. Tel 69931 (I).
Hilton International, Shahrah-i-Quaid-i-Azam. Tel 310281 (I).
• Moderate Hotels (Rs 400-1,000):
Faletti's Hotel, Egerton Road. Tel 303660.
Hotel International, Upper Mall. Tel 870281.

Ambassador Hotel, 7 Davis Road. Tel 301861-8.
Shalimar, Liberty Market, Gulberg. Tel 870331-3.
• Inexpensive hotels:
Hotel Liberty, Liberty Market, Gulberg. Tel 875232.
Orient Hotel, 74 Macleod Road. Tel 223906.
Uganda Hotel, 45 Macleod Road. Tel 56007.

Multan
Hotel Hushiana, Chowk Kutcheri. Tel 43520, 42026, 43536.
Hotel Sindbad, Nishtar Chowk, Bahawalpur Road. Tel 72294-6.
Mangol Hotel, L.M.Q. Road, Dera Adda. Tel 30164.
Shezan Residence, Kutchery Road. Tel 30253-6.
Silver Sand, 514 Railway Road. Tel 33061, 33062, 76800, 76900.

Murree Hills
Kashmir View Hotel, Ayubia. Tel 17.
Cecil's Hotel, Mount View Road, Murree. Tel 2247, 2257.
Blue Pines and Murree Inn's Hotel, Cart Road, Murree. Tel 2233, 2230.
Bright Lands Hotel, Imtiaz Shaheed Road, Murree. Tel 2270.
Mall View Hotel, Jinnah Road, Murree. Tel 2075.
Green's Hotel, Nathiagali. Tel 544.
Pines Hotel, Nathiagali. Tel 505.
Hotel Valley View, Nathiagali. Tel 506.

Rawalpindi
• Luxury hotels (Rs 1,000–4,000):
Pearl Continental, The Mall. Tel 66011-21, 62700-10.
Hotel Shalimar, off The Mall. Tel 62901.
• Moderate hotels (Rs 400–1,000):
Flashman's Hotel, PTDC, The Mall. Rawalpindi. Tel 64811.
Kashmir Wala's Tourist Inn, The Mall, Tel 583186-4.
• Inexpensive hotels:
Gatmell's Motel, Airport Road. Tel 65047, 65123.
Rawal Hotel, Committee Chowk. Tel 70121.
Sand Hills Hotel, Murree Road. Tel 70651-2.

New Kamran Hotel, Kashmir Road. Tel 582040.

BALUCHISTAN

Quetta
Bloom Star Hotel, Steward Road. Tel 75178, 70177.
Gul's Inn, behind Jinnah Road. Tel 70170, 70175, 74178, 70179.
Hotel City Baluchistan, Prince Road. Tel 70647.
New Lourdes Hotel, Staff College Road. Tel 70168-9.
Quetta Serena Hotel

Ziarat
PTDC Motel. Tel 15.

NORTHWEST FRONTIER PROVINCE

Abbottabad
Sarban Hotel, The Mall. Tel 2376-78.
Springfield Hotel, Mall Road. Tel 4834-4770.

Dera Ismail Khan
Midway Hotel, Indus River Bank. Tel 2900,3100.
Jan's Hotel, North Circular Road. Tel 3925 3926.

Dir
New Khyber Hotel, Timgara, District Dir. Tel 713.

Kohat
Green Hill Hotel, Near Police Line, Hangu Road. Tel 2220, 2577.

Peshawar
• Luxury hotels (Rs 1,000–4,000):
Pearl Continental, Khyber Road. Tel 76361.
• Moderate hotels (Rs 300–1,000):
Dean's Hotel, 3 Islamia Road. Tel 76481.
Green's Hotel, Saddar Road. Tel 76035.
Jan's Hotel, Islamia Road, Peshawar Cantt. Tel 76939, 70256.
• Inexpensive hotels:
Galaxie Hotel, Khyber Bazaar. Tel 72738-9.
Kamran Hotel, Khyber Bazaar. Tel 72345.
Khyber Hotel, Saddar Bazaar.

SWAT VALLEY

Saidu Sharif and Mingora
Swat Serena Hotel, Saidu Sharif. Tel 4215, 4504.
Hotel Pameer, GT Road, Mingora. Tel 4926, 4306.
Marghazar Hotel, Saidu Sharif Road, Marghazar. Tel 5714.

Bahrein
Abshar Hotel. Tel 22.
Bahrein Hotel. Tel 33.
Delux Hotel. Tel 15.

Miandam
PTDC Motel. Tel 10.
Pameer Guest House. Tel 1.
Karashma Hotel. Tel 4.
Miandam Hotel. Tel 11.

Maydan
Madyan Hotel. Tel 4599.
Mountain view. Tel 7.
Nisar Hotel. Tel 441.

Kalam
PTDC Motel. Tel 14 or book through PTDC Rawalpindi.
Hotel Falakshir. Tel 10.
Khalid Hotel. Tel 6.
Heaven Breeze Hotel. Tel 5.

KAGHAN, KARAKORAM HIGHWAY AND NORTHERN AREAS

Kaghan Valley
Taj Mahal Hotel, Kaghan Road, Balakot.
Park Hotel, Kaghan Road, Balakot.
Lalazar Hotel, Kaghan. Tel 22.
Vershigoom Hotel, Kaghan. Tel 12.
Lalazar Hotel, Naran. Tel 1.
PTDC Motel, Naran. Book through PTDC Rawalpindi.

Besham
PTDC Motel. Book through PTDC Rawalpindi.

Chilas
Shangrila Midway. Tel 69.
Chilas Inn. Tel 187-71.

Chitral
Mountain Inn, Ataliq Bazaar.

PTDC Tourist Complex. Book through PTDC Rawalpindi.
Fairland Hotel.
Dreamland Hotel.
Tirich Mir View Hotel.

Gilgit
Gilgit Serena Lodge, Jutial. Tel 2330-31. 3960-61.
Chinar Inn, PTDC Hotel, Chinar Bagh. Tel 2562, or book through PTDC Rawalpindi.
Hunza Inn, Babar Road, near Chinar Garden. Tel 2814.
Park Hotel, Airport Road. Tel 2679.

Hunza
Serena Lodge, Karimabad.
Hill Top Hotel, Karimabad. Tel 10.
Rakaposhi View Hotel, Karimabad. Tel 12.
Tourist Park Hotel, Karimabad. Tel 45.
Mountain View Hotel, Karimabad. Tel 17.

Skardu
Shangrila Tourist Resort, Kachura Lake, Skardu.
K2, PTDC Motel. Book through PTDC Rawalpindi.

OTHER ACCOMMODATION

Youth Hostels: The Pakistan Youth Hostels Association, 110 B-3, Gulberg III, Lahore maintains hostels which may be used by members of organisations which are affiliated to the International Youth Hostels Federation.

There are Youth Hostels in Abbottabad, Balakot, Kaghan Valley, Bhurban, Ketas, Khanpur, Lahore, Naran, Shogran, Taxila and Islamabad.

The **YMCA** and **YWCA** also have hostels in the major cities of Pakistan.

Pakistan Railways have some "retiring rooms" for passengers and tourists on major railway stations. These are open to passengers with air-conditioned and first class tickets for overnight stays.

The **Salvation Army** maintains excellent value hostels in Lahore and Karachi:

Salvation Army Hostel, 35 Fatima Jinnah Road, Lahore; and

Salvation Army, Frere Road, Karachi.

FOOD DIGEST

WHERE TO EAT

Where to eat depends on individual taste and how much the pocket allows. If a person likes western style foods, the luxury hotels can come up with an excellent international cuisine. They are, however, not expensive, by western standards.

There are a number of different "ethnic" restaurants – Chinese are popular, especially in Karachi but plenty elsewhere too. Islamabad has a super ice cream parlour, appropriately called "Yummy's". There is one in Peshawar too.

In the luxury hotels, breakfast menus offer an enormous choice of dishes enough to keep one going all day.

As a general rule, it is wiser to avoid food kept on warm /hotplates. The food might have been kept tepid for a long time, and may not be as fresh as it once was. Besides, the warmth makes it an ideal breeding ground for bacteria.

For hygiene reasons, the best places to eat are the five-star hotels and the *dabbas*, the truck driver's "boxes", pull-ups. What is available in a *dabba* may not be gracious living, but it has tasty and freshly cooked food.

WHAT TO EAT

Dal (lentils) are eaten practically at every meal. In Pakistan, orange-yellow *dal* are the most common, and they are usually prepared to a consistently thick soup. For the very poor, *dal* may be the main course. For the wealthier, they are a side dish served with other dishes.

Pathans are the "meat-and-potatoes men". It can be quite a problem for vegetarians anywhere in Pakistan. The villager will insist on slaughtering a chicken or serving eggs as meal, creating an agonising dilemma for anyone who doesn't take such food.

Kebabs come in various kinds. They are best bought fresh from roadside stalls. *Shami kebab* is mince meat on skewer. *Boti* means "chunks". *Chappli* means shaped like a shoe sole (The *kebab* is like a meat patty, a kind of spicy hamburger.)

The *chappli kebabs* come from Northwest Frontier Province, especially good at Nowshera. There is a jolly, well-upholstered *kebab* stallholder on the Bara Road leading out of Peshawar, whose *kebabs* are memorable. He will even produce some with a little less chilli for the children! *Chappli kebab* are grand with a *naan* (bread) bought from a neighbouring stall. One can sit in the park in Peshawar under the huge peepul trees and enjoy a memorable lunch.

Listed here are the local names of some common food items:

Alu – potatoes
Anda – egg
Badam – almond
Bheja – brains
Biryani – a rice dish with meat and vegetables
Chapatti, paratha, naan – bread
Chai – tea
Chini – sugar
Dahi – yogurt
Dudh – milk
Firni – a milk pudding, rice and milk
Gajjar – carrot
Gajrela, gajjar halwa – sweets made from carrots
Gobi – cabbage,
Gosht – meat. *Burra gosht* is beef and *chota gosht* is mutton.
Gurda – kidney
Halwa – a delicious sweet dish, comes in various flavours and colours
Kaleji – liver
Keema – mincemeat
Khir – rice pudding
Koftas – meatballs
Maghaz – brains
Nargisi Koftas – meatballs with egg; *Nargis* is a narcissus.
Masala – spiced
Macchli – fish
Mattar – peas
Murgh – chicken
Nimbu – lemon
Palak – greens, spinach
Pani – water

Paneer – cheese
Phulgobi – cauliflower
Seb – apple
Sag – spinach, mustard greens
Shahi tukre – a dessert made from bread, milk and nuts

Sometimes, two ingredients come together; *Keema matar* = peas and mincemeat. *Sag paneer* = spinach and cheese.

Here are some familiar items available in Pakistan:

Biscuits – There are an wide range of biscuits available: Bourbons, Rich teas, Wafers, Nice, Custard creams, Cheese biscuits, Crackers, Tuc and Ginger nuts (very comforting!).

There are also potato crisps – some in unusual flavour varieties (the children will demand them, but won't eat them). There are other pre-packed snacks, spiced *chanas*.

DRINKING NOTES

Stalls are found everywhere selling a variety of drinks in cans, bottles or in minicartons. Some internationally known drinks – Coke, Pepsi, Sprite, 7 UP, Fanta, mineral water, etc. – are easily available. There are also local drinks: Team, Qais, Sprite, etc.

There are also fruit juices. Shezan is a bottled mango juice. Apple, mango and orange juice, etc. often come in cartons. There are stall vendors of orange juice, cane juice, etc., on the streets and in the markets. They extract the juice on the spot. Nevertheless, it would be safer to buy the fruit and peel it yourself.

Water: Everyone says don't drink it. Everyone ends up drinking it. What else can be done? *Neau eau!* Bottles of spa water are unavailable in Pakistani villages, though bottled water is available in towns.

Use common sense. It is possible to encounter unclean water. No one in their right mind would drink it. The locals don't drink it either. On the other hand, the water in Islamabad is quite safe. Boiling it will merely concentrate the chemicals put in to purify it. Water in many places in the north is also safe to drink. On the other hand, Peshawar's water supply is under severe strain – the system was never designed to provide water for so many people – and there are open

INSIGHT GUIDES

SOUTH ASIA
Special

Available at all
leading
bookshops.

APA PUBLICATIONS

PAKISTAN

Explore it casually or extensively. Our offers include Safaris-on jeeps in the North or camels in the South-a boat trip down the Indus River, re-tracing the tracks of the Arians & Mughals left on the land, to remote and intriguing areas. Whichever way you choose to explore Pakistan, join us for the ultimate travel experience.

The ultimate travel experience

sewers in the town. It is probably wiser to drink, coffee, or a bottled drink. It is also sensible to bring some Puritabs or iodine.

Liquor: Visitors are not allowed to bring any liquor into the country. Non-Muslim visitors who wish to drink require a permit which enables them to buy liquor from hotels or authorised vendors.

THINGS TO DO

TOURS

Mass tourism in Pakistan is, as yet, not a very highly developed industry, though there are an increasing amount of tours for special interest groups, some organised by PIA and a few by other operators. There are also more and more operators abroad now including Pakistan on their itineraries. Some of the tours which last only a week or 10 days are very hectic indeed as the distances traversed are long. On a six-day tour, it is possible to visit Karachi, Lahore, Rawalpindi, Islamabad, Taxila Museum and Peshawar and the Khyber. But it would leave little time to linger.

There are tours to historical sites, Buddhist study tours, tours to the shrines of the mystics. There are some sports tours – squash and golf particularly. Some tours include trout fishing or hunting wild boar.

There are many adventure holidays and tours in the north: jeep safaris to Gilgit, Hunza, Skardu, etc.

There have been questions asked about the safety of these "adventures", but most people seem to agree that adventure holidays are not exactly cosy: Choose carefully – for example, a "Family Summer Escapade in Swat" can be suitable for some while a Rakaposhi-Nanga Parbat adventure package may be preferred by others. Some tours are better suited for a family or a holidaymaker. Some are only suitable for the very fit who do not mind taking things rough. In the

South, there are trips from Karachi to Mohenjo-daro, Quetta, Ziarat, Multan and Lahore. There are desert safaris in winter. Tours of Pakistan can be combined with another country (e.g. China or Sri Lanka.)

TREKKING

In common with other regions of the greater Himalayas, trekking in the Northern Areas of Pakistan has seen rapid growth during the past few years, though the onslaught of mass tourism has perhaps developed more slowly here than in Nepal. The mountains have proved to be the No. 1 tourist attraction for many visitors, a trend which has been exploited by a growing number of trekking agencies operating from Islamabad and Rawalpindi, which offer package tours lasting a few days to a few weeks. Similarly, an increasing number of specialist operators abroad now include parts of the Northern Areas in their "wilderness adventure" destinations. Here are some of the well-known trekking tour operators in Pakistan:

Pakistan Tours Limited (PTL), Flashman's Hotel, The Mall, Rawalpindi. Tel. 64811.

Travel Waljis Ltd., 10, Khayaban-i-Suhrawardy (Aapara Market), P.O. Box 1088, Islamabad. Tel. 28324/6.

Hunza Treks and Tours, No. 253, 23rd Street, E7, Islamabad. Tel. 28558.

Karakoram Tours, Baltoro House, 19th Street, F 7/2, Islamabad. Tel. 29120.

The Pakistani Government has actively participated in the developments, producing guidelines and leaflets designed to ensure that the situation does not get out of hand. Once a region for the exclusive exploitation of mountaineers, floods of trekkers from all over the world now explore the fragile domains of the Karakoram and Hindu Kush. Treks can vary from ambles along the river banks to ventures lasting much longer; over passes to some of the remotest valleys on earth; to the base camps of some of the highest mountains; to summits under 6,000 metres.

WAYS OF TREKKING

The majority of people who go trekking in the Northern Areas tend to book with a tour operator. Tents, porters, food and cooks are all normally supplied and all that the trekker has to do is trek. His every need will be taken care of. Porters' wages are protected to a minimum daily rate fixed by the Pakistani government, a small amount when compared to that which the individual has paid for his trip, particularly if it has been booked abroad. Only a minute fraction of the money reaches the people who do all the work, and not much more is changed to rupees.

Several men from any one village may be involved in an expedition. As a result, the once subsistence economy in the Northern Areas is now changing to one increasingly dependent on tourism, with the locals often forced to play an increasingly servile role. While mountaineering expeditions often require the largest numbers of porters, there is no doubt that large groups of trekkers also play their role in transforming the region, even when the only surface signs may be the large amounts of litter usually to be found deposited at the more popular camping grounds.

Some trekkers choose to "go it alone" in small groups, often carrying their own gear on their backs. If a guide is needed, then he can be hired at a locally negotiated fee in Gilgit, Chitral or Skardu. Should trekkers wish to go as a wholly independent group, then any assistance that is required for direction finding can be found in the valleys where friendly villagers are usually only too pleased to help out.

But trekking without a guide is not for the inexperienced, particularly when it comes to going anywhere off the "beaten track". And while a guide will always act as intermediary between the group and the locals, those who go it alone will have to establish their own contacts, whether it is asking a local shepherd for help, or enquiring of the local schoolteacher whether it is possible to pitch tent within the confines of the village. While increasing numbers of mountain people are acquiring basic English, a knowledge of the local language, or at least a smattering of Urdu, is a definite advantage. Individuals must be aware of the codes of the local people and not infringe on them. Despite developments, local traditions are still very strong. Nevertheless, most villages are very hospitable and the villagers themselves are normally happy to play host to a group of backpackers.

RESTRICTIONS

However one decides to go trekking, there are restrictions. Sensitive border regions, e.g. the Siachen Glacier and some parts of the northern Hindu Kush, are closed to outsiders. Other areas are deemed Restricted Zones, where expeditions need to be accompanied by a representative of the government, the liason officer. A permit is required and there is much red tape to overcome before such ventures can get underway. The cost too can be prohibitive. The liason officer needs his own porters and they have to be catered for. The party also needs to hire approved guides and porters who have to be catered for. There is a set amount of rations per guide/porter that the expedition is required to supply.

The most famous of all the Restricted Zones is the Baltoro Glacier, where anybody found without a permit will be airlifted out at his own expense by the army, which can provide enough helicopters due to its presence on the Siachen Glacier.

Most of the treks in the Northern Areas, however, lie in the so-called Open Zones, and apart from the Baltoro, one doesn't really need to go any further to savour the staggering beauty of the Karakoram and Hindu Kush. From Tirich Mir to the Hushe Valley, this is a trekker's paradise.

The Ministry of Culture, Sports and Tourism in Islamabad provides an annual booklet outlining all the treks approved by the government and the zones within which they fall. It also describes the formalities in detail one has to go through.

The booklet can be obtained from either Tourism Division, College Road, F-7/2 Sector, Islamabad, or Pakistan Tourism Development Corporation (PTDC), House No. 2, Street No. 61, F-7/4, Islamabad.

SEASONS

The best time to trek in the Northern Areas is from July to October, though the valleys are suitable from March-April onwards. Many treks involve crossing high passes however, and the dangerous snow cornices will not have disappeared until July or August, when the summer snowline rises to some 4,500 metres. Autumn is beautiful, though very cold at altitude.

ALTITUDE & FITNESS

There are no hard and fast rules of how the individual body responds at high altitudes. Even the fittest adventurer can have severe physical problems, and will be surprised to learn that a companion who is less fit at sea level can cope better. It is very difficult for anybody to function well if suddenly confronted with the atmospheric conditions which exist, say, at 4,000 metres, having come up from sea level. Listlessness, headaches and nausea are likely the result, with the first signs of altitude sickness caused by a lack of oxygen supply to the brain.

The body can get used to coping with altitude over a period of time, a period of acclimatisation, the length of which varies greatly from individual to individual. It is therefore important for the individual to have total control over the rate of his/her acclimatisation and that, if any of the symptoms mentioned arise, he/she should descend to recuperate immediately. For members of a large group, this can be difficult, particularly where there is a time limit. Peer pressure can be very strong. Organised trekking parties often have to reach a certain spot by a certain date in order to make sure they catch their flight home.

A week spent at 3,000 metres may prepare one for a week at around 4,000 metres, which may then enable one to go on and spend time at 5,000 metres. Certainly, for someone who is not acclimatised, going from 2,000 metres to 5,000 metres in two days is plain foolhardy!

FOOD

While supplies for organised parties are all laid on, individual trekking groups will need to take their own food along. As rations may need to last for a few weeks, it is advisable to take lightweight dried food containing as many carbohydrates as possible. Freeze-dried meals can be bought from any good mountaineering shop and there are even supplies of leftovers from previous expeditions available in Gilgit and Skardu. Garlic is very good for blood circulation. Dried fruits are available in abundance in the Northern Areas and they can either be eaten as they are or reconstituted with porridge meals. Salt is another impor-

tant element. Salty biscuits are available even in the remotest of villages. At lower altitudes water needs to be purified or boiled. Failure to do so may result in amoebic dysentry or gardia. Take along supplies of Flagyl or Fasygyn just in case.

EQUIPMENT

Food needs to be cooked and therefore one needs a reliable stove. Camping Gaz is good, though one is limited by the number of canisters one can carry. A better solution may be a liquid fuel stove with interchangeable nozzles to suit different fuels. Both petrol and paraffin are widely available in the Northern Areas – villagers need paraffin for their lamps.

Some trekkers just carry a bivvy bag for shelter. In summer and early autumn, there is normally very little precipitation. If you bring a tent, make sure that it is lightweight, with the least possible number of pegs.

Night-time temperatures can sink as low as -20°C at 4,500 metres in September. If you are going high, bring a warm sleeping bag. Summer treks at 3,000 metres do not require anything substantial.

Clothes should not be bulky. Changes in conditions can be adapted to more easily by using a lot of layers, starting with thermal underwear. A few more layers followed by a fleece jacket and wind/waterproof overalls should be enough for most conditions likely to be encountered. A pair of well-worn boots should be brought along. If you are contemplating an ascent of a minor peak under 6,000 metres (there is a lot of red tape for anything higher), then your boots should have some stiffener in the soles to accommodate crampons.

Quality sunglasses are a must, preferably those with 100 percent ultra-violet cut out. Glare from glaciers and snowfields can be very strong. It is also advisable to bring sunblocker for the face.

ORIENTATION

Most of the routes in the Northern areas, apart from those up minor summits or to basecamps follow well-established paths which have been used by shepherds or tradesmen for centuries. Particularly the routes over the main passes (e.g. Thalle La) are very well marked, though the final stages may be covered in snow. However, it is still necessary to have a good map and compass. Often there are so many paths that it is difficult to know exactly which one to take. The best widely available maps of the Northern Areas are those which were produced by the US Army in the 1950s and 1960s, The "US 502" series which have now all been updated and reprinted in colour. There are also maps of specific mountains which have been produced by various mountaineering expeditions, notably by the Germans and the Japanese. For further details of maps, contact a specialist map shop. The foreign maps department at Stanfords near Covent Garden in London has always been particularly helpful.

An altimeter is also a very useful tool, not only for determining altitude, but also for giving clues to weather changes. If there has been a sudden overnight rise in altitude, this would normally mean that the weather already has or is going to get worse!

N. B. If you intend to do any walking on glaciers, it would be very advisable to have a guide.

MOUNTAINEERING

As with restricted trekking activities, permission is required from the Department of Tourism. Applications must be made a year in advance, with the exception of applications to climb K-2, which requires two years. Royalties are payable for attempts to climb peaks. There are five peaks above 8,000 metres and 82 peaks above 7,000 metres. Some of the peaks are, as yet, unclimbed.

There is an emergency helicopter service. High altitude porters are also available upon payment.

OTHER ACTIVITIES

Skiing, Mountain Bikes:
Enquiries may be forwarded to the PTDC.
White water sports:
Rafting, kayaking and canoeing are possible at recommended sites:
1. On the River Indus – from Jaglot to Thalot;
2. Kunhar River – from Naran to Kaghan;
3. Swat – from Bahrein to Saidu Sharif;

4. Chitral;
5. Hunza – from Aliabad to Gilgit.
Expeditions require permission from the Ministry of Culture, Sports and Tourism and need a liaison officer from the Ministry to accompany the group.
Marathons:
The Himalayan Marathon is a new sport. The first was in 1985. The 1986 marathon started at Skardu at a height of 2,300 metres and covered an 80 km course up to Dasu, taking two days. A five-day marathon was held at the Askoro Pass, 5,127 metres up. The Himalayan Marathon is described as "the most difficult race in the world."

Camel safaris: The administrator, Lal Sohanra National Park, should have information on desert safaris by jeep, camel or by other means of transport. They are organised only in winter .

Note: Further advice on what to do and where to go can be sought from the Pakistan Tourist Development Corporation. The PTDC has offices in most tourist centres and in the larger cities. Apart from the headquarters in Islamabad, PTDC Tourist Information Centres are located at:

–Hotel Metropole, Karachi
–Faletti's Hotel, Lahore
–Dean's Hotel, Peshawar
–Flashman's Hotel, Rawalpindi
–Swat Serena Hotel, Saidu Sharif

as well as in many other smaller motels run by the PTDC itself.

While the PTDC has no offices abroad, it has appointed agents in London, Rome, Tokyo, Vancouver, Copenhagen and New York which disseminate literature and maps and give advice. PIA offices abroad also provide similar information.

CULTURE PLUS

MUSEUMS

Most museums open in winter from 8.30 a.m.–12.00 p.m., and from 2.00 p.m. until an hour before sunset.

In summer, they open from, 8.00 a.m.–12.00 p.m. and again at 2.00 p.m. until an hour before sunset. Here is a list of the museums in Pakistan:

- –Bahawalpur Museum
- –Bhambhore, Thatta. Archaeological Museum
- –Bhit Shah, Hyderabad, Sind. The Bhitshah Cultural Centre – Shah Abdul Latif Memorial Centre includes a mu seum and cultural centre.
- –Faisalabad. Agricultural Museum
- –Harappa. Archaeological Museum
- –Hyderabad. Fort Museum, Pucca Fort
- –Hyderabad. Sind Provincial Museum
- –Islamabad, Lok Virsa. National Museum of Folk and Traditional Heritage
- –Islamabad. National Museum
- –Karachi. National Museum of Pakistan
- –Karachi. Natural History Museum
- –Karachi. Quaid-i-Azam Birthplace Museum
- –Lahore. Allama Iqbal Museum
- –Lahore. Lahore Fort Museum
- –Lahore. Central Museum
- –Lahore. Faqir Khana Museum
- –Lahore. Holy Museum of the Badshahi Masjid
- –Lahore. Museum of Science and Technology
- –Lahore. Zoological Museum
- –Mardan. Guide's Mess, Museum and Cemetery
- –Mohenjo-daro. Archaeological Museum
- –Peshawar Museum
- –Rawalpindi. Army Museum
- –Saidu Sharif. Archaeological Museum
- –Sialkot. Library and Museum at Birthplace of Allama Iqbal
- –Taxila. Archaeological Museum
- –Umarkot. Archaeological Museum.

There is also the private collection of Mir Nur Muhammad Talpur, one of the chief Talpur Rulers. The collection is now maintained by his heirs and owned by Dr. Mir Nur Muhammad Talpur of Hyderabad. Call 25981 for an appointment, allowing a week's notice.

Plans are underway for the opening of a new museum to display artifacts unearthed during recent archaeological expeditions in the area of Bannu. However, there is no way of knowing when the museum will be ready.

ART GALLERIES

Art Galleries are rather rare. The Pakistan National Council of Arts (Idara Saqafat-i-Pakistan) runs two in Islamabad:

- –The National Art Gallery, House No 73, Street No 22, F 6/2.
- –Gallerie Sadequain. Street 25, F6/2.

Other galleries located in Karachi are:

- –Fayzi Rahmain Art Gallery, Denso Hall, Bunder Road.
- –Arts Council of Pakistan, Ingle Road.
- –The Gallery, Sindi Muslim Housing Society, off Drigh Road.
- –Pakistan Art Institute, P.E.C.H.S., Karachi.
- –Pakistan Art Gallery, opposite Lal Kothi, off Drigh Road.
- –Indus Gallery, opposite nursery, Drigh Road.

Artists tend to turn up at houses and show their work to the occupants in the hope of making sales.

Works of art are also displayed on the walls of some of the luxury hotels and restaurants. The grill room may be decorated with a collection of works by one artist. The works are usually up for sale.

MOVIES

There are a great many cinemas. Pakistani movies may not be to everybody's taste. In Islamabad, there are imported films from various sources. Watch out for the Yugoslav/Hungarian Film Week or similar film festivals.

CONCERT & OPERAS

There are not many. Watch out for advertisements in the newspapers. Probably this kind of entertainment will develop in the future.

There are some events held at U.S. Centres, British Councils etc., but these are very popular and are usually restricted by invitation only. Sometimes, it is possible to get invited.

FAIRS & FESTIVALS (MELAS)

There are a great many *melas* which are jolly occasions with fairs, circuses, pilgrimages, religious frenzy, people in catatonic trances, beating of drums, bagpiping and other activities held simultaneously. The most exciting religious *melas* are those marking the *urs* of the Sufi saints. The dates for most of these *melas* depend on the sighting of the moon and therefore they vary from year to year.

Other major events are the Horse and Cattle shows. The National Horse and Cattle Show is held in Lahore at the beginning of March each year, but the actual date is only announced a few months in advance. The same applies to the Horse and Cattle show in Sibi, held in February.

There are many folk festivals with colourful folk dancing marking the different seasons of the year. Spring Festivals are held in March all over the Northern Areas, and there is also the colourful Basant Festival held in Lahore, where kites take to the air.

NIGHTLIFE

There is no nightlife in Pakistan apart from eating out at restaurants. Islamabad is rather dead after nightfall and whatever happens, happens inside the houses! Lahore at night is livelier, as is Karachi. There are problems of returning to the hotel though, as taxis and rickshaws do not operate after nightfall, especially in Peshawar.

SHOPPING

The larger towns, and many shops even in out-of-the-way places can supply a wide range of goods. Mundane items for daily needs are (usually) easily available.

In the large towns, there are modern shopping malls which shouldn't pose any problems to shoppers. The old bazaars are laid out with specific trades occupying designated areas. In some places, there are still bazaars full of shoe shops, bookshops or other specialist trade.

WHAT TO BUY

Chiniot
Inlaid works; beautiful furniture; carved chests and doorways.

Chitral
Puttee, soft handwoven, woollen material; *chogas*, large warm woollen coats like dressing gowns (on which the latter are modelled), in soft brown tones, embroidered in black; *pakols*, the Chitrali hats which look

like pancakes; locally woven woollen rugs; bags, shoes and sandals; musical instruments, archaic weapons, precious stones; war memorabilia for ghouls and many ex-army surplus items like mountain boots, sleeping bags, groundsheets, etc.

Faisalabad
Good for shopping, especially for household items – linen, bedding, bedcovers; embroidered cotton fabrics; leather shoes, hosiery and cotton briefs.

Hunza
Chogas and embroidered hats (for women); dried fruits, particularly mulberries and apricots.

Hyderabad
Embroidered bracelets; lacquered furniture; handloom cloth – popular locally are Sousi, Ajrak and Rilli; shawls called *chaddars*, available in very colourful printed fabrics; bangles; Sindhi types of embroidery, such as *khusso* – mirrorwork.

Islamabad
Threadlines Gallery is a government-sponsored handicrafts shop. The profits from Behboob Boutique, and APWA Handicrafts go to charity. These shops sell a wide range of material at very modest prices. They offer good quality and excellent value for money.

The shops sell silverware, brass, copper, onyx, woodwork, embroidered items (such as bags, cushions, clothes, hats etc.), printed cloth, bedspreads, tablecloths, napkins, necklaces; *namdah* rugs made from chain-stitch embroidery on felt, with colourful designs are usually of animals and flowers; *Batiks* - lovely designs and hangings; embroidery to decorate the neckline of a frock, ready-made dresses, *kaftans*, shawls, *salwar kameez*, woollen *weskits* (waistcoats), *chogas*, hats – embroidered ones, some with *shisha* – mirror embroidery, and woollen chitrali caps; toys, shoes, tribal jewellery – and more. A real treasure house!

There are also shops selling carpets, jewellery, books, videos, tapes (including western pop music), household goods, perfumes, cosmetics, track suits, sweatshirts, teeshirts, shoes, fabrics, watches.

Is anything unavailable here? Practically everything one could ever want is on sale somewhere!

There are also people in all the cities who mend things! This is an almost forgotten art in the west. Look out for the *Mochi* who occupies a street corner, or perches, with his equipment under a tree. He is the cobbler and for a few rupees will sew, stick or otherwise mend a shoe and return it shining and looking as good as new. The watchmender will mend your watch, too.

Also, people can't afford waste; there are second-hand clothes vendors, sometimes selling lovely things. These can be found at Juma Bazaar (Friday market), Itwar Bazaar (Sunday market), Mangal Bazaar, Aabpara, Karachi Company.

Kaghan
Embroidered shawls and shirts. Handicraft items made from walnut. Wood carvings. Woollen blankets and rugs.

Karachi
Copper, brass, onyx, lacquered work, hand blocked printed cloth, applique bedspreads, embroidery, embroidered garments – Sindhi style traditional dresses with mirror work; old pieces of embroidery; jewellery, beaten gold and silver, glass bangles, shirts, *salwar kameez* – ready made clothes; shawls, silk, and saris; handwoven carpets available in styles of Iran, Afghanistan, Kurdistan and Baluchistan.

Lahore
Ivory, brass, woodwork, camel skin items, pottery, embroidery shawls and slippers in traditional designs, embroidered clothing, shawls, handwoven and embroidered *chunnis* (veils), scarves, bangles. Silk, saris, perfumes and cosmetics (get some *kajaal* - eyeblacks), carpets, rugs and books.

Multan
Multani *khussa* (shoes); embroidered clothes for ladies; embroidered *cholas* for men; earthenware pottery, painted pottery, camel skin ware (e.g. lamps); carpets, wooden products, especially lacquered wood. Multan has good shopping facilities.

Murree
There are many shops stocking goods for tourists along the Mall. Lots of souvenirs,

toys, (some locally made, some imported): shawls, *namdahs*, clothes, and locally made fur caps and coats.

Peshawar
Peshawari *chappals* – the popular footwear favoured by Pathans. They are men's sandals with a cross-over of leather and a square, peep-toe, fastened with a strap at the back of the heel. They are very sturdy and very comfortable too.

Belts, bandoleers, holsters; brass and copper; carpets, blankets, shawls, birds, fruit, cloth, bells and baubles, bangles and beads; hair braids, old weapons, military buttons, old coins, tribal jewellery, lapis lazuli, leather goods, printed cloth – block printing; very capacious shawls. Here is the best place to buy a *burqa* – the all enveloping garment worn by *purdah* ladies which leave them looking like little black pillar-boxes; capacious black coats and matching veils; woodwork, inlaid work, furniture and pottery.

Rawalpindi
Inlaid work in *shisha* and walnut – furniture; Kashmiri silver, Kashmiri embroidered shawls and jackets, embroidered woollen *kurtas* and *kaftans*; household linen; Potohari *jhutis* and *chappals* (shoes, sandals); cane baskets, leather, walking sticks; carpets – Kashmiri and Bokhara type; cosmetics, clothes, all manner of household and fancy goods.

Swat
Handwoven rugs, shawls, embroidered clothes, hats, silverware and precious stones, tribal jewellery, dried fruit.

Skardu
Local handwoven woollen cloth, embroidered linen, jackets, *chogas*, silver, carvings; wooden spoons.

Taxila
Pots, locally carved pestles and mortars.

Thatta
Hand blocked and hand dyed fabrics, beadwork, necklaces, rings and chains, Sindi embroidered clothing.

Ziarat
Shisha work – mirror-embroidered items.

Tourists are allowed to export or take out as personal baggage, exportable items up to a value of Rs 75,000 on surrender of foreign exchange against export permit. Remember to retain all receipts to avoid problems with the authorities and also retain the receipts for customs purposes on arrival home.

SPORTS

SPECTATOR SPORTS

The most popular spectator sport is cricket. The country has also produced notable champion teams of hockey players (field hockey).

Badminton and squash are other games in which Pakistan produces world champions.

In the north, polo is the game in summer, with competitions held in Chitral . There is also a tournament in November in Gilgit.

There are some shows, like the Lahore Horse and Cattle show, which include traditional sports like tent pegging. Horse and camel racing are occasionally staged in Sind and Baluchistan.

In the Frontier area, there is cock and quail fighting, but one is unable to watch these activities unless invited. Bets are high.

PARTICIPANT SPORTS

Most participant sports are organised through clubs and there are a number of established ones in Karachi, Lahore, Quetta, Islamabad, Rawalpindi, Abbottabad and Peshawar. Some sports make use of available local facilities.

For sailing fans, there is the Karachi Boat Club in Karachi. Deep water fishing is also possible.

In other cities, some clubs have facilities for golf, tennis, squash, cricket and indoor sports. There are also Race Clubs, Flying Clubs, and Boating Clubs. In some places, it is possible to hire horses through the Clubs.

It is possible to find a local playground or informal cricket or football ground where the local kids play – especially in Islamabad. Visiting children are usually welcome to join in. One can make a lot of friends too.

Fishing is especially popular in the north, in places like Gilgit, Swat and Chitral where there is plenty of trout. A fee is payable for a fishing permit. In some places, fishing rods can be hired.

Hunting and Shooting: Most wild species in Pakistan are protected by the conservation authorities. Snow leopards, musk deer, markhor, etc. are, rightly, protected species. There is a total ban on netting, trapping, poaching and exporting of wild animals. It is possible, though, to hunt wild boar in some places, especially in Panjab.

Swimming: Luxury hotels have pools. Do not swim in mountain rivers and streams. Other rivers are not recommended for swimming either. The currents can be dangerous. So are the water snakes and the crocodiles in the Indus! Every year people get drowned in Swat because they ignored warnings.

SPECIAL INFORMATION

CHILDREN

Children seem to do rather well in Pakistan. The people seem quite besotted with children, often making a fuss over them, and tend to spoil visiting infants.

THE DISABLED

There are no special facilities (e.g. special lavatories) for disabled people. But then there are not often toilets for other people either. And some parts of Pakistan would be frankly not possible in a wheelchair, though there are disabled mountaineers.

Nevertheless, being disabled isn't much of a problem in Pakistan, probably less than elsewhere. Pakistanis seem to show the same kind of respect for the disabled as they have for elderly people. Disabled people are probably not very likely to travel alone in Pakistan. When disabled people have visited relatives or friends, there have not been any particularly insurmountable problems.

Wheelchairs can be made available at the airport. Make arrangements through the airline. The airlines can also arrange "meeting" services for disabled travellers, to assist them through the bureaucracy.

PHOTOGRAPHY

There are many sights in Pakistan which are attractive to the photographer. However, it should be borne in mind that there are things which should not be photographed:

1. Military installations.

These sometimes include ancient Forts like Attock and the Bala Hissar in Peshawar. It is best to check that there are no objections.

2. Airports and bridges.

These are also prohibited. Breaking the law is serious.

Most books claim that village people do not often like to be photographed, especially women – though exceptions have been encountered. Occasionally, one is quite likely to encounter people who wish, or even insist, that their photograph be taken. This could happen in the case of female photographers who befriend the local ladies, or who get befriended. Men should not take photographs of women unless specifically invited to do so. There was one recent instance of a male journalist getting shot in the frontier districts for attempting to take photographs of tribal women! In general, it is unwise and unkind to photograph people unless they give consent.

Polaroids are handy because they give instant results. Colour film is available in cities, but it may not be in good condition.

Slides are especially difficult to find. It is wiser to take a supply along. There are processing services which are varied.

The major problem faced by photographers in Pakistan is the strong light during the day. Conditions for photography are best in the early morning, before 10.00 a.m. and in the late afternoon after 3.00 p.m. or 4.00 p.m. – though few people can wait about until the ideal time. The strength of the sun flattens the subject and colours lose their brilliance, so results can be rather disappointing. Landscapes can look perfectly miserable! What one recalls as a vibrant scene can turn out very dingy. Also, shadows can be very stark and black, and turn up in just the wrong places, unless great care is taken. A daylight filter is useful.

LANGUAGE

Urdu is the national language of Pakistan. There are also regional languages – Panjabi, Pushto, Sindi, Baluchi.

English is the official language of the country and is spoken among the educated classes. It can be met with even in remote places.

Urdu is an Indo-European language owing its origins to the languages spoken in Northern and Western India. It has absorbed much vocabulary from Persian, Arabic and in modern times, from English too. The name "Urdu" is closely related to the English word "horde".

USEFUL WORDS & PHRASES

Peace be with you (Greetings)	*Salaam alaikum*
And also unto you (Reply)	*Wa alaikum as salaam*
Hello	*Hello*
Goodbye	*Khuda hafiz*
Thank you	*Shukria*

What is your name?	*Aapka nam kya heyh?*
My name is Tony	*Mera nam Tony heyh*
How are you?	*Aapka (tumhara) kya hal heyh?*
I am well	*Teekh heyh* or *teekh takh*
Yes	*Ji han*
No	*Nahin*
I do not speak Urdu	*Main Urdu nahin bol sakta*
Do you speak English?	*Kya ap Anglesi bolte heyn?*
I do not understand	*Main nahin samjhta*
I do not want it	*Main yeh nahin chahta*
What is that?	*Yeh kya heyh?*
How much does this cost?	*Yeh kitnay paise heyh?*
How much do you want?	*Kitnay chahiye?*
Please give me	*Meherbani kar ke Mujhe deejiye*
enough	*Bas*
Never mind/ It's a pleasure	*Koi baat nahin*
Good	*Achha*
Very good	*Bahut achha*
Stop	*Tehriye*, or *Rukh Jao*
Go	*Challiye*
Wait here	*Yahan intazar kariye*
Go left	*Baien challiye*
Go right	*Daien challiye*
Go straight on	*Sidha challiye*
How far?	*Kitni dur?*
water	*pani*
ice	*barf*
hot	*garam*
Have you got hot water?	*Aapka pas garam pani heyh?*
cold	*thanda*
blue	*neela*
black	*syah*
white	*sufaid*
green	*sabz*
red	*lal*

Numerals:

0	*sifar*
1	*ek*
2	*do*
3	*teen*
4	*char*
5	*panch*
6	*che*

7	*saat*
8	*aath*
9	*nau*
10	*das*
11	*gyara*
12	*bara*
13	*tera*
14	*chaudra*
15	*pandra*
16	*sola*
17	*saatara*
18	*aathara*
19	*unees*
20	*beess*
25	*pachees*
30	*teess*
40	*chaleess*
50	*pachas*
60	*saath*
70	*sattar*
80	*assi*
90	*navvay*
100	*ek sau*
1000	*ek hazar*

FURTHER READING

Here is a list of suggestions. Inclusion does not imply that the contributors to this book are necessarily in agreement with the points of view expressed.

GENERAL

Fairley, Jean. *The Lion River: The Indus*. London: Allen Lane, 1975

Kureshy, K. U. *A Geography of Pakistan*. Karachi: Oxford University Press, 1978

Quraeshi, Samina. *Legacy of the Indus: A Discovery of Pakistan*. New York: Weatherhill, 1974

Qureshi, Ishtiaq Husain. *The Muslim Community in the Indo-Pakistan Subcontinent*. 's Gravenhage: –, 1962

Spate, O.H.K., and Learmouth, A.T.A. *India and Pakistan: A General and Regional Geography*. London: Methuen, 1954

HISTORY

Allchin, Bridget and Raymond. *The Rise of Civilisation in India and Pakistan*. Cambridge: Cambridge University Press, 1982

Baloch, Inayatullah. *The Problem of "Greater Baluchistan"*. Stuttgart: Steiner Verlag, 1987

Baluch, Muhammad Sardar Khan. *History of the Baluch Race and Baluchistan*. Quetta: Gosha-e-Adab, 1977

Berridge, P.S.A. *Couplings to the Khyber*. Newton Abbot: David and Charles, 1969

Collins, L., and Lapierre, D. *Freedom at Midnight*. London: Pan, 1977

Davies, C. *The Problems of the North West Frontier 1890-1908*. London: Curzon Press, 1975

Gascoigne, Bamber. *The Great Moghuls*. London: Jonathan Cape, 1971

Hardy, Peter. *The Muslims of British India*. Oxford: Oxford University Press, 1972

Moon, Peveral. *Divide and Quit*. Berkeley: University of California Press, 1962

Mosley, Leonard. *The Last Days of the British Raj*. New York: Harcourt, Brace and World, Inc., 1961

Spear, Percival. *A History of India. Part 2*. Harmondsworth: Penguin, 1966

Symonds, Richard. *The Making of Pakistan*. London: Faber, 1950

Thapar, Romila. *A History of India. Part 1*. Harmondsworth: Penguin, 1966

Wheeler, Sir Mortimer. *The Indus Civilisation*. Cambridge: Cambridge University Press, 1968

Woodruff, P. *The Men Who Ruled India*. London: Jonathan Cape, 1954

POLITICS & PERSONALITIES

Ali, Tariq. *Can Pakistan Survive?* Harmondsworth: Penguin, 1983

Bhutto Benazir. *Daughter of the East*. London: Hamish Hamilton, 1988

Bolitho, Hector. *Jinnah: Creator of Pakistan*. London: John Murray, 1954

Burki, S.J. *Pakistan Under Bhutto, 1971-1977*. London: Macmillan, 1980

Duncan, Emma. *Breaking the Curfew*. London: –, 1989

Zirling, Lawrence. *Pakistan: The Enigma of Political Development*. Sawson Westview, 1980

CULTURE, ART & LANGUAGE

Ahmed, Akbar, S. *Social and Economic Change in the Tribal Areas*. Karachi: Oxford University Press, 1977

Barth, Fredrik. *Political Leadership Among the Swat Pathans*. London: Athlone Press, 1959

Biddulph, J. *Tribes of the Hindoo Koosh*. Lahore: Ali Kamran Publishers, r. 1986

Burkhardt, Titus. *The Arts of Islam*. London: World of Islam Festival Trust, 1976

Caroe, Sir Olaf. *The Pathans*. London: Macmillan, 1958

Craven, R.C. *Concise History of Indian Art*. London: Thames and Hudson, 1976

Dar, Saifur Rahman. *Guide to the Lahore Museum*. Lahore: The Museum, 1984

Guillaume, Alfred. *Islam*. Harmondsworth: Penguin, 1968.

Harle, J. C. *The Art and Architecture of the Indian Subcontinent*. London: Penguin 1986

Huntington, Susan L. *The Art of Ancient India*. New York: Weatherhill, 1985

Institute of Folk Heritage. *Folk Heritage of Pakistan*. Islamabad: The Institute, 1977

Lewis, Bernard (ed.). *The World of Islam*. London: Thames and Hudson, 1976

Mitchell, George. *The Architecture of the Islamic World*. London: Thames and Hudson, 1978

Mumtaz, K. K. *Architecture in Pakistan*. Singapore: Concept Media, 1985

Pehrson, Robert N. *The Social Organisation of the Marri Baluch*. Chicago: Aldine, 1966

Qureshi, Ishtiaq Husain. *The Pakistani Way of Life*. London: Heinemann, 1956

Rahman, Fazlur. *Islam*. Chicago: University of Chicago Press, 1966

Sehrai, Fidaullah. *The Buddha Story in the Peshawar Museum*. Peshawar: The Museum, 1988

Shackle, Christopher (ed.). *South Asian Languages: A Handbook*. London: SOAS, 1985

Singer, André. *Guardians of the North West Frontier*. Amsterdam: Time Life Books, 1982

Spain, James. *The Pathan Borderland*. The Hague: Houton, 1963

Spain, James. *The Way of the Pathans*. Karachi: Oxford University Press, 1972

Welch, Stuart Cary. *India: Art and Culture 1300-1900*. London: Deutsch, 1986

Zainab Ghulam Abbas. *Folktales of Pakistan*. Karachi: Pakistan Publications, 1957

FICTION

Lambrick, H.T. *The Terrorist*. London: Ernest Benn Ltd., 1972

Kipling, R. *Kim*. London: Macmillan/Pan Books, 1976

Masters, J. *The Lotus and the Wind*. Harmondsworth: Penguin, 1956

Sidwa, Bapsi. *The Crow Eaters*. Lahore: Ferozeson's, 1982

Sidwa, Bapsi. *The Bride*. Lahore: Ferozeson's, 1984

Sinclair, Gordon. *Khyber Caravan*. London: Hurst and Blackett, 1936

Singh, Kushwant. *Train to Pakistan*. New York: Grove, 1961

TRAVEL NARRATIVES & ADVENTURE

Danziger, Nick. *Danziger's Travels*. London: Paladin, 1988

Matheson, Sylvia A. *The Tigers of Baluchistan*. London: Arthur Barker, 1967.

Keay, J. *The Gilgit Game*. London: John Murray, 1979

Keay, J. *When Men and Mountains Meet*. London: John Murray, 1977

Mayne, Peter. *Journey to the Pathans*. London: John Murray 1955

Moorhouse, Geoffrey. *To the Frontier*. London: Hodder and Stoughton, 1984

Murphy, Dervla. *Full Tilt*. London: John Murray, 1965

Murphy, Dervla. *Where the Indus is Young*. London: John Murray, 1977

Naipaul, V. S. *Among the Believers*. Harmondsworth: Penguin, 1985

Reeves, Richard. *Passage to Peshawar*, New York: Simon and Schuster, 1984

ART/PHOTO CREDITS

Bergendahl, Erik	304
Blanchez, Gilles	84
Bonington, Chris	122/123, 325
British Library	45, 48, 50, 53, 57, 203, 206, 236, 237, 238, 338, 341
British Museum, The	37, 172
Dhanjal, Beryl	202, 204, 216, 226, 228, 229
Evrard, Alain	20/21, 24, 88, 89, 176/177, 209, 213
Fantini, Piero	153R, 316/317
Fritz, Wolfgang	43, 65, 99, 105, 108R, 119, 121, 148L, 152, 212L, 212R
Grosse, Heinz	cover, 18/19, 27, 78, 79, 94, 102, 103, 110, 113, 118, 120, 128/129, 134/135, 136, 139, 145, 149, 150, 154, 157, 159, 164R, 165, 166, 170, 171, 175, 193, 194, 197, 198, 199, 217, 218, 227, 232/233, 239, 242, 243, 244, 245, 252, 262, 266, 267, 312, 336/337
Güler, Ara	9, 44, 49, 74/75, 82, 83, 90, 93, 101, 130, 142, 151, 160, 168, 182, 187, 189, 196, 200, 201, 208, 211, 251, 253, 278, 280, 283, 347
Halliday, Tony	47, 54, 186, 222, 270, 271, 273, 281, 286, 287, 294, 299, 300, 306, 313, 322, 323R, 324, 328
Höfer, Hans	22, 86, 91, 124/125, 144, 256, 260, 295, 307, 308, 311, 318, 319, 326, 330
Holmes, Jimmy	31, 71, 138, 162, 220, 258, 302, 305, 320, 321, 323L
Huges, Simon	41, 51, 52, 104, 111L, 143, 146, 148R, 214, 215, 219, 224, 225, 246/247, 248/ 249, 263, 264, 269, 327, 331, 332
Khan, Javaid	72/73, 76/77, 85, 96/97, 109, 126/127, 184, 190
Lambert, Anthony	334/335, 339, 342, 343, 344, 345, 346
Lawson, Lyle	14/15, 81, 106/107, 114, 268, 274, 275, 276, 282, 285, 290/291, 301, 314, 315, 329
Maier, Hermann	40, 116/117, 292/293
Masherbrunn, K.	288/289
Ministry of Information	25, 28, 33, 34, 35, 42, 56, 58, 59, 60, 61, 62/63, 64, 68, 69, 108L, 174, 261
Osborne, Christine	16/17, 111R, 112, 115, 141, 156, 158, 161, 163, 164L, 167, 169, 207, 221, 223, 230/231, 235, 240, 241, 250, 265, 284, 309
Palmer, Alan	192, 195, 272, 279, 333
PTDC	95, 191
Steiner, Ernst	26, 29, 36, 38/39, 98, 140, 153L, 155, 173, 178/179, 277, 348
Topham Library	66, 67, 80
Victoria and Albert Museum	46, 55
Wassman, Bill	87, 92, 298

INDEX

B
C
D
E
F
G
H
I
J
a
b
c

e
f
g
h
i
j
k
l

NOTES